IN THE JAWS OF HISTORY

To Robert Silano
with warm regards
& best wishes.

April, 1988

IN THE
JAWS
OF
HISTORY

BUI DIEM
WITH **DAVID CHANOFF**

1 9   8 7

HOUGHTON MIFFLIN COMPANY BOSTON

Library of Congress Cataloging-in-Publication Data

Bui, Diem.
In the jaws of history.

Includes index.
1. Bui, Diem.   2. Vietnam — History — 20th century.
3. Ambassadors — Vietnam — Biography.   I. Chanoff, David.
II. Title.
DS556.93.B85A3   1987   959.704′092′4   87-3417
ISBN 0-395-42637-5

Printed in the United States of America

A 10 9 8 7 6 5 4 3 2 1

This book recounts many conversations held over a long period
of time and reconstructed from notes or from memory. In each instance
the substance and tone of these conversations is accurate; the dialogue
is as precise as the notes and memory permit.

To my wife and children
for their love and support

Contents

Preface

I have written this book because I feel a duty, a duty not only to the hundreds of thousands of South Vietnamese who died on the battlefield in our struggle for independence and freedom in Vietnam but also to the millions of others, soldiers and civilians alike, who suffered the hardships of war for so long and now are suffering the consequences of defeat.

There is a former military cemetery not far from Saigon where many thousands of South Vietnamese were buried. Their graves have now been deliberately desecrated. But an even greater desecration will have taken place if the sacrifices and suffering of the countless thousands who dreamed of a Vietnam neither colonized nor communized are simply swept into the dustbin of history. In honoring my victimized countrymen, I ask the privilege to honor also the thousands of Americans, Australians, Koreans, and other allies who died trying to help us.

This book attempts to tell part of the story of modern Vietnam and its struggle for identity, independence, and freedom. My own upbringing and temperament made it feel unnatural to tell the story in the first person. Yet I realized that my life is part of the common life of all Vietnamese of my generation. To make this story live, I wanted to invite the reader to join us in living through these events and seeing them through our eyes, as if through his or her own.

I also wished to make my own modest contribution to the continuing search for the meanings of the war in Vietnam, about which there are so many misconceptions — both for Vietnam and for America — and to describe the lessons to be learned from this tragic, yet often heroic, period. Accordingly, in the Epilogue I have not hesitated to draw conclusions in the furtherance of what I believe to be truth, reconciliation, and resolve for the future.

I owe a debt of gratitude to Peter Braestrup, editor of *The Wilson Quarterly,* and Philip N. Marcus, former president of the Institute for Educational Affairs, whose encouragement and support were at the origin of this book.

Special thanks are due to my two old friends of the Vietnam era: Ogden Williams, who from the beginning helped me in structuring the book and the initial draft, and George McArthur, whose critiques and abridgments were of great value. I also wish to express my gratitude to my enthusiastic and knowledgeable literary agent, Muriel Nellis, whose valuable professional judgments I greatly relied upon.

My thanks also go to other American friends, in particular to William P. Bundy, who generously put at my disposal his unpublished manuscript on the Vietnam War.

I am particularly grateful to David Chanoff, whose enthusiastic assistance in the research, writing, and editing of the manuscript was invaluable.

Finally, I wish to gratefully acknowledge the Earhart Foundation, the Smith-Richardson Foundation, the Institute for Educational Affairs, the Woodrow Wilson International Center for Scholars, and the American Enterprise Institute, without whose support this project could not have been undertaken.

Many have thus shared in writing this book, but responsibility for all the conclusions and judgments expressed in these pages is, of necessity, mine alone.

BUI DIEM

IN THE JAWS OF HISTORY

Chapter 1

The Jaws of History

A THIN, PERSISTENT VOICE penetrated the static on the line: "Diem, this is Bob Shaplen, Bob Shaplen. I'm calling from Hong Kong." The voice kept repeating the name, but the deep sleep I had been in a moment before and the drugs I was taking for a vicious flu wouldn't let my head clear enough for recognition to take hold.

"Bob Shaplen, Diem. I've just gotten back from Saigon. Your friends need you, Diem. They have to know what's happening. Nobody has any idea what's going on. Thieu and Graham Martin are incommunicado. Nobody can get through to them. You're the only one. You've got to go to Saigon to tell them the truth. You've got to go immediately!"

By now my attention was riveted on this demanding voice, the first direct message I had received in weeks about conditions in Saigon. By the time Shaplen hung up I was wide awake and convinced he was right. I had to get back. The *New Yorker*'s veteran Far Eastern correspondent was knowledgeable and perceptive, not the sort for dramatics. He was also an old friend. He would not have called like that unless he felt compelled. I could still hear the urgency in his voice.

It was two in the morning in Washington, and though I lay back down in bed, there was no getting to sleep again. I had in fact been thinking hard about returning to Saigon for the last week. But then this knockout virus had hit. And South Vietnam's military disintegration in this spring of 1975 had been so unexpected, and so sudden, that it was hard to say how much time might be left. I certainly had no illusions about what would happen if I was caught by the other side.

Three weeks earlier President Nguyen Van Thieu had sent me to the American capital, the city where I had lived as South Vietnam's ambassador from 1967 to 1972 and where I had visited regularly from 1973 on as ambassador at large. My mission this time was to do what I could to unstop the $700 million in emergency aid that was bottled up in the U.S. Congress, aid that would give shells to South Vietnam's nearly silent guns and fuel to her grounded aircraft, as the nation's armed forces battled to hold back the flood tide of twenty North Vietnamese divisions that were engulfing the country at the rate of a province a day.

But it was now April 14. There was nothing left for me to do in Washington. At the crucial moment, with South Vietnam's existence in the balance, seven years of friendships and contacts with American presidents, cabinet secretaries, senators, and congressmen had proven insufficient to free up an extra penny of life-giving aid for my country. With the end approaching fast, it was time to return. My ninety-year-old mother was still in Saigon, living with my sister. I would get them out if it was humanly possible. But besides that, fate had given me a role in thirty years of Vietnamese political life, both in opposition to South Vietnam's governments and as their representative to the outside world. Although Saigon was doomed, my place was there. Who knew, maybe I could still help somehow, as Bob Shaplen had said. And if not, it would still be better than sitting in Washington watching the news describe the end, the marooned ambassador of a dying ally.

The next day I kept my luncheon appointment at the Empress with Ted Shackley, CIA chief for East Asia. Shackley had just gotten back from a special mission to South Vietnam for President Ford. He would have the latest information, and before I left I wanted to hear his assessment of the situation. Shackley's prognosis was grim. Saigon was already dangerous and would quickly become more so. Thieu was a lost soul, "numbed." The South Vietnamese president hadn't even been able to keep his mind on the discussion Shackley and Army Chief of Staff Frederick Weyand had had with him. A man overwhelmed by the immensity of the debacle.

By the following morning I was ready to leave for Saigon, with a short layover in Hong Kong to talk with Shaplen. At Washington's National Airport I said an emotional goodbye to my wife and three children: Luu, twenty-four; Giao, twenty; and Han, at eight too young to understand but old enough to sense the difference in this leavetaking. My wife was worried but as supportive as always. Though she had a sharp appreciation of the dangers, she also knew that if I didn't go I would regret it the rest of my life.

The Pan Am jumbo jet made its way west while I slept fitfully, exhausted in mind and body and only vaguely aware of the stops in San Francisco and Honolulu. Twenty hours later I stepped out of the plane at Hong Kong's Kai Tak Airport and went immediately to Shaplen's apartment. When I arrived it was afternoon. Till late that night I sat with him as he talked about the chaos in Saigon. "Nobody there knows anything about what's really happening, especially about American intentions. It's an absolutely critical situation. But they still have a lot of illusions about help from the United States, and about a compromise solution."

There were a million rumors, he said, and a general belief that the United States could not simply stand back and watch an ally of twenty years be destroyed by its Soviet-supplied Communist enemy. Somehow the Americans would even now save the situation. Fleets of B-52s were being sent to rip apart the fully exposed North Vietnamese divisions. U.S. marines were readying themselves to land in the Mekong Delta, to secure South Vietnam's rice basket as a new state. Kissinger was negotiating a further division of the country with the North Vietnamese, ceding the central provinces and promising massive economic assistance in return for a cease-fire. These were only a few of the stories making the rounds, stories that were affecting not just the morale of the population but of the government itself, which had become blind and paralyzed and beset by fancy. "They need the truth of it," said Shaplen. "That's why you had to come back."

"The truth of it," I told him, "is that as far as the United States is concerned, this war is over."

"Then that," he said, giving me an intense look, "is what you have to go and tell them."

The next day, April 17, I was on the Air France flight to Saigon. Landing at Tan Son Nhut at four in the afternoon, I was surprised by the relative calm. After Shaplen's description, I had half-expected to find myself in the middle of a madhouse. Then I noticed the crowd milling around the Air America restricted area, awaiting what was clearly a high-volume airlift outbound. On the ride into town, the traffic on the other side of the two-lane thoroughfare was piled up — lines of cars headed toward the airport.

In Saigon, the only outward indication that people were aware of the wave sweeping toward the city was the unusually nervous bustle of street crowds. Each face in the sea of movement seemed set and preoccupied. The ordinary air of diffuse energy and noise was gone, replaced by the determined expressions of people who had a lot to do in a hurry. That day, two hundred miles to the north, Phan Rang, President Thieu's native province, fell to the invaders.

At my apartment on Nguyen Hue Street my mother and sister were happy and relieved that I had come. They were growing anxious about the developing crisis and were at a loss about what to do. The only other member of our immediate family was my brother, a professor in Hanoi, who had remained in North Vietnam with my father when my mother and sister had fled south in 1951. Obviously, no help could be expected from that quarter.

As soon as we had embraced and I had assured them that I would take care of things, I put in a call to Thieu at the presidential palace. His chief of staff, Colonel Vo Van Cam, came on the line and said he would let the president know immediately that I was in Saigon and then get back to me quickly. A few minutes later Cam was on the phone again, telling me that "the president is very busy and very agitated by the loss of Phan Rang." Thieu had asked me to see the prime minister right away.

That message said everything necessary about how black the situation truly was. Thieu himself had sent me as his emissary to the United States. Now I was back, straight from the only possible source of South Vietnam's salvation. Whatever the news, hopeful or desperate, he needed to know it right away. Instead I was to see the prime minister, Nguyen Ba Can, a man Thieu regarded with barely concealed scorn. Always before, under far less critical circumstances, I had had immediate personal access. I thought of CIA chief Shackley's assessment — Thieu was "overwhelmed," "numbed" — and of Shaplen's report that Thieu (and U.S. Ambassador Graham Martin, too) was "incommunicado." "Who," I said to myself, "is running things?" How fast events had raced since mid-March and the marathon session I had had with the president before taking off for Washington — a brief three weeks before.

*   *   *   *   *

March 11 had been the beginning of the end, though nobody saw it at the time. On that day Banmethuot, a lightly defended provincial capital in the central highlands, was overrun by a surprise attack of three North Vietnamese divisions. In the Saigon government there was no panic. Banmethuot was a serious setback, but hardly a fatal one. We had recaptured larger cities in the past — Hue after the Tet offensive in 1968, Quang Tri after the 1972 spring offensive — and now crack South Vietnamese special forces were being mobilized for an attempt to take back Banmethuot.

At that time I had just returned from a fence-mending visit to New Delhi, one of the many stops that made up my itinerary as South Vietnam's ambassador at large, a diplomatic troubleshooter attempting to shore up my country's image, improve bilateral relations, and seek financial aid in Southeast Asia, Japan, India, France, and anywhere else a need or an opportunity presented itself.

This activity I combined with regular visits to Washington — my briefcase bulging with documents on military and economic necessities — lobbyist and public relations man for a cause that was growing less and less popular with each passing day. Now, on March 15, Thieu had asked me to come in, to prepare me for yet another mission to the United States, a more pressing one this time, with the North Vietnamese offensive in full bloom and the fallen Banmethuot a potential key to the strategic central highlands.

Typically, my meetings with Thieu were far-ranging affairs that would include blunt discussions of world politics as well as analyses of every important dimension of South Vietnam's domestic life. I had been drafted into the Thieu-Ky government back in 1965, directly from my job as cabinet-level chief of staff to Dr. Phan Huy Quat, the last civilian prime minister. As a convinced opponent of military rule, I had had few positive feelings about the generals who were then replacing Quat's administration with their own. But when Quat himself urged me to accept their invitation, I swallowed my reservations. South Vietnam needed every advantage it could muster in its dealings with the United States, its huge protector. As the Quat government's liaison with the Americans, for better or worse I had developed an excellent rapport with Ambassador Maxwell Taylor and Alexis Johnson, the top-ranking State Department official who served as Taylor's deputy. Besides that, I knew how important it was to the generals that they retain some highly visible civilian presence in their government.

When the Quat administration fell, I had been anxious to get back to private life and my job as editor and publisher of the *Saigon Post*. But the fact that the generals were so determined to keep me on suggested I would have the leverage to make my views heard in the new government. And if not, I could always quit. So I took the job, secure in my independence and willing to see if I could continue to serve in a way that would be compatible with my integrity and productive for the country.

The upshot was that my relationship with Thieu and Ky was blunt indeed. Thieu especially was not noted for his tolerance of criticism, and it was something of a wonder to both me and others that he could put up for so long with my regular harping on themes that were anything but dear to his heart. Foremost among these was the need for a government of national unity. As far as I was concerned, Thieu's cabinet was made up almost entirely of passive incompetents, many of them corrupt and none of them willing to do more than acquiesce to the president's wishes. Only a government of strong individuals who represented the country's various non-Communist political factions, including the opposition, could rally national support against North Vietnam and the Vietcong and begin to resolve the host of urgent social concerns.

It wasn't that Thieu was blind to the shortcomings of his administration. In our private talks that would follow the typically sterile and unproductive cabinet meetings his frustrations would break out. "Look at them," he would snarl in frustration. "These people are utterly worthless!"

These were the times to press the issue. "I've told you, Mr. President. You have got to change this government." But as the discussion warmed up, inevitably the response would come. "I'm considering it. I'll give it some thought." In the end, the dilatory, indecisive nature of the man always prevailed. To whatever extent he actually understood the vital need for change, that understanding would be lapped in a sea of temporizing, suspicious cerebration that precluded action.

Still, by March 15 Thieu had been in deep political trouble for months. And now, with the accelerating North Vietnamese offensive applying its own iron logic, the time had come for a showdown. I knew how critical our aid requirements were (though neither I nor anyone else suspected how quickly the enemy avalanche would descend), and I intended to use this moment for whatever leverage it could provide. So it was that when the president summoned me on the fifteenth, I sent back the clearest signal possible. I would of course meet with him, but I wanted to bring two others with me: my good friends Tran Van Do, former foreign minister, and the labor leader Tran Quoc Buu, both active politicians who were outside the government. With these men along, there could be no question about which issues I intended to address.

When Thieu's chief of staff called to say that the president would be pleased to see the three of us together, I knew I was in a position to push hard. In particular, I would hammer on the link between American public opinion and congressional responsiveness to our requests.

Thieu knew from years of briefings by myself and others that in the United States he was widely regarded as an oppressive militarist and dictator. It was, in fact, one of my greatest frustrations that I had been unable to impress on him the corrosive effect this perception had on our relations with the Americans. Typically, he would answer my dissertations on the ultimate importance of American public opinion by insisting that many of the U.S. criticisms were "exaggerated" and "unjustified." My response was always the same: "As long as you still need their help, you have to take their views into account. The moment you can say you don't need them — that moment you can tell them to go to hell."

Now, of course, Thieu's need for the Americans could not have been more graphic. The loss of Banmethuot was the most pointed kind of stimulus. With Do and Buu reinforcing me, I spent a good part of our five-hour meeting insisting on the necessity for immediately forming a government of national unity. Even at this hour such a change might affect the response I would receive at the White House and on Capitol Hill. At the very least, it would rally the spirit of the nation to resist. So tense were our discussions that word leaked out (as it was later reported by the CIA's Frank Snepp) that I had demanded Thieu's resignation. I did not; but everything short of it that I could do, I did.

Even then Thieu remained unreceptive. He went so far as to agree in principle to restructure the government. He even asked us to provide him with "practical formulas" for doing it. But underneath I knew he was still temporizing, promising as he had so many times before, with no intention of taking action. Even in his extremity he proved to be a man blindly wedded to power, incapable of accommodating himself to either the needs of his own people or those of his sole support, the ally by which he would live or die.

On March 22 I arrived in a Washington just beginning to come alive with the beauty of the spring. But the incipient bloom of azalea, dogwood, and cherry did nothing to lighten the mounting anxiety in my heart. Stopping over in Paris, I had learned of the disastrous retreat from the highlands. Instead of attempting to stabilize the military situation in the center after the loss of Banmethuot, Thieu had elected to pull back to the coast. With the main roads interdicted, the retreating South Vietnamese troops had been forced to use an old logging trail. There, in the heart of the highland forests, the fleeing columns had been cut in half and annihilated. Now North Vietnamese army units were attacking the coastal highway, isolating the major cities of Hue and Danang. What had been a limited local defeat was rapidly developing into a stunning military catastrophe.

The tragedy unfolding on South Vietnam's coast turned the $700 million in emergency funds — the object of my trip — from an urgent necessity into a matter of life or death. The continued existence of my country was now to play out its final act in the halls of Congress. In my years of experience with trying to move Congresses, I had developed a fairly standard series of steps that included preliminary meetings at the White House, the National Security Council, the State Department, and the Pentagon. After these I would get together privately with journalists on the Vietnam and congressional beats. By the time I completed my rounds, I could count on having a good feel for where senators and representatives stood on a particular issue. By then I would be well prepared to meet with the congressmen themselves, with friends to rally support, and with critics to urge reconsideration.

The day after I arrived in Washington, Hue, the old imperial capital, was cut off. Hundreds of thousands of refugees pushed southward down the coastal highway to Danang, fleeing the North Vietnamese spearhead.

In Washington, Congress had adjourned for a ten-day recess. Henry Kissinger was away, engaged in Middle East diplomacy. President Gerald Ford had gone on vacation in Vail, Colorado.

That day I met with Philip Habib, assistant secretary of state for Far Eastern affairs. I had known Habib for a decade, since he was minister-counselor at the Saigon embassy in 1965. A disciplined career diplomat, he was also a candid person who had the courage to be brutally frank. With the directness of an old friend he got right to the point. "The president is tied down by the War Powers Act. . . . I don't know how he can get through to them [congressmen]. . . . We have to impress them with the emergency, but he really has his hands tied."

Habib was grim and pessimistic, but no more so than George Aiken, the craggy Vermont senator who was one of my closest congressional contacts. Though a Republican, Aiken was good friends with Mike Mansfield, the antiwar Senate majority leader. Aiken's assessments of the mood in Congress were always acute. "The outlook," he told me in his office, "is bleak." As I called other congressmen, I had the sense that even friends were reluctant to see me, that those who did found it hard to look me in the eye.

On March 30, Danang, a hundred miles south of Hue and Vietnam's second largest city, was overwhelmed by a force of thirty-five thousand North Vietnamese troops. That night, the television screen pictured scenes of unimaginable horror: women and children being trampled by mobs of civilians and soldiers frantic to escape the noose tightening around the city. A million refugees clogged the roads leading south.

At this point communications between our Washington embassy and Saigon broke down. We were unable to get calls through to Thieu's office. We sent off one cable after another but received no responses. It was as if a curtain had fallen between Saigon and the outside world, shutting us off. Each night we watched the news in anguish, as one province after another disappeared from the map of South Vietnam. Each day Tran Kim Phuong, who had succeeded me as ambassador to the United States in 1972, and I would map out our schedule of calls and meetings, going through the paces in what we were increasingly sure was a futile effort. At the end of the day we would collapse in exhaustion, hardly remembering a thing of what we had done. Ten thousand miles away our world was dying, and we were helpless to prevent it.

At the end of March a momentary light glowed when President Ford sent Army Chief of Staff Frederick Weyand to Vietnam along with CIA Far East chief Ted Shackley and Erich Von Marbod, assistant secretary of defense for logistics, to assess the situation and recommend whatever further aid they thought necessary. I went to see Weyand on April 9, the day he returned. Although pessimistic, he felt the South Vietnamese army still had a chance to regroup and hold — if emergency military assistance could be delivered in time. He would support immediate passage of the aid bill.

By this time the entire North Vietnamese force, with its enormous quantities of Soviet and Chinese equipment, was spread out in the open, advancing in long columns along the major highways, more vulnerable to air attack than at any time during the war. At Xuan Loc, on Saigon's outer defensive perimeter, South Vietnam's Eighteenth Division was throwing back every assault their enemies launched at them. Intervention by American air power alone, the kind of intervention Nixon and Kissinger had so fervently promised in 1973, could have destroyed the exposed columns, crippling the Communists' war-making capacity for years. A resupplied and re-encouraged South Vietnamese army might then have taken back a great deal of what was lost.

Even as the darkness fell, Phuong and I grasped at visions like these, knowing that any chance at all depended on the Congress that was about to reconvene. And this was a Congress sick to death of war and tired of supporting an ally that so many of its members saw as weak and corrupt. After all the years of struggle and bloodshed it was this particular group of men that would have to weigh the final balance. A realist by profession, I knew, of course, that an American Congress would make an American decision. Damage to America's credibility and to her geopolitical posture would be cast in the scales opposite the treasure and blood the United States had poured into Vietnam over twenty years and the good chance that additional aid would simply prolong the agony. A decision would be made, and at worst a chapter of American history would come to an end.

All my political experience taught me not just to expect what was about to happen but to understand it, to appreciate the viewpoints of the lawmakers. And so I did. But deep in my heart I knew that the essential question had nothing to do with American credibility or the unfitness of Saigon's leaders. The essential question was the kinds of lives twenty million individual South Vietnamese would have to endure once this Congress had made its choice. Those lives and the lives of their children and of their children's children, *our* children's children — that was the real issue. But in 1975 this was not an issue that could be expected to move an American legislature. And so I could not help but rage inside at the unfairness of it. And in the privacy of my Washington home, I could not keep myself from weeping.

The glimmer of hope Weyand's mission had sparked died on April 11, two days after his return. On that day, the emergency aid bill was defeated. Pragmatists might have argued that by then it was too late anyway. But for Phuong and me the defeat put the final seal on America's abandonment of its ally. Unknown to the South Vietnamese troops still fighting valiantly at Xuan Loc and to the million South Vietnamese refugees fleeing the Communist advance, on Capitol Hill the sentence of death had been pronounced.

Since the presidency of Lyndon Johnson, I had been an ambassador, chief liaison between the governments in Saigon and Washington. Through five summit meetings, through Tet, Cambodia, the great Communist spring offensive, through the Paris negotiations and their aftermath, my life had been taken up with the business of state. But with this final act in Washington my role was finished. Cut off from communication with my government, with nothing more to be done in the American halls of power, I went back to my family in the home we kept in Washington's suburbs. There, with my wife and children, I glued myself to the television, mesmerized by the tragedy playing itself out on the screen.

I remembered a short vacation we had all spent together the previous year on the beach at Nha Trang, where the water was a translucent aquamarine and the sand sparkled. On that sun-washed beach I had thought how infinitely sad it would be to lose this lovely, lovely country. Other, older memories came back too, like sequences of a film. I saw myself standing in a rice field near my childhood home in North Vietnam in the early 1940s, watching an American P-38 with a double tail bombing Japanese installations near Hanoi. It was as if I had watched the American intervention in my country at its very beginning. And now I was witnessing its end. For better or worse, my life had been intertwined with the events that led inexorably from that point to this.

Chapter 2

Early Years

MY FATHER WAS BUI KY, the scholar, the mandarin, the man who didn't care if the sky fell. In accord with the old Vietnamese tradition, he had chosen a pen name that revealed his inner self: Uu Thien, literally, "He Who Fears the Sky Will Fall," but meant to be understood ironically, "He Who Doesn't Care in the Least If the Sky Falls." "Those people who worry about everything are foolish," he wrote in one of his better-known poems. "They worry about the sky falling / They worry about the earth trembling / They worry that the birds will forget their nests and the fish forget their streams. / Well, worrying like that, really, what good does it do?"

As a young man he had refused to serve the emperor, who served the French. Instead he had gone to Paris to spend time with Phan Chu Trinh and some of the other great Vietnamese nationalists of those days. But after two years, rather than becoming a revolutionary himself, he came back to Vietnam to start a school. He told me afterward, "These people's cause is good, their intentions are correct. I subscribe to them." But though he subscribed, and though he hated the French colonials, his characteristic attitude of detachment stopped him short of action.

Detachment was a temperament that ran deep in the family. In the 1860s my great-grandfather had been a high mandarin in the emperor's court. Like other scholars of his rank, he had been invited to choose his favorite flower in the emperor's inner garden, then had received its replica in gold and silver as a token of his status. But when the French came, he gave up the court to go back to his village, also to teach. He would not taint himself by collaborating. My grandfather, too, had achieved *tien si,* the highest degree of scholarship, qualifying him as a mandarin.

But like my great-grandfather, he too chose not to associate himself with the subservient Vietnamese court. So there was plenty of family precedent for my own father when he spurned French offers of an administrator's job in the colonial government and went off to become acquainted with the nationalists in France.

From my forefathers and my father I inherited a scorn for Vietnamese who served the French. I also imbibed the family's traditional disengagement, the air of weary aloofness from the transitory things of this world. One serves the people, yes. But — if service becomes too weighted with problems, if it begins to demand unacceptable compromises, then one goes back to the home village to teach, to write, to compose intricate Taoistic poetry, to observe events with the casual negligence they so eminently deserve.

But though I was heir to this tradition, I knew from an early age that for me the retired life of a scholar wouldn't do. Nor would the life of a government administrator, which was the main alternative for someone of my background. The world that Vietnam was in the 1920s and 1930s was so constricted, and I wanted to fly. I was filled with the desire to get out and see things, to visit foreign places, to explore the universe that beckoned from beyond the horizon. Simple and unformed though it was, that desire attached itself to me as a boy and quickened when I reached adolescence. I also began vaguely to understand that the path to my dreams lay through education. Though the connection was still unclear, I was sure that school would give me the wings I needed. If only I could do well enough.

In primary school I performed in a manner expected of the grandson and great-grandson of mandarins. At thirteen, already proud of my academic accomplishments, I entered high school, the famous Thang Long private school in Hanoi, which my father had helped found and where he taught. Although I didn't know it at the time, the school was full of people who also had their dreams of a world different from the rigid contours of colonial Vietnam. But where my own thoughts were of vague if exciting voyages abroad, these people were defining visions that would eventually transform the political and social landscape of the nation.

In fact, when I matriculated in 1936, Thang Long was seething with anticolonial feeling and Socialist debate about Vietnam's future. The faculty ("professors" to us) included such figures as Phan Thanh, founder of the Socialist party, Dang Thai Mai, later to become the Communist minister of education, Hoang Minh Giam, who would be North Vietnam's foreign minister, and Tran Van Tuyen, destined for a career as South Vietnam's leading opposition politician. Among these memorable personalities, the most intense was a small, driven man who taught us

French history — Vo Nguyen Giap. Although still years away from his world-shaking triumph over the French at Dienbienphu and his subsequent war against the United States, the future General Giap was already a man possessed by the demons of revolution and battle.

Giap's history course was supposed to cover France from 1789 to the middle of the nineteenth century. But from the first day of the semester, the whole class knew we were in for a different experience. "Look," Giap said, pacing back and forth at the front of the room, "there are a lot of books about this stuff. If you want to know about it, you can look it up. I'm only going to tell you about two things: the French Revolution and Napoleon."

So distinctive was Giap's teaching that even now, forty-five years later, his presentation and his subjects come to mind clearly: his detailed descriptions of Marie Antoinette's luxury and decadence that left us with no doubts about the justice of her fate; the rousing accounts of the Committee for Public Safety, the Paris Commune, and the lives and deaths of Danton and Robespierre. His admiration for the Revolution and its leading figures glowed in these lectures, and Giap spoke not as a mere historian but as a passionate advocate.

Even more remarkable were Giap's lectures on Napoleon. Nervously prowling the floor, he recounted in minute detail each of Napoleon's campaigns — the separate battles and even individual skirmishes, every action that demonstrated the development of Napoleon's tactics and strategy. Giap knew all of it by heart. He had studied this history until it had become part of him, and he talked about it as if compelled to impart his understanding of why this squadron of dragoons had been positioned here or why the Imperial Guard had charged at this particular moment. Back and forth he would pace, so carried away that it was mesmerizing. And Giap's excitement was contagious; the whole class sat still, riveted by his accounts. If he admired Robespierre and Danton, he adored Napoleon and dwelled with unfeigned love on the details of his career.

Along with Giap's French history course, the Socialist Phan Thanh taught us French literature. Vietnamese history was not even offered. No one so much as mentioned it. Despite the nationalistic fever gripping our professors, as far as the curriculum was concerned, our language was French and our ancestors were Gauls.

Nevertheless, by the time I was sixteen I had become aware of the political currents that swirled just under the apparently placid surface of school life. On occasion I would stop at Giap's home after classes to talk. In his library was a copy of Marx's *Das Kapital* in French, which he urged me to read along with other Socialist books. My math tutor, only a few years older than I, was a source for political tracts and brightly illustrated magazines from the Soviet Union. Of all my elders, it was Tran Van Tuyen, the future dean of Saigon's political opposition, that I was closest to. Neither a Socialist nor a Communist, Tuyen would tell me that "someday the situation has to change, and we are the ones who have to change it."

Presiding over his restive faculty, my father maintained a stance of disengaged sympathy. He himself had refused to go along with the French, and he liked the idea of encouraging activism. But his introverted, reflective nature dictated that his only mode of resistance would be passive. He supported the young teachers with friendship and advice, feeling toward them as he had felt toward the nationalists he had met in France. They were right to form their groups and spread their influence, to begin the struggle for independence. Theirs was a movement he subscribed to, even if he was unsuited by temperament to join it himself.

Meanwhile, together with my uncle, the historian Tran Trong Kim, my father began work on what was to become a definitive compendium of Vietnamese history (*Viet Nam Su Luoc,* still a classic and still in use). Working together each day, they filled the air in our house with discussions of the country's history, poetry, and philosophy. Every bit as patriotic as Giap and the others, they knew that their talents lay in the realm of scholarship and that the revival of Vietnam's national life was as much a cultural matter as a political one. Their days were taken up with their writing and the lectures they gave to the many students and scholars who gathered around them. Among their favorite subjects were Buddhism and the Taoist Way, which urged the achievement of serenity through a withdrawal from the meaningless flux of the world.

Whatever the unique chemistry by which I was becoming a man, it incorporated powerful elements from my family and teachers even as it ignored other influences. I was caught by my teachers' fervor for a new Vietnam free from the arrogant French, but the Marxist model that Giap and my mathematics tutor proposed left me cold and unconvinced. Perhaps I was too attracted by the living spiritual models of my father and uncle, for whom personal integrity required maintaining a steady distance from excess and mundane striving. Revolution was not part of their make-up. But at the same time, it was the world outside that called to me, not the carefully cultivated and guarded world of scholarship.

My adolescent fantasies led me to dream of faraway people and places. Now, in high school, I became addicted to the foreign press. I read the French papers religiously, obsessed with news of the war that Japan had brought to China. Photographs and reports from Nanking shocked me, and I felt a troublesome ambivalence about the horrors the Japanese army was visiting on the Chinese. I had learned to regard the Chinese as invaders, the age-old enemy of Vietnam. But I also studied Chinese characters each summer with an elderly teacher in our home village, and I felt at home with the classical literature and moral traditions that were part of China's pervasive influence on Vietnam. The Chinese being slaughtered wholesale in their villages and cities may have been historic enemies, but they were anything but alien.

By 1939 it was clear that war would not be limited to China. *Are We Defended?* played in Hanoi, a French film about the Maginot Line that set off a barrage of questions regarding France's ability to deal with the threat from Germany. Imminent war in Europe stimulated the growth of nationalist sentiment in Vietnam, where anti-French talk began to percolate more freely than before. In school we heard rumors that covert organizations were being formed to oppose France, that they were recruiting young men who loved the country and were willing to sacrifice themselves for it. No one seemed to know exactly what these secret societies were, and how one might contact them was a complete mystery. But there was no question that they existed. As Europe went to war in the spring of 1939, my friends and I were gripped in a mood of expectancy. We could feel the ossified ground of colonial Vietnam beginning to tremble under our feet.

That trembling soon became an earthquake. France, the all-powerful giant whose might had cowed Vietnam for so long, collapsed before the German army on June 25, 1940, after a campaign of only six weeks. Overnight our world changed. Mine was the third generation for whom the universe had been bounded by France, her language, her culture, and her stultifying colonial apparatus. Now, in a moment, the larger world had intruded itself on our perceptions. Our ears were opened wide, straining to pick up signals from the outside that would give us some hint as to what all this might mean.

Chapter 3

Secret Societies

WE DIDN'T HAVE LONG to wait. Immediately after France's surrender to the Third Reich, the Japanese began pressing the French colonial administration in Vietnam for concessions on the control of Vietnam's border with China. Without the military means to resist, the French governor general attempted to delay the inevitable, putting the Japanese off as best he could. After three months the Japanese tired of this game and staged two military demonstrations intended to impress the French with their seriousness. An attack on the border town of Lang Son and landings in Haiphong were sufficient to persuade the governor to capitulate. The French would be permitted to continue their control over Vietnam's domestic affairs, but Japan would establish bases and a military presence in the country.

Although the French colonials continued to act as though their *mission civilisatrice* would go on forever, no one could be blind to the Japanese troops who now made their appearance, setting up camps and doing precisely as they wished in spite of the hostile glances of the legionnaires. With the humiliation of our French overlords, we began to imagine for the first time that the French regime itself might be swept away, and not sometime in the dim future.

Now the secret societies began to mushroom, still underground or disguised as sports clubs and outing groups. The Communists were particularly active, setting up the traditional "National Salvation" associations and establishing what they called their "zone" in the mountainous areas of Cao Bang and Lang Son. Vo Nguyen Giap disappeared from his classroom, and in the school hallways it was whispered that he had fled to the mountains to organize guerrilla activities there.

Other political parties surfaced, among them the Quoc Dan Dang, Vietnam's version of the Chinese nationalists' Kuomintang. The VNQDD, as it was known, had organized the bloody Yen Bay rebellion against the French in 1930. After its brutal suppression then, many of the VNQDD leaders had fled to China. Other members had simply reverted to total secrecy, doing nothing overt. Now we heard that VNQDD partisans were again becoming active and that the party's émigrés in China's Yunnan province were arranging for aid from Chiang Kai-shek.

New nationalist groups were also forming — the League for Restoration (Phuc Quoc Hoi) and a number of different parties with the name Dai Viet (Great Vietnam) — some of which were said to be close to the Japanese, while others were rumored to have links with the VNQDD and the Chinese. Like my high school classmates, I heard about all of them. Although no one knew anything concrete about these parties, what their policies were, or even the names of their leaders, we were caught in a rush of excitement. We felt that our country was on the verge of striking out for its freedom, and there wasn't a soul who didn't want to be part of that.

As the secret parties gathered strength, the Japanese, too, began stirring the murky waters. It was the Japanese, after all, who were ridding Asia of white rule, offering in its place a "Co-Prosperity Sphere" of Asian nations dominated, of course, by themselves. In Vietnam there was nothing heavy-handed about their manipulations, at least not at first. Numerous Japanese students and cultural affairs people arrived in Hanoi, setting up friendship societies, free Japanese language courses, and discussion groups, making as many contacts among Vietnamese intellectuals and students as they could.

All this the French administration watched balefully. But the Japanese did nothing blatant, and the French security police, the Sûreté, would have been unable to act against them anyway. The Japanese troops were obviously strong and disciplined. It looked to us as if they could easily have swept the French aside had they wanted to. But for the Vietnamese, the Sûreté had never been anything to laugh at. Especially for Vietnamese students, who were prime targets of both the political parties and the Japanese, it was turning into a dangerous time — a time of joining, of choosing secret allegiances, of watching carefully what others were doing, and of watching for those who were watching you.

By this point, I was beginning to spend a great deal of time at my uncle's house, where he and my father were now collaborating on the history book. The three of us ate together frequently, and often the Japanese were the subject of our dinner conversation. Neither my father nor my uncle saw them as liberators. The Japanese army's ruthless behavior in China had been well covered by Vietnam's French press, and the Kempeitai, the Japanese secret police, were known to be brutally efficient. The Japanese were strict disciplinarians; once they stepped in, there were no half measures. Who could predict what would happen if they decided to eliminate the French colonial government? We didn't identify with them racially. We didn't know anything about their ultimate intentions. My father and uncle thought it was premature to get involved with them.

But though it might have been too early to get involved with the Japanese, it turned out to be impossible not to, at least for my uncle Kim. One afternoon an older Japanese student by the name of Yamaguchi showed up at the house and asked to speak with Kim. He was, he said in perfect French, a student of Vietnamese history. He had come to respectfully request that my uncle help him with his research on certain periods of Vietnam's Nguyen dynasty.

From that day on, Yamaguchi was a frequent visitor. Ostensibly, he came by to interview my uncle for his historical work. But what he really wanted was hard to say. Perhaps it was just to cultivate a relationship with my uncle. Although we didn't know what Yamaguchi was up to, it was clear that something was going on, and whatever it was, it had nothing to do with the Nguyen dynasty.

Meanwhile, Yamaguchi began showing up in other places too. He seemed to be everywhere, organizing meetings small and large, recruiting friends and students to attend, lecturing, making contacts with teachers. He would talk about the brotherhood of Asian peoples, about helping brother countries achieve their freedom. He touched on the theme of "Asia for the Asians" and nurtured the idea that Japan was Vietnam's friend and supporter. He said nothing harsh or inflammatory, or even concrete. Instead there were soft-spoken hints and insinuations. Japan and Vietnam shared a cause. Japan would prove a reliable comrade. I knew him perhaps better than most, because I saw him often at my uncle's house. One day he casually intimated to me that he belonged to the Black Dragon, the secret Pan-Asian tong that had helped Sun Yat-sen overthrow the last of the Manchu emperors and supposedly exerted its mysterious influence throughout the Orient. I didn't know whether to believe him about that or not. None of us, in fact, knew quite what to make of the Japanese. We knew only that they were incredibly active, talked a lot, sounded very serious, and made no promises.

At seventeen, I found the growing excitement and riskiness a tonic. But I did not allow politics to divert my attention from the overwhelming task that loomed immediately before me and every other last-year high school student: achieving the coveted *baccalauréat*. This was the academic degree one received after passing a monumental examination on virtually all the subjects covered in the high school curriculum. Without the *baccalauréat*, one's future would be suddenly curtailed; with it, there was a clear path to the university and to whatever lay beyond. Through the first half of 1941, I studied for this exam night and day, finally taking it that June. When the announcement came that I had passed — and on the first try — the family held a joyous celebration in our home village of Phu Ly. I had taken the vital first step into manhood.

The second step was to decide which course of study to follow at Hanoi University, the single institution of higher learning the French had seen fit to establish in Indochina. As far as I was concerned, the law school was out. Since the chances of a Vietnamese actually practicing law were almost nil, the only career available to graduates was in the despised colonial administration. Medicine, though, was a possibility.

Curious about whether a doctor's life would suit me, I attended an orientation session for medical students at Bach Mai Hospital. Whoever had come up with the idea for this session must have been a sadist. Our group of fifteen potential doctors was spared none of the horrors the hospital had to offer. We saw patients writhing in agony and despair, some crying uncontrollably in their beds, others swathed in blood-soaked bandages. I couldn't stand it. So, along with law, medicine dropped by the wayside.

In the end I decided on mathematics. I had always had a feeling for math, and this field was well insulated from either the forced collaboration a law degree would bring or the human misery that would be my daily diet as a doctor. With the decision made, I was accepted into an advanced mathematics course, along with fourteen French students and two other Vietnamese. Because it was an accelerated program, classes met for thirty hours a week; homework took longer than that. There wasn't a moment for anything else. The political world, recently so enthralling, faded from sight. In the *cours de mathématiques spéciales* it was just math, math, and more math.

I loved it: I loved the intricacies of equations, the elegance of abstract expressions. Here was an utterly pure world that could absorb all the intelligence and energy I had to give. For a year I saw little else, though I still followed the war reports and even began to understand that Japan's fortunes could be traced in the skies over Vietnam. For by 1942 American planes had begun to appear above Vietnamese targets.

The first one I saw was a P-38 fighter swooping through a blue sky to attack a Japanese camp near the train station outside my home village of Phu Ly. As the war pushed closer to the Asian mainland, more and more planes arrived. I got used to the air-raid sirens wailing in Hanoi and to the ambulances rushing through the streets, delivering victims to the hospitals. But after a while, these events became no more than a small distraction as my fascination with mathematics led me deep into an interior world.

At the end of the *cours de mathématiques*, the French students left to continue their studies at the famous universities of France. For my Vietnamese friends and me, with no family money to support us abroad and scholarships a concept that had not yet been invented, it was on to the University of Hanoi's regular math program.

Soon I moved from my father's house to the Cité Universitaire, the sprawling modern campus half a mile from Bach Mai Hospital. The change meant far more than just a different place to sleep. The political turbulence I had temporarily left behind had not subsided in the least. On the contrary. When I was in high school, I knew of the secret political parties mainly through rumor and secondhand sources. Somebody's cousin had joined one; someone else's father's friend had been arrested for membership in another. But now, a year later, the movement had gained strength and credibility. The Cité was alive with students who were Vietminh, Dai Viet, or VNQDD. Political discussions and party recruitment went on all the time against a background of the more diffuse but equally fervent nationalism of the university's Student Association, of which I immediately became an active member.

Aware that French agents and provocateurs were everywhere, the Student Association acted prudently. We avoided confrontation by arranging meetings and outings that were ostensibly innocent but in fact were intended to stimulate patriotic feelings. Our weekend bicycle tours always had historical and political connotations. We visited the Temple of the Ancestors, the Temple of the Trung Sisters, and other temples and sites associated with the great heroes of Vietnam's past who had routed and destroyed earlier foreign invaders. The parallels between their times and ours were not exactly subtle, but the French authorities could hardly object to such orderly excursions. Sitting around campfires, we would discuss how the Trung sisters had overthrown the Chinese occupiers of the first century or how Tran Hung Dao had smashed the Mongols twelve hundred years later. Afterward we would sing, so loudly the woods seemed to reverberate:

Brothers, students, stand up!
Answer the call from rivers and mountains.
Go forward, always forward.
Have no regrets ever
About sacrificing your lives.

These meetings touched something deep inside each of us. With the Temple of the Ancestors just out of sight in the dark, we could feel that we ourselves were part of the continuous, heroic flow of Vietnamese history. The Trung sisters, Tran Hung Dao, Le Loi — they all led up to this very moment, a moment that was about to witness the rebirth of the nation's struggle for freedom. Magically, this was taking place in our generation. It was our time. We felt within us the immortal strength of youth and youth's boundless emotion. You could see all of that in the faces lit by the flickering, dancing campfires. It was a moment as pure as crystal, when we were all united in the longing for independence and in the willingness to sacrifice ourselves for it without hesitation. It was a moment of innocence, the last one, perhaps, before the fratricidal war between Communist and non-Communist bore down on us.

In public the students were united. In private it was a different story. Gradually, each of us joined one or another of the parties that promised to mold a reality from the desire for freedom. At that time, in 1943 and 1944, few had any idea of the distinctions between these parties, or even a good concept of which was which. They all said they were fighting for independence; that was enough. What the VNQDD's social program was no one knew. The real differences between Dai Viet and Vietminh were something perhaps none of the students could define. It was not generally known, for example, that the Vietminh was Communist controlled. Ho Chi Minh was not a name anyone had yet heard of.

Without firm knowledge about the various parties, the students tended to see them as basically the same. We knew, of course, that some were aligned with the Chinese and others with the Japanese. But their overall objective was identical: independence. Consequently, which party an individual joined was largely a matter of chance connections. People chose a party because a friend or, more often, a relative had joined. Once one family member was Dai Viet or VNQDD or Vietminh, chances were good that others who were politically inclined would follow suit.

With my father and uncle sitting firmly on the sidelines, it was a friend, Dang Van Sung, who convinced me to enroll in his party, the Dai Viet. An added incentive was the fact that Dai Viet seemed to have a sizable student following. By the time I formally enrolled, though, it was 1944. All during the war I had avidly followed the battles in the Pacific, reading the daily accounts in Hanoi's French language newspaper, *La Volonté Indochinoise*. Throughout that time, at least after 1942, the French had taken an almost malicious pleasure in reporting the constant tale of Japanese failures. Now the conviction spread that the war was coming to an end. Whatever the outcome, it was sure to have serious consequences for Vietnam. Something major would happen, and among the university students, at any rate, there was a feeling that we had better be organized. Membership in the parties picked up; even the undecided joined.

On the day of my initiation into the Dai Viet, my friend Dang Van

Sung led me through the streets of a modest residential area to a quite ordinary home. Inside I met the man who would perform the initiation and would be my superior, my single link to the party hierarchy, a man who looked as plain as the neighborhood he lived in. The situation gave me an odd feeling. By that time I considered myself a person of some sophistication, yet here I was, about to swear allegiance to a party I knew next to nothing about, in front of a man who seemed unprepossessing, to say the least.

Adding to my uneasiness was the altar in front of which I was invited to take the party oath. It stood before a large map entitled DAI VIET, which showed not only Vietnam but all of Indochina and a good deal of the rest of Southeast Asia as well. On the altar candles burned, giving the scene a religious air. In front of the candles my Dai Viet contact placed a large black pistol. "This weapon," he said, "represents the discipline of the party. You are here to swear allegiance to the nation and to the party. If you betray either . . ." He gave a meaningful nod toward the pistol.

The ceremony was impressive, but I was not taking the whole thing too seriously. There was a bit too much of the nineteenth century about it, an air of romanticism and conspiracy. Nevertheless, I raised my right hand and pledged my loyalty. With this self-conscious act I entered the world of the Vietnamese nationalists, a world I was not to leave until its final destruction by Vietnamese communism thirty years later.

Chapter 4

The Dai Viet

SOON AFTER MY INITIATION I was introduced to the two other Dai Viets with whom I formed a cell. Ostensibly, I was to know only my cell partners and my superior as members of the party, and by code names only. For my own I chose Kim, the first name of the girl I had spoken to a number of times at my uncle's house, where she had come for tutoring. She had had a beautiful smile, and although I tried not to allow myself to think about her, somehow when I was asked what name I wanted to use, hers came to mind first.

With the cell established, we began to meet regularly, never in the same place twice. Because our cell belonged to the Dai Viet's "intellectual circle," our chief focus was recruitment. We trained ourselves as proselytizers for the party, discussing how best to approach others, how to appeal to their patriotism and play on their sense of guilt about "doing something" for the country. Other Dai Viet sections were concerned with security, information, and finance. This was no longer the amorphous patriotism of the Student Association but a revolutionary movement. Arrests by the French police were common, and from time to time someone would simply disappear without a trace. Often it was impossible to tell what had happened or who had been responsible, the French or some rival Vietnamese party. The clandestine nature of all our activities enhanced the atmosphere of danger and threat. Life suddenly seemed full of menace. I began to carry a pistol, which rode snugly in my back pocket.

The Dai Viet party I had joined was made up of several Dai Viet factions that had very loose connections with one another and with the Vietnamese Kuomintang, the VNQDD. One of these factions was Dai Viet Quoc Xa, which had close ties to the Japanese. Another espoused the three revolutionary principles of the great Chinese republican Sun Yat-sen: with the people, for the people, by the people. This Dai Viet group was thus closer to the VNQDD, though it did not have that party's direct links to the Chinese Kuomintang. It even called itself the Dai Viet Quoc Dan Dang. It was this faction to which I had sworn allegiance in front of that ceremonial altar with the candles and the pistol on it.

With its democratic principles and militant Vietnamese nationalism, the Dai Viet Quoc Dan Dang attracted a generation of Vietnamese students. Unfortunately, beyond its philosophical commitment to government with, for, and by the people, the Dai Viet Quoc Dan Dang had only the most nebulous ideas about social and economic development. It had been born at a time when Vietnam's passion for independence, suppressed during seventy years of French colonial rule, was smoldering toward an eruption. The party's very existence was an expression of that anticolonial fervor. Its raison d'être was national freedom, and it had neither the time nor the inclination to look far beyond that goal.

This lack of a well-formulated political program was a weakness the Dai Viet Quoc Dan Dang shared with all the other parties but one. The Vietminh, founded and controlled by a core of trained, clear-sighted, and committed Communists, brought to the struggle for independence qualities the nationalists were never able to match. Ho Chi Minh and his colleagues were absolutely certain about the nature of the society they envisioned for Vietnam. Equally important, they had mastered the organizational skills necessary to bring it about. And most significant of all, they were versed in the strategy and tactics of factional warfare.

By the mid-1940s Ho Chi Minh had been a Comintern agent for a quarter century. He had helped found the French Communist party and had studied at the Stalin Institute for Toilers of the East. He had been an original Krestintern (Peasants' International) member and was with the legendary Comintern figure Michael Borodin during Borodin's mission to assist the Chinese revolution. At the time the Dai Viet and its siblings were in their infancy, Ho Chi Minh had already mastered both the art of revolution and that of destroying political enemies. With lieutenants like Giap, Le Duc Tho, Pham Van Dong, and Le Duan, the Vietminh was quickly to develop into a buzz saw against which the national parties would find few defenses.

Whether the Dai Viet leaders were aware of what they were facing, I don't know. Mercifully, neither I nor my friends had any idea.

But as 1944 slipped into 1945, I did know that I was beginning to find my role in our four-man cell too constricting. I felt sure I could do more than was being asked of me, and I started agitating to meet Truong Tu Anh, the Dai Viet Quoc Dan Dang's chief, the man we called Eldest Brother Phuong.

At first I got nowhere. My party contact kept putting me off, telling me that it wasn't possible, that I would have to be very patient about meeting Anh. Without any way of circumventing this man, who was my only channel of communication with the party, it was a frustrating period. I was finding that I wasn't very tolerant of the concept of strict party discipline. How this might eventually have affected my allegiance to the Dai Viet, I don't know. As it turned out, I was to meet Anh quite by accident a short time later, a meeting that quickly led to an intense personal relationship and a crash course in party politics.

It happened during a gathering at a classmate's house. Typically for those times, I had not been aware that this classmate was also Dai Viet. But I did see a couple of other friends there whom I knew were in the party. There was also a thin, balding middle-aged man I didn't recognize who seemed to be holding court in one of the bedrooms. When I asked Phuc, one of my Dai Viet friends, if he knew who the man was, the answer came in a whisper, "That's Truong Tu Anh, the boss."

As soon as I heard that, I insisted that he introduce me. Phuc was shocked. "You can't just be introduced to him. That's not the way to do it. You've got to go through your superior." But I persisted. I had waited a long time for this opportunity, and now that I had it, I wasn't going to be put off. Finally, with a great show of discomfort, Phuc agreed.

Anh turned out to be personable and relaxed, not at all annoyed by the unexpected introduction. He smiled warmly at me and I noticed that his long face was lit by intense eyes, which seemed almost magnetic. He told me I should take the time to study the principles of the party, to understand exactly what the Dai Viet intended for the nation. I answered that I was eager to study exactly those things, because I did not have a good grounding in the party's philosophy.

"Your friend Phuc," said Truong Tu Anh, nodding toward the door through which Phuc had just left the room, "he's the one you can learn from about these matters. He's quite a decent theoretician."

I was surprised. "Phuc? He's an old friend, but how can I learn from him? In school I was way ahead of him in philosophy and everything else."

Whether it was this remark's brashness or its simplicity, I don't know. But something about it made Anh laugh. We talked a while longer, and then Anh asked me to meet with him privately several days later. I left the house feeling that Anh was someone I could put my faith in. And I knew I had made a good impression on him.

When I next saw him, Anh said he had several jobs for me, but the most important was to act as a contact between the party and my uncle Kim. Although Kim was a historian, not a politician, his work had made him a central figure in the reassertion of Vietnamese national culture.

Universally known and respected and committed to no particular group, Kim had become, willy-nilly, a public person. With his integrity, political neutrality, and public recognition, he would be a substantial asset to any party. Perhaps it would be best for me to stay close to Kim, Anh told me, to let him know that I had joined the Dai Viet Quoc Dan Dang, and to make myself available as a discreet liaison.

Although Uncle Kim was still hard at work on his books, in fact his life had changed substantially over the past year. The gathering political tide had succeeded in moving him somewhat away from his previously passive approach to the issue of independence. Yamaguchi, the Japanese operative, was more than ever a frequent visitor, and the Sûreté had mounted a close watch on Kim's house and movements.

Although I became aware of all this, I was still shocked when one day I showed up at his house only to be told by my aunt that Kim was no longer living there. "He's had to go away," she said. "He's afraid for his life now, with the French watching him like they are. So he's left for Singapore with Yamaguchi."

In the summer of 1944 the Allied armies were racing across France. By August 23 they had breached the Seine, and two days later General Jacques Philippe Leclerc's Free French had liberated Paris from four years of German rule. With Vichy France dead, the complicated situation in France's colony of Vietnam became even more so. In particular, the uneasy tolerance with which the Japanese had managed the French colonial administration turned increasingly ugly. Rumors flew about a Japanese move against the French. When it finally came, no one was surprised.

On the afternoon of March 9, 1945, I got a message from my aunt that Yamaguchi wanted to have dinner with me at her house. But when I arrived that evening, there was no Yamaguchi. We waited for a while, but shortly after dark the sound of small-arms fire began to crackle in the nearby streets. Suddenly Yamaguchi burst through the door and took me by the arm into a corner of the living room. "We're attacking the French tonight," he said. "It's already started. I need your help, you've got to come with me to the campus. There are going to be a lot of casualties, and I want to talk to the students about it. We'll need medical students especially. You've got to give me a hand."

With this breathless appeal, Yamaguchi began to steer me toward the door. But I wasn't quite as eager to go as he was. I certainly did not want to give the students the idea that I was cooperating with the Japanese in their action against the French. So I pulled away from his grip and faced him, ready to start discussing the situation.

But I didn't have a chance. "Look," he said, "there's no time for this. Don't you understand what's happening? We're attacking right now. It's not only the French who are going to get shot. There are going to be civilians involved in this. You people will simply have to help."

The way he put it, there didn't seem to be any choice. Before I knew it, we were in Yamaguchi's car, careening through streets alive with machine-gun and rifle fire. Somehow we made it to the Cité Universitaire without ever slowing down, let alone being hit. Once there, I tried to distance myself from Yamaguchi, though I did introduce him to the dormitory students, who were already milling around, trying to find out exactly what was going on. Most of them knew Yamaguchi at least slightly, since he had been enrolled at the university for years and had been so active on the Japan-Vietnam friendship front. So I told them that like all of us, I knew Yamaguchi, and that he had asked for our help.

Yamaguchi then gave a short speech and asked the students to help take care of the wounded, who even then were being caught in the firefights embroiling large parts of the city. Then he left. With the sounds of battle coming closer, we discussed what to do. As I had anticipated, many of the students assumed I was collaborating with Yamaguchi, and they wanted to know precisely what he wanted. But I told them I only knew him as a fellow student, the same as they did. Almost everyone wanted to avoid having it look as if the students were connected with the Japanese coup. But with all the noise going on outside, there was also no doubt that there would be many Vietnamese civilian casualties. We could hardly refuse to help care for them.

In the end we decided to adopt a neutral position. Teams led by medical students would go out on the streets, but with red cross arm bands prominently displayed. We would give whatever help we could but keep our contacts with the Japanese authorities to a minimum.

As it turned out, the specter of widespread fighting and great numbers of wounded never materialized. The Japanese had organized their takeover so well that in Hanoi the shooting was over by morning. With daylight, the French were gone and Japanese soldiers patrolled the streets in their place. It was an abrupt end to seventy years of French domination.

Now that the Japanese were in charge, the great question was, What would they do? Throughout their occupation they had avoided enunciating policies or making commitments, preferring to work through the ambiguous, silk-glove manipulations of agents like Yamaguchi. And by now it was clear to everyone that Japanese control, too, would be only a temporary affair. America's Pacific juggernaut was closing in on Japan's home islands, and the Co-Prosperity Sphere was obviously a dying organism. So whatever Japan's immediate plans for Vietnam, a golden historical opportunity had arrived.

Excitement swept the university. An overflow of patriotism mixed with the conviction that whatever was about to happen, we students, the flower of Vietnamese society, would have a major role to play. All of the emotion that had been building over the past years burst out in a frenzy of activity. Committees were formed, student newspapers burgeoned, celebrations and demonstrations of unity were planned. The energy that the French police had barely restrained now found an outlet. Nothing violent happened, no one was ready to challenge the Japanese directly, but we had the sense that the future was now in our own hands.

Before long, all this enthusiasm began to coalesce around plans for the Anniversary of the Ancestors of Vietnam. This national holiday was always a time for the expression of patriotic feeling, so much so that the French had never allowed public celebrations, afraid of the potential for violence. But now, with no explicit prohibition from the Japanese, the Student Association went all out.

At the Cité Universitaire the architecture students erected a huge monument to the Hung Vuong, the ancestors. The association sent groups of students into every ward of the city, to let people know about the celebration and urge them to come out. On the morning of the anniversary the field around the monument began to fill. The entire population of Hanoi seemed to be there, each family bringing a symbolic rice cake to place at the feet of the ancestors. The crowd grew in a huge circle around the monument, and the mountain of rice cakes rose higher and higher. Speeches rang out, each one a reaffirmation that we were Vietnamese, that we were a nation, that each of us must give himself for the sake of our country.

Perhaps only someone born and raised in a country colonized and brutalized by foreigners can imagine the emotion of that moment. After each speech the throng roared, "Long live Vietnam! Long live Vietnam!" Throughout the crowd, men as well as women were weeping. No one paid attention to the Japanese hovering on the outskirts, taking pictures of everything. Our vision had no room for them or anything else — only the nation.

When the speeches were over, the whole throng marched to downtown Hanoi waving banners and chanting "Independence! Independence!" Japanese soldiers stood stolidly along the streets, their faces impassive as the cheering columns flowed by. There was no hostility on either side. Eventually the crowd broke up into smaller groups, filtering back to their neighborhoods and homes, spent by the exhilaration of the day.

A few days later, Yamaguchi again asked to see me. My uncle, he said, was back from Singapore. Bao Dai, Vietnam's emperor, had asked him to form a new government.

Chapter 5

The August Revolution

THE EMPEROR BAO DAI was the last of the Nguyen dynasty. As titular ruler under the French from 1932 on, he exercised a power that was almost entirely ceremonial. But the man himself was complex. Highly intelligent and capable of considerable subtlety, he was also lethargic and addicted to hunting, gambling, and women. Although he felt keenly his responsibility to the cause of Vietnamese independence, his advocacy was timid and inconstant. Since ascending the throne, he had several times pushed France for reform and movement toward a national government. But he had always pulled back, too weak to sustain a courageous stand.

Now, encouraged by the Japanese, he declared Vietnam's independence and formed a national government. It was a surprise to everyone when Bao Dai appointed Tran Trong Kim prime minister. It was a surprise primarily because a real Vietnamese politician had kept himself close to the Japanese all along. That politician was Ngo Dinh Diem, the future first president of South Vietnam. To anyone concerned about these matters, it was self-evident that if the Japanese ever decided to throw out the French, Diem would be appointed to head the government. There was also no question that Diem was enthusiastically looking forward to just this eventuality. But for reasons of their own, the Japanese had decided to cast him aside.

This development took place just as the nationalist parties were busily preparing for an open power struggle. The Vietminh had consolidated their guerrilla bases in Viet Bac, and Dai Viet chief Truong Tu Anh had set up his own strongholds in Bac Giang and Thanh Hoa. When news about my uncle's appointment came, I had already received orders to report to the Thanh Hoa base, but now Truong Tu Anh asked me to go instead to Hue, the imperial court city in central Vietnam where my uncle's government would be installed. In Hue I was to keep an eye on the new regime and again serve as liaison between Anh and my uncle.

Suddenly my world had expanded geometrically. One moment I was a twenty-two-year-old mathematics student, active in politics yes, but not in any sense a leader. The next I was on a personal mission to Vietnam's new government. I asked myself whether it was real or whether, perhaps, the real Bui Diem wasn't somewhere else, observing with amused tolerance the pretentions of this political upstart. It was a sensation I was to experience more than once in my later life.

The trip to Hue was hair raising: three days down the narrow coastal highway on an antique, charcoal-powered rattletrap of a bus — or, rather, three nights. American air force bomb attacks had made the highway a road of death during the daytime, so we could travel only from sundown to sunup. But I couldn't see how night driving on that road in that vehicle could possibly be less dangerous than American bombs. Nevertheless, contrary to all my private predictions, after three days the bus wheezed safely into Hue, crossed the lovely Perfume River, and deposited us at the provincial-looking bus station.

The bus station wasn't the only thing about Hue that looked provincial. Compared to Hanoi, the imperial capital was a sleepy backwater, a serene country town dominated by the graceful nineteenth-century citadel where the emperor held court and by the imposing colonial palace of the former French *résident supérieur,* which now housed the new government.

Slinging my backpack over my shoulders, I walked briskly over the Trang Tien Bridge and made my way to the *résidence.* As I walked, my head kept ringing with the words *"doc lap"* — independence. The country was truly free — or so I believed. I was at the seat of Vietnam's first independent government since 1884. To the guards at the entrance I said with a touch of pride, "I'm the prime minister's nephew, Bui Diem. I'd like to see him." At this, one of them slipped inside, returning a few moments later to show me in.

Once inside the doors, I was astonished by the grandeur of the place, its long, elegantly furnished corridors, sweeping stairways, and ornate ceilings. I was staring in awe at this incredible luxury when my uncle Kim walked up behind me and said, "Look around, Diem. Look around carefully. Now you see why the French were so eager to hold on to their colony."

Soon we were having tea, and Kim was asking me to stay with him in the palace. The invitation didn't surprise me. I was a favorite nephew with whom he had always loved to talk. I had lived in his house in Hanoi from time to time, and I knew that in some ways he regarded me as the son he and his wife had never had. So, with a toothbrush and one change of clothes in my knapsack, I moved into the huge *résidence*.

Once I was settled, Kim told me the story of his appointment, which had been as much a surprise to him as to everyone else. Shortly before their coup against the French, the Japanese had flown Kim from Singapore (to where Yamaguchi had spirited him a year before) to Saigon. There they had put him up in a private home to await events. Ngo Dinh Diem was also in Saigon at that time and was also in constant touch with the Japanese, anticipating that developments might soon favor him.

One day the Japanese asked Kim to come to their administrative headquarters for a talk. There they told him that the emperor wanted to see him and that he should leave for Hue as soon as he could. They didn't mention anything about a new government, only that Bao Dai had asked to speak with him. When the message had been conveyed Kim left, thinking over its implications. But in the hallway he ran into Ngo Dinh Diem, who was waiting nervously for any news the Japanese might have for himself. Seeing Kim emerge from one of the offices, he rushed up to him and asked excitedly, "What's the news? What's the news?" He knew no more about it than Kim.

The next afternoon Kim was in Hue, listening as Bao Dai asked him to accept the prime minister's post and form a government. When he heard this, Kim's first response was, "Why me? Why not Ngo Dinh Diem?" To which the emperor answered, "Well, I've been trying to get in touch with Diem for over a week now. But the Japanese tell me they don't know where to locate him. Apparently, he's gone into hiding, and I simply can't wait any longer."

As my uncle told the story, it was obvious to me that the Japanese had been keeping both men available pending their reading of the situation. Even at that age, I was impressed by their smooth manipulation of both the French colonial government and the Vietnamese. Though I didn't understand exactly why, the Japanese clearly believed that the times demanded a reticent, scholarly figure as Vietnam's prime minister rather than a strong-willed and ambitious politician. As a result, Tran Trong Kim was living in the *résident*'s palace in Hue while Ngo Dinh Diem was still in Siagon, wondering what had happened.

In many ways my uncle Kim embodied the old mandarin approach to service. He brought to his new post exemplary scholarship, personal integrity, and faithfulness toward what he deemed the obligations of public office. With hindsight, it is easy to see that these were hardly the qualities that savage period called for.

My uncle's political orientation was mirrored by that of his cabinet, individuals drawn from the country's intellectual elite, the cream of Vietnamese society. A few of the ministers were, in fact, old professors of mine, including the education minister, Hoang Xuan Han, who had taught me mathematics, and the minister of youth, Phan Anh, my instructor in French literature. Because the government had just been formed, the ministers and their families were all staying at the *résidence* while trying to find houses for themselves. With everyone living together, it seemed like a cross between a huge family and a university campus.

At dinner the whole group would gather around the giant table in the formal dining room, and political discussions would flare up. But these were political discussions with a difference. Hardly one of these ministers had had a day's worth of practical political experience. Consequently, they approached the task of government from a theoretical point of view: if this was the way something was supposed to work, certainly this was the way it would actually work. They believed they could simply issue directives and their wishes would automatically be fulfilled. They were not in any sense puppets. Even though the real power was in Japanese hands, not one of them would have considered doing something that conflicted with his sense of duty or conscience, no matter who ordered it.

But though they did not take orders, neither did they have any clear idea of the political and military storm that was gathering around them. They did not, for example, yet have their own representative in Hanoi. In fact, in the spring of 1945 there was not even a telephone hookup between Hue and Hanoi, and the government had to rely on a telegraph link. They knew nothing whatsoever about the Americans, whom Ho Chi Minh was busily courting at that very moment. Nor, to my memory, did they ever discuss Ho Chi Minh himself or the Vietminh. It was as if they were living in a vacuum. Or perhaps, in the fashion of the old court, they considered themselves the center of the universe, with everything else revolving around them.

As for the Japanese, my uncle and his ministers seemed, to my mind, to have little more understanding of them than they had of the Americans. For one thing, Japan's imminent defeat did not appear to weigh heavily with them. One night, I remember, there was an especially lively discussion about the southern part of Vietnam, then called Cochinchina, which the Japanese had refused to include in the independent Vietnamese state. In the midst of the talk about how Cochinchina might be recovered, my uncle announced that he had already brought the issue to the attention of Yokahama, the Japanese ambassador, and that he had insisted on its return. Yokahama, according to Kim, had said he would have to get instructions from his government about it. He had also said that he would "do his best." That closed the subject for the moment. As long as the Japanese were "doing their best," my uncle thought, what else was there to do? The rest of the cabinet agreed with him.

As far as the business of governing went, Uncle Kim and his ministers were starting from scratch. With no experience to draw on, they began organizing a national army, reordering the educational system, and setting up a new government administration. They made steady progress in identifying major problem areas and moving toward solutions. But in the possession and exercise of power they had no interest at all. On the contrary, they viewed their presence in the government as a matter of duty, which they would happily relinquish whenever there was a legitimate request to do so.

I stayed in Hue for two months, observing the ministers, listening to their talk, and walking around the city till I knew all the historical sites intimately. By that time I was more than ready to go back to Hanoi. Fortunately for me, my uncle had just appointed a viceroy to represent the government there (Phan Ke Toai, an old mandarin with whom both my uncle and my father were on close terms). To my great pleasure, he then asked me to accompany the new viceroy to Hanoi. I was to serve as unofficial personal liaison between the viceroy and the government.

A liaison's job, I had already discovered, was not excessively burdensome. I had just spent two months as Truong Tu Anh's personal envoy to Uncle Kim without once delivering a message in either direction. Still, I would have seized on any excuse to get back, and this one would do nicely.

In contrast to Hue, Hanoi in late June 1945 was buzzing, alive with news, rumors, and intrigue. One thing clear to everybody was that Nippon's empire was near the end of its long slide toward oblivion. Whereas my uncle had thought there would be plenty of time to set up the government and then work things out in a civilized manner with the Japanese, everyone else was already scrambling for a strong position in anticipation of the next phase.

I quickly restored contact with Truong Tu Anh, who told me that the Dai Viet forces were now firmly established in their bases. But instead of going to one of the strongholds myself, I was to stay with him in Hanoi. I would, he felt, be more useful doing political work.

The closer I became to Truong Tu Anh, the more I was impressed with his competence. There was a touch of the mysterious about him; nobody knew precisely where he came from or what his family background was, but there was no question that he was a man of stature. Behind his quiet, reserved demeanor was an intelligent mind and a deep conviction in his own ability as a leader who could help shape the country's future.

In July Anh sent me back to my uncle in Hue. I was to deliver a message of support, assuring him that, in the developments that were bound to come, he could depend on Dai Viet backing. So again I braved the coastal highway at night; in the few weeks since I had last traveled the route, American bombing had become even more frequent. Not long before, my uncle's minister of health had been killed trying to make his way to Hanoi.

In Hue the atmosphere had not changed a great deal. My uncle received my message without visible enthusiasm. To me it seemed evident that he was not interested in participating in any struggle for power that might be in the offing. On the contrary, he had now heard about the Vietminh and wondered whether perhaps they might be the group that could most effectively lead the country through the troubled times ahead. He told me that it appeared this new party had the backing of the Americans. "If they really do," he said, "we will be willing to hand over power to them."

My uncle had, of course, heard the reports spread liberally by the Vietminh about their ties with the Americans. Making good use of his contacts with an Office of Strategic Services team that had been parachuted into a Vietminh-controlled area some months before, Ho Chi Minh managed to convince both potential supporters and even some of his enemies that he had gained backing from the triumphant Americans. Clearly, the United States was going to have a strong voice in determining the immediate future of Vietnam, and my uncle was not alone in believing that whoever had the Americans' confidence would be best placed to guide the nation during the postwar period. Although not all the leaders of the various factions shared his own Confucian attitude toward power, all of them were Vietnamese and all, thought my uncle, would have the nation's best interests at heart.

I was still in Hue on August 6 when the first atomic bomb fell on Hiroshima and three days later when the second dropped on Nagasaki. Word came that hundreds of thousands of people had died in an instant. A week later we heard that Japan had surrendered to the Allies. In Hue the atmosphere was ebullient, but also confused. Not having prepared adequately to exert authority once fate had overtaken the Japanese, my uncle's government was unsure how to proceed. Ho Chi Minh, on the other hand, had laid a careful groundwork for his own assumption of power. Within days, Uncle Kim would be faced with what had all the appearances of a Vietminh fait accompli.

As soon as the Japanese surrendered, Hanoi came alive with demonstrations and mass meetings engineered by the Vietminh. People poured into the capital from the surrounding villages to cry out their enthusiasm for independence. With the Japanese no longer interested, the French still absent, and the Allies not yet a presence, Hanoi was very nearly a political vacuum. Phan Ke Toai, the Kim government's viceroy, watched the crowds passively and then, prompted by his Vietminh son, stepped down. The Dai Viet factions and the VNQDD were still relatively unorganized, incapable of matching the armed propaganda teams, revolutionary committees, and hundreds of political cadres the Vietminh had positioned to orchestrate the mass outpouring of emotion.

On August 17 a large crowd gathered at the National Theater to support the Kim government. But the demonstration's organizers were powerless when armed Vietminh agitators took over the rostrum and raised the Vietminh flag, denouncing the "puppet government" and calling on the people to "rise against the fascist occupation forces." On the eighteenth the Vietminh brought more of their supporters into the city. With no competition, their propaganda campaign was taking a firm grip on the mood of the crowds, channeling the excitement. In strident shouts the street corner orators declared that the Kim government was full of collaborators. The Vietminh were the authentic representatives of the nation, taking power from the deposed, fascistic Japanese. Only the Vietminh were backed by the victorious Americans. Tension moved toward the breaking point.

On the nineteenth the crowds swarmed through central Ba Dinh Square, then marched off to occupy the official government residence, where the viceroy had earlier resigned his office. By that afternoon the Japanese authorities had agreed not to intervene, and the government's few civil guard units had disbanded. We heard that Emperor Bao Dai was receiving telegrams asking for his abdication.

It was on the nineteenth that Tran Trong Kim resigned as prime minister. At first, when news of events in Hanoi reached him, Kim had felt ambivalent. He was unhappy about the position the Vietminh coup had put him in, especially since he would have been amenable to an orderly, legitimate transfer of power. But he was not about to jeopardize American support for Vietnamese independence, and he believed the Vietminh had their support. About the Vietminh's plans for radical ideological revolution, he had not a single notion. His ignorance was shared by almost every individual marching under the Vietminh banners through the streets of Hanoi.

But the moment Kim made his decision, all the ambivalence disappeared. "Now I'm happy again," he told me. "Someone else will have to take charge of things. It's a great relief. Now let's leave."

A few days later, along with several of the other ministers, Kim moved to the little fishing village of Vi Da to observe developments. I went with him. Government authority had now been vacated, and aside from the Dai Viet and the VNQDD, there was no one left to oppose the party of Ho Chi Minh.

In Hanoi, on August 21, a series of meetings were held under Vietminh auspices which passed resolutions demanding Bao Dai's abdication. The most important came from the Student Association, now being led by Vietminh party members.

Motivated in part by his sincere desire to act in the best interests of national unity, and in part by his recognition that there was no realistic alternative, the emperor telegrammed back that he was prepared to step down. By August 26 a Vietminh delegation was in Hue, and on that day, in the great courtyard of the imperial palace, Bao Dai officially abdicated, saying as he did, "I would rather be a citizen of a free country than king of a slave state."

Three days later the provisional government of the Democratic Republic of Vietnam came into being. Along with avowed Communists, it included several ministers whose Communist affiliations were not then known and a few members from other parties. Clearly, the Vietminh leaders were attempting to play on the feeling of national unity that flowed through the country. But in Vi Da I felt uneasy about what was going on. The village had by then been taken over by a people's committee, which was organizing one mass meeting after another, beating the drums and calling the people together to support the new government. I was uncomfortable with the forced tone that hovered over these demonstrations and by the conspicuous manipulation of the villagers' emotions. On September 2, the day Ho Chi Minh read his declaration of independence in Hanoi, I watched as the villagers gathered, and I listened to their singing. But I did not feel the slightest enthusiasm for the provisional government and its people's committees. It seemed to me that an opportunity had been lost and that something ominous was in the air.

Chapter 6

British, Chinese, and French

A FEW DAYS LATER my uncle gave me permission to return to Hanoi.
By the time I arrived there, the political situation had become quite complex. Although World War II was officially over, there was still a formidable Japanese army in the country. To disarm these troops and maintain
public order in the south of Vietnam (the old Cochinchina), the Allies
had assigned the British. In northern Vietnam, that role had been given
to China.

As far as my Dai Viet friends and I were concerned, this was a time to
reorganize, to try to divine the future, and prepare for it. First of all, the
nationalist parties would have to devise a common strategy vis-à-vis the
Vietminh, who had so adeptly maneuvered themselves into power. But
before these discussions began, we heard reports that the British had allowed a contingent of French troops to land in Saigon. By mid-September
fighting had broken out there between the returning French and Vietnamese from both the Vietminh and nationalist parties. In Hanoi we
were expecting the Chinese occupation troops any day. For the nationalists it seemed an almost irresolvable quandary. On the one hand, we
did not trust the Vietminh. On the other, a Chinese occupation was enough
to give the shivers to any Vietnamese. And the thought of the French
reasserting their control made everyone's hair stand on end with anger
and anxiety.

Only two weeks into their new government, the Vietminh needed desperately to mobilize all the support they could. With his leadership hardly
secure, and forced to maneuver among Japanese, Chinese, French, and
British, Ho Chi Minh strove to shape alliances and keep emotions at a
fever pitch. Mass meetings and protests kept Hanoi's streets surging. Anti-

French demonstrations provided an outlet for profound antipathies, but any occasion would do for whipping up and uniting people in a common cause. There was even a demonstration against Spanish dictator Francisco Franco, though not one Vietnamese in a hundred thousand had ever heard of the man.

Amidst all this, one group of foreigners were universally admired — the Americans. That feeling was built on a gossamer hope that somehow the United States might yet save the situation. Vietnam's love affair with the United States had begun the previous year when rumors had circulated that President Roosevelt was in favor of a postwar trusteeship for Vietnam, to be followed by independence. Word of Roosevelt's concept had spread quickly through Vietnamese political and intellectual circles, where it made a deep impression.

Now, with the French and Chinese sharing the winner's circle, America was the only potential savior. Having emerged from World War II a shining giant, the United States was seen as a nation that hated colonialism and championed freedom. We could not understand why they had agreed to let the British and Chinese in, but the Americans themselves had representatives in Vietnam, and their presence sparked a wild hope that the United States was interested. And if they were interested, they might yet be prevailed upon to act.

It was a hope without any basis in reality. Still, it seemed real enough to those who cherished it. Whether Ho Chi Minh and his colleagues actually thought some arrangement could be made with the Americans, I don't know. Undoubtedly, at that point Ho would rather have dealt with them than with the French or the Chinese. But if he couldn't manage that, at least he could use the Americans' presence to buttress his own domestic position. Certainly, Vietminh propaganda made the most of every show of friendship the U.S. mission afforded them. Major Archimedes Patti and General Phillip Gallagher, the two most conspicuous American officers, were inundated with flattery by Ho's government, complemented by a very real flood of affection from the citizens of Hanoi. In a city plastered with slogans and banners denouncing imperialism, Major Patti's jeep, flying its American flag, was constantly mobbed by people who simply wanted to see and touch the representative of the United States of America.

Vietminh propagandists let it be known that Ho and Vo Nguyen Giap were negotiating with the Americans, ostensibly for recognition. A Vietnamese-American Friendship Society was created, and numerous receptions were held in Patti and Gallagher's honor. I remember the red, white, and blue flags that draped the hall of the one Friendship Society meeting I attended. The gathering was suffused with hope generated simply by the appearance of the two American officers, who looked so civilized and handsome in their uniforms that everyone, myself included, rushed to shake their hands. Throughout the affair, conversation revolved around the idea of an American trusteeship for Vietnam. And although neither Patti nor Gallagher said much of substance, it didn't matter. Their mere physical presence was encouragement enough.

Vietnam in those days could be compared to a young country girl repeatedly abused by predatory and unscrupulous masters. France, Japan, and China had mistreated her. Then, in the midst of her travail, a handsome and generous prince arrived on the scene. As far as Vietnam was concerned, it was love at first sight.

Unfortunately, the love was to go unrequited. Despite Major Patti's admiration for the Vietminh leaders, and despite those leaders' ostentatious use of the Americans' regard, it soon became evident that the American connection would produce nothing. For its own reasons, Washington was not going to do a thing to divert events in Vietnam from the complex and volatile course they were now taking. Ho Chi Minh and Vo Nguyen Giap were left to deal with the Chinese and French alone. For the rest of us, worries about the Vietminh's intentions were compounded by fears of what the French and Chinese might be planning.

In late September the Chinese occupation troops marched into Hanoi. They looked terrible — diseased, ragged, half starved. The Japanese had been all spit and polish. The Chinese looked as if they would steal anything not tied down. Almost immediately, they began to live up to the worst suspicions of them. They settled onto the country like a swarm of locusts, grabbing up everything in sight.

The arrival of the Chinese exacerbated the hunger that had already been raging through northern Vietnam for over a year. A combination of Japanese confiscations and several disastrous harvests had brought a killing famine to northern rural areas the previous year. By the fall of 1945 the situation had worsened. In Hanoi peasants from the stricken countryside roamed desperately through the streets. Bodies of people who had starved to death overnight littered the sidewalks and intersections. At the Cité Universitaire we organized teams of students who would go out each morning to assist in removing the bodies that had accumulated since the previous day's clean-up.

But though hunger was everyone's constant companion, it did nothing to dampen political activism. Each day the Vietminh would beat the meeting drums for one thing or another. With no money in their treasury, they organized what was called the Gold Week campaign, urging all the people to contribute their rings, jewelry, and precious gold taels to the government. With part of the proceeds Ho Chi Minh placated the Chinese occupation general, Lu Han, presenting the opium-smoking warlord with a golden pipe and a set of golden smoking paraphernalia. With the rest of the money the Vietminh bought arms.

At the same time he was cultivating the Chinese, Ho continued his efforts to generate mass backing for the Vietminh. For Ho and Vo Nguyen Giap, the university students were a priority, and they both scheduled tours of Cité Universitaire to whip up support. In early October I met Giap when he came to the campus one evening to give a talk about revolution and the events of August. With my knowledge of how the Vietminh had handled the Kim government and my memory of the people's committee in Vi Da, I was not a sympathetic listener. But I was happy to see him anyway, and after the talk I came down to shake hands and say hello. We hadn't seen each other since the day five years before when he had taken to the mountains instead of showing up for his history lecture.

Not long afterward, Ho Chi Minh himself came to visit the Cité. This was to be the first and last time I would meet him. Like Giap, he had scheduled this appearance because the student body had not been 100 percent enthusiastic about the Vietminh takeover. Many welcomed it, and of course quite a few, including the Student Association's leaders, were Vietminh party members. But many other students belonged to different parties and were ambivalent at best about Ho and his program.

Ho's tour was to include all the Cité's modern buildings, including the dormitories. One student on my hallway, whose name I remember as Hoan, was no supporter of Ho or of Ho's party, and the scene he engineered to embarrass him, which I witnessed, was unforgettable. Just as Ho entered our building, Hoan went into the bathroom to take a shower. A moment after the new president of the republic came into our hallway, the bathroom door opened, and there stood Hoan, dripping wet and completely naked. Acting surprised and abashed, Hoan did a nervous little dance replete with apologies and unsuccessful attempts to cover himself up.

But if Hoan thought Ho Chi Minh was going to be embarrassed by this display, he must have been severely disappointed. Ho just looked straight at him and laughed. "Oh, it's you, little brother," he said. "You're always looking for a good laugh, aren't you?" I was standing only a few feet from Ho, watching him carefully. Here he was, the chief of state, and the man didn't have a pretentious bone in him. Afterward he went from room to room, introducing himself and shaking hands with a familiar, natural grace. When he had met everyone, he gave a little talk. There was nothing special about it, nothing memorable or particularly persuasive. But I thought to myself nevertheless that this was a truly capable man, relaxed and unflappable — a consummate politician. It was an impressive performance.

In October, not long after the Chinese arrived, I said goodbye to my friends in Hanoi and traveled north to the province of Lao Kai. My Dai Viet military training — put off when I went to Hue — was about to begin. One consequence of the reorganization the nationalist parties were attempting after their belated recognition of the Vietminh's strength was a military collaboration between the Dai Viet and the VNQDD. Now the two parties had set up a joint training camp at Chapa in Lao Kai.

Strangely enough, the military instructors at this camp turned out to be Japanese. Supposedly disarmed by the Chinese occupation troops, at least some Japanese soldiers had ended up working for the nationalist parties. And they had brought their weapons with them. All the equipment we used in Lao Kai was Japanese. It was a sign of those intricate times that I simply shrugged off my initial disorientation and set about the business of getting used to Japanese military discipline.

The officers who ran the camp wore their Japanese uniforms, but for some inscrutable reason had adopted Vietnamese names. (None of them could speak a word of Vietnamese. Every order was transmitted through an interpreter.) The Japanese colonel in command called himself Hung ("the Hero"). His welcome to the three hundred or so trainees went something like this: "We are here to help you Vietnamese become masters of your country. We ourselves have lost everything. But we will now train you. With our help you will become Vietnamese samurai."

Our samurai training began the next morning. That morning and every morning thereafter, we were jerked out of sleep by a Japanese bugle call cutting sharply through the frigid mountain air. On the parade ground we stood at attention as the blue and white VNQDD flag was raised. Then, facing the sun rising from the east, we bowed our heads, renewing our inner commitment to the cause of the country.

Our devotions done, we gave ourselves over to a half hour of strenuous calisthenics and began a long day filled with marching, weapons handling, and eventually field tactics and strategy. The entire course was to last six months. At its end, the Dai Viet and VNQDD expected to have trained officer cadres to form and lead their combined army. But not many of us made it through the entire course. Events did not give the nationalists sufficient leisure to create the leaders they needed. As for me, by January I was back in Hanoi.

Truong Tu Anh, the Dai Viet chief, had called me back for a special mission. I guessed it would have something to do with my uncle Kim, and my assumption turned out to be right. Three or four weeks after he had resigned as prime minister, Uncle Kim had moved back to his old house in Hanoi. Although since his resignation Kim had been doing nothing overtly political, as the former prime minister he had become a kind of lodestone for anti-Communist sentiment. Nevertheless, the Vietminh, looking hard for consensus during this period, had as yet taken no action against him.

But Kim was a changed man, a good deal wiser politically than he had been a few short months ago. In June he had seriously considered supporting the Vietminh as the party with the best chance to guide the nation through the storm. By August he had resigned after being subjected to the blitzkrieg of Vietminh power politics. In September, with few illusions left, he found himself listening attentively to Truong Tu Anh's thoughts on counteracting Vietminh strength. Specifically, Anh was talking about the need for help from the outside world, from China.

Anh's thinking was based on two ideas. Inside Vietnam, he and his allies in the VNQDD would do their best to establish a strong military presence (hence the Lao Kai training camp). At the same time, they would attempt to solicit outside support. This was where Uncle Kim fit in. As the former head of government, he had a modicum of international stature. He also had a reputation for integrity. With these advantages, he would be the perfect individual to look for allies beyond Vietnam's borders. For his part, Uncle Kim's eyes were now wide open to the nature of Ho Chi Minh's revolution, and he had found in the Dai Viet leader a compatible and trustworthy ally. Now chief Anh was calling on me to organize Uncle Kim's journey to Hong Kong.

At the same time Bao Dai, the former emperor, had gone through a similar political evolution. He too had stepped down under Vietminh pressure, renouncing his hereditary title and becoming an ordinary citizen. His parting statement, that he would rather be "a citizen of a free country than king of a slave state," had been a noble and memorable gesture. Shortly afterward, in a demonstration of remarkable political adroitness, Ho had invited Bao Dai to come to Hanoi as "supreme counselor" to the Vietminh government. With this stroke, Ho managed to project a magnanimous image while publicly displaying the fact that he enjoyed the royal blessing. And not least important, Bao Dai would be where he could be watched closely and prevented from indulging any second thoughts about the transfer of power.

In Hanoi the supreme counselor was treated deferentially by Vietminh leaders. But as the months passed, their respect had apparently not prevented him from coming to resent deeply the way he had been trapped and used.

By the beginning of 1946 Bao Dai was eager to dissociate himself from the Vietminh. He was looking for a way out, and by this time Ho Chi Minh seemed quite willing to let him find one. After all, the former emperor had already served his main purpose: conferring the appearance of legitimacy on the Vietminh's seizure of power. But whatever Ho's thinking, in January he offered Bao Dai the opportunity to lead a delegation to China. It is possible that Ho suspected Bao Dai would stay in Chungking (then China's capital) once he was there, and that he didn't care.

When word about these developments got out, Dai Viet chief Truong Tu Anh decided the time was ripe to spirit Uncle Kim to China as well. This was the mission for which I was called away from my military training in Lao Kai.

Although Uncle Kim had not yet been threatened by the Vietminh, the subterranean war between Ho Chi Minh's party and the nationalists was becoming an increasingly murderous affair. By the turn of the year, the Vietminh had managed to assassinate many of their political rivals, including Huynh Phu So, leader of the southern-based Hoa Hao religious sect; Ta Thu Thau, leader of the Trotskyite party; Ngo Dinh Khoi, future president Ngo Dinh Diem's brother; and Pham Quynh, a scholar and cabinet minister at the imperial court. Good friends of mine had also begun to disappear. Quan Trong Ung and Dang Vu Chu, from the medical school faculty, were arrested by the Vietminh and never seen again. Two law students, Dang Van But and Dang Van Nghien, were gunned down at Yen Bay. Phuc, who had so reluctantly introduced me to Truong Tu Anh, was assassinated in Hanoi, shot in the stomach. Dozens of other Dai Viet colleagues died. Sometimes their bodies were found. More often they simply vanished.

While the underground war of terror picked up, Ho Chi Minh undertook a series of delicate negotiations with the Chinese and French. By this time, southern Vietnam had been embroiled in a full-scale guerrilla war for several months. The small British occupying force had allowed the French to bring in troops, and now most of the cities and major towns were in French hands, while the Vietnamese resistance had been forced back into the countryside and inaccessible base areas. In the northern half of the country, the 200,000-strong Chinese occupation army had prevented the French from attempting a return. But by the end of February it was known that French and Chinese representatives in Chungking were negotiating the return of French forces to northern Vietnam in exchange for France's renouncing its prewar concession rights in China.

Ho understood that circumstances would soon force him to deal with the French directly. The Chinese occupation had worked well for him, giving the Vietminh almost six months to build up their strength. Their presence had kept the French out of the north — exactly what the British had failed to do in the south. But the Chinese were a mixed blessing to Ho. No Vietnamese could regard China's ultimate intentions without suspicion. And the Chinese had also given aid and comfort to Ho's rivals, the VNQDD and the Dai Viet.

Consequently, in February of 1946 Ho opened talks with French representative Jean Sainteny. In the Dai Viet we knew negotiations were going on, though we were in the dark about the details. We were furious at Ho for what he was doing, outraged at the prospect of seeing the French army once again come into our country. And though we couldn't complain about it openly, the departure of the Chinese would be a severe blow to our own build-up. For just as the Chinese troops had given the Vietminh a buffer against the French, so they had given us a measure of protection against the Vietminh.

On March 6 Ho and Sainteny reached agreement. France would recognize Vietnam as a free state "within the French Union," and the Vietminh would permit a French military force to be based in the country for five years. It became known that Ho had defended the agreement to his Vietminh colleagues by declaring that he "would rather sniff French shit for five years than eat Chinese shit for a thousand." But in every quarter, anger about allowing the French back ran deep. Two weeks later I was standing on the balcony of the Phu Doan Hospital in Hanoi with a group of doctor friends, some of whom were Dai Viet. On the street beneath us fifteen thousand French troops under General Jacques Philippe Leclerc were marching by. Watching them brought the taste of gall to our mouths. It seemed the return of Vietnam's colonial enslavement. On the sidewalks French civilian residents of Hanoi stood cheering. On the balcony each one of us was brushing away tears.

Chapter 7

The Terror

AS THE FRENCH ARRIVED, the Chinese occupation army was pulling out. All the movement and confusion gave me the perfect opportunity to spirit Uncle Kim away. My first step was to get in touch with the right VNQDD people, to make use of their channel to the Chinese. Through them I made arrangements to evacuate Kim by plane. With all the plans set, Kim and I waited at his house for the signal. But as a week stretched toward ten days with no word, we finally decided we could wait no longer. Each passing day brought with it the increased chance that we would be discovered by the Vietminh security squads.

Now I decided to try my own luck with the Chinese. During the occupation, many Vietnamese women had "married" Chinese officers. Some of these were real unions, others simply affairs of convenience. I knew one of these women, who had managed to captivate a Chinese general. In return for a small gift, she agreed to use her influence with her husband to obtain a safe conduct pass and transportation for Kim.

She was as good as her word. On the given day an old black Citroën pulled up in front of my uncle's house. In it were a driver, the general, and a Dai Viet doctor, who was to make the trip with my uncle. We threw two suitcases into the trunk, squeezed into the car, and started the long drive to the Chinese border. Outside Hanoi both sides of the road were choked with columns of bedraggled Chinese soldiers carrying on their backs live chickens, iron pots, and sacks full of goods of every kind. The substance of northern Vietnam was accompanying them back to China.

Amidst this huge, unruly mob no one paid any attention to the black Citroën. By dusk we had reached the border at Lang Son. There I said goodbye to Kim and promised I would shortly make arrangements for his family to join him in Hong Kong, where he planned to establish himself as nationalist Vietnam's representative to the outside world.

Returning to Hanoi by bus, I began looking for a way to get my aunt, her daughter, and her daughter's family out of the country. But movement was becoming more difficult every day. Even as the Vietminh continued to negotiate peace with the French, they were moving hard against the nationalists. In April and May the terrorist war picked up. Nationalist strongholds along the Red River girded themselves for the Vietminh offensive that was about to erupt.

With outright war between the Vietminh and the nationalists in the offing, getting my uncle's family out became an urgent business. The tentative peace agreement with the French had given Ho at least a temporary respite, and he was using it to ruthlessly put his own house in order.

In April follow-up negotiations in Dalat between the Vietminh and the French ended in fiasco. The French high commissioner, Admiral Georges Thierry d'Argenlieu, seemed intent on preserving southern Vietnam as a French colony, and he refused to clarify what Vietnam's status as a "free state" would mean. After Dalat, Ho Chi Minh could have had few illusions about French willingness to carry out the agreement he had originally reached with Sainteny. But in May he left for France anyway, for what turned out to be five months of extended talks. He might have hoped that his presence there would rally the French left to support Vietnamese independence. But he was also buying time. Along with him, Ho took most of the Vietminh leadership. Vo Nguyen Giap, however, stayed behind, working feverishly to strengthen the Vietminh army. While Ho was in France, it was Giap who would deal with the Vietminh's troublesome domestic opponents.

Vo Nguyen Giap's methods were blunt. In the Red River provinces his forces launched all-out assaults against nationalist bases. At the same time, Vietminh urban units tightened their security nets in Hanoi and Haiphong. Nationalist party members went underground or tried to escape to China through the Vietminh control grid. Many were caught and imprisoned; others disappeared under circumstances that left no doubt about their fate. Panic struck the parties as Giap's reign of terror swept their ranks with a force that dwarfed previous assassination campaigns the factions had launched against one another. While Ho and the French colonial ministers danced a slow minuet at Fontainebleau, site of the increasingly futile independence negotiations, thousands of nationalists in Vietnam died quietly.

I was luckier. On the Haiphong docks I secretly met the captain of a Swedish freighter. Speaking a combination of French and English, I made a deal with him to carry me, my aunt, and her family to Hong Kong. No questions, no declarations, no travel documents — you pay, you go. Money in exchange for a spot on the freighter's deck, where we were welcome to sling up a canvas awning to protect us from the weather.

The freighter slipped out of Haiphong harbor under a full moon. Never having been on a ship before, this seemed to me the most beautiful, romantic thing I had ever done. But as soon as we cleared the harbor's protection, I became violently ill. Out on the South China Sea, the moon that had cast its luminous glow over our departure vanished behind a storm front that was to envelop us for the entire voyage.

To avoid mines left from the war, the freighter was forced to head first toward the Philippines instead of taking the direct route for Hong Kong. What was ordinarily a three-day trip turned into seven days of agony on the open sea. When at last we disembarked, I was so thankful I kissed the ground.

Once I set up my aunt, her daughter, and son-in-law in a Hong Kong hotel room, I went out to locate Uncle Kim and the emperor Bao Dai. With no contacts or prearranged plans, it was only after a good deal of searching that I was able to ascertain that they were not in Hong Kong at all but in Chungking, Chiang Kai-shek's capital city. The lack of coordination was all too typical. Hong Kong was already the center of a small community of Vietnamese nationalists who had fled the Vietminh-controlled north. But though they had the idea of developing an outside base of operations, they had yet to form an effective organization. It was not an auspicious beginning.

For her part, my aunt was deeply disappointed. When a week passed with no news from Uncle Kim, we had to make a decision. We had little money, and there was no one we could turn to for help. "The best solution," I said to her, "is for you to take all the money while I go back to Hanoi to try to arrange a way of getting you more. Uncle should be back soon, and I'm sure you'll be all right."

The voyage back was just slightly less traumatic than the trip out. Somewhere in the middle of it I took a solemn vow never to set foot on a ship again. Landing in Haiphong, I again slipped through the security control points and patrols and found my way to Hanoi, where I reported to Truong Tu Anh. I described the disorganization I had found in Hong Kong and emphasized the need to set up some regular supply channel. But first of all, my aunt and uncle needed money.

To help with this, Anh introduced me to the Dai Viet counterfeiting operation, through which he financed a portion of the party's activities. The piasters produced by the counterfeiters were not exactly works of art, but they were adequate to sell at a discount to currency black marketers, who obviously had their own outlets for it. A counterfeit one-hundred-piaster note could usually be sold to these people for sixty pias-ters of real money.

At least initially, additional funds for my aunt and uncle would come through this system. I was to make the pick-up, sell the notes, and find a way of getting the money to Hong Kong. My education in underground politics was growing fast. With another party member, I went to the address Anh had given me. But when I looked at the stacks of bills, I was appalled. They were brand crackling new, and they were terrible. A child could tell they were hot off the press. There was no way I could sell them to even the dimmest black marketeer.

That afternoon, my partner and I spent hours getting the bills to look presentable. We reasoned that the main problem was that they looked so new. To remedy this, we decided to put them through a rapid aging pro-cess. We laid all the bills on the floor of the house and rubbed each one with rice, using the grains as if they were coarse sandpaper, taking the shine off and, we hoped, giving the notes a patina of age and authenticity.

It wasn't a bad job. When we were finished, the twenties looked like the real thing. But even to our unpracticed eyes the hundreds still seemed phony. In the end, we got 80 percent for the twenties but felt lucky to sell the hundreds for fifty. I was more successful in setting up a supply link to Hong Kong through a Thai tourist agency that had branches throughout the region.

Not long after I had worked out the currency transfers, Truong Tu Anh ordered me to organize another escape to Hong Kong, this time for Do Dinh Dao, the VNQDD general who had commanded the ill-fated Dai Viet and VNQDD forces along the Red River. He had been unable to stand up to Vo Nguyen Giap's onslaught, and with his troops crushed he was being removed to a safe haven from where he could plan a re-grouping effort. An expert at these things by now, I was able to arrange his passage from Haiphong. But this time I didn't go myself; I had had enough of ocean voyages.

The summer of 1946 was a difficult one for the nationalist parties. Ho Chi Minh's negotiations outside Paris were going nowhere. But in Viet-nam his lieutenant, Vo Nguyen Giap, was having great success in elimi-nating the competition. In the field, nationalist forces had been routed or pushed back into the mountains. In the cities, Giap's security squads had made life in the underground very chancy. I never slept in the same house more than one night. I watched everything and everyone carefully. I had grown used to the feel of the pistol in my back pocket.

Truong Tu Anh was living the same way. The Dai Viet chief was a hunted man. He spent his nights hiding in different safe houses and seemed to run the party through an ongoing series of meetings with one or two people at a time, held at locations only they would be informed of. I met with him frequently during the summer and came to like and respect him more and more.

By early September it was clear that Ho Chi Minh's talks at Fontainebleau had failed completely. In the end, Ho and French overseas minister Marius Moutet signed what was termed a *modus vivendi,* a kind of agreement to disagree, obviously a last-minute attempt on both sides to buy more time before the momentum toward war achieved a critical mass. Rumors — later enshrined as history — had it that as Ho initialed the agreement, he remarked that he was signing his own death warrant.

If Ho actually did make that remark, it was more an example of his superb showmanship than an expression of genuine anxiety. In fact, even with the *modus vivendi* signed, Ho was in no rush to get back to Hanoi. Instead of flying, he chose to return aboard a French ship whose leisurely passage from Toulon to Haiphong took more than a month. It was not the act of a frightened party boss unnerved by threats from his subordinates. In fact, Ho was, as always, in full control. Whatever slim hope he might have had about winning independence at the negotiating table had not materialized. But his second aim — to gain time for Giap to destroy the nationalist opposition and establish firm Vietminh dominance over the northern half of the country — that motive had borne excellent fruit.

Though I had no special insight into the details of what had happened at Fontainebleau, I watched the destruction of the nationalists from a victim's perspective. In the fall of 1946, as the Vietminh made feverish preparations for war against France, we, the Dai Viet survivors, were unable to show our faces. It was a confusing and desperate time for us. Because of relentless pressure from the Vietminh police, we had great difficulty setting up secure meetings, whose chief purpose was to find ways to maintain contact with one another. Party activity was reduced to a kind of census taking. How many were still alive? How many were alive but had dropped from sight? What kind of connections still existed in the provinces? In Ho's absence, Giap had done a thorough job, utterly crushing the combined Dai Viet–VNQDD military forces and setting up a systematic countrywide security apparatus. Even before the war of independence began, northern Vietnam had been effectively transformed into a modern police state.

Amidst the debacle, Truong Tu Anh somehow managed to control what must have been a mounting personal despair. On the surface, at least, he seemed calm — almost too calm — and he usually kept his plans to himself. There was certainly very little room to move, but we had the impression he was figuring out how we could regroup and once again become active. One option was to build up the Dai Viet infrastructure in the south, where Vietminh control was not yet so tight. Another was to temporarily transfer the locus of operations outside the country, to the little party group that had gathered around Uncle Kim in Hong Kong. Anh even asked me if I would go back there to help, but I kept putting the move off. Kim already had with him Dang Van Sung, the friend who had introduced me to the party, and Tran Van Tuyen, my high school professor and the future opposition leader in South Vietnam. I thought my presence would be superfluous. I could see no point in leaving Anh, despite the pressure we were under in Hanoi.

One day in early December I went to one of the usual secret meetings with Truong Tu Anh. He never showed up. That had happened once or twice before, but there had always been a message. This time there was none. I waited for three hours, growing more and more nervous, afraid that Vietminh security would pick me up. The next day a friend told me that he, too, had had a meeting scheduled with Anh, and that Anh hadn't shown up for that either. Truong Tu Anh was never seen again. But there was no question about his fate, or about who was responsible.

Chapter 8

In Hiding

TRUONG TU ANH'S DEATH was a terrible blow. I should say his "disappearance," for of course there was no proof he was dead, and along with everyone else I struggled to nurture a hope that he might yet surface. As the weeks passed, though, whatever illusions we managed to cherish crumbled to dust. By this time a great many of my friends had been killed, some on the Red River, some in Hanoi. Others, like my uncle, had escaped to China or had been driven into hiding. My father, too, had moved out of Hanoi, back to our home village of Phu Ly. I was living underground with few contacts and friends, no family, and, worst of all, no direction. I felt like a lost soul.

For a while I stayed with a party friend who lived on the outskirts of Hanoi and rarely went out. Two or three other Dai Viets were there too, making the house a little party outpost. We all suffered from a siege mentality. With nothing to do, we sat around and talked listlessly about where to go from here, discovering that none of us had a decent idea on the subject. Looking back, it seems we were in a state of shock. Occasionally, one or two of us would sneak out of the house to buy food or visit colleagues who were holed up in their own enclaves. But mainly we just stayed put and waited, our thoughts growing increasingly morbid.

One day my friend and I decided to break the monotony by visiting a female cousin of his in a small village not far from the city limits. The trip would involve some hazards, but both of us were experienced in avoiding patrols and getting through checkpoints, and we felt the outing would be worth the risks. The confinement was making us stir crazy and more than a little paranoid.

The day was lovely. Just getting out lifted my spirits. At my friend's cousin's house we had tea, talked, and strolled together in the garden. It was a moment of relaxation that both of us were grateful for. But the return trip was not so serene.

On our way home that evening, we were stopped at several control posts, but each time the "self-defense" volunteers examined our forged papers and let us through. At the last one, though, something about the papers looked fishy to one of the teenagers on duty, and we were arrested and marched down to the local police outpost. My friend acted outraged. He was, he told everybody in hearing range, the prosecutor from Vinh. I was his associate, the deputy. What did they mean by arresting us? Unable to check this claim and nervous about the not-so-veiled threats my friend was making, the locals finally decided to let us go.

Back at the house, we grabbed our things in a rush and moved in with the family of another Dai Viet colleague. The next morning we got word that during the night the police had searched the house where we had been living. Sure now that we were being tracked, my friend and I split up. I began moving from place to place, staying with relatives of friends and party comrades in a succession of cramped rooms and dingy hiding places.

It was while I was a hunted fugitive that the news came: war had finally broken out. With the failure of negotiations in France, in the fall of 1946, tensions all over Vietnam had picked up. A series of incidents in Haiphong led, on November 23, to a pitched battle between French soldiers and Vietminh militia while French planes bombed the city and a French cruiser in the harbor turned its guns on Haiphong's neighborhoods. After that, the slide toward all-out war quickened. On December 19 Ho Chi Minh issued a proclamation. "Compatriots," he said. "Rise up! . . . We would rather sacrifice everything than lose our country!" Almost all the people of Vietnam responded to Ho's call to arms. Among those who did not were the Dai Viet and VNQDD who had been slaughtered by Vo Nguyen Giap along the Red River or tracked down by Vietminh security squads in Hanoi and Haiphong.

For me the war began with an explosion that I at first thought was a giant thunderclap. I was sitting with friends around a table at one of the houses I was using, savoring a bowl of noodle soup someone had ducked out to buy at a street stand. Suddenly, a roar shook the ground and the lights flickered and went out. It took us a minute to figure out that someone had blown up the central power plant, and another to understand that the war was really on.

The outbreak of war against France created the confusion I needed to escape the Vietminh hunters and make my way into the countryside, one among tens of thousands of refugees. As the battle for Hanoi raged, a refugee exodus streamed out of the city. Hordes of people trudged along in the blackness of the night, the city dark behind them, its lights extinguished. An atmosphere of suspicion and fear permeated the crowds. You could hear whispers about *"Viet gian,"* Vietnamese traitors and collaborators who would betray us to the French. Along the route I ran into an old school friend, and we decided to travel together, though neither of us had any idea where to go.

I wanted badly to return to Phu Ly, where my father and mother were living. But I knew the Vietminh were searching for me, and if I showed up at home I would be caught. With nowhere to go we just wandered, moving aimlessly from village to village along with the streams of refugees. Finally, we hadn't a penny left between us. I traded the extra shirt I was carrying for barge fare down the Day River and two potatoes, which made our dinner. We didn't know when we would eat again. It was a cold, bleak night on the river, the first of many I would spend first with my friend and then, when he went his own way, alone.

That barge floating down the Day River was typical of the flotilla of boats that provided transportation on northern Vietnam's navigable rivers. About twenty feet long, its central section was sheltered by a flimsy roof under which the cramped passengers stretched their legs in close communion with their neighbors, total strangers whom they nevertheless huddled against in an effort to ward off the water's chill. My thoughts, as villages glided slowly past, were as bitter as the winter. Vietnamese were at that moment fighting heroically against the French in a war that I wanted desperately to join, that was by rights *my* fight. But "they" had made it impossible, the Vietminh who had crushed my friends and sent me wandering south down this river instead of standing where I belonged.

The frustration of it was almost unbearable. I thought about my fellow passengers, this one returning to his family, that one off on a marketing trip with his few pitiful wares. None of them, I thought, was suffering the way I was. I remembered a Paul Muni film I had seen a few years ago in Hanoi, *Je Suis un Évadé (I Am a Fugitive)*. I felt as alone and hunted as Muni's character, and I felt the injustice of it as perhaps only a young man can who sees his cause slipping away while his need to act is stifled by circumstances he cannot control.

Among the refugees on the barge, and in the riverside village markets where we stopped, fear of *Viet gian* traitors grew. Local militia units were everywhere, arresting anyone who appeared suspicious. Possessing a pocket mirror was grounds for arrest; it could be used to signal French warplanes. Red, white, and blue articles of clothing (the colors of the

French flag) were a sure sign that the wearer sympathized with the colonialists. Those arrested were questioned interminably to establish their identities. I lived in fear of arrest and of the inquisition that would inevitably reveal who I was. I even began to feel a creeping shadow of guilt that maybe in some sense I was a traitor, sneaking away from the very people who were carrying on the battle.

At one point the barge stopped at a landing little more than a kilometer from Phu Ly. My mood was compounded of depression, anger, and loneliness, and it was all I could do to suppress the temptation to leave the barge right there and join my family, whatever the consequences. But instead I continued downriver, arriving eventually near the village of Gian Khuot. Taking a short walk around the dock, I suddenly realized that a school friend of mine came from Gian Khuot. By this point the barge had left the war zone. This fact and an additional one, that I now had neither money nor anything I could trade, convinced me to take the chance of going into the village to see if I could locate him or at least his family.

Before long I had succeeded in finding the place where my friend was still living. His family, a wealthy one by village standards, had a large home and enjoyed good relations with the local Vietminh. For the time being I was safe.

I stayed in Gian Khuot for almost a month. Inexorably, though, the French pushed out from Hanoi, driving Giap's poorly armed troops before them and, little by little, expanding their area of control. As they closed in on the village, I realized it was time to move again. I borrowed money from my friend and renewed the journey down the Day River. My goal now was to reach Bai Thuong, on the Laotian border, where I had a clan of distant relatives whom I knew were Dai Viet sympathizers. I felt sure they would take me in.

Day and night I drifted southward, the same cold and lonely voyage I thought I had left behind for good a month before. After several days I found myself in Phat Diem, the center of northern Vietnam's Catholic population and a region especially inhospitable to the Communists. Here Vietminh security was much less in evidence. For the first time in ages, I felt able to drop my guard.

From Phat Diem I went to Thanh Hoa by bus, the same breed of charcoal-burning wreck that plied the road from Hanoi to Hue. At first we drove through flat farmlands, an endlessly peaceful landscape of rice paddies and villages unfolding outside the bus's grimy windows. In all of this, the only hints of war were the occasional little crowds of peasants parading in the distance under their red and yellow Vietminh flags. As we neared Thanh Hoa, the flatlands turned hilly, and before long the gentle hills began to merge into the mountainous highlands on the Laotian border. In Bai Thuong, I found my way to my relatives' house, where I was welcomed warmly by my surprised older cousin and his family.

The war had not yet reached this backwoods village, which stretched out along the sparsely populated hills, each house three or four kilometers from its neighbors. Farmers cultivated sweet potatoes and manioc and kept pigs along with the inevitable water buffaloes. In these border lands, families lived predominantly self-contained lives. For me it was a perfect situation. Living with my cousin, I could stay abreast of what was happening in the neighborhood while keeping myself hidden from prying eyes. I lived in a room with my cousin's two sons and became part of the family routine, working in the potato fields and reading in my spare time.

From this vantage point, I watched Vietminh-controlled Bai Thuong, amazed at the organization they had managed to bring even to this remotest of places. The village was run by a newly installed people's committee, which held popular meetings and disseminated news and propaganda. The committee kept track of who went where, of who was talking to whom, and of the political allegiances of each villager. Those, like my cousin, who were known sympathizers of other parties were watched especially closely. Every so often committee members would arrive at the house for "a little chat." When the cry of *"can bo, can bo"* ("cadre, cadre") echoed up the road, I would sneak out to the fields and hide till they were gone. Usually, they would stay for hours, sipping tea and asking my cousin questions about his sons, his relatives in the area, his thoughts on the war. These talks were never overtly hostile. On the contrary, my cousin maintained good relations with the cadres. But underneath the veneer of neighborly relations, the people's committee was extending its control over the private lives of each of Bai Thuong's families.

I hid in the village from February 1946 to January 1947, almost a year of enforced idleness. I still had not sorted out the future. I had no idea if I would be able to get back in touch with the Dai Viet, or even if there still was a Dai Viet. Truong Tu Anh's disappearance had devastated the party, and I had been out of touch for a long time. I had become, I realized, a political animal. But with my brand of nationalism and my dislike of the Vietminh revolution, what political future was possible? What future at all, for that matter? In my cousin's living room I had found a copy of Somerset Maugham's *The Razor's Edge*. It was about a young American who was searching for truth. His journey took him through Germany, France, Greece, and finally to India as he looked for some explanation for the mysteries of life and death. At the end of the story he found serenity, if not the answers to his questions, in an ashram. The novel was in French, and I read it over and over that year. I sympathized with the American hero. I was not looking for truth, perhaps, but for a role to play in the liberation of my country. It was a quest to which I could as yet see no resolution.

By 1947 the war had become something of a stalemate. French forces occupied the cities; the Vietminh owned the countryside. I was now corresponding with my father, who had become a cultural figure in the Vietminh administrative committee in "Zone 3," where Phu Ly was located. He wrote that he would try to get me home safely, that all I needed was to find a way to "usefully serve the nation." The Vietminh-nationalist conflict had calmed down considerably, so, eager to be away from Bai Thuong, I moved to Yen Mo, a small town not far from the Catholic center of Phat Diem.

There I set myself up as a mathematics teacher, giving small private classes and making just enough money to survive. Eventually, I received word from my father that I could now legitimize my status. All I had to do, he wrote, was join the local Vietminh cultural committee, which would be prepared to accept me. This seemed like a reasonable option. The committee would give me the credentials I needed to feel safe from the police. Meanwhile I would be keeping an eye out for some way of contacting my old friends.

My father had laid his plans well. Before long I was introduced to the Yen Mo Vietminh as the son of Bui Ky, the old scholar on the Zone 3 administrative committee. Whether the local cultural people knew about my past or not, I wasn't sure. But whatever they knew or suspected, it was evident they were at least going to tolerate me.

Work on the Vietminh cultural committee involved a blend of entertainment, news reporting, and propaganda. Together with a team of cadres, I made the rounds of all the villages in our region, giving speeches, setting up exhibitions, and leading audiences in patriotic songs. We showed photographs of how the war was going and what progress was being made in liberated areas. We described recent battles and political developments and talked about how Uncle Ho was valiantly leading the country toward independence. But even as I was propagandizing for the Vietminh, I was looking hard for a way out. I felt keenly that what I was doing was fake and that I couldn't go on doing it for long.

Only ten miles or so from Yen Mo, Phat Diem seemed to offer the best chance of linking up with other anti-Communist nationalists. It was a predominantly Catholic city of thirty thousand, containing hundreds of churches, parochial schools, and seminaries. Stretching out around Phat Diem proper was a region inhabited by another hundred thousand or so coreligionists, making this the densest concentration of Catholics in the country.

The spiritual leader of this enclave was Monsignor Le Huu Tu, a man

known for his strong anti-Communist views. Tu's influence and authority were paramount in Phat Diem and throughout the area, and to avoid
any open hostility, the Vietminh treated him with kid gloves, allowing
the region a kind of tacit semiautonomy.

It was to Phat Diem that I went searching for nationalist friends, or at
least for news of what had happened to the parties. At first the Catholic
zone seemed a strange, exotic place, full of priests in cassocks and youth-
ful seminarians dressed in the distinctive white pants and black tunics of
their orders. After a few trips, though, the novelty wore off, and I began
to think about settling here rather than keeping up the pretense with the
cultural committee. With the right contacts, I thought it would be easy
enough to live a relatively normal life in Phat Diem, without constantly
looking over my shoulder for the Vietminh police.

But when several visits to Phat Diem had not turned up any old friends
or party contacts, I began to get discouraged. Then one day when I was
wandering down one of the market streets, I noticed a little sundries
stand whose owner I recognized. It was the sister of Kim Ngoc, the girl I
had been so taken with at my uncle's house several years before and
whose name I had adopted as my own party code name. As it turned out,
not only was Kim Ngoc's sister in Phat Diem, but Kim Ngoc and the rest
of the family were too, having been driven out of Hanoi by the outbreak
of war. Her mother, I recalled, had not been too fond of me. I had seemed
a bit overadventurous to her, the type who might easily wander off somewhere. But that didn't diminish my enthusiasm one bit. Before long, I
had renewed my acquaintance with Kim Ngoc and was paying considerable attention to emotions I had never before experienced.

From that point on, I made the ten-mile hike to Phat Diem whenever I
had a free day. Spending more time in the Catholic zone, I also began to
make the contacts that had previously eluded me. I was overjoyed to find
two of my closest university friends living in the city, refugees as I was
from the disintegration of the nationalist parties. They were as happy to
see me as I was to see them. They too had been leading an aimless existence, the main object of which was to stay clear of the Vietminh security
people. With these two friends to help, I made arrangements to disappear
from Yen Mo and my job as a cultural cadre and lose myself among the
crowded neighborhoods of Phat Diem.

Blending in in Phat Diem was not difficult. In the Catholic zone, all the
priests, seminarians, and students wore cassocks or uniforms, and anyone in that clothing could count on being taken for one of the religious
brotherhood. Outfitting myself in the obligatory tunic and pants, and
moving into the home my friends shared with a group of seminarians, I
fit right in.

Among the various political groups in the zone was a militant faction that supported Ngo Dinh Diem, the ambitious nationalist whom Uncle Kim had so unexpectedly supplanted as prime minister in 1945. Ngo Dinh Diem was a zealous Catholic. His older brother was bishop of Vinh Long, in southern Vietnam, and he himself lived an ascetic, devout life. (In fact, several years later, Ngo Dinh Diem moved into an American monastery, living like a monk and cultivating the friendship of New York's Francis Cardinal Spellman.)

Soon my two friends — Le Quang Luat and Nghiem Xuan Hong — and I began meeting with some of Diem's backers to talk about setting up a combined nationalist front. The three of us had been separated for a long time from our parties, and we were anxious to get things going; none of us wanted to simply sit around and watch the Vietminh tighten its control. There was plenty of anti-Vietminh sentiment in Phat Diem, and it seemed worthwhile to try to harness it.

Our first step was to recruit and train cadres. With help from the pro-Diem people, we interested fifteen or twenty seminarians and students and set up a training course for them. Our curriculum was composed of lectures on communism, its theory and techniques, and the necessity of fighting against it. Both Luat and Hong brought forceful personalities and real intellectual stature to this enterprise, and as we taught our courses, we ourselves struggled to formulate a comprehensive rationale for non-Communist nationalism. We did not just react to the malevolent way the proponents of communism used power in Vietnam. It seemed to us that as an economic and political program, communism could never provide a solution to the problems of a small, underdeveloped nation. At the same time, capitalism offered little in the way of a moral basis for the kind of society we were groping toward. The three of us spent days and nights passionately discussing these questions. But a clear, logically coherent concept around which we could marshal a movement always remained just out of reach.

When we would finally tire of all the talk about politics, we would discuss literature. When we tired of that, we would recite poetry or read aloud to one another. By then it would be time to teach our classes. What with the constant intellectual stimulation and the nervous energy generated by starting something new, it seemed that none of us needed sleep. I was a young man, busy with urgent work and busy, too, with the first stirrings of love. It was a marvelous time.

Few of the Catholics in our classes and among our associates knew that I was not a believer. In my student's tunic they took me for a senior seminarian, one who was, no doubt, on the verge of ordination. Out of respect, they addressed me as *"thay gia,"* "reverend master," and on one mortifying occasion even asked me to say prayers. Frozen with fear, the only thing I could dredge up from all the praying I had listened to since arriving in the zone was the closing expostulation *"lay cha,"* "we bow to God." Prayers that evening were said in an incomprehensible half-whispered mumble, at the end of which rang out a loud and distinct (and thankful) *"lay cha!"*

Sometime toward the end of 1948, news started to percolate through Phat Diem. The French were talking about recognizing an independent Vietnam, but a Vietnam not controlled by the Communists. Specifically, the French wanted Bao Dai to resume his role as chief of state and form a new government. The reports said that Bao Dai was interested. He had no sympathy for the Vietminh, but he was also insisting to the French that he would only head a government that was truly independent.

At the same time, other reports were making the rounds. Uncle Kim had apparently moved back to Vietnam from Hong Kong and was now living in French-controlled Saigon. Ngo Dinh Diem was also in Saigon, but for the moment, at least, was keeping carefully distant from anything inspired by the French. With the war now two years old and no military resolution in sight, it was obvious the French were looking for an alternative approach. How far were they willing to go?

In the relative isolation of the Catholic zone, Hong, Luat, and I kept our ears wide open. We had enough wisdom to know that our attempt to organize a political movement ourselves was unrealistic, a stopgap born of frustration. We could never provide our own solution to the nationalist's problems. But it was possible that an initiative by Bao Dai might do exactly that. The emperor had never been energetic or decisive. But if he was not exactly a forceful political leader, he did enjoy a kind of vague popular sympathy. His abdication demonstrated that he was at least capable of putting the nation's interests above his own. And his declaration about preferring to be a citizen of a free country than king of a slave state was something we all remembered.

In an attempt to find out more about the situation, activists in the zone sent representatives to Hanoi and Haiphong, and to Ngo Dinh Diem in Saigon to get his assessment. For all the nationalists — Diem's supporters, Dai Viet, and VNQDD — the great dilemma of our political lives was coming to a head.

We were, we knew, caught in a trap. On the one hand, we desperately wanted independence for our country; that was the goal of all our actions. On the other, we had become strangers in the fight against France, because we knew that even if independence could be achieved, we ourselves would be eliminated by the Communists. Whatever their differences, all the nationalists shared this conviction. We had seen the Vietminh's colors already — the people's committees, the security apparatus, the assassination squads, the compulsion to arrogate all power to themselves. Once they achieved full control, the Vietminh would never let us live.

Under these circumstances, we might be able to reluctantly accept a Bao Dai government. The thought of collaborating in any way with French authority was repugnant. But so was the idea of giving the nation, and ourselves, over to a future ruled by Ho Chi Minh, Vo Nguyen Giap, and the Indochinese Communist party.

For months Hong, Luat, and I agonized about what course to follow. We listened intently to the news broadcasts, which were never fully intelligible through the static in the earphones of our primitive radio set. We heard that the French had explicitly and publicly promised independence to the Bao Dai government, a term they had never used in their talks with the Vietminh. In the end we decided that we could not rely on other people's reports about what was going on between Bao Dai and the French. We would have to see the situation first hand before making any decisions. And that meant getting ourselves through the Vietminh-controlled countryside around Phat Diem to Hanoi, occupied by the French. But I decided I would first have to see my father.

In the spring of 1949 my entire family — my father, mother, older brother, and sister — was living in a small village not far from where Phu Ly had been. Phu Ly itself had ceased to exist. It had been burned down by its own people, a victim of the scorched-earth tactics ordered by Vo Nguyen Giap. By this time my father had become a notable figure in the Vietminh zone. My brother — seven years older than I and a professor of literature — had also joined the Vietminh. But regardless of the different political paths we had taken, the war had done nothing to loosen the family bonds between us.

At the end of April I sneaked out of the Catholic zone on a barge going upriver toward the old Phu Ly district. At their new home I spent three days in the bosom of my family, our happiness marred only by the knowledge that the war would separate us again, perhaps for an even longer time. I confided to my father that I was planning to go to Hanoi, wondering what his reaction would be. I told him I was simply unable to stay with him in the countryside, pretending enthusiasm for the revolution when in fact I had the deepest objections to it.

Like me, he was upset by the implications of this trip for the family. Once we were divided by the French-Vietminh battle lines, who knew when we could be together again? But he also understood my feelings and did not try to dissuade me from them. Instead, he accompanied me on the first leg of my barge trip back to Phat Diem, drawing out our parting as long as he could. When we finally said goodbye on the shores of the Day River, we shared an uneasy intuition that it would be for the last time. To our sorrow, it was a feeling that turned out to be true. The events that were to tear the nation apart would not spare us any more than they would hundreds of thousands of other Vietnamese families.

Back in the Catholic zone, Hong, Luat, and I planned our trip north. From Phat Diem we would have to make our way through the heavily patrolled coastal strip, then go by boat to Haiphong. Because the area was under such close Vietminh control, we decided to go separately. The smaller the party, the less chance there was of being spotted, and we did not want to run the risk of being grabbed all at once.

At the beginning of May it was my turn to leave. On a dismal rainy night I followed a Catholic security cadre with a Sten gun along a path toward the shore. In the dark I couldn't see a thing. Suddenly, my guide stopped, listening intently. Then, without even a signal to me, he jumped off the path toward the beach. From the darkness I heard his voice, low but sharp. "On behalf of the Vietnamese nationalist movement, I order you to help us." A moment later I was next to him, helping to push off a little fishing boat manned by two frightened fishermen. With the rain pouring down on us, it took three hours before we found the junk that was waiting offshore for my arrival.

Even on board the junk, I could not shake the premonition that I was in for another horrible experience at sea. After a relatively mild first day, my fears were realized. Rain lashed the boat from side to side, and the rough sea crashed down on the deck. Late in the second day, the main mast snapped off, leaving the ship drifting uncontrollably toward shore. Aboard the junk the passengers were panicking, terrified that we would be driven aground and captured by Vietminh patrols. But working frantically, the crew managed to rig a small jury mast and head the unwieldy craft once more to sea.

Powered by the substitute sail, it took us three days to reach Haiphong. Once there, my happiness about being on land again was tempered by the fact that the territory I was standing on was French occupied. It was an extremely uncomfortable feeling.

Chapter 9

The Bao Dai Solution

THE MOMENT WE LANDED in French-ruled Haiphong, the police picked me up for questioning. The search and interrogation were superficial. I had come in from Phat Diem on a boat full of Catholic refugees, so the police were prepared to believe that I was not Vietminh. But while the questioning was going on, I began to experience a physical revulsion for the Vietnamese police who were working for the French, and for their masters. I could feel myself bristling at the French officers parading around the police station giving orders to everyone. It was an outrage. Here was the full-blown colonial apparatus on its feet again and functioning as if the euphoria of independence had never been. And I was in the middle of it, in a sense even acquiescing to it. I wondered how wise this carefully thought out decision of mine had actually been. After several painful days in Haiphong among the colonialists, I left for Hanoi.

Fortunately for my mental state, in Hanoi I found a different story. Almost immediately, I ran into Phan Huy Quat, the doctor who had served as my uncle Kim's cabinet secretary during his five months as prime minister. Dr. Quat was busy with his private medical practice but also kept attuned to the political situation. After talking a bit, he confided that he, too, was part of the Dai Viet circle. The party had in fact reconstituted itself, though not exactly as the formal entity it had previously been. No one had been able to reorganize the party hierarchy or to take the place of the murdered Truong Tu Anh. But the Dai Viet's amalgam of democratic principles and Vietnamese patriotism was attracting a new generation of members, many of them politically sophisticated professionals like Quat.

As I began to meet these people, I realized that they were less revolutionary than the students who had made up the core of the party during the conspiratorial days when I had joined. These people were older, more diplomatic. It seemed to me they more nearly resembled the mandarin administrators of my uncle's cabinet than the passionate, gun-toting activists who had worked under party chief Anh. But not all of the former Dai Viet types had disappeared forever. In the spring of 1949 many survivors were slowly filtering into Hanoi from their sanctuaries in China and their hiding places in the remote provinces. Like me, they had been drawn back by rumors that Bao Dai might be able to wrest real independence from the French. And in such a promise they, like me, glimpsed a path to salvation for both themselves and the nation.

From Dr. Quat I heard that my uncle Kim had indeed left Hong Kong for Saigon, but that he was now living in Phnom Penh, Cambodia. The last time I had seen Kim was on the Chinese border, three years before, when I had arranged his escape from the Vietminh. Now that I had the freedom to move around, I wanted badly to get back together with him. Over the years, our relationship had developed an almost father and son closeness. I felt I needed to see him. I wanted to know what had happened to him since our parting and, especially, how he assessed the latest developments between the French and Bao Dai and what he himself intended to do.

Borrowing the money from various friends, I flew from Hanoi to Saigon, and from there to Phnom Penh on an old Air France Dakota. Phnom Penh was one of the sleepiest places I had ever seen, the perfect spot for anyone looking for a quiet retreat. This, in fact, was precisely the reason Uncle Kim had established himself there. In Phnom Penh there was nothing to do and nobody to bother him while he rested and took stock of events in Vietnam.

As soon as I arrived, I moved into the cottage Kim was renting in the suburbs. In the mornings we ate dorians, a pungent white fruit popular with southern Vietnamese and Cambodians. Then we would walk together through Phnom Penh's lazy warmth down to the great Mekong flowing sluggishly through the capital. Sitting on the riverbank, we brought each other up to date on the last three years. I told Kim about Anh, my flight, my work for the Vietminh, and my attempt to organize a movement in Phat Diem while he described the vicissitudes he had experienced in China.

He had had a rough time of it in Hong Kong, Kim told me. The supply channel I had set up worked fitfully for a while, but with chief Anh's death even that was closed off. Kim had been left with no money, the representative of a party in shreds. At times Bao Dai supported him, but the emperor, too, was an unsteady source. In the end it was evident that nothing could be done in China, and Kim moved to Saigon to stay with relatives. But in Saigon the French refused to leave him alone, pressuring him to start taking an active role in politics. Though they knew how he felt about them and their administration, they also knew he could be a powerful voice for the Bao Dai solution, if only they could move him in that direction.

That was the reason Kim had moved to Cambodia, to escape the constant French harassment. His outlook was pessimistic. He had a clear understanding of both the Vietminh's strength and the nationalists' weakness, and he believed that a real solution through a Bao Dai–French agreement was unlikely. And even if an accord along these lines was possible, it would only come about in the distant future. With these misgivings, he was not about to lend his name to the accommodation that was being arranged.

Although I largely shared Kim's viewpoint, I refused to accept his pessimism. I was more and more convinced that there were only two choices: either to give up completely or to hope that a Bao Dai solution could actually work. After two weeks of discussing these things with my uncle in Phnom Penh, I flew back to Hanoi to wait and see what would happen, praying that French concessions on independence would go far enough to justify supporting the emperor.

Through 1948 Bao Dai and the French gradually came together, and in June they signed a pact, known as the Accord of Ha Long, in which France formally agreed to "solemnly recognize the independence of Vietnam."

Here was the essential point, the one thing I and others like me had been waiting for. Never before had the French put the word "independence" into an official document. Ho's preliminary agreement with Sainteny, for example, the one France refused to confirm in the summer of 1946, referred to Vietnam as a "free state . . . belonging to the Indochinese Federation and the French Union." We spent hours scrutinizing the text and debating its meaning. To all appearances, it seemed as if Bao Dai had secured through negotiations what the Vietminh had not begun to achieve in two years of war.

In short order more evidence came that the emperor was playing a strong hand. One negative side of the accord was its stipulation that the southern part of Vietnam — Cochinchina — would remain a French colony unless returned to Vietnam proper by vote of the Territorial Assembly. And since the assembly was composed of French settlers and prominent Vietnamese who had flourished under French rule, such a vote was anything but a foregone conclusion. But despite French pressure on Bao

Dai to re-establish residence in Vietnam (during the negotiations he had been living in France) and reassume the throne, he refused to budge until the Territorial Assembly actually voted to integrate Cochinchina with the rest of the country.

This finally took place in December. Only then, after he had signed the Élysée accord formalizing the integrity of Vietnam, did Bao Dai consent to resume his status as emperor and chief of state. With this success behind him, in January of 1949 Bao Dai moved back to Vietnam and began structuring the government that would negotiate the de facto transfer of power from the French colonial authorities to the Vietnamese.

Shortly after signing this agreement, Bao Dai moved into a villa in the southern resort town of Dalat. From there he sent out invitations to all the politically significant groups and families in Vietnam, asking them to come to Dalat for consultations. In response to one of these invitations, early in the spring I flew to Dalat from Hanoi, together with Dr. Quat and Dang Van Sung, the old school friend who had first persuaded me to join the Dai Viet back in 1944.

On the morning of our appointment, the three of us arrived at the emperor's villa, where we were shown into an anteroom to await our meeting. Despite the fact that I had been living with my uncle in Hue while Bao Dai was in residence at the city's imperial palace, I had never actually seen the emperor, although of course I knew a great deal about him, and was extremely curious about what he would be like in person.

A moment after we walked into a well-furnished room through one set of doors, Bao Dai appeared through another. He was dressed in a white European-style suit, and from the moment he came in, I was struck by his relaxed air. He seemed to me a friendly, easygoing person, in no particular hurry to break off the amiable small talk and get down to business. It was all we could do not to show how impatient we were to hear exactly what arrangements he had made with the French and what he wanted from us.

Finally it came out. "We have a framework for independence," he said. "I couldn't get everything I wanted from them. But at least we have a framework, a state of Vietnam. From now on, it depends more on them than on us, but on us, too. . . . Do you think you can help me put together a government? Can we cooperate together with this framework?"

This was exactly the question we had been asking ourselves, but Bao Dai didn't press us for an immediate answer. "We'll be in touch about it," he said. Then he asked me to send his regards to my uncle and added, "We have to be very careful this time around — tell your uncle this — or else we'll be cheated like we were last time." I knew he was referring to the Vietminh takeover, when he had been maneuvered into legitimizing Ho Chi Minh's revolutionary government and accepting the meaningless title of supreme counselor. He was hinting that not just he but all the nationalists had been cheated — suggesting that just as we were in the same boat then, we were still in the same boat now. This emperor might appear a bit detached, I thought, but there is nothing stupid about him.

Although our first conversation with Bao Dai was casual and friendly, in subsequent talks he became more insistent. "Look," he told us, "it was only because of people like you and your friends that I went forward with the French. It's no secret that all of you wanted me to. Now that I've done it, you have got to support me. So I didn't get everything I wanted, but I got something! What am I supposed to do now if you refuse to help me?"

It was an agonizing decision, not only for us but for all the nationalists who had been called to Dalat by the emperor. We were so reluctant to accept these frail promises from the French, who we all knew would do everything in their power to temporize or even renege on their agreement if they saw a way to do it. Anyone who participated in this government would surely be regarded as a collaborationist later on.

On the other hand, the British and the Americans had already recognized the Bao Dai government, and we were sure that the Americans, at least, would force the French to move steadily toward granting real autonomy. The United States had even opened an embassy in Saigon and appointed an ambassador. They certainly had no love for the French colonial system, and since they were the chief financial support for France's military efforts, they would have substantial leverage in this situation. Our assessment was that the Americans had always been in favor of Vietnamese independence, and that we would be able to rely on their backing. In 1945 when the United States had refused to get involved, they had had no investment in the country. Now, with formal diplomatic recognition, they were giving a clear signal of affirmation for Vietnam's freedom.

Besides, Bao Dai was planning to keep pushing the French, and if we didn't put our hands to this work, who would? Could we in good conscience keep our distance and wait around for the French to deliver the country on a platter? On the contrary, if we accepted the principle of a gradual transfer of authority now, we could demand more as time went by. In the not too distant future the government could even press France to turn over the auxiliary Vietnamese armed forces to its control. When that happened, we would be in a good position in the event of new negotiations with the Vietminh. We shared the conviction that France's days in Vietnam were numbered. All this we balanced against our repugnance for entering into any kind of partnership with the colonialists.

In the end we decided that with the French on one side and the Communists on the other, a successful Bao Dai solution was the only chance we had. We would be forced to accept the risk of being branded as collaborators. Still, we decided to move cautiously. After days of discussion, Sung and I conveyed to Bao Dai that "in general terms, we support the government," even though we did not feel the time was exactly right to serve in it. But Dr. Quat, the most prominent man in our group, would join.

Although all three of us had agreed on this step, Quat, in fact, felt as much discomfort about participating as we did. He considered that he was sacrificing himself for the common good while Sung and I got to keep our hands clean. There was no way I could have divined that fifteen years later, when the military government of Nguyen Van Thieu took power, I would be repaying the personal debt I owed to Quat for this act of self-abnegation.

We were all intensely aware of the dangers in what we were doing. We knew we were drawing a heavy burden onto our backs and would be stigmatized by many as collaborators. This was to be a continuing tragedy for Vietnam's nationalists, that in an especially xenophobic period, we would be associated first with the French, then the Americans. But we knew the Communists, too, and knowing them, we were sure we had no alternative. It was a tragedy from which there was no escape.

Of all the prominent nationalists of that time, the only one who kept a distance between himself and the Bao Dai government was Ngo Dinh Diem. Reading the situation perhaps better than we, after some initial meetings with the emperor, he left Vietnam for Europe and eventually the United States, where he cultivated the support that was to serve him well in later years.

There was one development that could make the Bao Dai solution universally popular and give real strength to our fight against the Vietminh: true independence. If France could be brought quickly to implement the transfer of power, the political balance inside Vietnam would change dramatically. Should that happen, we — the nation's non-Communist nationalists — would have accomplished through peaceful means what the Communists had failed to do in four years of violence and bloodshed.

The more likely scenario undoubtedly was that the French would transfer power only inch by painful inch in response to continuous pressure from Bao Dai, the nationalists, and the Americans. But as we studied the situation, we realized that there was one way to break the French lock step, and that was for Bao Dai to turn on them. If the emperor would not ask but demand the immediate implementation of French promises, the colonialists would be in a dangerous dilemma themselves. They badly needed the Bao Dai government to provide a Vietnamese alternative to the Viet-minh and to marshal all the anti-Communist sentiment they could. Even more important, they had to convince the Americans, their backers, that they were proceeding in good faith on the independence issue.

But just as they were using Bao Dai, there was no reason he could not use them. Now that the French had worked so hard to establish Bao Dai as an emperor with the appearance of power, why could he not demand real power and declare that he would resign if it was refused? It was an intriguing idea with real potential. If Bao Dai could be induced to make a giant fuss on this issue, the French would be faced with the choice of either going along or squandering their entire investment in Vietnamese nationalism and revealing their naked, reactionary intentions to the Americans. But such a ploy hinged solely on Bao Dai himself. Could the emperor be brought to play such an explosive role?

The more Sung, Dr. Quat, and I discussed this concept, the more we liked it. In the end, I was chosen to present it to Bao Dai. First, though, I wanted to talk it over with my uncle Kim, who had just gotten back to Saigon from his retreat in Phnom Penh.

"Listen," I told him, "everybody is impatient about the French. We're in an embarrassing situation with the people because of this collabora-tion business. Meanwhile, Bao Dai is in Dalat not doing anything at all. He has his women there and his hunting. He's hunting all the time. Now our friends have asked me to go up there and try to wake him up. What do you think?"

My uncle, though, had not lost his pessimism — or, rather, his realism. "Diem, you don't understand Bao Dai," he said, smiling at me patiently. "Bao Dai is an emperor, not a revolutionary. All his life he's been raised so that he'll behave in a very passive way. That's his life — passivity. Nothing you can do is going to change that."

My uncle's words were like an ice-cold shower. I knew his understand-ing of Bao Dai's character went far deeper than mine, and he had good reason to be skeptical. But even so, I was not going to be deterred from trying.

It took a month for me to arrange an audience with the emperor, but finally I had my chance to speak with him privately. One day while I waited in Dalat for the call, Bao Dai's military aide came down to the house where I was staying and said, "Sire is having a hunting party to-morrow, and he'd like you to join him." So the next morning I found myself traveling with the emperor's entourage into the forests of the cen-tral highlands.

Hunting was a passion with him. In the highlands was one of his hunt-ing boxes, with its series of camouflaged treetop enclosures where he and his party would sit all day long and watch for game to appear. Spread out in a huge circle two or three kilometers in diameter, the Montagnard tribesmen who lived in this area started beating their drums and slowly driving the animals toward the center, where the emperor waited for them, hoping for a tiger to emerge from the jungle. As the drums closed in, I was waiting, too, in an enclosure not far from Bao Dai's. Though my hunting companions were poised and ready to shoot, I was intent on Bao Dai a few trees away, wondering how I might get a few moments alone with him and present my proposition.

Despite the noise and commotion, that day Bao Dai got nothing. When it was all over, the party returned to the box. Shortly after we got back, I saw Bao Dai sitting alone on the veranda sipping a drink. Regardless of the inauspicious events of the day, I saw that this might well be my only opportunity, so, screwing up my courage, I walked up to him and started right in. *"Ngai"* ("Sire"), I said. "I've just come up from Saigon a few days ago. I have to report to you, Sire, that many people there are complaining about the French. They are simply not keeping their promises, and it is very hard to continue doing nothing about it."

Without a moment's hesitation, Bao Dai shot back, "In politics we should know how to be patient." Obviously, he had been thinking about these things as well. Perhaps he had even guessed what I was there to talk about. After a strained silence he said, "Yes, I know. The French are really behaving very badly. But I am so lonely. . . . Tell me, what do you see on the American side?"

"Well, Sire, Dr. Quat has contact with them from time to time. But there's nothing clear from them yet."

"Yes," he said, "that's my impression too."

"Still, Sire, how long can we continue like this?"

"I'm not sure," came the reply. "Why don't you come back and see me in a few months? We can talk about it then."

At this point, I felt I couldn't push the conversation any further. So that was it, the proof that Uncle Kim was right. Deeply depressed, I returned to Saigon knowing that there was no way we were going to get out from under this burden. After a few days, another piece of information came that completed the jigsaw puzzle. From Bao Dai's cabinet, word began to spread that several weeks before a large sum of money from the French was transferred into one of the emperor's foreign bank accounts. When, a few days later, a French Communist newspaper reported exactly the same thing, the story seemed incontrovertible.

With this news, the French strategy became evident. On the political level, they were playing a game of obstruction, refusing to negotiate sincerely on the transfer of power. At the same time, on the personal level, they were doing whatever they could to mute Bao Dai's demands. And Bao Dai, by his weakness, played right into their hands. As shrewd as he was, he could not turn down the money.

At the age of twenty-seven, I had learned another lesson. And though I was not conscious of it, a pattern was emerging of my career as a politician. I had found in Dai Viet chief Truong Tu Anh a man I could serve. But his career had been cut short by the Vietminh. For a brief period I believed that Bao Dai might be able to rise to the role of Vietnam's leader. But the day at the hunting box had put that thought to rest. For two and a half decades more I would serve various South Vietnamese leaders, searching always for the man who could meet the nation's needs. Fortunately, in 1950 I could foresee none of this. And so I did not sense that my search, which was also the quest of Vietnam's nationalists, was touched by doom.

Chapter 10

Alpine Interlude

AT THE BEGINNING OF 1951 I had, of course, no intimations of what my future would hold. And even though in my own mind Bao Dai had failed the test of leadership, I still rejected the detached pessimism that my uncle espoused and that my family background should have disposed me to embrace. Instead, I plunged fully into political activities.

First on the agenda was the establishment of a new party. Though the spirit and something of the fervor of the Dai Viet had come to life again, the party structure had died with Truong Tu Anh. Now we took the old northern Vietnam Dai Viet and formally re-established it under a new name: Quoc Gia Binh Dan, the Popular Nationalist party. We also started up a party daily newspaper, *Quoc Dan,* of which I became editor in chief.

Before long *Quoc Dan* became one of the most widely read and influential newspapers in the French zone. For me it was a marvelously busy period. I found backers for the paper, wrote editorials, managed production, organized debates and public meetings, even looked after the business end. The paper spoke for the party, and I took pride in our straightforward advocacy of the party's positions against communism and in favor of immediate, full implementation of independence. Interestingly enough, although occasionally we were constrained to use more diplomatic language than we would have chosen, the government censors never pressured us about our constant harping on the theme of "freedom now."

While the paper published what I regarded as hard-hitting editorials on independence, I also had the chance to watch Bao Dai from a distance as he maneuvered — slowly, almost surreptitiously — toward the same goal. For all his character flaws, I began to appreciate that Bao Dai was in essence a true Asian monarch, with a subtle grasp of politics and an instinctive ability to manipulate men. His primary tool in dealing with the French was his management of government — or, rather, of governments. Bao Dai operated on the basis of an ever evolving sense for how far he could push the French at any given time. As chief of state, he had the sole power to choose prime ministers, and each prime minister, according to his view, had to be appropriate for each particular phase of the ongoing negotiations with France.

The overall idea was to bring increasing pressure to bear on the colonialists. Initially, Bao Dai wanted prime ministers who were close to the French. Their function was to firmly establish a cooperative relationship between the French and Vietnamese governments and to get the ball rolling gently in the direction Bao Dai wished it to go. The transition from one stage of negotiations to the next required a change of government. As the hard issues of independence were broached, harder, more forceful leaders would be needed; if a tactical retreat became necessary, the proper man must be found to lead that. Eventually, I even came to suspect that Bao Dai planned his governments several turns in advance.

The emperor also selected his prime ministers carefully to ensure that they would not have complete control of their own cabinets. To prevent that, he larded each government with strong, independent-minded nationalists, men he could rely on to counterbalance the prime minister's power and provide continuity when it came time to replace the current prime minister with another.

Each time Bao Dai changed governments, the nationalist parties would debate intensely whether to join the next regime. Would the new government be strong enough to justify working with it or would participation damage the party's credibility? Was it necessary to have a representative in government regardless of the possible damage? What did the emperor really have in mind this time around? Whatever the decision, various nationalist figures moved in and out of Bao Dai's governments, including Dr. Quat and Tran Van Tuyen, my former teacher and mentor.

Quat, who had emerged as our group's leading public figure, was in Bao Dai's first government as minister of education. The second time he served, it was as minister of defense, a vital post, because perhaps *the* central issue on the table between the French and Vietnamese concerned the establishment of an independent Vietnamese armed force. This was a vexing subject. The French fully grasped the necessity of creating a separate Vietnamese army, but they also regarded such an army as a threat to themselves, and rightly so. The Vietnamese, of course, were pushing as hard as they could to get control of their own forces. It was during the very sticky talks on this topic that an event took place that spirited me as far from the political scene as if I had been suddenly whisked to Mars.

* * *

About a year earlier, I had gotten married to Kim Ngoc, the girl I had met first at my uncle's home and then in Phat Diem. Her family, too, had eventually moved from the Catholic zone to French-controlled Hanoi. Here we had again resumed our friendship, though at that point neither of us was contemplating marriage. Then one day, for no apparent reason, my uncle Kim took me aside and asked if there wasn't perhaps someone who had attracted my attention, someone I would consider sharing my life with. At first I told him no, I wasn't thinking of marriage, I was much too busy for anything like that. But over the next few days, he came back to the topic several times. As puzzling as Uncle Kim's interest was, his persistence somehow started me thinking: maybe there was something to it, maybe it was time to think about settling down. After all, I was already twenty-eight, and if my life hadn't exactly fallen into a dull routine, at least I was no longer hiding in safe houses with a gun in my pocket. In the end, I confessed that I did have someone in mind: the girl Kim Ngoc whom I had met in his house years before. If I was going to marry anybody, she would be the one.

Uncle Kim seemed especially happy to hear this news. He was acquainted with her family and heartily approved of my choice. Before I knew exactly what was happening, my aunt was dispatched to make the proper overtures to Kim Ngoc's family, and shortly after that, the match was arranged and sealed. That was how I became a family man, a circumstance I was almost immediately happy with and which I have been happy with ever since, despite its somewhat odd inception.

Had I known the real story behind Uncle Kim's sudden interest in my marital status, I would have thought it a good deal odder. Like many other Vietnamese, Uncle Kim had a taste for the occult. One day, he had invited a renowned physiognomist to his house. I had come by that day, and although I was not aware of it, the famous man had looked carefully at my face. What he saw disturbed him, and when my uncle heard the news, he was considerably more than disturbed. Apparently, there was an ominous shadow across my features. I was, the physiognomist told my uncle, leading a dangerous and event-filled life. The chances of my surviving it more than another year were not good. The only way he knew that might short-circuit my imminent and unpleasant fate would be for me to get married. In that event, my wife's future line might mingle with mine and deflect it, preventing the worst. It was the very next day that Uncle Kim had asked about my prospects.

Whatever the validity of the physiognomist's predictions, in one way at least our marriage at that point turned out to be fortuitous. Not long after Kim Ngoc and I had set up house, I received a message from my father that my mother and sister were coming to Hanoi from the Vietminh zone. Would I be able to put them up? My mother, it seemed, had developed a persistent, nervous fear of the French bombing that regularly disrupted life in the Communist-controlled areas. In an effort to get her away from the danger, my father had made arrangements to move her through the lines. Would I be able to provide a place to live for her and my sister? I wrote back immediately that he should send them through. And so it was that our new family of two suddenly became a family of four.

A year later, in May 1952, my wife gave birth to our first daughter, Ngoc Luu. Although the delivery was normal and the baby healthy, shortly afterward Kim Ngoc became ill with tuberculosis. Dr. Quat, who had been deeply involved in politics for a number of years (and was at the moment negotiating with the French), was also our family physician. After studying the X rays and test results, he informed us that Kim Ngoc's illness might easily develop into "galloping TB." For this disease there were no therapeutic facilities in Vietnam. If I valued my wife's life, I would take her immediately to France, where she could be treated by specialists.

The news shook us badly. To make matters worse, Quat emphasized that we should not take our baby with us. There was simply no way Kim Ngoc could physically care for her. After several rounds of bitter tears and arguments, we gave in to the inevitable. We would leave Luu with my mother and sister, who, together with Uncle Kim and my aunt, would serve as a temporary foster family.

With that decision made, we began to arrange the trip. My uncle gave us some money, I sold my gold watch, borrowed more money from friends, and managed to obtain travel documents. We left as soon as we could, on an Air France Skymaster that made the flight from Saigon to Paris in three days. I had finally fulfilled my childhood dream of going overseas, though not exactly under the circumstances I had envisioned.

Still, Paris in the spring of 1952 was a revelation to me. On the one hand, I felt I knew everything about it. I had been so immersed in French culture for so long that France and its people seemed as comfortable as old clothes. On the other hand, here I was in Paris, abroad for the first time in my life. I looked around and there was the Eiffel Tower, the Champs-Élysées, the Louvre. I gawked at the city and its sites, as if I were some strange hybrid: a French-educated intellectual staring at the capital through wide-open peasant eyes.

As soon as we arrived, we checked into a no-star hotel near Montparnasse and got in touch with a cousin of mine, a physician who had lived in Paris for many years. After doing his own examination, my cousin made arrangements for Kim Ngoc to visit a specialist, who performed a pneumothorax operation, in which the affected lung was surgically collapsed. Afterward the doctor prescribed an extended convalescence at a sanatorium in the Alps near Chamonix.

The sanatorium turned out to be an accommodating place that accepted not only patients but their families as well. In a short time Kim Ngoc and I were comfortably installed, she for her lungs and I to help with her care. It was unique, this environment for sick people, designed so that there was as little to do as possible. Tranquility was the order of the day, all day, every day. I walked around in the fresh mountain air and watched Mont Blanc loom over its neighbors. News did not penetrate easily here. The universe outside faded into obscurity. Vietnam, with its seething politics and vicious fighting, began to seem a distant land indeed.

With nothing to do, I decided to resume my mathematical studies. The University of Grenoble was only an hour and a half away, and the mathematics faculty there offered a correspondence course, with examinations and occasional meetings in Grenoble. I enrolled and again found myself immersed in a world of pure abstraction. Somehow Chamonix, with its monumental and unchanging serenity, made it easy to adjust to this sudden and radical transformation in my way of life.

At the sanatorium we ran into another couple who were there under circumstances similar to our own. The wife, convalescing from tuberculosis, was attended by her husband, an English professor from Berne University. Before long Kim Ngoc and I became friendly with Paul and Paulette Savarit, and Paul agreed to tutor me in English, which I had studied in high school but had rarely used. While our wives basked in the sun and mountain air on the sanatorium's veranda, Paul and I hiked and climbed our way through the nearby mountains, speaking English the whole time.

When it came to the English language, Paul Savarit was a perfectionist. English to him meant the king's English, not some "awful American dialect." "Speak perfect English," he would tell me, correcting my dismal half-French, half-Vietnamese accent. I wrote essays for him as well, first on the situation in Vietnam, a subject he knew nothing about, then on Somerset Maugham, then on *Hamlet* and *Macbeth*, which the professor had me read. I worked hard, progressing far beyond the "My tailor is rich" textbook paradigms, which were about all I remembered from my school days.

After three or four months of living at the sanatorium, Kim Ngoc and I moved to a small apartment in a nearby chalet. Since she was strictly forbidden to do anything but rest, I became a househusband, responsible for all the cooking, cleaning, washing, and shopping. Life was serene. Except for occasional trips to Grenoble for the math course, we stayed right where we were, marveling at the first snowfall on November 1 (neither of us had seen snow before) and amazed as the advancing winter brought additional piles of the stuff, which was eventually heaped as high as our windows.

As removed as we were, I did not completely lose touch with Vietnam. By the start of the winter, I was in weekly correspondence with my uncle. As far as I could determine, though, nothing earthshaking was happening, or at least nothing he was telling me about. Mostly he wrote that there was no need to worry about events at home and that I should take all the time we needed for Kim Ngoc to make a full recovery.

In the spring of 1953 it was evident she was on her way to exactly that. With the prognosis so good, in early May Kim Ngoc went with me to Grenoble, where I was scheduled to take my final examination. Shortly after we had checked into our *pension,* I received a telegram from Dr. Quat in Vietnam. Bao Dai had just installed another government, and Quat had again been named defense minister. It was clear to everyone that serious negotiations were now in the works. Could I come home?

I spent the night thinking about it. If my wife thought she should stay longer, I would have a difficult decision to make. Despite my uncle's regular reassurances, it seemed that events in Vietnam were starting to come to a head. Quat never would have telegrammed otherwise. But how could I go back if my wife still needed me here?

I could have saved myself the night's worry. The next morning, over coffee, Kim Ngoc looked at me and said, "I know how much you want to go home." As soon as she said it, I knew that she had made up her mind to come with me. I was elated. I completely forgot about the math certificate I had been working toward all year, and we checked out of the *pension* to go back to our apartment and make arrangements for the trip back. A few days later we were booked on the now familiar Skymaster for the three-day flight to Saigon.

Chapter 11

The French Dig In

THE DAY AFTER WE ARRIVED in Saigon, I was appointed deputy chief
of staff for Quat's ministry. As suddenly as I had been spirited out of
politics to spend a year on a French mountainside, just as abruptly I
tumbled back into the thick of things. As defense minister, Dr. Quat was
the key figure in this most recent Vietnamese government, and it appeared that his assessment of France's willingness to negotiate seriously
was accurate. As always, the military side of these talks would be pivotal.
Would the French at last accede to an independent Vietnamese army? If
they would, the other problems would resolve themselves with relative
ease.

To handle the military negotiations, Quat put together a small team
headed by me and Colonel Le Van Kim. (Kim was subsequently pro-
moted to general and was one of the three senior commanders who, a
decade later, engineered the coup against Ngo Dinh Diem.) By September
we were sitting down with the French commander, Henri Navarre, to
decide the principle of Vietnamese military autonomy. Unfortunately, despite our initial optimism, the talks quickly assumed the usual agonizing
routine. Regardless of their protestations of sincerity, the French remained ambivalent when it came to making the hard concessions. In this
case, the specific issue was the right to train and command battalion-level
Vietnamese forces. In the end we won: they would be our battalions, but
the French insisted on retaining overall control.

Even at this date (we were nearing 1954, which would see the end of
the war), the French were still trying to hold on to every shred of authority they could keep their hands on. They talked a great deal, for example,
about Vietnam's independence as part of "the French Union." No one

ever knew precisely what that meant. They never bothered to define the term specifically, so it simply aroused suspicions. As far as my friends and I were concerned, we did not want any part of a French Union. We were discouraged by Navarre's attitude during the military negotiations and by the ingrained colonial mindset it was part of. The French approach seemed so shortsighted and destructive, for themselves as well as for us. We needed independence desperately if we were ever to counteract the Vietminh. In order to face Ho Chi Minh from a position of strength, we had to show that we had won true national freedom at the negotiating table. But, bent on salvaging whatever power they had over their colony, French statesmen and commanders seemed quite willing to ignore the potential consequences of their stubbornness.

In September Bao Dai decided the time had come to bring additional pressure to bear on the French. The vehicle for this would be a three-day National Congress, to which would be invited representatives of all the significant political and religious factions outside the Vietminh. Uncle Kim would run the congress, which would obviously generate heated nationalistic sentiment and help swell public opinion behind the drive for independence.

When the congress opened, no one was disappointed by the enthusiasm of its members for full and immediate autonomy. Toward the end of the three days, a hot debate developed around a resolution against joining the so-called French Union. Proponents were calling on Bao Dai to insist on complete independence; there should be no accommodation that would include Vietnam in any form of French-dominated commonwealth. The debate was vehement and was conducted openly, which meant that it was drawing widespread public attention.

But perhaps the debate's most serious ramifications were not known to the public. I had been quite active in the congress, as a delegate and as behind-the-scenes manager for Uncle Kim. I also maintained contact with the Americans, who by this time had taken an active interest in the congress. Now, with the final debate nearing an end, George Hellyer, director of the United States Information Agency (USIA) in Saigon, asked me to stop by and see him at his home. When I arrived, he questioned me about what I thought would happen with the resolution. When I described the strong feeling against accommodation with the French, he said that if we wanted to hear the American position on the issue, he would arrange for me to meet with Ambassador Donald Heath. I told him that of course we would be interested in hearing from the ambassador, so we made an appointment for the same evening, this time at Heath's residence.

As soon as I left Hellyer, I sat down with Dr. Quat and Uncle Kim to try to prepare for the meeting. It seemed a bit strange that the Americans wanted to convey their message indirectly instead of through government channels. But whatever Heath's reasons, each of us knew that what he said would be an important factor in our future considerations. Like other nationalist politicians, Quat, Kim, and I had long looked to the United States for moral support and (we believed) as an eventual source of material help as well. With its anticolonialist and democratic predispositions, we viewed the United States as a natural ally in our efforts to clear a distinct path between French colonialism and Vietnamese communism.

Rightly or wrongly, we had invested substantial hopes in the American connection. And these hopes had been encouraged, not officially but through a continuing series of informal contacts with the USIA, the CIA, and embassy personnel. At receptions, private get-togethers, and social visits, Americans and Vietnamese had gotten to know one another and had developed relationships. Although it was true that nothing was said on the record, still, to our minds, the pattern of contacts held its own evident meaning. In hindsight, perhaps we wanted too much to be encouraged, or perhaps the characteristic Vietnamese sensitivity to the suggestive and indirect misled us. But the truth appeared to us then, as it still appears to me today, that on one level at least it was American policy to encourage Vietnam's democratic nationalists in believing that the United States would stand behind their drive for complete independence. On another level, American policy took a different tack, as I was to find out that evening at the home of Ambassador Heath.

As Quat, Uncle Kim, and I had immediately understood, Hellyer's overture to me meant that the pending resolution on the French Union had real significance in American eyes. Enough so that they felt compelled to reveal at least something about the basic direction of their thinking on Vietnam. And this Heath did, diplomatically but without a trace of ambiguity. He told us that the United States supported Vietnam, that it was in favor of independence for Vietnam. But at the same time, the United States was allied to the French. The relationship between France and Vietnam, Heath said, should be a smooth one. That was the reason he thought this resolution went too far. There simply wasn't enough room for flexibility in it. Heath went on to say that relations between the United States and France were "multifaceted." He alluded to the European alliance and counseled that we should be "moderate" rather than "extreme."

I felt a wave of disappointment at these remarks. I told Heath that it was late in the day for advice of this sort, and that I could not predict what would happen on the floor of the National Congress. Back with

Kim and the others after the meeting, it felt as if we had each received a kick in the stomach. I remember Quat saying angrily, "They ought to be more forthcoming than that!" The depression among Bao Dai's staff was palpable. A huge weight had settled on all of us.

We all recognized that the significance of Heath's remarks went far beyond the debate on the French Union resolution. Although Heath did not say so directly, his mention of Europe and of the "multifaceted" nature of Franco-American relations clearly referred to the European Defense Community proposal and the ongoing American difficulties with France on this subject. His signal was that although Vietnamese independence was a goal the United States favored, in fact Vietnam constituted only a small segment of American geopolitical policy. Other considerations carried greater weight — a united allied defense in Europe, for example. If French cooperation on that front could be affected by American pressure on Vietnam's obstreperous nationalists, then pressure there would be. In other words, life and death issues for us were merely bargaining chips in the Americans' pursuit of their global policy. This was a surprising lesson in the fall of 1953, primarily because we had made an inordinate investment in what we understood as the idealistic thrust of American foreign affairs. It was a lesson we would relearn at far greater cost later on.

The upshot of the American position was that the following day a weaker resolution passed. As the hands went up to vote, I was thinking to myself that the Americans had obviously talked to far more people than just Quat, Kim, and me. To what extent this episode undermined the Bao Dai government as it entered the final stages of negotiations with the French is impossible to accurately estimate. There is no question, however, that strong American support for Vietnamese independence would have enhanced the credibility of the nationalists just as it would have undercut France's diehard colonialism. Few of Vietnam's non-Communists thought the Bao Dai solution would provide a feasible counter to Ho Chi Minh without significant progress at the negotiating table. In the event, the emperor's passivity and French recalcitrance combined to produce a drawn out, tortuous failure. In the early 1950s the key to a different outcome lay in American hands. But United States policy, then as later, played a contradictory role, encouraging and ultimately disappointing the hopes of its friends.

When the congress ended without having its intended impact, the military negotiations moved from Saigon to Paris. Along with Colonel Le Van Kim, I now found myself in the middle of a dismal French autumn, facing a tiresome and dubious round of talks with a group of niggling, superannuated French generals. Neither the colonel nor I could generate much enthusiasm for any foreseeable consequences our labors might bring. On a cold November day, a telegram from Saigon interrupted one of these interminable sessions with the news that my uncle Kim was dead. He had died suddenly in Dalat of a heart attack. That grim and disappointing National Congress had been his last political act.

I arrived back in Vietnam just in time to board the plane flying my uncle's coffin from Dalat to Hanoi for a national funeral. There we buried him. The procession from his house to the cemetery stretched for half a mile behind the monks in their saffron robes and Kim's numerous family dressed in the traditional mourning white. Before the open grave, the eulogies followed one another under a lowering sky. The speakers lauded Kim as a philosopher, historian, and patriot rather than as a political figure. By the time he died, his short-lived government seemed an event in the distant past. His books, however, were already considered classics in the intellectual life of the nation.

Tran Trong Kim had been so much more to me than an uncle. We had shared a good part of our lives, both our political lives and our personal lives. Over the years, I had come to think of him as my spiritual father, closer, because of the circumstances of war, than my real father. To a certain extent, he was influenced by my father's mocking disregard for the capriciousness of the world, and that made him in some ways an unlikely politician. At a deeper level, he was a man of rigid honesty who systematically refused to make deals he thought out of keeping with his role as a servant of the people. Some historians have considered him too passive in his relations first with the Japanese, then with the Dai Viet. In a sense they are right; he was not a forceful leader of men or movements, nor did he think of himself in that way. His strengths lay elsewhere, in a rich inner life suffused by Vietnamese culture and in an unrelenting sense of public duty. He was perhaps Vietnam's last true mandarin, a man who embodied the best values the old heritage had to offer. The subsequent history of the nation was to demonstrate how sorely those qualities would be missed.

After the funeral I returned to Paris to resume the exercise in futility we were conducting with the French generals. Again I found myself sitting at the same heavy mahogany table, arguing for hours about the same endless procession of tedious and irrelevant details. It was all becoming increasingly surreal. Around that table the French negotiators were waging a vicious rear-guard action against Vietnamese nationalism while ten thousand miles away, the Communist noose was already tightening around Dienbienphu. The failure of the Bao Dai solution meant that we were negotiating abstractions in a vacuum; the realities lay elsewhere.

Chapter 12

The Emperor's Choice

ALTHOUGH THE BATTLE of Dienbienphu was developing badly for the French, in early 1954 no one was thinking in terms of a French military collapse (in fact, there was no military collapse even with Dienbienphu's destruction). It was clear, though, that the time had passed when an agreement between the Bao Dai government and France would be meaningful. Already there were rumors of an international conference of Indochina, to take place in Geneva. Such a conference would explicitly recognize that Vietnam's problems were too complex to be resolved by bilateral agreements between France and Bao Dai or France and the Vietminh. They required solutions of a more inclusive nature.

When the formal announcement of the Geneva conference came in February, we were unsure of what to make of it. On the one hand, we knew little about international politics and consequently felt uncomfortable with the idea of this wider forum. On the other hand, Geneva would be a good opportunity for us to free ourselves at last from the French orbit. Our experience with France over the previous years had been maddeningly frustrating; it had been a crucial period whose opportunities the French had crassly squandered. At Geneva we would be full participants. After the failure of the Bao Dai solution, the conference might give us another chance to establish a viable, internationally recognized Vietnamese nationalist government.

Within this new, wider context, the agreement we were now finishing up with the French negotiators assumed an unanticipated importance. With all of the details of Vietnamese independence worked out at long last, Bao Dai had become in every sense the legitimate head of a sovereign state, and it was that status we would be taking with us to Geneva.

The emperor did not personally represent his country at Geneva. For that he picked Nguyen Quoc Dinh, the foreign minister, who was a professor of international law at the University of Paris. Establishing quarters at the French border town of Evian, Bao Dai watched the early proceedings closely and received emissaries from various parties to the conference, conspicuous among them the American delegate Bedell Smith.

It was at Evian that Bao Dai began to plan his next government. Whereas up to this point the emperor had chosen each successive prime minister with an eye toward relations with the French, the new government would have to be constituted on a far different basis. Vietnam would now need a real national government, fit to operate competently not only in the domestic arena but in the international community as well. One way or another, after Geneva the country would enter a radically new political period.

By June Bao Dai had moved from Evian to the French resort of Cannes. At Dr. Quat's request, I followed the emperor there so I could confer with him about the post-Geneva government. Bao Dai knew, of course, what my purpose was. Quat was a strong and experienced politician who had served twice as minister of defense and had good relations with the Americans. Just as important, he was a committed democrat who could work closely with all of the nationalist groups in molding a consensus government. There was no question in my mind that Quat would be the best choice for prime minister, and I hoped I could bring Bao Dai to the same opinion.

At first Tran Van Do was with me in Cannes. Do, a good-natured southerner, had handled the political negotiations with the French that paralleled the military talks Colonel Kim and I had carried out. Characteristically, he had managed the French political hagglers with far more patience than I had been able to muster for the dyspeptic generals. Now he was lending his support and advice to the delicate business of moving Bao Dai in our direction.

One day, as Do and I were having lunch together, we noticed a very short Vietnamese come into the restaurant. Do pulled my sleeve and whispered, "Look, that's Ngo Dinh Luyen. What's he doing here?" Luyen, whom I had never seen before, was Ngo Dinh Diem's youngest brother. There was obviously nothing accidental about his presence in Cannes. While I waited at the table, Do went over to talk to him, then returned to introduce the two of us. It was clear that Luyen was in town on behalf of his brother, to try to discover what Bao Dai was planning and if possible to convince him to appoint Diem as the next prime minister.

Over the next two weeks Luyen and I did a careful two-step. Though we talked often, neither of us referred directly to the competition between Diem and Quat. Instead we discussed the future. I found this an easy thing to do. For years I had nurtured the idea of a union among all the nationalists, in which they would pool their resources for the fight against the Vietminh Communists. As long ago as my Phat Diem days, I had, in fact, espoused exactly that. So my approach to Luyen was: Look, we need a united front, and we need to agree at least in principle on a program of social and economic reforms. Without some kind of government of national unity, we will just not be able to stand up to the common enemy. In my heart, of course, I was firmly convinced that Quat should have the prime minister's job. But I did not feel there was anything to be gained from an outright confrontation between Luyen and me on this point. My paramount concern was simply the need for unity.

I soon discovered that Luyen was not of the same mind. When I first raised the subject of national unity, he seemed positively scornful. He found it difficult to mention other nationalists without deprecating them. *"Les intellectuels à la noix,"* he called them, "the do-nothing intellectuals." I found his attitude arrogant, to say the least. The man combined an extremely high opinion of himself with a contemptuous disregard for anyone outside the Ngo family. It was an unfortunate outlook that, as I was to learn later on, Luyen shared fully with his brothers, Diem and Nhu.

But regardless of Luyen's views, national unity was not a subject I could back away from. I had seen quite enough of the Vietminh to appreciate what formidable and merciless opponents they were. I understood Ho Chi Minh and Vo Nguyen Giap, and I had witnessed first hand the results of their organizational genius. I had not the slightest illusion about the dedication, ability, and strength of our enemies. I had, as well, a vivid sense of the Vietminh's popularity in the countryside, where they had just spent eight years leading the fight against France. And I had, of course, long been sensitive to the nationalists' vulnerability to attack as collaborators while the Vietminh were regarded as patriots. To me, these factors together meant that whatever the outcome of Geneva, our chances in protracted struggle against the Communists were not good. Only a unified government that could rally support from every non-Communist segment of the population would succeed. Dissension in our own camp would surely be fatal.

This was the debate I took up with Luyen at every opportunity. He gradually softened to my arguments, until by the end of my stay we arrived at a general agreement. Though we did not actually decide who would fill the cabinet posts, we reached a firm understanding on the need for a national unity government, and we concurred in principle on the social and economic programs such a government ought to pursue. Before I left for Vietnam, Luyen gave me a sealed letter addressed to his brother Diem that I presumed spelled out the nature of our understanding.

While we were carrying on these discussions, each of us was also talking to Bao Dai. What approach Luyen took with the emperor I did not know, although I was aware that Bao Dai and Luyen had been classmates and that they enjoyed a good rapport.

My own talks with Bao Dai were simple and friendly. By nature and training I favored indirection, so I did not make an explicit case for Quat's candidacy. Besides, by now I understood something about Bao Dai's cast of mind, and I knew that he was expert at deflecting any uncomfortably blunt way of posing issues. Instead, I tried to sound out his positions. We talked in general about Vietnam's situation after Geneva and what sort of man would make the best leader. "What," I asked him, "do you think of Ngo Dinh Diem?"

"Well," said Bao Dai, "he's a possibility. What do you think of him? Do you think he has support from the Americans?"

"Why don't we try to find out from the Americans?"

"Yes, I will do that, I am doing it. Could you also do your best to discover what they are thinking?"

This kind of exchange was typical of our discussions — probing, indirect, noncommittal. It was only after Bao Dai had chosen Ngo Dinh Diem as prime minister that I allowed myself a confrontation with him. But it was not over his choice. I was disappointed by that, of course. But as yet I had no strong feelings one way or another about Ngo Dinh Diem, and I had reached what I felt was a satisfactory understanding with Diem's brother Luyen on the all-important national unity issue. At that point, Bao Dai's choice of Diem meant only that the rest of us would have to work hard for inclusion in the new government. But there was no doubt in my mind that my friends and I, as well as other nationalists, would somehow be participating.

My confrontation with the emperor was on another issue. After his decision, I stopped by to pay my respects before returning to Vietnam. I asked when he himself was planning to go back to the country. Bao Dai's answer was elliptical. "When I returned from China in 1948," he said, "I promised I would bring independence and unity to the people. But it seems to me that now the nation will be cut in half." (The Geneva Conference was already moving to create a North and South Vietnam.) "As long as it is divided, I do not think I will be coming back."

I was irritated by this remark. As far as I was concerned, Bao Dai had an important role to play as a political arbiter, a role that might well become vital in keeping the new Diem government moving toward political accommodation. The emperor's absence from the country would be a problem; without him there would be no "higher authority" to appeal to for help in resolving whatever difficulties might arise in the coming period.

This man is simply lazy, I thought to myself. What he really wants to do is stay in France and avoid dealing with unpleasant problems. For the first time I allowed myself to express what I really felt.

"Sire," I told him, "permit me to say that I believe you are avoiding this burden. What you have said seems to me just an excuse. Excuse me for saying it, but if you don't come back to the country now, I think you will never come back."

Bao Dai averted his face and just sat there without speaking. Finally, after two or three minutes, I broke the silence. "Anyway, I hope you will come back. At least that will give me an opportunity to see you again." With that, I left.

Bao Dai's choice of Ngo Dinh Diem over Phan Huy Quat was one of the key events in modern Vietnamese history. The two men could not have been more different in their approach to government, though in 1954 no one knew that Diem would prove an imperious and jealous ruler and that his pathologically narrow view of power would eventually destroy both his government and himself.

The question of why Bao Dai decided on Diem is of some historical interest. There is little doubt that American pressure had something to do with the emperor's decision. Diem had lived in the United States; there he had created alliances and garnered the support of several congressmen and a small group of influential Americans, including Francis Cardinal Spellman. His disdain of the French was also an attraction. But whatever the American influence was, it seemed to me at the time that in appointing Ngo Dinh Diem, Bao Dai was doing little more than following one of his standard techniques of governance: using a front man to deal with particular situations. I knew that he saw himself as an emperor, that is, as one whose special skill was knowing how and when to use others. Bao Dai was raised in the culture of France, so he knew the French well. But he did not know the Americans. And though the time of the Americans had arrived, he did not see their role clearly yet. In this murky phase, he needed someone who did understand Americans and could deal with them. I believe he saw Ngo Dinh Diem as this man, the proper man for the time.

As it turned out, Bao Dai dug his own grave when he appointed Diem prime minister. But I believe he had no intimation that Diem, who in the early thirties had served briefly in Bao Dai's imperial cabinet, was capable of deposing him. On the contrary, the new prime minister was to him someone who would himself be replaced once his usefulness was past. It was the kind of thing Bao Dai had done many times already. Nor was I any more aware than the emperor of what a dangerous unknown quantity Diem really was. It was a lesson I was to learn considerably earlier than Bao Dai.

One of Diem's first acts as prime minister was to appoint Tran Van Do foreign minister. To me this indicated that the rough framework Luyen and I had worked out was already in place. Do was related to Diem by marriage (he was Diem's sister-in-law's uncle), but he was also a charter member of Quat's political circle. In fact, as soon as Do got word of his appointment, he asked me to accompany him to Geneva, where he would now be heading the Vietnamese delegation. But instead of going with him immediately, I wanted first to return to Saigon to go over the situation with Dr. Quat. I was also eager to meet Diem, give him Luyen's letter, and review the understanding Diem's brother and I had reached.

Back in Saigon I saw Quat, who was quite disappointed by what had happened, and arranged an appointment with Diem. I was not expecting this meeting to bring any surprises. I had a good deal of respect for the new prime minister, and I believed that above all he was an astute politician. Specifically, I anticipated a full discussion of the issues I had so painfully thrashed out with his brother, after which we would decide how best to move toward a coalition of forces.

These perhaps naïve expectations were rudely upset during the brief encounter I had with Diem at Gia Long Palace at the end of June. From the moment I stepped into his office, it was evident that Diem was not ready for a serious exchange of views. His attitude was formal and correct, but he did nothing to hide the fact that he was a busy man. Ngo Dinh Nhu, Diem's younger brother and his chief adviser, was constantly in and out of the room, interrupting us to hold whispered conferences with Diem or draw his attention to papers that needed his signature. When I handed Diem the letter from Luyen, he glanced at it and gave it to Nhu, who read it over quickly. But neither of them wanted to discuss it. Instead, they told me they would have to talk to me about it later and indicated that the meeting was over. As I turned to leave, I told them that Do, the foreign minister, expected me in Geneva soon, and consequently, I hoped we would be able to get together at an early date.

For the next three or four days I waited for a call from Diem. But when word finally came, it had nothing to do with a meeting. Instead, one of his aides let me know that I was not to return to Geneva but should wait in Saigon for further instructions. So I canceled the trip to Europe and waited. After a while I realized there were not going to be further instructions. Diem and his brother Nhu did not want me back in Geneva, nor did they have anything to say to me in Saigon.

Needless to say, I was deeply disturbed by these developments. I had been unhappy about my failure to have Quat appointed prime minister, but I had masked this disappointment behind the cheery conviction that we would play a significant role in the Diem government anyway. Now that illusion had been brusquely stripped away, leaving my inadequacies in handling this situation painfully exposed. At the age of thirty-one I was still an apprentice, I reflected, too simple and idealistic by a good margin. In the political world, things were always different from what I thought they should be. The requirement for a broad-based national unity government seemed so obvious, as did the need for social and economic reforms that would draw popular support. But objective political considerations and the personal desires of leaders were two very different things. With my own roots in the self-effacing mandarin tradition of government, this was a tough lesson to learn. I began to consider that perhaps the art of public service was knowing how to insinuate one's viewpoint into the minds of those to whom fate has given the reins of power. It was a skill I would have ample time to practice later on, during the ascendancy of Nguyen Cao Ky and Nguyen Van Thieu.

With the signing of the Geneva agreement, the de facto division of Vietnam into a Communist-controlled and a French-controlled zone (called the State of Vietnam, under Bao Dai) was formalized. For Vietnam's nationalists, the division was an opportunity rather than a loss, a chance to establish a sovereign, non-Communist, international entity where earlier there had seemed little hope of successfully opposing the Vietminh's drive for power. Curiously, the Communist victory at Dienbienphu aroused mixed feelings — a reluctant pride that Vietnamese had defeated France so decisively, even if the victors were our deadly enemies. But the division of the country that followed Dienbienphu, that was nothing but a blessing full of promise.

It was a promise, however, that depended for its fulfillment on Ngo Dinh Diem. And unfortunately, my initial experience with Diem and his brother Nhu typified the way they worked with anyone they considered an outsider, which meant, in essence, anyone outside their family. Over a period of time, I came to understand that this secretive and alienating method of governing was exemplified best by Nhu, though Diem himself was hardly averse to it. All the independent-minded nationalists felt the brunt of their disdain. As a result, the support that could so easily have been mobilized in 1954 and 1955 was converted by Diem and his family into hostility and opposition.

For the newly created country of South Vietnam, it was a national tragedy, another opportunity squandered by the failure of leadership. Just as Bao Dai's human weaknesses had aborted the possibility of a successful nationalist effort against the French, so the character flaws of Ngo Dinh Diem and Ngo Dinh Nhu thwarted the chance to build a democratic nationalism that could have counterbalanced Vietnamese communism. The consequence was that South Vietnam created a tradition of authoritarian rule that had only the negative virtue of anticommunism to recommend it. The two-decade-long history of the country was to demonstrate that as a principle of social cohesion, anticommunism by itself was dismally inadequate.

From the beginning, the Americans realized that Diem's jaundiced view of open government was causing problems. Consequently, even as they helped him establish his regime, they pressured him to broaden participation in it. Edward Lansdale, who was serving as Diem's personal adviser, was careful to keep his lines of communication open with the nationalists as well.* He and General Joseph Collins, President Eisenhower's special envoy, talked to Quat from time to time, meetings that I attended as well. They asked our opinions and noted our criticisms. Though they were never harsh with Diem, they kept up their effort to get him to accept outsiders into his government.

In 1956 Lansdale and Collins even attempted a reconciliation between Diem and Quat that would have included making Quat defense minister. He had served twice in this capacity under Bao Dai, had initiated the first Vietnamese-commanded national forces, and was expert on the problems of building a military capacity. His appointment would have brought sorely needed experience to these problems, and might well have begun a healing process between the nationalists and Diem. At one point during the negotiations, Lansdale left me a note stating that things were proceeding "along the lines we have discussed." But despite all Lansdale and Collins's efforts, in the end the deal fell through, torpedoed, we all believed, by Ngo Dinh Nhu.

With this failure, I finally realized that my own hopes of playing a role in Vietnam's national life were also dead. I had been sitting and waiting, hoping for a development that would have allowed me some sort of participation. But with Diem's final rejection of Quat, I saw that nothing like that was going to happen. I had been so close to the center for so many years, but now I was completely shut out. This meant, among other things, that I would have to find some way to make a living outside politics. While I went about doing this, I watched Ngo Dinh Diem and his family take the country's political apparatus entirely into their own hands.

---

* Lansdale was a former air force and OSS officer who had served in the Philippines and had advised President Ramón Magsaysay during the Huk rebellion. He was sent to Vietnam in 1954. Later he served as special assistant to Ambassadors Henry Cabot Lodge and Ellsworth Bunker.

Chapter 13

Diem and the Opposition

AS THE DIEM GOVERNMENT took hold, we nationalists talked incessantly among ourselves about how we might begin to open the political process, or how the Americans might be brought to move Diem in the right direction. Meeting followed meeting, even after the Lansdale-Collins initiative had failed. We hoped for an open assembly, for free elections, for some way of fulfilling our need to participate in building the nation and protecting it. For individuals whose lives had been dominated since World War II by visions of an independent Vietnam, it was intolerable to think that we would simply be excluded from the new nation's political life.

But there were no openings. Diem presented a stone wall to every overture while Nhu constructed his own personal political apparatus, designed to formally exclude every independent voice. I was now truly a spectator rather than an actor. I had entered the political wilderness, where I would stay until 1963. So it was from the vantage point of a frustrated outsider that I watched the events of Diem's early years in power.

Ngo Dinh Diem's first challenge was from the Binh Xuyen crime syndicate and the Cao Dai and Hoa Hao armed religious sects. These groups Diem's forces attacked and crushed, eliminating whatever claims they may have had to autonomous power. I had an aversion to the sects' armies; private military forces owing allegiance to their own commanders was not something a sovereign state could tolerate. But at the same time I thought Diem's methods were bound to create unnecessary problems. My instincts told me that negotiations were always the best route, that serious talks could well bring compromises and draw adversaries into the framework of the central government. When it was pointed out to me that Diem's use of military force had worked, my answer was that he may have succeeded in the short term, but that the hostility he created would do no good at all for the real fight, the one against the Communists.

In the summer of 1955 Diem also decided to rid himself of Bao Dai. The instrument for doing this would be a nationwide referendum on transforming Vietnam from a monarchy to a republic. Many of the nationalists believed that Nhu was responsible for the move to depose the emperor. We had already come to view Diem's brother as a truly Machiavellian character. It was likely he was more sensitive to the threat Bao Dai posed than was Diem, who was known to respect the tradition of monarchy, whatever he might have thought of Bao Dai himself. Edward Lansdale, the American liaison with Diem, was also heavily involved in this referendum. If Nhu was eager to eliminate any potential political threat, the Americans' motives (as Lansdale told me years later) were simply that this was a first, necessary step toward building a South Vietnamese democracy. On October 23, when the referendum was finally held, 98.2 percent voted in favor of Ngo Dinh Diem and the republic. The vote count might have suggested that Diem was a strange figure around whom to try and build a democracy.

Another major episode of Diem's first years in power was what he called the Denounce Communists campaign, a nationwide police offensive against former Vietminh fighters who had stayed in South Vietnam after the Geneva agreement. Although it was true that the Vietminh had left an underground infrastructure behind when they regrouped their forces above the seventeenth parallel, Diem's shotgun approach to the problem seemed designed to create widespread and unnecessary antagonism. Beyond that, the style of the thing was repugnant. This campaign pressured people into informing on neighbors and acquaintances, exactly the kind of propaganda and fear-inspired pogrom the Communists themselves were so expert at.

As disturbing as his methods were, during Diem's first several years of rule, he seemed successful in each significant step he took. He severely mauled his armed enemies, neatly disposed of Bao Dai, and excluded political rivals from the government. At the same time, his brother Nhu created the Can Lao, a new political party that monopolized the political process and owed allegiance to the Ngo brothers personally.

Watching all this passively was a devastating experience. To my mind, Diem was pursuing precisely those courses of action that would most weaken the nation. Every move he made generated alienation rather than cohesiveness, isolation rather than interdependence. No possible good could come from creating bitter enemies within, especially when those without were so implacable and deadly. One after another, Diem's policies were increasingly depressing for those of us who were forced to sit on the sidelines, activists transformed into *attentistes* — waiters and watchers — though exactly what we were waiting for no one could tell.

By 1956 I had used up my ability to wait any longer for anything. By that time my wife and I had spent every penny of our savings. Somehow I would have to make a living. It was while I was casting around for something to do that a friend of mine suggested the idea of making a movie. A war movie with a political message, he thought, would have excellent prospects, especially if it was a high-quality effort. Vietnamese movies at that time were not up to international standards of production, and if we could combine a first-rate technical job with fast action and a solid story, we could well have a hit. All the advice I got corroborated my friend's opinion, and the idea of doing the project excited me. That, of course, meant first raising money.

Surprisingly, I was quickly able to put together enough in loans from banks, friends, and private investors to bankroll the film. When I looked at the list of backers, it seemed that I owed money to half of Saigon. Not content to owe money only to Vietnamese, I hired a director and technical crew in the Philippines, the idea being that the Filipino production people were experienced in the latest film-making techniques. In addition, we felt we could make a simultaneous Filipino version, giving us access to that very large movie market.

Making the movie took a year and a half. We got cooperation from the South Vietnamese army for some of the battle scenes, and despite the usual traumas of producing a commercial film, in the end we thought we had created something worthwhile, the first feature-length movie made in Vietnam and shot to the highest standards.

Despite the quality of *We Want to Live,* marketing it turned out to be a disaster. For a variety of reasons (some of which I do not understand to this day), the Filipino version never made a profit, and box office receipts in Vietnam were far below production costs. When the dust finally settled, I was millions of piasters in debt.

It was not the moment to take more chances. Faced with hard times, Kim Ngoc and I both went out to work. She took a job as a salesperson for a pharmaceutical house, and I found a position as a mathematics teacher in one of Saigon's private high schools. The psychological transition was as hard as anything we had ever done. But at least we both had steady incomes, and very slowly we began to dig ourselves out of the hole I had gotten us into.

By the late 1950s practically the whole country had become politicized by Diem's arrogant authoritarianism, and the high school where I was teaching was no exception. Every faculty member, from the principal down, opposed the regime to one extent or another. Completely by accident, I found myself working in the middle of a kind of dissident political brotherhood. One of the teachers whom I eventually became very friendly with was in fact an anti-Diem militant who had organized an effective and violent underground network with followers all over South Vietnam. His name was Phan Chau, and he taught Vietnamese language and literature. But teaching was only a cover, though it was hard to tell just how effective a cover it was. Certainly the entire faculty was aware of what he was doing.

Phan Chau became one of the best-known non-Communist revolutionaries in the country, head of an extensive underground network that was active especially around the coastal city of Nha Trang. He harbored a burning hatred for Diem and had set himself the mission of attacking the regime in every way he could. He thought of nothing but revolution. After we got to know each other, he occasionally spent nights in my apartment, at times bringing with him sacks of pamphlets and once a satchel loaded with plastique explosive. My wife was scared to death whenever he showed up — always, it goes without saying, unexpectedly. One day he did not arrive at school to teach his classes, something he never did without calling in. The whole faculty was worried that the worst had happened. We never did hear from him, and sometime later his car was found abandoned in a backwater area of the delta south of Saigon. Eventually the secret police let it be known that they had simply eliminated him, a not so subtle warning to others who might have been similarly motivated.

As bizarre as someone like Phan Chau might seem to people unfamiliar with Vietnam, in fact he represented a characteristic element in our society. At once an intellectual, revolutionary, outlaw, and patriot, he was a man devoted heart and soul to his cause and to the country. In more peaceful times he might have lived a quite ordinary life, but for him circumstances had simply made ordinary existence impossible. He was enraged by injustice and stretched his considerable abilities to the limit in the attempt to destroy the Diem regime root and branch. Although a part of him — the teacher who punctually called in his absences — was anchored in the workaday world, his rage had transformed him into an adventurer-patriot who was capable of anything. Phan Chau was absolutely pure in his intentions, a character worthy of Dostoevski. But if he was more famous than most, he was hardly unique. In those turbulent days such specimens lived right under our civilized noses.

* * *

By 1960 Diem's policies were generating all the destructive consequences the nationalists had been predicting. The government had become, in essence, a family-run oligarchy. Both the civil administration and the army had been undermined by the corruption, jealousy, and demands of personal loyalty Diem used to maintain his control. The financial life of the country was centered more and more in the hands of Diem's friends and supporters, widening the already large economic disparities. In the countryside, not only were there no effective reform programs, but large numbers of peasants had been organized into labor corvées to build *"agrovilles,"* new, "secure" agricultural hamlets into which people were forced to move and which they, for the most part, cordially hated. Hanging over everything like a pall were the police state measures that kept the jails filled and silenced dissident voices. And all this was complemented by an expanding guerrilla war, organized by the remnants of the Vietminh infrastructure but drawing on the support of badly disaffected people at every level of society.

Without any way of influencing the regime's policies, in April 1960 a group of well-known independent nationalists decided to appeal directly to Diem. Quat, Tran Van Do (who had resigned as foreign minister shortly after his appointment in 1955), my old teacher Tran Van Tuyen, and twenty or so others formulated a letter to the president that spelled out in polite but clear terms our assessment of the state of the country, whose fault it was, and what must be done about it. I helped draft the letter, which stated in part: "You should, Mr. President, liberalize the regime, promote democracy, guarantee minimum civil rights, recognize the opposition so as to permit the citizens to express themselves without fear, thus removing grievances and resentments. . . . When this occurs, the people of South Vietnam, in comparing their condition with that of the North, will appreciate the value of true liberty and of authentic democracy. It is only at that time that the people will make all the necessary efforts and sacrifices to defend that liberty and that democracy."

The letter was signed by eighteen prominent people in the group and was sent confidentially to Diem. The idea was to be as private about this as possible in the hope of provoking a discreet dialogue. But there was absolutely no response; it was as if the letter had never existed. When it was clear that Diem was not going to acknowledge this approach despite the group's willingness to enter into an informal, quiet dialogue, the letter was made available to the press. It caused an immediate sensation. One political reporter called the signers the Caravelle Group, after a Saigon hotel in whose dining room some of the principals had been meeting, and the letter became known as the Caravelle Manifesto. The prestige of the group, their record as non-Communist nationalists, and the straightforward but constructive tone of the letter drew instant public support.

Diem reacted furiously. Police began rounding up the signers and throwing them in jail, despite their prominence. Even Tran Van Do, Madame Nhu's uncle, was imprisoned.* Quat hid in my apartment for a week and a half (I hadn't signed the letter and so was safe from the immediate wrath) before the situation calmed down enough for him to go home. One of the nationalists' elder statesmen, a distinguished writer named Nguyen Tuong Tam, committed suicide, leaving a letter declaring that he could no longer live in a country ruled as South Vietnam was. His act shocked the entire nation, and the funeral drew thousands of mourners.

The Caravelle letter was little more than a manifestation of the general perception that Diem's regime was by now bankrupt. By the time it was written, the government had forfeited the last shreds of the respect and good will with which it initially had been greeted. Diem's claim to govern was now based all too obviously on brute force alone. Instead of welding together a nation with the unity and morale to fight for its existence, Diem and his family had created a volatile mix of groups that at best despaired of his rule and at worst detested it. And for none of this feeling was there any outlet.

On November 11, 1960, several paratroop colonels who commanded units in the Saigon area took matters into their own hands. They besieged the president and his brother in the presidential palace and began to negotiate with Diem by telephone. Like the Caravelle Group, they urged Diem to reform, to broaden his administration and liberalize his policies. For hours Diem kept them on the line, acceding to the thrust of their demands and talking at length about the details of the policy changes he would make. But all the agreeable discussion was simply a clever ruse to put the colonels off and buy time until loyal units could be brought into the city from the south to disperse the rebels. When it was over, Diem simply reneged on the promises he had made.

But although the paratroopers' coup failed, its ultimate consequences were fatal to Diem and Nhu. However poorly organized and naïve the colonels had been, in effect their few units had been in control of the palace area for almost thirty-six hours. All of a sudden it became obvious that the thing was doable, that a small number of strategically placed troops could topple the regime. Knowing now that Diem would never bring in reforms, civilian dissidents and unhappy military people began to wonder when the next coup attempt would take place. After November 1960 it was in the air.

At just about the same time, opposition-minded people began to hear about a new antigovernment organization called the National Liberation

* Madame Nhu was Ngo Dinh Nhu's wife. Since Ngo Dinh Diem was unmarried, she served as the regime's first lady. Her shrill, abrasive manner made her widely disliked.

Front. Headed by Nguyen Huu Tho, a Saigon lawyer, the NLF was supposedly made up of disaffected South Vietnamese who wanted to overthrow Diem. For those of us who came from what was now North Vietnam, it was immediately evident that the NLF was really a creation of the North Vietnamese Communists, a political mechanism meant to enlist southerners of good will who were unhappy with Diem (and who wasn't?) in a front organization that would be manipulated from within by the party.

The NLF had all the telltale marks of Ho Chi Minh's organizing genius. No one who knew his techniques could miss it, and all the northern refugees were painfully familiar with them. We had been through it, and we had no illusions about what an apparently liberal, nationalistic front organization really meant. Even the name, Mat Tran Giai Phong, Liberation Front, was all too reminiscent of the various fronts with which Ho had attempted to draw in the nationalists during the forties. But for some reason we could not get many of our southern friends to believe us. I think they just did not know enough about Ho and his background, about the Communist party's constant strategy to "rally everyone who can be rallied." Instead, they seemed enthusiastic about this new movement, which at last would bring mass pressure against Diem's oppressive rule.

Unfortunately, arguments about the NLF went on against the background of traditional suspicions between northerners and southerners. For the southerners, here was simply more proof of the cynical, suspicious northern psychology, and for the northern refugees, southerners were yet again demonstrating their naïveté and romanticism. The reasons for our inability to persuade went beyond regional contentiousness, but whatever they were, it took a number of years before the true relationship between the NLF and the party was obvious to everyone.* Meanwhile, we warned Diem through intermediaries that his policies had led to extreme polarization and that many people were choosing to go into active, illegal opposition. Needless to say, there was no more response to this warning than there had been to any of our other messages.

The NLF was formally inaugurated in December of 1960. For the previous year, Vietminh troops had been infiltrating into South Vietnam across the demilitarized zone and down what would eventually be called the Ho Chi Minh Trail. As an outsider, I did not know the details of these developments or what their full significance was. I did know that

---

* North Vietnam maintained until the end of the war that the NLF and its younger sister, the Provisional Revolutionary Government, were the "sole legitimate representatives of the southern people." After the war, when the fiction was no longer necessary, party general secretary Le Duan announced that "our party is the unique and single leader that organized, controlled and governed the entire struggle."

as 1960 merged into 1961, the guerrillas had made serious inroads into the life of the countryside. Prior to that, it had been easy to get around in rural areas. You could drive from place to place without fear of attack. But by 1961 ambushes and mine explosions were everyday occurrences. One drove carefully or not at all. In the cities, too, public order was threatened. Street demonstrations were becoming commonplace, and an omnipresent atmosphere of tension seemed to have taken hold.

Despite the mounting public anxiety and the obvious brittleness of the regime, for some reason the American embassy, under Ambassadors Frederick Reinhardt, Elbridge Durbrow, and then Frederick Nolting, stood rigidly behind Diem (although Durbrow, on occasion, seemed uncomfortable with his stance). Whereas earlier, Lansdale and other American officials had openly kept in touch with Quat and a number of other democratic nationalists, now anything that looked like official communication was carefully avoided. The embassy attitude had become one of strict "legality." It was no longer "appropriate" (a favorite American word at this time) to have ties with the opposition. Of course, Diem's police were constantly watchful for contact between any of us and the Americans, and they kept the homes of Quat, Tran Van Tuyen, and others under surveillance.

From Diem we expected the worst, but we were furious at the way the Americans had locked themselves into his regime. We knew there was a strong current of American feeling for democratic procedures, open government, and social, economic, and military reforms. We could understand why the United States had supported Diem so effectively at the beginning, when the nature of the man was not evident. And we appreciated the fact that through Lansdale and Collins, they had at least tried to pressure him toward a more inclusive government. But by this time it was clear beyond any doubt that Diem was a hopeless oligarch whose repressive methods had led to domestic turmoil and military incompetence.

Under these circumstances, it seemed incomprehensible to us that the Americans would acquiesce to Diem and his brother and that they would keep at arm's length those who were so much closer to their democratic goals. I thought so then, and I still think that the United States should have made it brutally clear to Diem what its expectations were. And if these were not met, it should have withdrawn its support, even if that had temporarily increased the chances of a Communist victory. Diem was an autocrat and a failure, all too obviously under the sway of his Machiavellian brother. It seemed absurd to us that the United States would place its influence and prestige behind such a man. Among ourselves, we said that the Americans must be blind, that they had their heads in the sand, that despite their immense strength, they were allowing themselves to be manipulated in their own worst interest.

Our anger was fed by our impotence. The Caravelle incident had provoked a crackdown on dissidence of any type. Many were arrested, and political and media opposition, even such as it was, was caught in a vise. People became more cautious about what they did and said, more aware of being watched and of how the watchers might interpret what they saw. A sense of isolation and helplessness started to take hold. We began to think that if anything was to be done, it would have to be done by the military.

So the idea of another coup began to invade the political climate. The military men sensed it, too, and began talking among themselves, slowly getting used to the thought that eventually something was going to happen. It was in this atmosphere that the Buddhist crisis blossomed, raising to violent life all the latent religious, political, and military dislike of Diem and his rule.

Chapter 14

The Coup

THE BUDDHIST CRISIS that enveloped Vietnam in June of 1963 was provoked by the Diem regime's favoritism toward Catholics. Diem's family was Catholic, and while he was living in the United States, Diem had spent time in an American monastery. He naturally felt more comfortable around Catholics and more sure of their loyalty. By itself this might not have created insurmountable problems. But Diem's oldest brother, Thuc, was bishop of Vinh Long and then archbishop of Hue, and it was he, more than Diem himself, who was responsible for the religious explosions that took place that summer.

As the senior member of Diem's family, Thuc wielded tremendous influence and inspired a good deal of fear, especially among career government officials and army officers. Buddhists and nonbelievers felt constrained to attend Catholic ceremonies and celebrations, and in general to demonstrate their subservience to the family religion. As far as Buddhist religious demands went, Thuc spurned the idea of making even reasonable concessions. In the process, he poisoned the country's religious climate. It is likely that without his arrogant and confrontational approach, the crisis could have been avoided. But as it was, violence only awaited an opportunity.

May 7, the traditional birthday celebration of the Buddha, provided the spark. In Hue, the Buddhist center of South Vietnam, the event drew hundreds of thousands of people to hear the leading monks preach. Tension was high, because the provincial authorities had forbidden the Buddhists to fly their flag. Meanwhile, just a week earlier Catholics had openly flown their own flags in celebrations marking the twenty-fifth anniversary of Archbishop Thuc's consecration. This brazen discrimination set off a storm of Buddhist anger. When the provincial governor forbade the traditional broadcast of Buddhist sermons, a crowd gathered in front of the radio station. Before long, government troops pulled up in jeeps and armored vehicles and attacked the demonstrators. In the mêlée that followed, eight people were killed, including a number of children. Soon Hue was enveloped in rioting and clashes between police and demonstrators, and the city's great Tu Dam pagoda became a fortress, with soldiers besieging the monks and their leaders.

As the clashes in Hue progressed, Buddhist activists in Saigon began a campaign of public sermons, agitation, strikes, and street demonstrations in support of their comrades. By early June Saigon was alive with turbulence. On the eleventh, a Buddhist march from the An Quang pagoda stopped on Le Van Duyet Street near the Cambodian embassy. An old monk named Quang Duc stepped away from the crowd and sat down in the street. Then he soaked himself with gasoline and lit a match. It was the first of the Buddhist public immolations, and it sent a shock through everyone who heard about it or saw the pictures. It also brought the confrontation between the regime and the Buddhists to its first climax.

As the Buddhist crisis burgeoned, the vague background talk about an eventual coup became louder and sharper. The first real news I heard that something was actually being planned came through an old friend of mine, General Le Van Kim. I had known Kim for years, and his wife, Gabi, and my wife were close friends. I had served with Kim on the military negotiating team at Élysée in 1954, when he was a colonel. But because he was no Diem sycophant, he had been in perpetual disfavor, despite — or perhaps because of — his honesty and intelligence.

One day in early July my wife and I had dinner at Kim's house, something we did from time to time. Always a somewhat reserved person, that evening he seemed unusually somber. As we talked about the situation (in those months everybody was talking about "the situation"), Kim suddenly looked at me and said quietly, "Diem, you know the Americans pretty well. What do you suppose they think about everything that's going on?" The implications of this question struck me immediately. With hundreds of coup rumors making the rounds, the single thing everyone agreed on was that whoever might be planning a revolt would need to get American approval. So the common wisdom was that any serious group of conspirators would have to discreetly probe the U.S. embassy first. Under these circumstances, Kim's apparently simple question suggested more than innocent curiosity.

At this point, I began testing the waters on my own. One American I had known for a number of years, Rufus Phillips, was in charge of the rural aid programs run by the U.S. Operations Mission. Rufe Phillips had come to Vietnam with Edward Lansdale, and we considered each other good friends who shared the same overall views. We occasionally got together socially and discussed our concerns, which now included the Buddhist crisis as well as the deteriorating situation in the countryside and Diem's suicidal rigidity. I knew that Phillips was far from happy with the direction events were taking, so I felt comfortable about touching on the more general subject of perceptions at the embassy. From Phillips I began to pick up hints that the Americans were now less sure of themselves, that they were beginning to worry about Diem's viability. Evidently, their commitment to "legality" was being strained by the Diem family's maladroit handling of the Buddhists and by the damaging worldwide publicity it was generating.

Meeting with General Kim over the next few weeks, I discovered that he was part of a group of military people who had decided that the time had finally come to get rid of Diem. A coup was in the works, though as Kim described it, they had not yet developed any firm plans. What they needed, he said, was more information about how the Americans would react and what might be expected from them afterward.

As Kim knew, over the years I had cultivated a number of good contacts in the American press corps, including Neil Sheehan of UPI, Malcolm Browne of the AP, and David Halberstam of the *New York Times*. Through them I was able to get a sense of the mood in Washington and to make at least some educated guesses about what was going on inside the U.S. embassy. At first, though, I was careful to keep my distance from embassy personnel, since we had the idea that there was still a good deal of pro-Diem sentiment there.

On the night of August 20, whatever residual support Diem had in the embassy must have crumbled dramatically. That night Ngo Dinh Nhu's security police attacked the Xa Loi pagoda in downtown Saigon. The city's largest pagoda, Xa Loi had become the headquarters of the Buddhist opposition, and much of the leadership was inside when Nhu's police suddenly surrounded the compound. Firing tear gas, the police stormed the pagoda and broke into its main sanctuary, where they found almost four hundred monks sitting cross-legged around the giant Buddha statue, directly in front of which sat the ancient grand patriarch. They arrested everyone there. In other important Buddhist centers around the country, thousands were being arrested in simultaneous raids.

Perhaps even more significant than the Buddhists' rage was the fact that Nhu's attacks were alienating the army as well. The security police who carried out the raids had been dressed in army uniforms, and the government attempted to ascribe the anti-Buddhist measures to the military. Against this background, whatever minor reservations the coup's plotters might have had about the wisdom of deposing Diem evaporated. Final plans were being made and coordinated with the Americans, who by now were thoroughly disgusted with Diem themselves.

By September, every day brought with it new clashes between police and the various pressure groups who had taken their opposition to the streets. What before had been angry demonstrations now turned into a public frenzy against the government. Street fights, Buddhist marches and sit-downs, student demonstrations, and several additional immolations contributed to a sustained hysteria. Many believed a revolution was in the making, or perhaps the first stage of it had already begun.

It had. As the pace of planning picked up, I decided the time had come to arrange for Kim to get together with Rufe Phillips. With a good deal of fear in my heart, I made plans for the three of us to meet at Kim's house, which was in the center of the city just behind the heavily guarded presidential palace. With that location, I thought the chances of the house's being under surveillance were minimal. Besides, Kim himself was keeping a very low profile and, as far as we knew, had not aroused any suspicion. For me, on the other hand, as a conspicuous member of the opposition, this would be a potentially dangerous affair. I knew by this time that I was being watched by the secret police.

On the day we were to meet, the whole city was in an uproar. The streets were choked with Buddhist monks, demonstrating students, police, and tens of thousands of sweltering onlookers. To avoid being seen with Phillips, I arrived at Kim's house more than an hour beforehand, watching carefully to see if I was being followed. As soon as Rufe got there, the three of us sat down to review the situation. Kim described it from his perspective, and then asked Phillips about attitudes at the embassy.

Neither Kim nor I considered Phillips a conduit between the coup's plotters and the Americans, certainly not in the way CIA agent Lucien Conein had become a go-between for Ambassador Henry Cabot Lodge and Kim's fellow conspirator General Tran Van Don. He was, however, a parallel source of information and a kind of sounding board for us. Most important, he was an honest man and a personal friend. We knew he would be direct in his opinions, and we had no fear that he would betray us.

When Phillips left, I waited for fifteen or twenty minutes, then walked out of Kim's house. In my back pocket were the notes I had taken on the meeting. About a hundred yards down the street, immediately in back of the palace, I stopped to light my pipe. As I cupped the flame into the bowl, I suddenly heard someone shouting at me from the palace grounds, "Hey, you, hey!" I froze. Two plainclothes guards were walking quickly toward me. They've been watching me, I thought. They know everything! I could barely bring myself to look at them. Then they both held out cigarettes, indicating the Zippo in my hand, and asked for a light. When they walked away, I grabbed the first taxi that came by and collapsed on the back seat, drained.

By now I was involved up to my neck. Kim had asked me to continue providing assessments of American policy and, more important, to give consideration to a post-coup government — how it should be set up and what its overall goals should be. Although I had agreed with Kim that there was no point in my knowing any of the details of the plot, I was impressed with his approach, and specifically with his awareness that unless the coup was followed by something more productive than the present regime, it would be a failure. Ideally, replacing Diem would allow us to start over, instituting the type of government that had been denied the nation for the last nine years.

There was no great secret about what was needed, and Quat and I, together with Tran Van Do, the former foreign minister, and Dang Van Sung, my old Dai Viet friend, began to discuss plans for a constitutional, national unity, civilian government that could be established once Diem was gone. If anything, our commitment to these principles had been strengthened by the experience of Diem's authoritarianism. My own political philosophy had a very simple basis. I just did not believe that you could successfully force your ideas on others. For whatever reasons in my nature, I bridled at the attempts of others to impose their will on me. That was what had given me my instinctive dislike of the Communists. I knew that behind Ho Chi Minh's suave charm was a world-class manipulator whose method of managing human beings was manifest in the people's committees and in Vo Nguyen Giap's iron fist. That was also the reason I found Diem so unappealing. His dictatorial personality thoroughly informed his government, and it was unbearable.

My period of political exile had led me to reflect, perhaps more than I would have otherwise, on the way my personality shaped my political views. As a person who took naturally to argument and persuasion and detested imposition, I saw that democracy was the political expression of these predilections, and constitutionality was a protective framework for them. National unity embodied the belief that in the face of the threat to South Vietnam's existence, rational people could find a community of interest that would supersede whatever differences separated them.

Unfortunately, Quat, I, and the others did not have time to flesh out our concepts into a workable plan of action before events overtook us. As the coup plans progressed, it became too dangerous for Kim and me to meet. I began communicating with him through his wife, with whom

I worked out a kind of private code. It was not an effective method of coordinating our strategy with the military's. Then, in late September, even this tenuous contact broke down when I was forced to go into hiding.

For months I had known I was being watched. As a charter Dai Viet activist, a member of the Caravelle Group, and especially as a man with numerous American friends, I was, of course, a prime candidate for surveillance. But beyond that, I had been warned through Tran Kim Tuyen, chief of Diem's secret police, that though I was being tolerated for the moment, I had better watch my step. Tuyen was not exactly a friend, but we had known each other for years. He was a northern Catholic who had been a student in Phat Diem back in the days when I was hiding from the Vietminh. He had, in fact, been one of the first enrollees in the seminars I set up there with my two nationalist friends.

But Police Chief Tuyen left his post in June, supposedly to become consul general of South Vietnam in Cairo. The story behind the story was that Ngo Dinh Diem and his brother Nhu had become suspicious that Tuyen himself was involved in a plot and they exiled him. With Tuyen out of the picture, I felt really exposed. While he was chief, I was reasonably sure I would at least get warning of any real danger.

The warning came anyway. At the end of September a friend of mine with links to the secret police told me that the new chief had prepared a list of dissenters to be eliminated, and my name was on it. I knew I had to get out immediately. The first person I went to was Ogden Williams, who lived in an apartment across the square from mine. Williams was with the U.S. Economic Mission. He understood the needs of a developing country and had a great deal of respect for the Vietnamese people. Beyond that, his opinion of the Diem dictatorship was similar to mine. In the nine years he had been in the country, we had become warm friends. When I somewhat hesitantly asked if he could help, he shot back in his usual gruff tone, "Hell, Bui Diem, you can come live with me."

That same night I snuck out of my apartment and crossed the square to Williams's. Visions of the revolutionary schoolteacher Phan Chau danced in my head. I remembered all the times he had stayed the night at our place. I also thought about his fate. Early the next morning I watched from Williams's living room window as my wife left our building to go shopping. She was wearing a red kerchief on her head, the signal we had agreed on to indicate that everything was normal. Each morning for the next week and a half she left at the same time, always wearing the red kerchief. Williams went out to work in the morning and returned at night with news of the latest developments. I just stayed put, my initial excitement fading into a boredom just barely relieved by anxiety.

After ten days my daughters, eight and twelve at the time, came with a message from my wife. They had made their way around the square through the labyrinth of adjoining cellars, alleys, and rooftops of the neighborhood buildings to tell me that I should come home. My wife had seen nothing unusual at all and thought it would be better if I returned. I was not eager to spend what was beginning to seem an eternity at Williams's either, so that night I found my way home through the back ways, careful to stay out of the glare of the street lights.

I kept inside our apartment from then until the coup two weeks later. On October 31 at 1:30 in the afternoon General Kim and his colleagues, Generals Tran Van Don and Duong Van Minh (known as Big Minh), launched their attack. In my apartment we suddenly heard machine-gun fire and the roar of planes. I remember looking at my wife and saying, "Well, that's it." I had no doubt the coup would succeed, and inside I was full of enthusiasm. Now, I thought, we will have a chance to do things right.

By 3:00 the radio was full of the news. It seemed that almost all the generals were either participating in the coup or supporting it. Many of their voices crackled across the airwaves. They had acted to "liberate the country," to save the nation from the constantly deteriorating situation, to rescue it from the oppressive rule of one family. Together they had formed a military committee that would now exercise temporary authority.

By the next morning it was all over. The only disquieting report was that Diem and Nhu had been killed, though at first it was unclear exactly how that had happened. (It turned out that they had given themselves up and afterward had been assassinated, according to some unverified accounts, on the personal orders of Big Minh.) Later that afternoon General Kim called and asked me to have dinner with him. Quat, he said, was being flown back from the delta, where he had been on tour. "So you see," he told me, "it's done. Now it's up to us to get moving on all the things we have been talking about."

Chapter 15

Beyond the Coup

AT THE TIME OF THE COUP, I had spent nine lean years of political exile watching Ngo Dinh Diem and his family strangle the concept of a united and democratic South Vietnam. With the coup's success, I felt a swell of hope that those wasted years might not have been fatal after all, that we could now begin where we should have begun back in 1954. I was encouraged by the fact that General Kim had started consulting us months before on the structure of a new regime. Quat and our circle of friends, together with other nationalist politicians, would have real leverage in the government that was about to take shape. Although we had not had time to put together formal plans for the post-coup period, we had given substantial consideration to these matters. As far as I knew, nobody else had. In addition, I had been Kim's colleague on the military negotiating team at Élysée, and Quat, as minister of defense, had been our boss. I knew it would not be easy for Kim to ignore these past relationships.

At the dinner meeting Kim and I had the evening after the coup, my hopes at first were buoyed. He made a point of telling me that a special plane had been sent to pick up Dr. Quat and that we were now going to do all the things we had set out for ourselves. But then, quite abruptly, the vision I was enthusiastically nursing of a new start disintegrated. When I asked Kim who the generals were thinking of for prime minister, he answered Nguyen Ngoc Tho, the man who for years had been Diem's vice president. When I heard this I was startled. In an agitated voice I told Kim, "Listen, we have a wonderful opportunity here, a historic opportunity. But what we need is a clean slate. How can you possibly think of taking this guy back?" "Well," he answered, "it was a given as far as Big Minh was concerned. Tho would have to get the job."

At this I lost my temper and started shouting at Kim. If they had made this revolution just to put their friends in office, then what was the use of the whole thing? Kim tried to calm me down, describing how complicated the situation was and mentioning that Quat would be invited in as minister of health. That was the last straw, offering Quat, with all his stature and experience, the ministry of health, as if throwing a bone to a dog. I told Kim that, and I told him there was no point in discussing it any further, that Quat wouldn't even consider it.

During the following week I met with Kim a number of times. It became evident that whatever promises the generals had made to each other, Kim was determined to bring Quat, myself, and some other friends into the political process one way or another. If we could not participate as members of the cabinet, then perhaps we would help with "extragovernmental problems." For example, would we consult on methods of moving from rule by the military toward elections and a new constitution?

Despite my unhappiness over the make-up of the generals' government, and especially over the cronyism that was already marking their style, I knew that creating a constitution was the most important step the new regime had to take. As far as I was concerned, remaining aloof from this process was not an option, no matter how serious my reservations.

From then on, in my sessions with Kim we discussed how to bring an element of participatory politics into the new regime. The Diem-era constitution had now been suspended, and the military committee was ruling by decree. I understood that the coup had made this necessary, and that it would take some time to organize elections, especially since there was no existing mechanism for them (there had never been a free election in the country's history). Nevertheless, I argued, in the interim we had to have a forum that would allow open debate of the issues and symbolize the government's commitment to the democratic process.

These discussions led a month later to the creation of the Council of Notables, a group of seventy leading political figures who represented the entire non-Communist political spectrum. Practically all of the Caravelle Group participated, as did representatives of the Buddhists, the Catholics, and the Cao Dai and Hoa Hao sects that Diem had suppressed.

Though it had no formal powers, the Council of Notables was the closest thing to a democratic deliberative assembly South Vietnam (let alone North Vietnam) had ever seen. Under Diem the National Assembly had been nothing more than a rubber stamp. The council, on the contrary, was filled with outspoken individuals who reflected a variety of distinct political views. They had no hesitations about criticizing the government in the sharpest terms, and they had access to a vigorous and combative national press. The generals quickly found they could not easily ignore the council's views.

Privately, I was quite pleased with my part in establishing the council. I saw it as a check on the generals and as a significant step toward a constitution and a real assembly. I was eager to do everything I could to help nurture it. But I was also reluctant to draw too much attention to myself. I was, after all, a northerner in South Vietnam, and all my long-term political associates were also northerners. There was nothing to be gained from arousing latent tensions between northerners and southerners, particularly since I hoped we were proceeding toward a national unity government. Consequently, I accepted the position of deputy general secretary of the council and agreed that the general secretary's post should go to Tran Van Van, a southerner. This maneuver succeeded in circumventing at least some of the diehard regional suspicions. Unfortunately, my efforts along these lines would not always work out as well.

As the council got under way, I kept pressing Kim about the need to appoint effective outside people to important posts and to move expeditiously toward constitutional government. Already it was clear that despite the general joy and relief that followed Diem's overthrow, the military regime was now facing serious problems that could only be allayed by creating a normal civilian administration.

The generals' popularity was, in fact, waning quickly. In the first place, killing Diem and Nhu had done them a great deal of harm. The two brothers had controlled every aspect of government for nine years, installing their supporters to run the bureaucracy, and the assassinations created a deep and lasting antagonism between these appointees and the newcomers. The result was a partial paralysis from the central administrative bureaucracy down to the province chiefs. The entire civilian apparatus that stood behind South Vietnam's war machine was disrupted.

Second, the coup had inadvertently exacerbated the religious conflict. The revolt had grown out of the Buddhist crisis, and because Generals Le Van Kim and Tran Van Don were Buddhists, it seemed as if the coup was in some way an attempt to rescue the Buddhists and reverse the Diem regime's religious discrimination. It was understandable, then, that many Catholics felt animosity toward the generals, which was aggravated by the brutal treatment Diem and Nhu had received.

The central problem, though, was the generals themselves. The members of the junta had no cohesive vision of government or society, no real thoughts about how to rebuild the nation. As the Vietnamese saying goes, they were in the same bed, but they had different dreams. And even the dreams they had were unfocused and lacked the spur of urgency. Consequently, the generals were content to drift.

Le Van Kim was in a perpetual state of angry frustration over the incompetence and lethargy of the junta. A strong, capable person himself, he could not tolerate Big Minh's laziness. There were too many factions, he told me, and no sense of direction. Nothing was getting done. Someone had to take charge of the war, which was going badly, and someone had to provide the political leadership. But it wasn't happening. Everything had to be done through Minh, who had placed his own men in vital positions and was incapable of motivating even them.

Finally, Kim got so fed up with his co-conspirators that he asked to be relieved of his political responsibilities so he could focus his attention on military matters. As a result, in mid-January he was named chief of staff. Unfortunately, even this step added to the mutual suspicions. Some interpreted Kim's move as an attempt to consolidate his own power. In addition, Tran Thien Khiem, the general Kim replaced as chief of staff, developed a grudge that would shortly add a new dimension to the confusion. Although I considered the Council of Notables a small spark of light against a dark and disheartening background, by the end of 1963 it was clear that the "new start" was to be no revolution at all, only a transfer of power. Yet another opportunity was to be wasted, perhaps the last we would have.

The three months after the coup slipped through the generals' fingers like water. In that time the widespread happiness that had greeted Diem's overthrow dissipated and was replaced by apathy and mistrust. The honeymoon had been brief. No one could say how long the nation might have endured the listless drift it had now embarked on. But in the absence of leadership and ideas, three months was enough time for people to begin to sense that disaster was in the wings.

On January 30, 1964, the disaster revealed itself in the person of General Nguyen Khanh. Early on that morning Khanh and a number of co-conspirators — including General Tran Thien Khiem, the man Kim had replaced as chief of staff — launched a coup against the junta that succeeded without a shot being fired. Khanh arrested the generals who had overthrown Diem, though he did not harm them, and put on the mantle of leadership himself.

With this development, the purposeless rule of the generals gave way to the buffoon antics of a man whose serious moments were rare. If the generals had lacked stature and vision, Khanh was little more than a clown whose only claim to rule lay in his capacity for scheming. As far as I could judge, he was simply an intruder into South Vietnam's troubled political life whose unstable notions were bound to embarrass the nation.

With Khanh in power, I thought it was time for me to return to private life again.

During Diem's time there had been an English-language daily in Saigon called the *Times of Vietnam*. The *Times* was considered the mouthpiece of the government and often ran anti-American diatribes inspired by Ngo Dinh Nhu and his wife, Madame Nhu. After the generals' coup the newspaper's offices had been ransacked and the paper shut down.

It seemed to me that there was still a market for an English-language paper in Saigon. I knew something about the business, having served as editor in chief of the Dai Viet newspaper in Hanoi back in 1951, and was able to put together the money to start a new paper, the *Saigon Post*. Building the newspaper from scratch was a consuming effort that, for months, demanded every ounce of energy I had. Happily, it was also a labor of love. My time was taken up writing editorials, choosing articles, marketing the paper, even overseeing the typesetting, which was done by hand according to the best nineteenth-century techniques. Generally, I would have my last look at the next day's edition at about three or four in the morning, then go home and collapse into an exhausted but abbreviated sleep before the next working day began.

But though I was once more out of public life, I had not exactly cut myself off from politics. Short of moving back to the Alps, there was perhaps no way I could have done that. Politics was the lifeblood of my newly chosen profession as editor and editorialist. My previous, short-lived career as a movie producer had also had its political side in the themes I was working with. Even my teaching, carried on amidst the brotherhood of dissidents who constituted our faculty, was shadowed by current affairs. I had been a participant in the political world for twenty years now, and maybe it was just impossible to wean myself from it. In this regard my life was not really different from the lives of every other Vietnamese. From the mid-forties on, the nation's history left no one in peace and not a single family untouched. In one way or another we had all become political victims. And that, of course, is even more true today than it was in 1964.

In retrospect, the regime of Nguyen Khanh put an end to the idea of bringing alive in South Vietnam a democracy vital enough to ward off the political and military challenges of the Vietnamese Communist party. As I saw it then, Vietnam's nationalists, the only bearers of this particular torch, had had several opportunities to make the dream a reality. The first came in 1948, when the French offered Bao Dai a "solution." The second arrived in 1954, when the Geneva conference created an independent South Vietnam. The third opened up in 1963, when the generals brought down Ngo Dinh Diem. In each of these instances, Vietnam's leaders themselves aborted the prospects. Just as the Vietnamese Communist party seemed blessed in its leaders, its opponents — those responsible for the fate of a free Vietnam — were burdened by flaws and weaknesses that made them unequal to the struggle.

In that sense the Vietnamese brought their fate down on themselves. There is no particular mystery about why men like Bao Dai, Ngo Dinh Diem, and Nguyen Khanh failed. There is a great mystery, though, about why and how the United States, committed as it was to both a strong and democratic Vietnam, abetted the failure. For each opportunity presented to the Vietnamese nationalists was also given to the Americans. Nurturing democracy in Vietnam was not only a Vietnamese concern; it was a concern of the United States as well. And just as the Vietnamese failed at it, so did the Americans.

If Vietnamese failures were mainly due to inadequate leaders, America's failures seemed to me primarily caused by inadequate policies. To the Vietnamese, America presented an inconstant, often self-contradictory face. In particular, the United States always seemed to be tiptoeing along a delicate tightrope between intervention and nonintervention. The U.S. government never seemed to quite figure out whether or not it was proper to intervene, and as a result it brought itself and its Vietnamese ally the worst of both positions.

The anti-Diem coup was a conspicuous part of this failure in conception that would haunt both Washington and Saigon until the end of the Vietnam War. The generals who plotted Diem's downfall were especially careful to avoid having the coup appear "American made." * But regardless of the generals' wish to keep the operation wholly Vietnamese, the fact was that it would never have gone forward without American approval. For months prior to the coup, the generals were discreetly sounding out American opinion, a process I had participated in. They needed, or felt they needed, the Americans to tell them that economic and military aid would not be disrupted were Diem to fall. And in the end the United States gave them the green light, first through tacit signals from Washington, then explicitly through CIA agent Lucien Conein.

Although the conspirators and the Americans carefully shielded their

---

* That was one reason they kept the plans secret from the American embassy until the last minute. Lucien Conein, the CIA's contact with the conspirators, was only informed of the details on the morning the coup was launched. The plotters were also suspicious that pro-Diem people in the American mission would learn what was afoot, so there was a tactical reason for secrecy. But the generals also sincerely wanted to act independent of the Americans.

complicity, when it was all over, every Vietnamese on the street took it for granted that the United States had had a hand in events. So when the coup's success brought with it a flood of joy that Diem was gone at last, the United States was widely regarded as a friend of democracy. As far as South Vietnamese public opinion was concerned, it was quite natural that the United States had intervened. And the intervention was applauded, because it was in accord with the general aspirations of the people.

The generals' coup was the first instance where the Americans had intervened directly in South Vietnam's internal affairs, but as I have pointed out, U.S. policies had been influencing Vietnamese political affairs for years. At each significant phase, America had played an ambiguous role. On the one hand, every Vietnamese nationalist with democratic views had been looking to the United States as a friend since the waning days of World War II, and the Americans had indeed provided support and advice. But at the same time, they had also done much to frustrate nationalist efforts.

During Bao Dai's time the United States had consistently refused to back a nationalist solution, preferring to acquiesce in the French game of incremental concessions that so severely undermined nationalist credibility. During Diem's time the Americans supported the dictator for years after he conclusively demonstrated his antipathy toward open government. Pleading "legalities," they even went so far as to cut off contact with the democratic opposition during periods of intense government suppression. To South Vietnam's nationalists, these policies came as body blows, effectively depriving them of vital encouragement and leverage.

I reflected at the time, as I have since, that this policymaking "in a double key" indicated that America was unsure about where its vital interests lay. On the one hand, American policymakers apparently believed that geopolitical realities required one set of actions: support for French colonial policies and for Diem's consolidation of power. On the other, moral and idealistic considerations seemed to call for a strong anticolonialist stance and for the nourishment of a national democracy. It was as if the United States could never quite decide what policy to pursue.

I wondered if the Americans understood, either then or later, that whatever policies they adopted constituted active intervention. There was no avoiding it. The stature of the United States after World War II ensured that whatever it did or did not do would affect the internal affairs of Vietnam. For this reason, during the Diem period I found specious the refusal to communicate with us on the grounds of "legality" and "nonintervention." Other than by reverting to blind isolationism, the United

States simply could not divorce itself from involvement in Vietnam. As long as American policymakers believed that the fate of nations was intertwined and that the vital interests of the United States were linked to a stable world, it was involved, like it or not. Once that was accepted, the only thing left to decide was what form the involvement would take. Not whether to intervene but how to intervene, that was the question.

Up until the generals' coup, American involvement took the form of "noninterference." But the consequences of noninterference turned out to be so destructive for South Vietnam that by the summer of 1963 there seemed no choice but to reverse the policy and interfere. But even that the Americans did with an air of coy reluctance. After they finally flashed the green light to the conspirators, that was the end of their active involvement. It was as if they had said to themselves, "Circumstances have forced us to intervene, but we will intervene as little as possible, and we will deny that we did so."

But intervention, like pregnancy, is not a matter of degree. In their effort to limit the extent of their involvement, the Americans — Henry Cabot Lodge in particular — did not consider what kind of leadership should come after Diem. They decided to change horses without knowing anything about the new horse. Instead of helping to formulate a policy for the post-Diem period, they took no pains to shape what was to come. The result was first the fractious military junta, then the egregious Nguyen Khanh. In the end the Americans were both blamed for the coup's success and damaged by the plotters' subsequent ineptness. It was clumsy statesmanship.

And it was not necessary. Had the United States had the courage of its democratic convictions, its representatives might have approached their tasks differently. Instead of debating in the White House and the embassy how best to interfere in Vietnamese affairs without appearing to, they might have considered what they wanted for Vietnam and how they could best move the Vietnamese in that direction.

In the event, Lodge told CIA agent Conein to convey assurances to the conspirators that the United States "would not attempt to thwart" a coup. But he might have said something different. He might have said discreetly to the conspirators, "Listen, it is true we are unhappy about Mr. Diem. But do you yourselves represent a better alternative? We do not want to know the details of your plans for a coup. But what exactly will you do afterward? You are talking to us about the future of your country, and we, of course, have a stake in that too." The generals who planned the coup were not stupid. They would have listened to this quiet but direct approach. They would have had no choice.

Even with the benefit of hindsight, it is not possible to judge whether there should have been a coup against Diem. No one can say what might have happened had Diem and his family stayed in power. But what can be said is that without making the effort to ensure that something better would follow, the prize was not worth the effort.

The same contradictory pattern marked the United States' relations with the military junta once it had taken power. On the one hand, Lodge continued his laissez faire attitude, watching from a distance as the generals drifted from incompetence to incompetence. On the other, despite their refusal to interfere, the Americans demonstrated all the angry impatience of an older brother whose younger brother is acting impossibly irresponsible. Not only did there seem to be no program and no planning, but with the amorphous junta in power there was not even anyone specific to blame it on. In December 1963, an angry Robert McNamara walked into a conference with the leading generals, looked around with blood in his eye, and said, "O.K., which one of you here is the boss?" The generals bit their tongues in rage. The moment epitomized the American tendency to antagonize their allies instead of tactfully but firmly using their immense leverage productively.

Unwilling to provide unambiguous guidelines, yet angry and frustrated over the self-destructive actions of the Vietnamese leaders, U.S. policymakers were stirring a witch's brew. With the Americans' unhappiness about the generals all too evident, but with no clear signals from them of the desired overall direction, the stage was set for the coup of Nguyen Khanh. Although Lodge himself had nothing to do with this one, his final comment on the disappearance of the junta was "good riddance!"

He might more reasonably have voiced some doubts about the new man upon whom America's worldwide prestige was now to ride. But neither Lodge nor, for that matter, President Lyndon Johnson was looking for anything more than a firm hand at the helm. At all costs they wanted stability; they were desperate for it. And so they were willing to accept anyone who looked promising, again without ensuring that change would lead to the kind of government worthy of their support. Once again they were jumping on an unknown horse.

As a result, Khanh was treated from the start as a strongman who enjoyed America's staunch friendship. Defense Secretary Robert McNamara was even sent to South Vietnam to stump the country with him, as a visible symbol that the United States stood beside the new leader. (This kind of performance did not come naturally to McNamara. On one occasion he grasped Khanh's hand and declared, *"Vietnam muon nam!"* Unfortunately, whoever taught McNamara the Vietnamese phrase had neglected to also teach him the proper intonation. So instead of saying

"Long live Vietnam," what he actually said, to the vast amusement of his audience, was "Vietnam wants to lie down!") But underlying Khanh's supposed strength was a fragility that derived from the utter lack of consensus for his government and his personal remoteness from the very idea that such a thing might be desirable. So when McNamara raised his hand together with Nguyen Khanh's, it was obvious to everyone that the American secretary was keeping his fingers tightly crossed. But that was hardly a substitute for the kind of powerful diplomacy that alone could have addressed the root causes of Saigon's instability.

Chapter 16

The Government of General Khanh

BY THE SPRING OF 1964 Nguyen Khanh was getting nothing accomplished quickly, making meaningless pronouncements about his objectives and shuffling ministers and officials around without apparent rhyme
or reason. Among his other acts, in June he disbanded the Council of
Notables. Council Chairman Tran Van Van and I were called in one day
to hear Khanh tell us, "There's no use for the Council of Notables. I have
other ideas about the whole business." Then we were dismissed. It was
like getting an official notification that we were dead.

On a brighter note, the *Saigon Post* was through its start-up phase and
had established itself as a viable newspaper. Although I still found the
work exciting, the days had passed when every aspect of the paper needed
my personal attention.

With my family's finances finally on an even keel and with the political
scene offering only disheartening prospects, I began to feel a strong urge
to leave the country, to look around abroad and perhaps come up with
a different perspective on Vietnam's unhappy situation. From Barry Zorthian, director of the United States Information Service, I learned that
from time to time the USIS invited foreigners to visit the United States as
part of something called the Leadership Program. When I asked Zorthian
if he thought I might qualify, he said there would be no problem. All I
had to do was apply.

The whole thing was arranged quickly. In short order I received a letter
from Ambassador Lodge inviting me to come to the United States and a
similar one from the British Council welcoming me to Great Britain. As
plans materialized, I realized how eager I was to get away. I had not been
able to travel since 1954, when I had been forced to cancel my trip back

to Geneva, and the years since then had been full of personal difficulties and political frustrations. This trip would provide a welcome change of pace. More important, I would be able to see the United States first hand and have a look at Americans on their home ground.

In some ways this would be a dream come true. It was not exactly that I had been longing to visit America, but the United States and what it stood for had long ago invaded my imagination. As a schoolboy I had read avidly about Franklin Delano Roosevelt and the way he had kept the Allies alive during World War II. John F. Kennedy, too, had been an inspirational figure. I was so attracted by the idealism he projected. I had followed his election closely and had been taken by his inaugural address, with its vision of an America that would "bear any burden, pay any price." To my mind that had been a model speech, articulating a sense of what the United States represented in the world and of the energetic, confident role it had carved out for itself. For a young nationalist from an underdeveloped and threatened land, Kennedy's sentiments reinforced hopes of what might be and perhaps would be.

So, even though I had acquired a somewhat jaundiced view of U.S. policies in Vietnam, I was intrigued by Americans and by the promise the United States held out. I was in fact so expectant that when my plane flew over California toward our landing in San Francisco, I felt disappointed. Looking down, I saw the hills and fields and grass, and I thought, Well, there doesn't seem to be much difference. It doesn't look so unusual after all.

In San Francisco I immediately changed planes and flew to Washington, D.C. There I asked first to be taken to Arlington National Cemetery. I stood in front of Kennedy's grave in Washington's summer heat, feeling that this man had symbolized the clear-sighted idealistic and moral side of America, and thinking about the other side as well, the one I had seen perhaps too much of at home.

I spent the next few weeks in the capital visiting journalists and other friends I had made in Vietnam, then rented a car with a Vietnamese friend and drove off across the country. I had been invited to watch the 1964 Republican convention in San Francisco's Cow Palace, and I thought this would be a wonderful chance to kill two birds with one stone. I would first get to see the entire country up close, and then I would be able to observe the American political process first hand.

In our rented Chevrolet we headed north from Washington to Niagara Falls, then west to Detroit and on across the Plains. The summer heat shimmered in the fields, creating fluid mirages on the asphalt. On either side vistas of corn and wheat stretched to an endless horizon. It was immense. It was also unbearably hot the entire twelve or thirteen days we drove relentlessly onward, stopping to see sites and staying nights in little motels.

But the food was even more of a problem than the weather. A constant diet of hamburgers and hot dogs at roadside stands soon had our stomachs doing somersaults. We wondered how we could get a bowl of rice in that vast expanse, which seemed to contain only American faces and only American food. Soon, though, we discovered a system that almost always worked. No matter where we were, the moment we stopped for the evening we went straight to the nearest public telephone and searched the yellow pages for a Chinese restaurant. Sometimes the only one would be off in the next county. But often we found one right in town.

West of Denver, though, we ran into trouble. There, in the remotest hinterlands, it seemed the Chinese had never penetrated. The phone books had neither Chinese restaurants nor even Chinese names, no Changs or Fongs or Lees. Once, after several straight days of hamburgers, mashed potatoes, and gravy, we had again been disappointed by a phone book and were walking back to our motel in dejection when we saw a little Chinese boy running across the street. We followed him to a laundry, and when we described our plight to his parents, they immediately produced two plates of fried rice, which tasted to us like ambrosia.

We hit California at Bakersfield, then drove up the coast through Carmel and Big Sur, arriving in San Francisco in time for the convention. Here I was to have my first experience of American democracy in action. It turned out to be confusing, to say the least. I don't know exactly what I had expected to see as the Republicans went about nominating their presidential candidate, Barry Goldwater — some sort of austere deliberative assembly, I suppose. But whatever I had imagined certainly had no relation to the chanting, chaotic mob that thronged the floor of the hall, waving hats and banners and wildly applauding the dancing girls who appeared now and then from nowhere. When I said to my American guide that this didn't seem very serious, he told me that what I was watching was just the show, the visible part. The real decisions were being made behind closed doors, but of course we could not get in to see any of that. I left the convention thinking that, however the nominee was actually chosen, the Republicans had certainly evolved a strange way of expressing their political feelings in public.

By the time I got back to Washington, it was already August. The television and newspapers were screaming about the North Vietnamese assault on the destroyers *Maddox* and *Turner Joy* in the Gulf of Tonkin. According to the reports, the American ships had been on patrol duty in international waters and had been attacked on two separate days by North Vietnamese patrol boats. Now Congress was thrashing out what would become the Tonkin resolution, giving Lyndon Johnson extraordinary war powers in Indochina. I heard Johnson's speech on television as he described the incidents and the need for retaliation. In San Francisco I had listened to Barry Goldwater enunciate his stand on communism, and now here was Lyndon Johnson expressing himself forcefully in action as well as words. Immediately after the president's address, I sent an article back to the *Saigon Post,* to which I had accredited myself as a special correspondent. I wrote, "It appears the entire country, Democrats and Republicans alike, are joining in the fight against communism."

At the end of August I left the United States for Great Britain, impressed by the firmness of the Tonkin resolution (it had passed the House unanimously and the Senate with only two dissenting votes). It was clear that the Johnson administration was deeply committed and that on this issue it had the full cooperation of its Republican rivals. There was no question in my mind that the United States would lend strong support.

When I arrived in London, I found that the British Council had arranged a full program of visits with various Foreign Office and other government officials. But after a day or two of this, I began to find the tight schedule oppressive, especially after the easy comings and goings in the United States. As a result, the program officer to whose care I had been assigned lightened the load, and I started enjoying England as a tourist.

But not for long. After four days in London I received an urgent cable from the *Post* telling me I was needed immediately in Saigon. In my absence the newspaper had run a number of editorials attacking Nguyen Khanh's government. The writers had not been gentle, and now Khanh was moving to shut the paper down.

When I got back, I found myself in an all-out struggle to keep the *Post* alive. Khanh was not in the least happy about the paper's editorial stance, and the fact that he knew my opinion of him did nothing to make the task easier. Despite everything I could do, the paper was shut down temporarily, and would undoubtedly have been closed permanently except that by this time Khanh was so involved in trying to save his political skin that he neglected to follow up on the situation.

As distressing as the *Post*'s problems were, they were swallowed in the vortex of confusion that Saigon had become. From September through November one Khanh government was chased by the next while demonstrations rocked Saigon's streets every day. Catholics, Buddhists, students, Hoa Hao, Cao Dai, labor unions — Khanh had managed to alienate them all, and they were all screaming their demands at him, creating a continuous state of chaos that surpassed even the conditions during Diem's last months of rule. Amidst it all, Khanh ran around wildly, fleeing from some confrontations, standing up to others, warding off the Americans, trying to deal with the series of coups and mini-coups that shook his regime like recurring earth tremors, and all the while searching desperately for some key to stability.

The whole thing was just a mess — a civil mess, a political mess, and most dangerous of all, a military mess. During this period Communist forces had capitalized on Saigon's weaknesses and launched a concerted offensive aimed at gaining control of territory and population centers and cutting the country in two. Already, 1964 had seen major gains by South Vietnamese guerrillas, aided now by a steady stream of North Vietnamese regular army units infiltrating down the Ho Chi Minh Trail, which had been under construction since 1959.

In many areas the South Vietnamese army was battling courageously. But the political chaos and resulting problems at the army's command levels meant that the soldiers were fighting under impossible circumstances. At that moment it seemed that the guerrillas might succeed in dramatically upsetting the military balance.

I was struck by the irony of the situation. Just as Washington was girding itself for a major commitment to the war, Saigon was coming apart at the seams. Lyndon Johnson was gathering support for a concerted effort at exactly the moment Nguyen Khanh had succeeded in bringing the South Vietnamese government to a shuddering standstill.

Of course, this ironic correlation was not entirely accidental. As South Vietnam's ability to pursue the war deteriorated, the United States was being forced to take on the burden. But this development I blamed, in part, on the Americans. In some ways it seemed as though they had brought it on themselves. From the beginning they had been unwilling to put themselves squarely on the line for democracy and national unity in South Vietnam — and for the sincere social and economic reforms that could derive only from democratic government. They had been satisfied to support a succession of dictators and generals from whom they expected stability but who had given them widespread dissension and governmental breakdown instead.

The whole degenerative process had taken ten years — Diem had been appointed in 1954 and it was now the fall of 1964 — but it had finally reached its nadir. And now that it had, the United States was in a corner, and American leaders were debating the need to intervene in an Asian land war. True, this development had come about partly because a relentless enemy was bringing increasing military pressure to bear in South Vietnam. But it was also due to the fact that the Saigon government was a shambles. And for this, American diplomacy (or the lack of it) was as responsible as a decade's worth of Vietnamese autocrats and militarists.

The American policy of boosting whoever happened to grab power, for the sake of an elusive stability, was now reaping its harvest.

If there was any discernible pattern through the storm of South Vietnam's domestic politics in the fall of 1964, it was the emergence of a group of young military men, the so-called Young Turks. Among them Nguyen Cao Ky, the thirty-five-year-old commander of the air force, was the most visible, although another, General Nguyen Van Thieu, was thought to be steadier. Like most people close to politics, I was aware of this group. But I did not know any of them personally. They were a new force on the horizon. By this time, the older generation of generals — Kim, Tran Van Don, Big Minh, and the others — had been relegated to the background, and I had heard that the younger men were pressuring Khanh to ease out the senior officers altogether, in favor of the new blood they themselves represented.

Though not overtly rebellious, the Young Turks were one of the factors that made life trying for Nguyen Khanh. Then in December they were involved in an incident that led directly to his political demise. The background of this episode was in the fact that long before it happened, Khanh's flighty and unpredictable behavior had lost him the Americans' confidence. Maxwell Taylor, who had succeeded Henry Cabot Lodge as ambassador, was especially concerned with somehow getting Khanh moving toward a civilian government. As time passed, he became more and more impatient and increasingly peremptory. Finally, in September Taylor had had to spell out to Khanh the necessity of creating a constitutional framework for governing. Feeling constrained, Khanh labored and gave birth to what he called the High Council, a small group of mostly elderly politicians who were charged with drawing up a constitution. Phan Khac Suu, an old nationalist who had been a member of the Caravelle Group, was named president of the High Council and then was appointed titular head of state as well.

Not long after the council was established, the Young Turks began pressuring Khanh for a decree that would formally retire the senior generals, who were the chief objects of their displeasure. Khanh acquiesced, but because Phan Khac Suu was now chief of state, the decree required his signature. Suu refused to sign.

Afraid that Khanh was not completely in control of this difficult situation, Maxwell Taylor invited the Young Turks to dinner at the residence of General William Westmoreland, the overall commander of American forces. His goal was to impress them with America's determination to see the South Vietnamese government achieve at least a minimal level of stability. With Westmoreland and Deputy Ambassador Alexis Johnson present, Taylor admonished the young officers in very strong language, telling them the United States simply could not go on supporting South Vietnam as long as the government was so unsteady.

But the ambassador's remarks had less than the desired effect. Increasingly annoyed at council president Suu's obstinacy, the Young Turks decided on a straightforward solution. On December 20 they simply kidnapped the council members and shipped them and a number of other civilian politicians off to Pleiku under guard.

Taylor was livid. He summoned air force chief Ky, General Thieu, and several other young officers to the embassy and read them the riot act. He began this ill-fated meeting by asking them if they could speak English (at Westmoreland's house he had addressed them in French). When Ky responded sourly that they could understand well enough, Taylor went on to tell them that apparently the dinner with Westmoreland had been a complete waste. (Ky told me later that when Taylor said this, he and Thieu had first thought the American ambassador had meant the food had been wasted on them.) This kind of thing could not be tolerated, Taylor said. Now look what a mess you've made. He was bursting with fury and frustration.

Whatever Taylor hoped to accomplish with this chewing out, the most obvious result was that he had humiliated Ky, Thieu, and the others present. Nguyen Khanh, who was neck deep in trouble with various militant factions, quickly took advantage of Taylor's treatment of the young generals, making it a *cause célèbre* to rally nationalist feeling behind himself. He sprang to their defense, publicly denouncing American interference. He even went so far as to call for Taylor's withdrawal as ambassador for having meddled in Vietnamese affairs.

When he heard this, Taylor was beside himself, as were the State Department and the White House. They could hardly believe that Khanh would have the temerity to air something like this in public. It was bad enough that the man had been incapable of providing South Vietnam with anything approaching rational leadership, but this was just beyond credibility. Khanh was told that if Taylor had to be withdrawn, that would be the end of American support. For all practical purposes, that would be the end of Nguyen Khanh. But, of course, while this tragicomedy played itself out, a ferocious war was raging throughout the country, and Communist forces were closer than ever to winning it.

Nguyen Khanh was not finally removed from public life until the middle of February in the new year of 1965. After his effort to rally the Young Turks by posing as their defender failed so embarrassingly, he tried one last ploy to salvage at least a remnant of power. On February 14 he dissolved the then current government and asked Dr. Quat to form a new civilian regime in which he, Nguyen Khanh, would retain control of the army. It was Khanh's last throw of the dice. If Quat could establish a credible government, perhaps it would shield Khanh from the disgust of the Americans and the hatred of the Buddhists, Catholics, and other Vietnamese who were screaming for his scalp.

But it was past time for measures of this sort. The day after Quat accepted the position of prime minister, the last of the anti-Khanh military coups triggered off. Units commanded by General Lam Van Phat and Colonel Pham Ngoc Thao* surrounded Khanh's home, the army headquarters, and the radio station. In the confusion Khanh himself escaped and eventually ended up at the air force headquarters of Nguyen Cao Ky, who agreed to protect him.

Under American auspices, a meeting was arranged between Ky and the leaders of the revolt which resulted in General Phat and Colonel Thao's abandoning the coup in return for Khanh's ouster and permanent exile. This agreement was, of course, quite acceptable to Ky, whose Young Turks would now become the predominant military faction in the new Quat government. To the Americans who sponsored this meeting, Khanh's imminent departure must have brought sighs of relief. By this time Taylor could not bear the sight of him. Nor could many others, Vietnamese or American.

The morning of the coup — his first full day as prime minister — Quat asked me to join him in his office, where we spent several hours talking over plans. Then in the afternoon he was asked to come to air force headquarters for the discussions that were going on there. When he returned, it was about eight in the evening. The deal for Khanh's departure had been hammered out.

The following day Nguyen Khanh arrived at the government offices to say a formal goodbye — the departing strongman had insisted on a full ceremonial leavetaking. Quat set up the ceremony but declined to go down to the front of the prime minister's office to review the honor guard with Khanh. Instead, I was delegated to handle this chore. Afterward, I brought Khanh upstairs for the briefest of partings with Quat, then downstairs again for a final review of the troops. When this was done, Khanh looked at me and said, *"Maintenant les cartes c'est a vous de jouer"* — "Now the cards are yours to play." To the end he regarded the whole business of government as little more than an exciting game. It was not until he turned around and left that I stopped clenching my teeth. But though there was an immediate sense of relief that this individual was gone, no one was optimistic about quickly repairing the damage he had left behind.

* Thao was later revealed to be a Vietcong agent. His full story is told in *A Vietcong Memoir* by NLF Minister of Justice Truong Nhu Tang.

Chapter 17

The Americans Intervene

Dr. Phan Huy Quat was a man who combined long experience in government with intelligence, determination, and decency. His politics was characterized by a deep commitment to social justice and democratic procedures. Quat was a product of the old mandarin culture (he had served as chief of staff in my uncle Tran Trong Kim's government), and public service was in his blood. From his several tenures as defense minister, he was also familiar with military affairs. He was as stable and competent as Nguyen Khanh had been mercurial and deficient.

Quat might have been the best man available to head South Vietnam's government as Nguyen Khanh made his ignominious exit. But even his solid talents inspired little hope that the political and military situations would now take a dramatic turn for the better.

Of course, Quat himself felt otherwise. Whatever his other characteristics, he was a true political animal with great faith in his own abilities. For long years, many of them spent in the political wilderness, he had had his eyes fixed on the prime minister's job. Now that the opportunity had arrived, he was not about to turn it down. But beyond that, he believed he was capable of bringing the Saigon government back to order. The central problem, as he saw it, was the military, particularly the Young Turks. And he thought he could handle them.

But the odds against Quat were daunting. If a "new start" had been feasible in 1954 and again in 1963, by the turn of 1965 events had irretrievably altered the political face of the country. Religious and political factions whose differences might once have been reconcilable in an open, inclusive government were now locked into fratricidal conflict. Military people, once subordinate to the government, had come to regard politics as a field of endeavor every bit as legitimate as warfare. And the generals themselves were divided into competing cliques. Each of them thoroughly distrusted the others, though they all shared a hearty contempt for civilians, a sentiment that civilian politicians returned with interest. Catholics were suspicious of Buddhists and vice versa, and southerners had little love for the northerners who lived among them. Perhaps worst of all, in the tortured year and a half since Diem's fall, the very notion that a strong and decent central government was possible had itself been discredited in the minds of the people.

In this poisoned atmosphere Quat began his work without the one thing that would have given him good hope for success. Despite his many years as a leading nationalist politician, he had no personal power base to provide him with backing and leverage. One of the destructive consequences of a decade's worth of autocracy was that none of the nationalist parties had gone beyond being a loosely affiliated circle of political colleagues. None of them had ever had the opportunity to develop the kind of strong popular roots necessary to give them and their programs real weight. Indeed, it was precisely to thwart this that Diem had proscribed the parties. For their part, the generals who succeeded Diem had never given more than a passing thought, if that, to such supposedly insignificant nuances of the democratic process. The result was that as hard working and judicious as Quat was, he lacked the political muscle to deal with his problems. His assets as prime minister consisted of little more than his experience and his friends.

Of his friends, I was among the closest. Because our relationship went back so far, I was happy to offer him whatever advice and suggestions I could. But when, on February 14, Quat formally invited me to join his administration, I felt a good deal of reluctance. I was torn between my understanding of how bleak this government's chances were and my conscience, which told me that I could not refuse to make the effort regardless of the probable outcome.

Knowing my feelings, Quat argued strongly that with his background as defense minister, he was the only civilian who stood a chance of quieting the military. Once that was done, he would have a leg up on dealing with the religious and political factions. At the same time, we would be working toward a constitution that would embody the ideals of government we and our circle had been committed to for so long.

Despite the seductiveness of these arguments, my sense of reality suggested that Quat's scenario was unlikely. But when he finally said, "Look, apart from all the political reasons, we have been together for so long you simply cannot desert me now," I knew I had no alternative. With that, I accepted Quat's offer to become his chief of staff, technically, minister to the prime minister's office with cabinet rank.

With this decision, a train of events began that would lead to the most crucial and event-filled decade of my life, a time during which I would be exposed to national and international politics as a middleman between the various Vietnamese factions as well as between the South Vietnamese and American governments. When I entered the Quat administration, it was with no great hopes of either success or political longevity. With our other friends, whom Quat also brought in, I shared a "grit your teeth" determination simply to do my best. I had no intimations that I would be witness to large and dramatic events in both American and Vietnamese history that would lead from hope to final convulsive tragedy. I certainly had no sense as I began work that the war's most crucial and also its most questionable decision had already been made in Washington, and that as Dr. Quat's liaison with the Americans, I would shortly be called on to legitimize it.

American military involvement in South Vietnam had begun with advisers sent to assist Ngo Dinh Diem's fledgling army in 1954. Between 1961 and 1964 their number had grown from 900 to 23,000. But although this assistance had become substantial, American trainers and field advisers played only a narrowly defined instructional role in South Vietnamese army operations. As advisers, their numbers could be increased or decreased at any time and their presence in Vietnam was due to a long-term "advise and assist" policy that did not in any way suggest formal American military intervention.

The first independent American combat operations in Vietnam (other than the retaliatory air strikes after the Gulf of Tonkin incident) were carried out by U.S. air force and navy planes in February 1965. By the time Dr. Quat was established in office, Operation Rolling Thunder was already under way, striking at targets in North Vietnam and on the Ho Chi Minh Trail, running along the Laotian and Cambodian borders from north to south.

This bombing campaign had been planned in December, when Nguyen Khanh's reign was entering its terminal breakdown. But the Rolling Thunder attacks turned out to have far greater consequences than their planners ever intended. No one foresaw that they would constitute the first step in what quickly became a massive American military involvement in South Vietnam.

For the United States, this intervention arguably has been the most significant episode in its post–World War II history. For Vietnam, it led to a cataclysm whose consequences can hardly be exaggerated. Yet the distinct steps toward intervention were taken in confusion and amidst an almost complete lack of understanding between the two governments that they so dramatically affected. Between December 1964 and June

1965 the United States decided to fight a major land war in Asia despite the accepted wisdom after the Korean War that such a thing should never again be attempted. Over the same period America's Southeast Asian ally accepted the large-scale deployment of foreign troops on its territory. This against the better judgment of its political leaders and despite the fact that its own people were still recovering from eighty years of hated foreign domination, only recently ended by a long and bloody rebellion. How, then, was such a thing allowed to happen?

To answer this question, a number of firsthand accounts are available. Among these, the most revealing on the American side is in the unpublished manuscript of William Bundy, then assistant secretary of state for East Asian and Pacific affairs, chief coordinator for the major U.S. policy papers of late 1964, and a leading participant in policy discussions right through this period of decision. On the Vietnamese side, from the time just after the inception of American air attacks on North Vietnam, the main participants were Dr. Quat, who has left no record of events (Quat died in a Ho Chi Minh City prison in 1981), and I, Quat's chief of staff and liaison with the United States embassy. The primary sources for the following account are the Bundy manuscript and my own collection of documents, including cables, memos, notes, daybooks, and agendas, as well as my recollections from the period. These have been supplemented by other written records, such as *The Pentagon Papers*, the Gareth Porter collection of documents, and the memoirs of President Lyndon Johnson, Ambassador Maxwell Taylor, and Deputy Ambassador U. Alexis Johnson. In addition, I have interviewed most of the participants on the American side, as well as those surviving South Vietnamese who were in a position to know any significant details.

From the various sources it is possible to put together a picture of how the climactic decision to intervene came about and how it was seen by some of the chief American policymakers and by those of us in the South Vietnamese government. Putting the two views side by side, one cannot help but be struck by the lack of clarity in the process, the absence of understanding and communication between the two allies, the un-self-conscious arrogance of the American approach, and the impotence of the South Vietnamese response. Considering the momentousness of the decision, it is an appalling picture.

At the State Department the idea of mounting independent U.S. air operations against North Vietnam had been under consideration even before the Gulf of Tonkin incident. Although several options were outlined in working papers drawn up by Bundy's policy planning group, until the last week in November 1964, no firm decision had been made. At that point Ambassador Maxwell Taylor returned to Washington from Saigon. He had come back to brief Bundy's group while they were in the process of preparing their final position paper for submission to the president.

Taylor was the man on the spot, and his views were crucial. The report he gave on November 27 in front of the principal American policymakers was frank and pessimistic. The "chronic weakness" of South Vietnam's government, he said, was a "critical liability." "Without an effective central government with which to mesh the U.S. effort, the latter is a spinning wheel, unable to transmit impulsion." According to Taylor, in order to change the situation, the first priority was "to establish an adequate government in South Vietnam." *

When Secretary of State Dean Rusk asked what exactly could be done to get the Saigon government to perform better, Taylor said the Vietnamese leadership had to be given "the right message," one combining U.S. resolve and readiness to act (he emphasized that) with "a real fight talk." This kind of message, he thought, might well be the one thing that would encourage them enough to improve their effectiveness. At that point Secretary of Defense Robert McNamara asked whether the United States would be justified in bombing North Vietnam even if, regardless of what was said to them, the Saigon government did not improve. McNamara's own answer was that it would. Taylor agreed with him, saying that in a desperate situation really strong action might be enough to pull the South Vietnamese together.

According to William Bundy, who drew up the final position paper on the basis of what was said, the exchange between McNamara and Taylor about strong American action pulling the South Vietnamese together was "electric." "The idea of a last gasp effort — the 'pulmotor' treatment, as Taylor called it — had now been judged conceivable." **

Four days later, on December 1, Lyndon Johnson formally accepted the concept embodied in the working group's position paper, namely, that the United States should undertake a program of progressively greater pressure against North Vietnam, including air strikes that might eventually reach all major military targets in the country. But first, said Johnson, Taylor would have to do everything he could to "get these people [the South Vietnamese] to work together." "If you want this bombing program," the president told Taylor, "you must get the Saigon political leaders into shape." †

* Neil Sheehan, Hedrick Smith, E. W. Kenworthy, and Fox Butterfield, eds., *The Pentagon Papers* (New York: Bantam Books, 1971), pp. 370ff.
** William Bundy, unpublished manuscript, chapter 19, p. 7.
† Bundy, chapter 19, p. 14.

This was the message Taylor took back to Saigon with him. But only a month later the ambassador sent a long cable to Washington that signaled his failure to whip the Vietnamese side into shape. After Johnson's pointed directions about bringing political stability and harmony to Saigon, Taylor had returned to Vietnam just in time for the fiasco with General Khanh, the Young Turks, and the kidnapping of the national High Council. Despite the ambassador's best efforts, the obstreperous South Vietnamese simply could not be made to understand the necessity for teamwork. Instead, a *sauve-qui-peut* attitude reigned in Saigon, stemming perhaps, Taylor thought, from the feeling that the nation was doomed and that the United States would likely do nothing to save it. Bundy recalled Taylor saying, in effect, "The strongest drugs had not worked. Now the patient must be operated on." "Overwhelmingly," said Bundy, "the Ambassador's case for bombing rested on its effect on morale and political performance in the South." *

Other factors affected the decision to implement the bombing plans that President Johnson tentatively approved on December 1: reprisal for specific Vietcong attacks on American facilities, a desire to demonstrate American determination, and especially the attempt to pressure North Vietnam into reining in the Vietcong. But the record indicates that Taylor's "pulmotor" argument, which he first made to the working group in late November and reiterated strongly in January, was a key factor to Bundy and other policymakers. Something dramatic was needed to get the South Vietnamese to work together and to stiffen their backs.

One last note on Maxwell Taylor's rationale for recommending American air attacks on North Vietnam. Though the ambassador favored bombing the North, he did so partly because it was a step that could be taken without inextricably involving the United States in combat. In fact, as Deputy Ambassador Alexis Johnson put it, "We in the Embassy had one other hope for Operation Rolling Thunder: that it would quiet the growing push from Washington for the commitment of American ground forces." ** By February the ambassador and his deputy were under pressure to accept the idea of American ground forces in South Vietnam. A bombing program, they thought, might help to calm the hawks.

These extended deliberations among the Americans were not complemented by parallel procedure in Vietnam. Amidst the falling debris of yet another of his governments that December, Nguyen Khanh was hardly the man to consider carefully the ramifications of the planned American air strikes. He was not in a position to either accept or reject them — at

* Bundy, chapter 20, p. 18.
** U. Alexis Johnson, *The Right Hand of Power* (Englewood Cliffs, N.J.: Prentice-Hall, 1984), p. 427.

that point he was barely on speaking terms with Ambassador Taylor. Nor, contrary to Taylor's opinion, did the South Vietnamese generals need to have their backs stiffened. In the waning days of Nguyen Khanh's rule, their lack of cohesiveness did not derive from a *sauve-qui-peut* attitude, as Taylor thought, but from antagonisms created by their own political ambitions and jealousies. To the South Vietnamese military leadership jockeying around against each other and against Khanh, the new American bombardments were simply a godsend that they would never think to question. As a result, the first insertion of U.S. combat might into the Vietnam War was carried out on a unilateral basis, without even a modicum of joint American-Vietnamese governmental consideration.

For all the potential consequences of this step, when the new South Vietnamese government took office on February 18, it did not review the situation. It is my strong impression that Nguyen Khanh did not even inform Dr. Quat of the American plans. I remember only a brief conversation that took place sometime during our first week in office, when Quat casually mentioned to me that Ambassador Taylor would soon be by to brief us on the bombing. Thereafter, twice each week Maxwell Taylor and Alexis Johnson would arrive in the prime minister's office with a roll of maps to let us know what targets were being bombed. The issue of an independent American combat role was so taken for granted that the South Vietnamese cabinet never even scheduled it as an item for discussion at its weekly meetings. There is no record of it in their agendas from that period, nor is there any mention of the subject in the agendas that Minister-Counselor Melvin Manfull and I drew up for the regular Friday meetings among Quat, Taylor, and their chief subordinates.

By the same token, the decision to use U.S. air power in South Vietnam proper (as distinct from North Vietnam) was also made without any special notice being taken. It now seems all but incredible that such a step, with its momentous political implications and devastating impact on the population, was made without any official discussion between the Vietnamese and American governments. But acting under pressure of circumstances, the military establishments of both countries did not think it important, let alone necessary, to raise the subject with the Saigon government. And the regime, struggling with all too few resources to clean up the mess it had inherited, was so preoccupied with keeping its head above water that it simply allowed the military to run the war as it saw fit.

But as significant as the decision to use American air power was, the landing of marines at Danang on March 8, 1965, was vastly more so. For the United States this event signaled the start of a new American land war in Asia. For the South Vietnamese it meant the presence once again of foreign soldiers on our own territory.

Phan Huy Quat was considerably more than a boss to me; our close friendship over fifteen years had made us "political brothers," and we habitually discussed all the most sensitive issues with each other. As far as the presence of foreign troops in Vietnam was concerned, we were of one mind and had been for quite a long time. Whatever the military need, neither of us doubted that bringing foreigners into the fighting would be a heavy handicap indeed. We both bore the scars of participating in Bao Dai's French-dominated government, and we remained painfully sensitive to the fact that outsiders would give the Communists the most powerful propaganda weapon they could hope for. To be openly accused of being puppets was not just personally insulting; it was a wedge that would be driven between the government and the people. Accepting American troops could be justified only in extremis, if the nation was otherwise faced with extinction.

It was against this background that, in early March of 1965, I expected some sort of request from the Americans to bring combat troops into Vietnam. Such a request would come as a logical outgrowth of the air war that had started up. The primary U.S. air base was at Danang, on the country's northern coast, and it seemed probable that General William Westmoreland would want the base's security to be handled by American units. But because of my killing work schedule, this expectation was hardly uppermost in my mind; I merely thought that at some point we would be fielding this idea during one of the weekly meetings between Quat and Taylor, the agendas for which, as I have noted, were set by Manfull and me for the principals.

Events happened otherwise. Early on the morning of March 8 I received a phone call from Dr. Quat, asking me in a strained voice to come to his house immediately, something urgent had come up. When I arrived, I found Melvin Manfull already there. The American diplomat looked all business, but Quat was obviously nervous. Without asking me to sit down, Quat said that marines were at that moment coming ashore at Danang to take up defensive positions around the base. Manfull and I were to write a joint communiqué announcing the landing. "Be as brief as possible," Quat told me. "Just describe the facts and affirm our concurrence."

The news itself was not an overwhelming surprise, because in the back of my mind I knew that Westmoreland would soon be pushing for something like this. But the abruptness of the thing and the lack of preparation for it were upsetting, to say the least. Taking Quat by the arm, I guided him into the next room. As soon as we were away from Manfull, I said, "Is there something going on on the military front we don't know about? Something that's making them do this so suddenly?"

Quat did his best to project an air of calm, but his voice was tense. "Listen," he told me, "they are landing on the beaches right now. They are already ashore. Please, just draft the communiqué and we can talk about the situation later."

Within half an hour, Manfull and I had prepared a text announcing the arrival of two battalions of U.S. marines, "with the concurrence of the Vietnamese government." But as soon as the American diplomat left, I got back to the point with Quat. He told me that several days earlier he and Ambassador Taylor had had an "exchange of ideas" about the need to reinforce South Vietnam's defenses. As part of this exchange, which Quat had considered no more than an initial, general discussion, Taylor had broached the subject of bringing in the marines. Quat had then told Taylor he was reluctant to see an "Americanization" of the war. Although he had not requested American troops, Quat told me, neither had he explicitly opposed the idea. For his part, Taylor, as Quat put it, "had shared many of my views on the matter."

When I asked Dr. Quat why we faced this sudden development, he answered, "I think Taylor himself was taken by surprise by a quick decision from Washington. This morning he tried to present it to me as a strictly limited military move that had to be taken because conditions were bad around the base."

The same misleading impression of joint consultation given in the communiqué was conveyed more vividly the following day in Saigon's newspapers, where front-page pictures showed battle-ready marines being greeted on Danang's beaches by lovely Vietnamese girls dressed in native *ao dai* dresses and carrying leis. It seemed like a well-prepared official welcome. Few who saw the pictures knew the facts behind the open arms and smiling faces.

From the Bundy manuscript, as well as from Alexis Johnson's, Taylor's, and Westmoreland's memoirs, it is clear that Taylor himself had "grave reservations" about deploying the marines and conveyed Quat's reluctance about it in a cable to the State Department on February 22. "On the whole question of ground forces," said Bundy, "he was flatly negative, with only a possible future exception for a security force at Danang."[*]

As Bundy recalled, Taylor was eloquent about the drawbacks of using

* Bundy, chapter 22B, p. 31.

American troops. Yet two days later, on February 24, Westmoreland sent an independent recommendation to Washington that two battalions of marines be landed immediately to provide security at the Danang base, at the same time indicating that Taylor would go along with this.

Westmoreland's proposal went to the Joint Chiefs of Staff, who seized the opportunity to up the request to an entire expeditionary brigade of 5,000 men, complete with heavy artillery and fighter planes. When Taylor and Alexis Johnson heard this, they were, in Johnson's words, "appalled." Such a scheme went "far beyond anything we envisioned or the military requirements could justify," and they flatly refused to approve it. That night a compromise was reached in which Johnson and Taylor agreed to bring in 3,500 marines. They did so "reluctantly" and only "on the condition that there would be no more and that these would be withdrawn as soon as Vietnamese replacements were available."* On February 26 the Defense Department presented this proposal to President Johnson at a luncheon meeting. The president approved it then and there. According to Bundy, the State Department staffs had not been consulted.

Among the Americans an impressive gap had opened between President Johnson's civilian and military advisers. The military was not reluctant to contradict civilian assessments or to use its independent access to the president. It was clear that the landing itself came as a surprise to Taylor, who was not informed of it in advance by the Joint Chiefs. He expressed his anger about this to Westmoreland, even going so far as to explicitly remind the general who outranked whom. Taylor was further upset when he discovered that the marines were bringing ashore tanks, self-propelled artillery, and other heavy equipment whose necessity for "base defense" was hardly evident.

Taylor must have felt he was being manipulated. He strongly opposed the use of American troops, then had grudgingly agreed — initially, to only one marine antimissile battalion for the Danang defenses, then to a second battalion that would defend the first. Overnight, these two battalions had grown to 3,500 men, and Taylor and Alexis Johnson must have counted themselves lucky to have had it limited to that. The president's approval for this deployment came only two days later, without Taylor's State Department colleagues having had a chance to review the proposal from the Joint Chiefs of Staff. To cap off the process, the Joint Chiefs had not informed him ahead of time about the landing, and when the marines did come ashore, they stage-managed it to look like an Iwo Jima beach assault instead of keeping the low profile Taylor had in mind.

* Johnson, *Right Hand of Power*, p. 427.

The record shows that Maxwell Taylor voiced his deep reservations about the introduction of American troops at every step in the process. But he was overruled in Washington and in the end had no choice but to go along. Taylor then turned around and asked Dr. Quat to concur in a decision that was already being implemented. It was a hasty and furtive procedure, the destructive consequences of which would become evident in due course.

Whether Dr. Quat could have delayed the move, or perhaps rejected it outright, was another matter. Because he was dependent on his own military and was only three weeks in office, the fact is that he did not. Taylor had argued in all sincerity that the marines would play a limited defensive role and, he hoped, a temporary one. For the moment at least, Quat decided to satisfy himself with that and acquiesced. Perhaps he should have done differently. But looking back, I cannot honestly say that had I been consulted at the final hour, I would have advised him to take a stand against both the Americans and our own generals. In light of our still tenuous grip on the reins of government, and considering the manner in which the American decision was made and carried out, that kind of opposition would not have been particularly realistic.

Once the Rubicon was crossed, however, the ensuing steps followed with a natural inevitability. With military intervention, as with political intervention, there was no such thing as being "a little bit pregnant."

Barely two weeks after the 3,500 marines landed at Danang, U.S. army Chief of Staff Harold K. Johnson submitted a formal request to President Lyndon Johnson to authorize the deployment of three divisions, two American and one Korean. Again Maxwell Taylor objected. Having reluctantly gone along with the introduction of the marines as a strictly local defensive measure, he was especially unhappy about the prospect of large-scale intervention. The details of what passed between Taylor and Dr. Quat on this subject I do not know, but Quat told me repeatedly that he and Taylor agreed wholeheartedly on the necessity of limiting the marines' role at Danang.

In response to General Johnson's call for more troops, Taylor cabled the White House that he would go no further than to "round off" the marine battalions at Danang. Called back to Washington for consultation at the end of March, he continued to argue his position tenaciously. By now he was clearly at loggerheads with General Westmoreland, who, along with General Johnson and the Joint Chiefs, was advocating expanded deployment of U.S. forces. But Taylor was not alone in his opposition. Indeed, his skepticism was shared by virtually all the civilian elements in Washington.*

At the National Security Council meeting of April 1, President Johnson gave both his civilian and military advisers some of what they wanted. Instead of the three divisions requested by the Joint Chiefs, only two additional marine battalions would go to Vietnam. This was Taylor's position, backed, according to Bundy, by a consensus of the president's civilian advisers. However, the marines in Danang would now be allowed to pursue more than simple "base security," the job for which they had been brought in. They would also be permitted to take a "more active role" in the fighting.** In addition, the new marines would be accompanied by 20,000 support and logistical personnel. It was a compromise, but Ambassador Taylor had won a victory of sorts in at least temporarily delaying a major deployment of American combat soldiers.

Of all these decisions, the most critical was the one authorizing the marines to expand their role. With this, the "base security" theory, which served as the initial rationale for the marine landing, had evolved into an "enclave strategy," which permitted them to fight up to fifty miles from the base. In addition, the marines were to be made available for emergency use on South Vietnamese request, as U.S. field commanders might deem proper. For the first time, American ground forces would be taking an aggressive role on the battlefield.

During the first week of April Taylor came back to Saigon and presented Quat with a request for "concurrence" with the National Security Council decision to bring extra support troops and marine reinforcements with expanded duties. At first Quat simply did not know what to make of it. We were completely in the dark about what the Americans intended by bringing in these additional 20,000 support troops and by enlarging the marine detachment and changing its mission — all this only weeks after we were surprised by the initial two-battalion landing. He knew that Taylor had been unenthusiastic about the first deployment, and now the ambassador was presenting him with something far more ominous.

Being the professional he was, Taylor gave us no indication of the conflicts that had spawned the National Security Council compromise. Nor did we even know it was a compromise. Certainly Taylor did not say to us, "Look, we are just as confused as you are about what may improve things. We don't really know what to do and we're having a lot of arguments. This seems to be the best we can come up with, although

* Bundy, chapter 23, p. 19.
** National Security Council memorandum #328, April 6, 1965.

I myself am not too happy with it." And because we were unaware of the background and intent of this new American plan, we were not able to evaluate it in a meaningful, or even rational, manner.

We suspected, though, that the Americans were operating from some carefully devised master plan that they had simply chosen not to share with us. We did not know in any detail their assessment of the overall situation, and we did not know what the various groups of presidential advisers thought about our needs, although we certainly knew what we ourselves thought our needs were. Above all, we needed political strength so that we could achieve governmental stability. That was the prerequisite for everything else, the one thing that would provide a foundation for the war effort and for the social, political, and economic development that was the key to the country's long-term survival. We needed to find ways to overcome the fractious mess left by Diem and the generals which was still threatening daily to suck us under.

We also needed military help, of course. But in March and April we were not sure what form this assistance should take. Both Quat and I were opposed to an Americanization of the war, but how best to utilize the help our giant ally stood ready to provide was a subject we were only then beginning to consider. And it was just at this point that we were faced with the American decision to begin moving significant numbers of troops into the country.

As far as this new American request was concerned, we simply did not know what it portended. And although we had almost boundless confidence in our ally's capabilities, we did want to know what they had in mind, and especially what this new troop request meant in the larger scheme. At least as unhappy as Taylor with the idea of deploying additional troops, and disturbed by our friends' lack of candor, Quat asked me for an assessment of American intentions.

Although South Vietnam did have an embassy in Washington, the ambassador at that moment was General Tran Thien Khiem, who had helped Nguyen Khanh foment his coup and whom Khanh had eventually shipped off to Washington so that he would be as far from Saigon as possible. Since General Khiem was a political intriguer of little practical use, I was forced to do my best with the resources available in Saigon. I talked to everyone I thought might be helpful, from Taylor, Manfull, and Alexis Johnson, to my other friends in the American mission, to my numerous contacts in the American press corps — especially those (like Jerry Rose of *The Saturday Evening Post*) who knew both Vietnam and the Washington scene. But I felt like the proverbial frog at the bottom of a well, who has only limited vision and even that is distorted.

At any event, even such as it was, my assessment had hardly begun when the U.S. embassy pointed out that the request for concurrence was urgent and required an immediate response. Consequently, on April 6 Dr. Quat felt constrained to agree, on behalf of the South Vietnamese government, to the additional troops and to their new role.

With this concurrence, the crucial decision had been made: to give American combat troops an independent part in the ground war. It was what William Bundy called "a break point." On the American side it had been made largely out of despair about what else might be done and out of a feeling that the situation could not continue as it was. The United States had to take some action, and to the military — Generals William Westmoreland and Harold Johnson and the Joint Chiefs — the combat option recommended itself. To the civilians — particularly Maxwell Taylor and Alexis Johnson — it did not. But theirs was a rear-guard action that of necessity traded principle for compromise. Meanwhile, on the Vietnamese side the American decision was accepted by a government distracted by a volatile domestic political situation, a government that did not have the confidence or (its principals felt) the ability to withstand U.S. pressure. The record does not show either that the American decision makers understood our perspective or that we understood American intentions. The Americans apparently did not believe such an understanding was necessary, and we, their allies, felt too weak to insist on achieving it.

From air strikes to "passive base defense" to "aggressive base defense" to a general combat role — the steps led from one to the next with a relentless logic. Within the next nine months, the original, embryonic unit of marines would be transformed into an army of over 200,000 American and allied troops, all there according to the demands of the same reasoning.

If the president's decision of April 1 in favor of logistical troops, more marines, and an expanded marine fighting role was a compromise between the administration's civilian and military planners, it was a compromise the military did not regard as permanent. Unhappy with the decision against the Joint Chiefs' request for two divisions, on April 11 General Westmoreland cabled Admiral Ulysses Grant Sharp, Jr., commander in chief of the Pacific fleet, that he still wanted at least the army's 173rd Airborne Brigade. After high-level discussions among the military, on April 14 the Joint Chiefs ordered the 173rd to be deployed.

When Maxwell Taylor arrived back in Saigon after his strenuous battle in Washington, he felt that his arguments for restraint had been accepted by the president. Now he was upset to learn that apparently this was not the case. The stilted language he used in a cable to Secretary of State Dean Rusk on April 14 did not completely hide his irritation. "Recent actions relating to the introduction of U.S. ground forces have tended to create an impression of eagerness in some quarters to deploy forces into South Vietnam which I find difficult to understand. . . . This comes as a complete surprise in view of the understanding reached in Washington [on April 1]." *

The next day Taylor received a cablegram back from Assistant Secretary of Defense John McNaughton that could not have improved his mood. "Highest authority believes the situation in South Vietnam has been deteriorating and that, in addition to action against the North, something new must be added in the South to achieve victory." McNaughton's message included, among other recommendations, the prompt deployment of the 173rd Airborne. "It was quite a cable," said Taylor, "particularly significant to me because few of these proposals had originated in the Embassy." And Deputy Ambassador Alexis Johnson wrote later, "We were inundated [with proposals]. The dike was springing more leaks than we 'go slowers' had fingers." **

To counter these unwelcome developments, on April 17 Taylor sent a long cable to both Dean Rusk at State and McGeorge Bundy at the White House in which he reviewed the confusing, quickly changing scenario with which he was faced. Among the many problems the ambassador envisaged was Quat's likely opposition to new troop deployments. "I badly need a clarification of our purposes and objectives," he wrote. "Before I can present our case to GVN [Government of Vietnam], I have to know what that case is and why. It is not going to be easy to get ready concurrence for the large-scale introduction of foreign troops unless the need is clear and explicit." †

The increasing divergence of views between Taylor and the Joint Chiefs resulted in a tense meeting in Honolulu on April 19 that was chaired by Robert McNamara and included the senior military commanders as well as Taylor, William Bundy, and John McNaughton. In two days of "vigorous" discussion, Ambassador Taylor was persuaded to go along with the military consensus and recommend a substantial increase in the number of GIs (to 82,000) and the introduction of "third-country" troops totaling 7,250. It was, said Alexis Johnson, a "reluctant consent." Again Taylor was able to win a concession in return for his agreement. The

---

* Secret cable #3384, quoted in Larry Berman, *Planning a Tragedy* (New York: Norton, 1982), p. 60; and in Sheehan et al., eds., *Pentagon Papers*, p. 404.
** Sheehan et al., eds., *Pentagon Papers*, p. 404; Maxwell Taylor, *Swords and Plowshares* (New York: Norton, 1972), p. 342; Johnson, *Right Hand of Power*, p. 428.
† Sheehan et al., eds., *Pentagon Papers*, p. 445.

American forces would still not be permitted a free-ranging offensive latitude, but instead would be limited to operations within the coastal enclaves where they were to be based. According to Bundy, the civilian advisers actually believed that Westmoreland's new troops could be kept in this defensive posture. But he also thought that "our military colleagues probably had a more skeptical (and realistic) view of what would happen to such arbitrary limitations." *

For the Vietnamese April was a month of cascading American demands. On April 6 Dr. Quat agreed to the additional marine battalions and the 20,000 support troops that were the subject of the April 1 NSC memorandum. By the next week rumors were circulating about a push for even more troops, some of them from other nations. While Taylor was struggling to limit the various grandiose plans for increasing U.S. troop strength with which Washington was "inundating" the embassy, Quat was feeling more and more nervous about the whole situation. Circumstances had forced him to go along up to this point despite his deep reservations. He knew, I think, that with the marines' new action-oriented mission a dividing line had been crossed. But there were still relatively few American soldiers in the country. There was little doubt, though, that the Americans would soon press for more. How could we respond to this other than by simply acquiescing?

The answer seemed to depend first of all on a full examination of the military situation by our generals. If the war effort was truly in danger of falling apart in front of the Vietcong and North Vietnamese forces that had made their way south, then we would, of course, have no choice. But if the commanding officers thought the situation more stable than that, then we would be in a better position to confront the pressure.

I was already consulting with the generals when Taylor returned from his meeting in Honolulu. On April 24 the ambassador presented Dr. Quat with the consensus reached in Hawaii. Quat understood completely the gravity of what was about to happen; for some weeks he had been anxious over just this development. Quat told Taylor that he needed time to consider the military and political implications of such a dramatic increase. Immediately after Taylor left, Quat rushed into my office, visibly shocked, and practically shouted at me, "What's happening on the battlefield that we don't know about? Are we on the verge of collapsing?" He simply could not imagine any other reason why the Americans would think they needed an offensive force of that size in the country.

My own feelings mirrored Quat's. Although I had been meeting with

---

* Johnson, *Right Hand of Power*, p. 428; Bundy, chapter 25, p. 7.

the military people just prior to this latest request, it was clear that we would have to consult them in more detail before deciding what to do. We had to review all the problems and implications, and we had to do it quickly, since it was obvious that something of a juggernaut was on the loose here.

That weekend Quat and I plunged into a series of intensive meetings with all the South Vietnamese senior commanders. We asked each of them to assess the short- and long-term military prospects. We also expressed our own doubts about the wisdom of bringing in more U.S. troops and solicited their views on the subject. At the time our new government had nothing like the National Security Council through which to review problems, so these talks were informal. But we also sounded out some of the mainstream political leaders in Saigon as well as the generals.

There was nothing pro forma about these consultations. Quat and I knew that from a political as well as a military standpoint the generals' advice, whatever it was, could not easily be by-passed. But beyond that, we were also testing our own reservations. I was especially aware of the problems a major troop build-up would bring with it. As Quat's chief of staff, I was handling all the complaints about the Americans who were already in Vietnam, from their trucks killing people to a wide variety of crimes and lawsuits. So I was attuned more than most to the problems of sovereignty and jurisdiction. In addition, the Élysée negotiations with the French in the early 1950s involved a range of disputes similar to those that would be created by a large American force fighting alongside the South Vietnamese army. As secretary of defense back then, and my boss, Quat was as sensitive to these problems as I, perhaps hypersensitive, we both thought. So it was in search of perspective, as well as to feel out the political situation, that we set about the business of consultation.

As far as the military people were concerned, the answers were perhaps predictable. For the present, they felt, we were in no particular danger, despite the major battles that were beginning to shape up. But the long-term outlook was a different story. Elements of at least two regular North Vietnamese divisions, the 324th and the 304th, were already fighting in South Vietnam, and the infiltration rate was increasing. Improvements in our own forces to match this trend would be difficult because of man-power shortages and the training time necessary before new soldiers could be fielded. The conclusion? More U.S. troops would be a big plus, regardless of the political difficulties their presence would undoubtedly cause.

The reactions of the civilian politicians were, somewhat surprisingly, not too far from those of the generals. Some of the diehards positively relished the idea of an international war against communism. Others seemed relatively unconcerned about the negative side of a large American involvement.

In our own evaluation of all this, Quat noted that, to a certain degree, our senior officers were under the influence of their American advisers. It was to be expected, then, that their opinions would coincide with the conventionally hawkish judgment of their American counterparts. And like the U.S. commanders, they were used to seeing things in narrow military terms. By training and experience they were poorly equipped to consider the long-term psychological and social effects of an American influx. But from a national security standpoint it would be very difficult to reject their views. And from a political standpoint it might be impossible.

When it came down to making the final decision, Quat was starkly alone. He was the new prime minister of an embattled nation, exerting authority from a fragile and threatened seat of power. At this precarious moment, he had as his guide, as he said to me at one point, "only my conscience and my political instinct." In theory he might refuse the American request. But actually he was under immense pressure from his giant ally — with whom his own military, an important part of his power base, was in agreement.

In the end Quat followed his political instinct, reserving the hope that if the military situation improved, he would have the ability to maneuver, which at the time he so clearly lacked. On April 28 he informed Taylor that South Vietnam concurred with the new American request. The floodgates were now wide open.

In fairness to Lyndon Johnson and his administration, it must be said that even as the American military build-up began, the United States was also attempting to engage North Vietnam in negotiations. But for the South Vietnamese government, American peace explorations in 1965 were as shrouded as its military intentions. In one way, America's decision not to tip its hand was understandable. With its unstable past and unpredictable future, the Saigon government may not have seemed any more likely a partner for serious consultation on the diplomatic than on the military front. However, the South Vietnamese could hardly have been expected to contribute much when they were kept ignorant of decisions, and of course these were decisions that affected the very life of their country.

We were, of course, kept informed of the American peace initiatives that went forward in public: President Johnson's address at Johns Hopkins on April 7, for example, and the bombing pause on May 10. Even earlier, in March, Alexis Johnson briefed our foreign minister, Tran Van Do, about the possibility of a reactivated Geneva conference, with Great

Britain and the USSR presiding.* But we knew very little about the substance of unofficial "feelers" the United States was putting out through Canadian Ambassador J. Blair Seaborn of the International Control Commission; through the Chinese embassy in Warsaw; through French channels; and to Mai Van Bo, the North Vietnamese representative in Paris. We knew that various avenues were being explored but could only speculate about what the United States had in mind as a negotiated settlement. It was not so much that we distrusted American intentions, but ignorance, as always, bred suspicion.

In the event, neither the United States' public overtures nor its secret approaches were put to the test. Hanoi turned a cold shoulder to all of them. Consequently, everyone's attention reverted to the military and political situations that confronted the Saigon government in that season of escalation.

The Americanization of the Vietnam War, which took place so abruptly and imperiously in the spring of 1965, had a long, significant history. It was a history of the perennial failure of American diplomacy to foster a vital South Vietnamese democracy capable of handling its own affairs and worthy of partnership in the common struggle against communism. I do not mean to suggest that the United States bears sole blame for this catastrophe. The people who held power in South Vietnam have to bear the prime responsibility. They share this with the fractured South Vietnamese nationalist parties that were simply too weak to do for themselves when outside help proved unavailable.

But specifically in terms of American diplomacy, the first eleven years of the United States' relationship with an independent South Vietnam set a deadly pattern. The Americans first watched the rise and fall of civilian and military dictatorships without attempting to use their influence decisively for something better. Then, horrified by the resulting mess, they took the whole ball of wax into their hands, intervening with massive military might. They did this suddenly and unilaterally, without consulting their ally in any meaningful way. In effect, they had worked themselves into a corner from which they could only escape — or so they thought — by making the war American. Later they would discover that

---

* Subsequently, Do and the American deputy ambassador held a series of meetings to formulate a South Vietnamese peace position. In the end Do, Quat, and I worked out aims similar to those of the 1954 Geneva agreement: an end to aggression and subversion, freedom to shape our own destiny in accord with democratic principles, and the removal of all foreign forces. We did not mention reunification. We considered it a natural aspiration of all Vietnamese, but we saw no practical way to accomplish it, given the nature of the two governments.

Americanization, too, was a cul-de-sac. At that point they just as imperiously moved out and began searching for their own peace solutions, again keeping their ally, whose country it was, on the periphery of the process.

By chance I would be present at the abdication of responsibility, as I was at the assumption of it. It seemed a strange and destructive way to conduct the work of an alliance.

Chapter 18

Dr. Quat and the Generals

THE WHIRLWIND that transformed the war from an internecine killing field to an international one was not the only event that occupied Dr. Quat's attention in the spring of 1965. When he originally took office, his personal agenda had been, first, just to survive, then to gain some control over the military, deal with the wildly unstable factional warfare in Saigon, carry out local elections, and write a constitution. In broad terms, these were his priorities, but of course the complexity and turbulence of the government-military-civilian political tangle was such that almost everything seemed to be happening at once. And this was above and beyond the war itself and the table the Americans were busily setting for us.

Looking back on that period, it all seems to have taken place in an instant, a burst of furious activity that consumed four months in a flash. Henry Kissinger perhaps best evoked what we felt when he described a statesman as someone constantly forced to make choices "not only without knowledge of the future, but usually even without knowledge of what is going on in the present." It was only on rare occasions during those days that I thought I could see the outlines of the forest through which we were frantically toiling.

Nevertheless, Quat, in his workmanlike manner, did manage to keep at least part of his mind on the agenda. As he saw it, the military people were the key. If he could persuade the Young Turks to attend to the war and leave politics alone, that would be a half step. If he could do that and muster some of their influence behind himself, that would be a whole step. Of course, he would have to do these things while at the same time quieting the political sharks sufficiently so they would not tear our fragile boat to pieces.

In dealing with the generals, Quat had a number of advantages. First was his own credibility. As a former defense minister, he knew the military and their problems and was able to develop an excellent rapport with some of the key officers. For their part, the generals tended to regard him as a serious, stable individual with whom they could work, unlike most of the other civilians. Second, ever since February, Taylor and Alexis Johnson had been prodding the generals about their political involvement. If they wanted to be politicians, that was fine. But in that case, the Americans suggested, they should hang up their uniforms and put on suits and ties. Third, and probably most important, whatever the generals thought about a civilian government, not one of them was willing to see a brother officer take power. To avoid that, it was better to allow Quat to run things. They had, in effect, overbid the game.

With these three factors conspiring in Quat's favor, he and I got together with the senior officers at the beginning of May and persuaded them to dissolve the Armed Forces Council, through which they had been exerting their influence since the regime of Nguyen Khanh. The end of this council did not exactly signal the end of the military's political sway, but it was certainly a step along the path.

Quat had less success with the civilian political factions. It is possible that the dissolution of the Armed Forces Council had made him a bit careless. Certainly some of us in the government thought he was not putting sufficient effort into courting the various groups of real and potential civilian antagonists, though it is hard to fault him for focusing first on the military. But one man he should have been more attentive to was Phan Khac Suu. Suu was the octogenarian figurehead chief of state who the previous December had refused to sign Nguyen Khanh's order dismissing the older generals and, in so doing, had precipitated the Young Turks' kidnapping of the national High Council.

In May the ancient Suu was still president and still just as cantankerous. Late in the month he set afoot his second governmental crisis. This one started with a rice shortage caused by the Vietcong's disruption of the roads between Saigon and the provinces. Prices in the capital suddenly skyrocketed, and within days the government was forced to intervene. A week, then two weeks, passed with no resolution. By then it was evident that the officials responsible (the ministers of interior and economy) were not up to dealing with the crisis. By the third week Quat was fuming at their incompetence and took the problem into his own hands. Acting decisively, in an almost American fashion, he replaced the two ministers. It was a fatal error in judgment.

Unfortunately, Quat had not taken effective steps over the preceding months to placate his political enemies. The most dangerous of these were the southern regionalists who were deeply aggrieved to have a northerner in power and had been looking for a chance to reverse that situation. In firing the two ministers, Quat gave them their opportunity. The cantankerous Suu gave them their lever. Although the chief of state's job was entirely ceremonial, Suu did have to sign the orders of dismissal. But, encouraged by the *"sudists"* — the "southernists" — joined now by a group of Catholics fearful of a Buddhist resurgence, he refused to sign. Soon we were in the middle of a full-fledged ministerial crisis.

As the government ground to a halt over the impasse, Quat tried everything he could think of to break Suu's hold over the machinery of state. But with no constitution, there was no procedural way to do it. Suu, for his part, remained adamant. He had not budged for Nguyen Khanh, and he was not about to budge now. Behind him, the southernists were swearing that whatever came of this, they would at least have Quat's scalp. For a mediator, Quat turned to Tran Van Do, our foreign minister and a southerner by birth. Unfortunately, despite Do's natural talent for conciliation, he had lived in northern Vietnam for a good part of his adult life, and his pleading fell on deaf ears.

With the crisis persisting and no one willing to back down, it was perhaps inevitable that the generals would step in to resolve it. In fact, Quat had spoken with some of them as he was casting around for some way of breaking the deadlock, but he had been unable to muster their support. On the contrary, their attitude was quite clearly, "Look, we removed ourselves from politics, and now that we have, you people can't control things." It is possible that Quat might have persuaded some of the generals to go along with him and add their weight to his position. But behind the Young Turks were *younger* Turks, ambitious colonels with field commands who were not happy about their newly circumscribed political horizons. For them this was the ripe moment for a return to military control. It was a constituency the senior generals could not ignore.

The impasse was ended at a marathon meeting held on June 11 in the prime minister's office. Everybody was squeezed into one room: forty or fifty generals, Quat and his backers, Suu and his. Quat made a last, token attempt to appoint the two new ministers, but the generals insisted that the deadlock be broken then and there. They would not, they said, stand by while the government remained paralyzed. Quat knew this was coming, and in the middle of the shouting he announced that he would voluntarily step down and dissolve the government. This he did, pulling Suu down with him and clearing the stage for the generals to come in with their own regime. In short order two military committees were up and running: the National Leadership Committee with General Nguyen Van Thieu as chairman and chief of state, and the Central Executive Committee with Air Marshal Nguyen Cao Ky as chairman and prime minister. It was a bitter way to end South Vietnam's final experiment in civilian government.

Immediately after the fall Alexis Johnson told me he was "very, very disappointed." I understood that the Americans had begun to invest a good deal of hope in Quat's effort to bring a normal political life to South Vietnam, and they were deeply frustrated by the failure. It seemed, too, that their unhappiness was compounded by a sense of humiliation, because they had found themselves powerless to help. They had been like bystanders watching a disturbing incident about which they could do nothing. And now they were faced with yet another round of military strongmen. It had been only several months since Ambassador Taylor had gone through his unpleasant encounters with the Young Turks, prominently including Thieu and Ky, and he could not have been enthusiastic about the prospect of having to deal with them as government leaders. (As Taylor wryly phrased it in his memoirs, "There was not much cause to hail his [Ky's] advent to the premiership with excessive optimism.")

Whatever the future held for those who had taken over, I suddenly felt myself crashing down from four months of constant tension and crisis. Physically and emotionally, I was exhausted, but I also felt a surge of relief. However dubious this transfer of power was, it seemed that a giant weight had been removed from my chest. It was time for a long rest, somewhere far away.

Since the school year was just ended, we decided on a family vacation at the little seaside resort of Nha Trang, three hundred miles north of Saigon. On the lazy white sand beach there I would be able to relax with my wife and two small daughters and forget for a while about the existence of war and politics.

There could not have been a more perfect setting for it than Nha Trang. Mornings we all got up early and puttered across the bay to a tiny offshore island that was home to a small colony of fishermen. There we would wander along the shore under the coconut palms, watching them tend their early nets as an incandescent sun made the sea shimmer with light. I was a free man in what might easily have passed for paradise. I felt so good I even began thinking again about reorganizing the staff of the *Saigon Post*, which I had been planning back in February when Quat asked me to join his government.

The last thing I expected was the message I received, five or six days after I arrived, from the new prime minister, Nguyen Cao Ky, requesting my immediate return to the capital. As closely associated with Quat as I had been — his alter ego, according to some — I refused to believe that Ky was going to ask me to participate in the new government, though that was what this summons suggested. I didn't know him all that well, though as Quat's liaison I had met with him from time to time on issues involving military affairs or the Armed Forces Council. As with his colleague Nguyen Van Thieu, my relationship with Ky was cordial and correct, but certainly not close. And after what had just happened, I would be a distinct political liability, a man who should be allowed to disappear peacefully into his private life.

Consequently, I was shocked when I returned to Saigon and heard Ky ask me to become his special assistant for planning and foreign aid. He had talked to Dr. Quat about it already, he said, and no doubt I would be hearing from my former boss later in the day. He described the grave military situation and hit on the absolute necessity of maintaining continuity in our ties with the Americans. That had been my job before, and it would be best if I could continue doing it. When he was finished explaining why I was needed, Ky let me go off to think about it. He did not even bother to ask whether I would accept.

I spent the rest of the day touching base with friends in the political world and talking to Dr. Quat. As Ky had implied, Quat advised me to accept the offer. Like Ky, he pointed out the need to keep communication with the Americans as smooth as possible, and he took it as a good sign that the generals were so attuned to this. Quat also felt that, as he put it, "It would be better if we could keep at least some kind of eye on these guys." That remark, among others, suggested that Quat was not quite ready to write an end to his own political career. Though he did not say it outright, I got the impression that he wanted to maintain his own connection with the military, and that this was one of the reasons he wanted me to accept. I knew that at heart he was bitter about what had happened, and I suspected he did not really want me to collaborate. Nevertheless, he had ceded power to Thieu and Ky voluntarily and had stepped down on good terms with them. If he had any hope at all of coming back, it was essential to keep up that relationship. Recent experience suggested that the new government might not be around long, and who could tell what might happen afterward? "Besides," he told me, "after you've proved your good will for six months or so, you can always resign for health reasons."

I thought I understood Quat, but I also had my own considerations to take into account. First of all, I had extreme reservations about working with these generals, whom I thought of as trigger happy, intemperate individuals with no discernible concept of government. Second, I knew that regardless of Quat's urging, it would not look right for his chief assistant to stay on in the regime that replaced him. That was the kind of thing which would provide the Saigon rumor mongers with a lifetime's worth of speculation about who had really done what to whom. On the other hand, I had had just enough time in Nha Trang to lose the edge of my fatigue, and the idea of keeping my hand in government was tempting. I was only forty-two, hardly the age to step voluntarily into limbo. After spending the better part of the night weighing the choices, the following morning I was in Nguyen Cao Ky's office, accepting his offer.

My first weeks with Ky were uncomfortable ones. He and his inner circle of officers took pains to treat me with consideration, but there was no doubt I was a stranger in their midst, in some ways an intruder. In this atmosphere I kept myself occupied with my own area of responsibility, preparing brief memos for Ky on urgent foreign policy matters and going to see him only at his request.

But this situation did not last long. I had been brought in primarily because of my experience with the Americans and because I would be a known quantity for them to deal with during a period of necessarily unsettled relations. It was no surprise, then, that the embassy turned to me first on a wide range of problems requiring the prime minister's attention. By the same token, Ky also found it convenient to use me as a conduit to the Americans, to sound out their reactions to steps he had in mind. From there, it was a natural progression for the prime minister, with no personal experience in government or foreign affairs, to begin looking to me for advice. As we began to develop a closer working relationship, he made an effort to put me at ease, frequently inviting me to have lunch with him in his office as I briefed him on one issue or another.

Contrary to my expectations, I found Ky quick to grasp problems and well disposed to listen. Although clearly not a profound man and still unsteady as a politician, there was a charm and natural sincerity about him that was difficult not to like. He had a disconcerting habit of making rash statements, and his flamboyant style was at odds with my concept of how a public figure should comport himself. Yet I could not help feeling that, despite his impetuosity, he was essentially well meaning and honest.

On the subject of American troops, I laid out for Ky what had gone on during the preceding months. I also explained Quat's concerns about deploying large numbers of Americans in the country. Ky acknowledged Quat's misgivings, but he was heavily influenced by the series of large-unit enemy attacks in June and especially by the vicious terrorist bombing of the My Canh waterfront restaurant in Saigon, which caused dozens of civilian casualties. Ky argued that the most important task was to get the military situation under control, and for that we badly needed American ground forces.

Neither of us was aware that even prior to the change of government, General Westmoreland had asked for an additional increase over the number of troops agreed on by the two governments in April. And as usual we were completely in the dark about the debate Westmoreland's request had reignited in Washington among advocates of escalation like Secretary of Defense McNamara, "hang on" middle roaders like William Bundy, and the lone but strong voice of Undersecretary of State George Ball, who had already started talking about cutting losses. For the Thieu-Ky regime, as for the Quat government that preceded it, the controlling assumption was that the Americans knew precisely what they were doing and had made plans to achieve their objectives. It was a misconception, of course, and one that was to become a dominant factor in the relationship between the two countries and eventually in the outcome of the war.

In the meantime, the American military was already changing the face of the war. During the last days of June we learned that the newly arrived 173rd Airborne Brigade had attacked Vietcong strongholds in War Zone D, a dense jungle area northwest of Saigon. It was the first offensive thrust initiated by U.S. ground forces. Just as significant, the assault was preceded by bombing runs made by B-52s flying from Guam. The laborious decisions about deploying American troops, made over several months, had now been implemented. In a way it was anticlimactic. Not much contact was made with enemy troops, and since the remote jungles in Zone D were only sparsely inhabited, not much notice was taken of the huge strategic bombers. But almost all the South Vietnamese who did know of the American action felt reassured. It meant that now our ally was truly in the war and could be counted on. Any aversion to having foreign troops on Vietnamese soil was swallowed in the vast relief that a military defeat under the Communist onslaught no longer seemed possible.

On the other hand, many problems associated with the U.S. build-up began to surface. Supplies and equipment flooded the country, swamping the available distribution systems. The port of Saigon was jammed with ships waiting to unload while people argued about priorities. Giant construction projects seemed to be sprouting everywhere, with all the inevitable difficulties. Matters of jurisdiction between Americans and South Vietnamese had to be resolved — procedures for working together and for settling disputes.

Sometime during the second week in July the usually frenetic activity was interrupted by news that Secretary of Defense Robert McNamara would be arriving on the sixteenth. In preparation for the visit, Ky asked me to put together a memorandum summing up the questions he should raise with the secretary. It was a job I needed no urging to do. To my mind, McNamara was one of the American administration's stars, perhaps the most important of Lyndon Johnson's advisers. I was in some awe of this man and anxious about the impression we would make. But his visit would provide an important opportunity for Ky to review the Johnson administration's overall war strategy. We knew, of course, that approximately 80,000 U.S. soldiers were now in the country and that the Americans were at least testing out offensive tactics. But what, precisely, were their military aims? What did they want to achieve and what were they willing to settle for? What war strategy had they developed? Drawing on my experience from March and April — the marine landings and the subsequent quick increases in troop strength — I prepared a comprehensive memorandum for Ky on July 14 that included the following policy questions:

· What are overall U.S. war objectives: outright military victory? negotiated settlement?
· If negotiated settlement, what are negotiation positions and objectives?
· If outright victory, how is victory defined: Formal surrender by Vietcong? By North Vietnam? Conquest of North Vietnam? Simple cessation of Vietcong and North Vietnamese aggression?
· What are desires of U.S. concerning joint military command or unified command?
· How many troops will U.S. deploy in South Vietnam? For what length of time?

These and other questions regarding how U.S. intentions would affect South Vietnamese political and economic development were meant to guide Ky on a *tour d'horizon* with the American secretary. From a historical perspective, perhaps the most interesting thing about the memo was that it spelled out those major dimensions of the joint war effort about which the South Vietnamese had almost no information in the summer of 1965. I suggested that Ky should push hard to get the answers that I considered vital to planning our own course of action.

When Secretary McNamara arrived in Saigon, he brought with him Henry Cabot Lodge, who had come to replace Maxwell Taylor as ambassador. We knew Lodge from his first tenure in Saigon in 1963–64. McNamara had also been in the country before, in 1964, when at Lyndon Johnson's request he had gone on tour with Nguyen Khanh. Despite that episode, McNamara's reputation preceded him: he was a man of high intelligence, with a computerlike mind. He was perceived as the most influential individual in the American administration. So it was with a good deal of anticipation that I attended the meeting in Ky's office immediately after the secretary's arrival for a joint review of the war.

Along with McNamara sat Lodge, Westmoreland, Earle Wheeler (chairman of the Joint Chiefs of Staff), Alexis Johnson, and other officials and aides. Ky, Thieu, and I were on the opposite side of the table, along with several other South Vietnamese government and military people. I was poised to pass notes to Ky as we went along.

McNamara seemed unbelievably alert for someone who had just completed such a long trip. As soon as he started the meeting, it was clear that he was going to follow his own exclusive agenda. Precise but affable, scribbling notes on a yellow pad as he went, he fired his questions about numbers, organization, management, and logistics as if he were bent on assembling all the factors and components for the solution of some grand mathematical equation. Apparently preoccupied by his own line of thought, he paid little attention to those around him. As far as I could judge, he made absolutely no effort to size up Nguyen Cao Ky, who was sitting directly across the table from him. I wondered if Ky simply did not particularly matter to him.

By the end of the meeting McNamara had touched on U.S. plans to secure and build up the countryside and had given some general assurances about the continuation of American support, but not a single one of the policy questions I had so carefully outlined had even come up. Perhaps Ky was too timid or inexperienced to ask them. It seemed as if McNamara and his team were far more interested in collecting data than in revealing their policies or plans. I was disappointed by that, but I also recognized that these issues were perhaps too sensitive to discuss at a large meeting. Consequently, I suggested to Ky that he should seek private talks with McNamara, in order to provide a more comfortable setting. But though Ky and McNamara did sit down together, no clarification of the problems noted in that memo was forthcoming. When McNamara left the country, we knew precious little more than we had when he arrived.

Later, however, we learned that while McNamara was in Saigon, he received a cable from Cyrus Vance, his deputy in Washington, telling him that President Johnson had agreed to Westmoreland's request to raise the number of American troops to 125,000. On July 28 the president announced this decision in a press conference at the White House. It was our official notification as well.

Chapter 19

Toward a Constitution

EXACTLY TWO DAYS after President Johnson's July 28 press conference the Joint Chiefs of Staff requested the deployment of 193,000 troops, up almost 70,000 from the figure the president had just announced. Approval followed shortly thereafter. The tide that had been building since February was now irreversible; Washington's compromisers and "go slowers" had decisively lost the battle to General Westmoreland and the Joint Chiefs.

In retrospect these decisions are not difficult to understand. Already, by June, the Americans were feeling rather desperate. They had invested a great deal in the South Vietnamese, and now, just as it seemed they might be clearing up their political mess, the whole thing had unraveled once more. Again there was a new government. And not just a new government, but precisely these same disagreeable Young Turks who already had such an unreassuring track record. As Bill Bundy commented later, "The outlook was gloomy and forbidding. If [South Vietnam] had stood alone, I have no doubt whatever that the United States would have pulled back and said 'enough.' "* But strategic considerations (which accounted for 90 percent of U.S. aims, according to Assistant Secretary of Defense McNaughton) precluded this option. The war was now indisputably an American enterprise.

Toward these developments, so momentous by July, the new Saigon government displayed an almost complete passivity. The Americans came in like bulldozers ("When we want to do something," Dean Rusk said to me some time later, "we do it!"), and the South Vietnamese followed

*Bundy, chapter 28, p. 1.

their lead without a word of dissent, for the most part without even a thought of dissent. After July 1965 the American build-up was so massive, so irresistible, and so fast that it simply left no room for doubt or second thoughts of any kind.

The marshaling of forces by the world's greatest power was an awesome sight, one that could not help but instill a sense of security in the South Vietnamese. The combined Vietcong and North Vietnamese army (NVA) spring–summer offensive that had been so threatening only a few weeks before simply evaporated in front of it. A new and unaccustomed feeling of confidence filled the air, and the entire country began gearing up to cope with the multitude of problems created by the arrival of the GIs.

U.S. army tent camps — small towns, actually — sprang up everywhere. Around them swarmed Vietnamese businessmen and small-time entrepreneurs vying to provide necessary services and take advantage of the thousands of new opportunities the situation offered. Construction boomed. It seemed the Americans wanted to build everything at once — warehouses, barracks, roads, bridges, helipads, ports, airports. They began changing the face of the country. U.S. contractors who arrived in the army's wake recruited thousands of workers overnight, sucking the labor pool dry. Traffic jammed the streets; prostitutes were all over the place. Transport planes and jet fighters roared in and out of the airports with a constant maddening din.

Paradoxically, while all this American activity heartened every Saigonese opposed to a Communist victory, it tended to divert people's attention from the war. Aside from the boom of the jets at Tan Son Nhut airport and the green-uniformed U.S. soldiers in the streets, it was hard to tell there was a war going on. Saigon appeared more like a city in the midst of some out of control economic miracle. The construction frenzy was complemented by an inundation of consumer goods, many of which the Saigonese had never seen before. They stared at the giant PX warehouses stacked full of appliances whose uses they could only guess at, and they wondered what kind of army this was that trailed such opulence with it. The citizens were reminded of the war, of course — by the black-bordered lists of names published regularly in the newspapers and by the funeral processions that occasionally snarled downtown traffic. But somehow one had the impression that there was little connection between the vicious fighting in the countryside and the boomtown life of the capital.

The biggest beneficiary of the changed shape of things was the Saigon government. Firmly entrenched behind the ever-growing American shield and invigorated by the thought that the country could now look to the future with at least some confidence, Thieu and Ky for the first time felt the helm steadying under their hands. A moment ago they were just another regime in a land where six had fallen in two years. Now they were leaders whose immediate military problem had dissolved and who were gaining substantial credibility with their countrymen, all of whom could see (or so they thought) where this American influx was taking them.

With the breathing space provided by the destruction of the Communist offensive, Thieu and Ky embarked on an ambitious program of reinforcing and reorganizing South Vietnam's armed forces. With American financial and logistical aid, huge training centers were created in Nha Trang and Vung Tau, and thousands of new recruits pushed through the doors. The South Vietnamese army began to reach toward the number of troops it would need to match those of its enemy.

At the same time, the Americans took full responsibility for waging war. They systematically brought in and deployed their troops, engaging the Communist main forces wherever they could find them and permitting the South Vietnamese army to concentrate on pacification activities. In several major engagements U.S. forces mauled Vietcong and NVA units, forcing the enemy over a period of time to switch tactics and regroup along the Cambodian border and in the dense, impenetrable jungle areas. General Westmoreland, the U.S. field commander in chief, formulated a three-pronged strategy that consisted of "search and destroy operations," then "clear and hold," or mopping up, operations, and finally "securing operations," in which Saigon troops would establish authority over pacified villages.

From a strictly tactical standpoint, almost all the early operations initiated by the American high command could be considered victories. They hit the enemy, inflicted casualties, and forced them to flee their bases. Yet in fact the successes were only partial. Main-force enemy units were often able to avoid combat altogether, and even when they were brought to battle, they had a disconcerting ability to slip away. Beyond that, Westmoreland's troops were prohibited from pursuing them into their sanctuaries in Laos and Cambodia, where the enemy could rest and regroup and fill in their ranks with reinforcements from North Vietnam.

As a result, the mobility and immense firepower of the Americans never was decisive. As long as the enemy could escape detection or melt into the jungle, as long as they had inviolable sanctuaries along the borders, it was they, not the Americans, who could dictate the tempo and level of confrontation. For the Communists, the whole Indochinese peninsula was a battlefield, while the American ground forces restricted themselves to South Vietnam.

This enormous, self-imposed disability gave the enemy the strategic initiative. With twenty years of hindsight, American military thinkers now speculate that in 1965 the U.S. army should not have poured hundreds of thousands of troops into Vietnam to take over the ground war. Instead, say people like Colonel Harry Summers, who wrote *On Strategy*, the highly regarded study of the war, American forces should have limited themselves to helping the South Vietnamese stabilize the military balance and then establishing an effective barrier to interdict the flow of men and supplies from North Vietnam.

For their part, South Vietnam's high command had serious misgivings about the American approach early on. But here, as on the political front, the Vietnamese did nothing, or more accurately, could not do anything to convey their doubts. General Cao Van Vien, chief of the South Vietnamese Joint General Staff, was only one of a number of senior officers who consistently advocated breaking the Ho Chi Minh Trail supply lines. A veteran of Laotian operations during the French war, he understood in detail what effective use Communist forces made of the sanctuaries. After the war I asked him why the South Vietnamese military did not press their views on the Americans. His answer reflected the psychology of our commanders at the time. "We did not have the strength to wipe out the sanctuaries ourselves," he told me, "and we had no say at all in the deployment of American forces. Besides, we depended so heavily on the Americans for almost everything that it was difficult to get our opinions taken into account."

The fact is that though it was our war and our country that was at stake, we were so junior a partner in the effort that our voices carried no weight. Undoubtedly, one reason for this was an inferiority complex we brought to the alliance. Another was our blind confidence in the United States, which suggested that however grave our doubts about a particular policy, in the larger scheme they were probably not consequential. The United States possessed such vast power and resources that it would do what it wanted regardless, and we believed it would be successful.

The fact was too that, reservations about Westmoreland's strategy notwithstanding, it did bring some victories. Whenever enemy troops were brought to battle, they suffered heavy casualties and were compelled to withdraw. And that gave us precious time to strengthen our own forces and extend government control into areas that were previously beyond our reach. The effect was not dramatic, but it was steady. And as the military situation improved, so did the political situation.

It was in this upbeat atmosphere of nascent success that President Johnson decided to invite Generals Thieu and Ky to a summit meeting in Honolulu — the first of its kind between the American and Vietnamese heads of state. To at least some of the American press, now beginning to show signs of cynicism toward its government, the idea of a summit seemed little more than a Lyndon Johnson public relations improvisation to deflect attention from the televised hearings of antiwar Senator William Fulbright's powerful Foreign Relations Committee. The fact that the invitation was formally delivered barely a week before the conference was to begin does suggest spontaneity. But whatever the motivation behind it, the summit could not have come at a more opportune moment for the Saigon government, and particularly for the two men who headed it.

In February of 1966 Nguyen Van Thieu and Nguyen Cao Ky had been in power only six months. They had first come to public attention scarcely six months before that, as leaders of the Young Turks, who had done at least their share to undermine the erratic rule of Nguyen Khanh. Then they had taken over after the serious but unfortunate civilian government of Dr. Phan Huy Quat. Though Thieu and Ky had certain military credentials, their potential as political leaders had not been altogether apparent to anyone. Now, a half year into their regime, they had achieved a measure of success, particularly in strengthening the armed forces and setting up a coordinated pacification program. In addition, although the religious and political groups that had shaken previous regimes to pieces had not completely abandoned their militancy, at least they were no longer demonstrating in the streets or threatening the government with imminent destruction. For the South Vietnamese, these were not insignificant achievements.

As a result, Thieu and Ky were at a turning point in their careers, making the transition from warlords to legitimate political leaders. So the summit was an especially important event. It gave them the opportunity to sound out U.S. intentions at the highest level, something that had been egregiously lacking until now. It also could not help but enhance their stature and perhaps affect their self-image as leaders of the country.

How each of them reacted to this transition would, of course, differ. Although Thieu and Ky had emerged together as by far the most substantial and intelligent of the Young Turks, as individuals they had practically nothing in common. In 1966 Thieu, a southerner, was forty-two years old and Ky, a northerner, only thirty-five. They were neither classmates nor even friends. In personality, temperament, and approach to problems it would be hard to find two people who differed so thoroughly. The South Vietnamese used to say that if the two were put in a blender, what came out would be a good deal better for the country than what went in.

Thrown together by compromise and necessity, their government operated by consensus among Thieu, Ky, and their military colleagues without the benefit of either electoral mandate or constitutional authority. Within the government Ky held the limelight; he was the prime minister, the chief executive officer who handled the day-to-day business of state. The real power, however, belonged to a loose group of military men usually called the Directorate, and their chairman was Nguyen Van Thieu.

A quiet man, more mature than the boyish Ky, Thieu had been around longer and was more politically experienced. Having witnessed many changes of government, he was more sensitive than Ky to the dangers of peaking too soon, while the ground was not yet solid underfoot. Ky, on the other hand, was naturally brash and incautious. He had no qualms at all about drawing attention to himself. For example, he commuted to work by helicopter — though he lived only two miles from the prime minister's office — engulfing the entire government complex in a deafening roar each morning as he arrived. He was always ready to talk off the cuff to the first newsman who happened by. But while Ky ran the government and drew the lion's share of publicity, Thieu was at work behind the scenes, cultivating his power base and exerting his influence on policy decisions.

The alliance between Thieu and Ky was obviously a temporary one; from the start the two saw each other as rivals and were constantly jockeying for position. But at the same time they shared a tacit understanding that as long as the war was critical, they would stay together and make sure the hybrid formula through which they shared power remained intact.

For these two men, just now coming into their own as leaders, Honolulu was a major event. The day the invitation was received, the entire government was mobilized to prepare for the meeting. The Joint General Staff was assigned to analyze the military situation and list our current and projected needs for aid. The energetic new minister for rural construction, General Nguyen Duc Thang, was to write a detailed report on the revised pacification program. I immersed myself in the work of coordinating the overall presentation and, even more important, of drafting the formal address that Prime Minister Ky would deliver to the assembled delegations.

Given the short notice and all the arranging that had to be done, Ky's speech was a great challenge. But I also considered it an opportunity. I had by that time fully reconciled myself to working with the military government. Over the past months I had come to regard Thieu and Ky as basically well-meaning individuals. Their commitment to governmental stability, for example, was as important to them as their personal ambitions and jealousies. Moreover, they were riding a wave of success brought about by the American intervention. And they were taking advantage of it, especially by beefing up our country's armed forces.

But in spite of these strengths, their government still lacked any real political direction. They were military people, and they had simply never given much thought to political or social concerns. Nevertheless, in my judgment they were also open minded, at least to an extent, even somewhat malleable — Ky substantially more so than Thieu.

I had, in fact, already quietly begun to do what I could to direct Ky's attention to the concept of social and economic reform and constitutional government that had been the consistent goal of Dr. Quat and the rest of our circle for almost two decades. In speeches I had written for him, I had been able to emphasize such themes as social justice, educational and economic opportunity, religious liberty, and certain other "inalienable rights." I had even dared touch on the subject of moving toward democratic government. As a speechwriter I tried hard not to obfuscate the hard facts that the regime was still an oligarchy, that progress was slow in coming, that the diseases of the past were difficult to cure. But the overriding aim was, as one of these speeches phrased it, "to have something to fight *for,* not merely against communism, but *for* a nation of progress nurtured by personal liberty."

As far as I was concerned, these were not just words. They were concrete goals that had to be achieved in good measure if South Vietnam was to find a purpose and cohesiveness that would enable it to survive the onslaught of a murderous and ideologically committed enemy. For the most part these ideas were not yet embodied in programs, but that was partially because Thieu and Ky were just beginning to awaken to the issues.

Surprisingly, Ky was responsive to discussions of such ideas. To a certain extent he was attracted to the fundamental concepts of democracy — enough to talk about them openly and perhaps even enough to slowly commit himself to them. Each time he put himself on record, it was another step away from rule by strongman and toward something better. The public record was not something easy to retreat from or treat cynically.

It was against this background that I began drafting the speech Ky would give in Honolulu. Although Ky was receptive to the concept of social revolution, neither I nor my friends knew to what extent he would be willing to fight for its adoption by his fellow generals. But if, at a summit meeting with the American president, the military leadership publicly committed itself to reforms and a schedule for implementing them, the course of events could not afterward be reversed.

With this in mind, I wrote the strongest speech I felt had a chance of being accepted by Ky. Along with the necessity of winning the war, I talked about the ideals of nation building, the creation of a constitution, and a return to civilian government. I trod a very fine line between what I would have liked to have Ky say and what I thought he would go along with, appealing implicitly to his heroic tendencies, his willingness to champion ideas for the sake of their drama as well as their substance. At the same time I diligently avoided initiating contact with Thieu's people, who I knew would take a jaundiced view of making such things explicit.

It was a delicate process. Thieu had carefully reviewed previous speeches I had written for Ky, and as a cautious man who habitually resisted making commitments, he had not liked whole sections of them. Typically, his aides would call me about this or that part of a draft, indicating the changes and deletions they considered necessary. At that point I would backtrack to Ky, asking him to take these subjects up with Thieu so we could retain important headings and phrases. Sometimes Ky would and sometimes he wouldn't, and then I would have to back off. Much depended on the complex relationship between the two of them, so I could never be completely certain what the outcome would be. But in the Honolulu speech, the one that really counted, the essentials were retained: the commitment to social and economic reforms and to the return of civilian government.*

In addition to the speech, I also prepared a long memo listing all the important questions I thought Ky should raise during his scheduled private conversation with President Johnson. This memo was consistent with the one I had written a few months earlier for the McNamara visit, stressing again our need to know America's long-term strategy and commitment.

At the conclusion of this intense week I was on the whole quite satisfied with our preparations and confident that the South Vietnamese delegation would make its case well in Honolulu. I was equally pleased, and somewhat intrigued, that during our consultations on the summit, the U.S. embassy had exerted little pressure on us. I had informed my two good friends at the embassy — Edward Lansdale and the new minister-counselor, Philip Habib — about the content of Ky's speech. Although they were pleased with our intention to commit publicly to constitutional government, they seemed more interested in the new pacification pro-

---

* Stanley Karnow wrote in his book *Vietnam: A History* that this speech was composed by Ky's American advisers. This is completely untrue. The ideas were developed by me and an informal civilian study group I had helped set up during the first months of the Thieu-Ky government. The only person who worked with me on the speech itself was Nguyen Ngoc Linh, then director of the Vietnam press.

gram and in counseling us about how to handle the international press that would be covering the summit.

U.S. Information Service Director Barry Zorthian in particular spent time briefing me about what questions to expect from journalists, emphasizing their aggressiveness and the need for careful preparation. The full-scale press conference was one aspect of the summit that I was really nervous about. I had never dealt with American reporters before, except on an individual basis. I did not trust my English, and Ky's English was terrifying. I told him repeatedly that if he ran into trouble, he should ask me and I would jump in to correct or elaborate. But I knew the man had no fear at all. With reporters especially he was a loose cannon.

Full of expectations, on February 6 we left Tan Son Nhut in a plane President Johnson had provided for the occasion. Henry Cabot Lodge and other embassy personnel traveled with us to what we believed would be a historic meeting. Still a novice at these things, I was impressed by the meticulous care with which the Americans had handled all the preliminary arrangements. I was also impressed by the list of people who would make up the American delegation: Rusk, McNamara, Rostow, Harriman, Wheeler, and other luminaries in addition to the president. This would be a gathering of most of those David Halberstam would later call "the best and the brightest." Reading over the names, my old friend Foreign Minister Tran Van Do said only half jokingly, "What an odd bunch of Lilliputians we are to be going into the land of Gulliver."

When the plane landed at Honolulu's military airport, the impression was reinforced. In the middle of a vast expanse of tarmac stood a welcoming platform planted with flags. As I watched from the sidelines, the tall American president towered over the two Vietnamese generals standing next to him, as if to provide a symbolic reminder of the respective roles played by the two governments. But if Johnson's physical appearance seemed out of scale, his welcoming address suggested the man's warmth and humanity. He spoke not only of "victory over aggression" but of "victory over hunger, disease, and despair." He talked about "health, education, agriculture, economics," and about "a better life for the common people." Of course it was a political speech, but the sentiments it expressed seemed heartfelt, and it encouraged those of us who also had a vision for South Vietnam after the war, one not too different from what we were hearing.

Not that there was much time to dwell on these reflections. As coordinator for our delegation, I went about making sure that everything was in place for the next day's formal sessions. Then in the early evening I joined my American counterparts to write the joint communiqué that would be released at the summit's conclusion. As every participant in international conferences of this sort knows, drafting the joint communiqué is the most tedious and least productive chore one can be subjected to, especially because it is usually written before the conference begins. But never having participated in such an affair before, I went into this meeting full of enthusiasm and sure that I was helping to make history.

Nothing about the communiqué made me change my opinion. Entitled the Declaration of Honolulu, the final draft pledged both sides to "defend against aggression, to work for social revolution and free self-government, and to seek peace." For the Vietnamese side the most demanding commitment was "to formulate a democratic constitution in the months ahead, to take it to the Vietnamese people for discussion and modification, to seek its ratification by secret ballot and finally to create, on the basis of elections, a representative government." When I took this back to Thieu and Ky for their approval, it was with a good deal of trepidation. The more general statements about defending against aggression and even working for social revolution would not cause problems. But getting Thieu and Ky to pledge themselves to a constitution and elections in the near future was another story.

To my great surprise and pleasure, however, neither of them balked at all at the wording, specific as it was. They were simply in too euphoric a mood after the day's events. So I quickly became euphoric myself, for they were now committed in black and white in an international document on which they could not possibly renege.

The conference was formally opened the next day in an auditorium at Pacific Command headquarters. The two delegations were spread around a huge oval conference table, but for everyone in the room it was clear that only one person counted. Lyndon Johnson completely dominated the session. His imposing stature, the attention he commanded among his advisers, and the sheer weight of his office all combined to create an undeniable aura of leadership. Leaning forward over the table to emphasize his points, the forceful, energetic president was in full display. The Vietnamese could not have been more impressed.

Johnson listened intently to Ky's speech, then heard General Thang describe the pacification program. On occasion he interrupted Thang to ask a question or give instructions to one of the aides sitting behind him. His comments were persuasive and to the point. Some were also colorful. At one point he said that he wanted to see "the coonskins on the wall," a colloquialism that left the Vietnamese delegation mystified. Several people leaned toward me, the supposed expert in English, and asked, *"Ong ay noi cai gi the?"* ("Just what is this gentleman talking about?")

But exactly what words he used did not matter. The overall message could not have been clearer. He wanted concrete results from both the Americans and the South Vietnamese. His intensity was unmistakable, as was his impatience to get things accomplished. On the Vietnamese side, Thieu spoke little, preferring for his own reasons to let Ky play the lead role. Rusk, too, sat silent with his Buddha face while Secretary McNamara, as always, scribbled away on his yellow pad.

We broke for lunch with everyone feeling we had gotten off to an excellent start. In the afternoon the two delegations split up into working groups while Thieu and Ky met privately with Johnson.

As far as I could see, the Texan president, at the height of his powers, had almost nothing in common with the two Vietnamese generals whose country was so dependent on American aid — except, of course, that all three were deeply and mutually engaged against the same enemy. But the personal chemistry was favorable that day, and after two hours of private talks, the three leaders emerged smiling. The two Vietnamese were completely seduced by Johnson's sincerity and folksy manner, and he seemed to have gotten along well with them, too — especially with Ky. The two of them were seen huddling cozily over cups of coffee, as if they had been buddies for years.

Despite the fact that there was no comprehensive review of issues, the Honolulu conference was considered a success by all. Lyndon Johnson had had an opportunity to meet with all his senior advisers and military commanders and to impress upon them the importance of pacification. He had had a chance to listen to the South Vietnamese leaders and size them up. The president had also gotten a commitment from them to write a constitution and hold elections.

Most important, perhaps, Honolulu was a public relations coup for Johnson. In answer to the criticism from doves that he was relying solely on military might to solve what were essentially political problems, Johnson emphasized health, education, textbooks, fertilizer, and rural electrification. And it was evident that behind the talk was a commitment to rebuild the countryside and an understanding that without a positive program to win the loyalty of the people, all the force in the world would not suffice.

Thieu and Ky could not have been happier. They had received the full backing of the American administration, not only for waging the war but for consolidating their regime. Ky was especially elated. He had hit it off with Johnson and had basked in the full light of the media. He had been so happy with the way the conference developed that he had not even bothered to raise with Johnson the themes I had outlined in my memorandum. When I asked him about that on the eve of our return to Saigon, he brushed my concerns aside, saying, "Look, the old man is so sincere you can't doubt for a minute what his plans are."

Despite this, I, too, had reason to be pleased. Not only had the speech been delivered, putting the government on record as I had hoped it would, but Johnson had taken special notice of it. In private he had even asked Ky to elaborate on the "social revolution" part of what he had said. Since the speech had struck a chord with Johnson, Ky realized that, in effect, I had been instrumental in boosting his image with the president. To some degree at least, the result was that my own position with Ky had been consolidated. From here on I would be less of an outsider.

With these developments, I experienced my own kind of elation on the return trip. I had worked hard for this moment, spurred by my obsession to create conditions that would preclude the suicidal anarchy of 1963 and 1964. Now, after all the chaos of the preceding years, I had by chance found myself at a kind of confluence of history, a moment when American goals and the development of democratic politics in Vietnam were finally in overt sympathy. Circumstances were at last conspiring toward stability rather than disintegration.

Chapter 20

Second Step

OUR SATISFACTION at the end of the Honolulu conference was boosted even further when Johnson asked Vice President Hubert Humphrey to accompany the South Vietnamese delegation home. Humphrey had not been at the conference, but now Johnson thought he could keep up the momentum by dispatching him on an Asian tour to inform the region's leaders of the new direction of American policy as defined in Honolulu. So Humphrey flew out from the United States, planning to stop first in Saigon and then in the region's other capitals. At that stage of the war, the vice president was still in a positive mood, and the emphasis on social and economic programs fit right in with his own brand of liberalism. His presence on the flight back brought an additional vigor and ebullience to our group, reinforcing the confidence the summit had generated.

Unfortunately, the added prestige Thieu and Ky were now enjoying did not put them completely out of reach of the domestic broils that had brought down all their predecessors. Given the tradition of intrigue and coups d'etat that had ingrained itself in South Vietnam's political life, it was predictable that the two generals would have to face down at least one major attempt to unseat them. That attempt occurred in March 1966, scarcely a month after their triumphant return from Hawaii. Again it was the Buddhists who triggered it, this time in conjunction with the powerful and ambitious military commander of South Vietnam's northern war zone, General Nguyen Chanh Thi.

The confrontation had in fact been simmering for months. This General Thi was something of a maverick who in his day had participated in a number of coups and countercoups. He had headed the failed coup against Ngo Dinh Diem in 1960, which had, in a way, initiated the whole idea of coup making. He had lent his support to Nguyen Khanh in the coup that brought down the anti-Diem generals in 1964. Then he had switched his allegiance to the Young Turks in the internal war that ended with Khanh's ouster in 1965. With this distinguished background, and with warlord powers in his northern domain, General Thi considered himself at least as qualified to rule as Thieu and Ky.

Hue, the capital city of General Thi's Military Region One, was also the stronghold of the militant Buddhists and their leader Thich Tri Quang. Although the Buddhists had been relatively quiet since Thieu and Ky's ascendance, they had not been happy. Their consistently antimilitary disposition was now seriously aggravated because they had no entrée whatsoever in this government. Thieu was Catholic, and although Ky was Buddhist, he had no time at all for the militant variety of monks.

In early March the combination of General Thi's brooding anger and the Buddhists' political frustration ignited the crisis. On a trip to Hue, Nguyen Cao Ky was snubbed by the resentful northern warlord, who was overheard saying loudly to one of his aides, "What is this little man doing here anyway?" Furious, Ky took the remark not just as a personal affront but also as a direct challenge to the government. That, at least, was how it appeared. Or perhaps Ky was looking for an occasion to confront the obstreperous general. In any case, returning to Saigon, the prime minister got approval from the rest of the military leadership for Thi's dismissal. But this act gave the Buddhists in Hue their opening to launch demonstrations and demand the resignation of the military government. These were events only the most rabid coup hounds could enjoy, and perhaps only Gilbert and Sullivan could do full justice to.

By March 26, what had started as a potentially insignificant personal incident had grown into a full-scale rebellion in the northern region. The radio stations in Hue and Danang were taken over by demonstrators, and the area's civil authorities declared their neutrality between General Thi and the Buddhists on one side and the central government on the other. A military confrontation was only barely avoided when Prime Minister Ky sent intermediaries to the Buddhists, promising a constitutional assembly and a civilian government by the end of the year.

Although Ky succeeded in thus defusing the rebellion, residual demonstrations died down only slowly. And because Ambassador Lodge had supported Ky during the crisis, Buddhist anger was now directed at the United States as well. The final episode of the drama, which began on May 4, was the result of a typically injudicious remark made by Ky to a reporter. Asked about the constitutional assembly he had promised the Buddhists, Ky answered that although it would be held, his military government would not immediately relinquish power but would stay on until a constitution was formally promulgated. While no one knew for sure the details of the assurances Ky had given the Buddhists a month earlier, Buddhist leaders now denounced him for cynically reneging on his promises, and the protests began anew.

This time a military confrontation was unavoidable. In Danang Ky moved in quickly with his crack marine battalions, and after several days of fighting, most of the Buddhists and dissident soldiers had been routed. A scary situation developed when U.S. General Lewis Walt opposed the use of the South Vietnamese air force to bomb the rebels and threatened to shoot down any planes that tried. But in the end Ky gave in and mopped up the remaining opposition using only ground forces. After a dangerous week the situation in Danang was almost back to normal.

Hue, though, was a different story. There the confrontation continued, reaching its peak when Buddhist crowds burned the U.S. Information Service library on May 26 and the U.S. consulate on May 30. For some time the demonstrations had been taking on an increasingly ugly anti-American tone, and the two buildings were natural targets. Although after Danang there was no chance that the insurgents would succeed in any of their goals, the conflagration in Hue was not completely extinguished until mid-June. At its conclusion, the original instigator, General Thi, left the country for exile, needless to say, in the United States.

Although the Hue uprising had lasted, in varying degrees of intensity, for more than three months, when it was finally over, it marked the end of what might be considered South Vietnam's adolescent rebellion. After the fall of Ngo Dinh Diem, we had suffered from a three-year bout of self-destructiveness, the legacy of a decade's worth of autocracy and repression. But the end of the Buddhist crisis was also the beginning of a period of relative political stability that would last until the final days of the Saigon regime in April 1975.

No one then, however, anticipated that this would be the start of a new phase. On the contrary, it was an extremely trying period that gave no reason to expect any future amelioration. At the same time other disturbing concerns were surfacing on the battlefield.

In the first place, South Vietnam's army had become a close witness to the American style of waging war. Vietnamese soldiers, no less than Vietnamese civilians, looked with amazement on the logistical miracle that sprang into being to serve the GIs. They saw the vast PXs with their dazzling array of goods aimed at easing the hardship of American soldiers who were fighting ten thousand miles from home. They saw the endless stream of military supplies that were funneled into the American units — though not, they noted, into their own. They knew the Americans were spending vast sums on bombs and shells, which they used with such prodigality. They were, on the one hand, resentful. On the other, they were already acquiring the idea that this was the correct way to fight a war. It was a style to which they would become habituated in a short time, and that would prove disastrous to them when the Americans eventually withdrew their support.

Beyond that, with General William Westmoreland's search and destroy strategy moving into high gear, by the spring of 1966 the American-inspired pattern of warfare began to create very serious problems in the countryside. The U.S. army rule of thumb for engagement was "expend shells, not men." Among other things, this meant that practically every operation of any size was preceded by "softening-up" bombardments by artillery or naval gunfire, or by B-52s or other air strikes. One consequence was that the element of surprise was almost always lost, and huge operations often turned up only a few enemy snipers and the remnants of bases. More important, the lavish use of firepower also resulted in horrible casualties for the villagers and peasants in areas where these operations took place.

This possibility had been anticipated, and originally Westmoreland's strategy was to utilize his forces away from populated areas and try to find and kill the enemy in the sparsely inhabited highland regions or along the Laotian and Cambodian borders. In addition, detailed rules of engagement (ROEs) were worked out in cooperation with South Vietnamese authorities which were designed to minimize casualties and the destruction of property among civilians.

As worthy as these intentions were, their implementation proved problematic. It was not so easy to find the elusive enemy in the places Americans chose to look. One of the guerrillas' main tactics was to conceal themselves among the peasants who lived in the countryside. Knowing the American habit of responding to contact with overwhelming firepower, they often deliberately provoked shelling or air strikes on villages to foment hatred of the GIs. Beyond that, although U.S. bombardment of suspected enemy concentrations technically had to have the advance approval of South Vietnamese provincial authorities, in fact officials often gave their permission automatically, without taking the local inhabitants into account. As a result, inaccurate and indiscriminate shelling and bombing frequently caused incalculable suffering.

Given the nature of the war, with no established lines and guerrillas mixing with noncombatants, the military people were making very little headway in trying to prevent needless casualties. I and others met with Westmoreland many times to discuss our deep concerns about the situation. We knew that the human tragedy was immense and the effect on international public opinion devastating. But we were fighting a war whose venue and circumstances were largely defined by the enemy. It was a constantly frustrating paradox: although the Vietcong and the North Vietnamese were conducting what they called a people's war, which by its nature drew the civilian population into the carnage, blame for the massive destruction and the consequent uprooting of the rural population all devolved on the Americans and the South Vietnamese. It was a burden we would carry for the rest of the war.

In 1966 the mounting American and civilian casualties and the devastation in the countryside created an increasingly hostile climate of world public opinion. In June the sharp but occasional criticism of U.S. policy in Vietnam among America's European allies suddenly became an open rift, particularly after a series of bombing attacks against industrial and petroleum storage areas in the vicinity of Hanoi and Haiphong. Prime Minister Harold Wilson declared that the British "disassociated ourselves from the bombings," and Charles de Gaulle condemned the attacks as "a reckless escalation of the Vietnam conflict."

Within several years, the use of massive bombing and firepower in inhabited areas — with all the horror and population displacement that resulted — would create a swell of international protest about the immorality of the war. It proved impossible for foreign journalists and television reporters to see the strategy and tactics of the Communists, whose theory of revolutionary struggle counted noncombatants as essential elements in the war. And because they did not see this side of things, neither did their readers and viewers. As a result, the debates about morality raged on in a completely one-sided forum, which in mid-1966 was just beginning to be heard from.

The emerging pattern of warfare — the inconclusiveness of the search and destroy strategy and its impact on civilians — was a deepening problem. But other, positive developments were also taking place. With the Buddhist crisis finally over, in June the government was able to focus its attention on elections for the promised constitutional assembly.

For nations with long democratic traditions, voting may be a relatively simple procedure. For South Vietnam, new to the whole idea, it was not. Consequently, the first item on the agenda was to publicize the concept of elections and impress people with the importance of going to the polls. To this end, the government enlisted the services of the country's actors, comedians, musicians, and singers to spread the word. Popular songs were ingeniously adapted to promote the idea. The radio was full of music and sketches on the subject, and troupes toured the countryside, putting on shows and concerts aimed at getting out the vote. These efforts were amusing and, I thought, quite wonderful. As one of the songs put it, in a refrain everyone heard over and over, "Our future depends on democracy." For several months the country was inundated with that message.

While the popular campaign was going on, a special committee was chosen from among the various political parties and religious groups to draft an election law. Before long, the committee was involved in a fierce debate over who could run for the assembly. There was no controversy at all about excluding Communists, but there was about candidates who had "neutralist tendencies." Eventually, the hard liners won on this issue, and no one who "openly advocated a solution in favor of the Communists" was permitted to run. It was a poor resolution to the problem, but I was not greatly concerned; not that much was riding on it. This would be a short-lived assembly whose only purpose was to draw up a constitution. After that it would be dissolved. In the end a wide variety of candidates stood for election: lawyers, professors, farmers, retired military men, and journalists, along with politicians and representatives of religious groups.

September 11 was election day. Despite threats of violence from the Vietcong and a Buddhist warning about a possible boycott, there was a great show of enthusiasm from the people. They came to the polls en masse, most of them wearing their holiday clothes. Of the seven million registered voters, more than five million cast ballots for 117 assembly delegates out of 630 candidates. Although there were occasional irregularities, on the whole the voting was a great success. For a country in the middle of a war, with no electoral tradition, it was a remarkable event fraught with significance for the future. As one of my American friends put it, "There is a joyous, festive, and optimistic mood in the air, and it gives us hope."

It gave me hope as well. Once instituted, democratic procedures tend to develop their own momentum. As soon as people get the idea they have a say in government, when they see that politicians are forced to court them, new configurations of power inevitably emerge. Of necessity, mechanisms spring up to chart and influence the popular will. Political energy is channeled into open confrontation in the struggle for consensus instead of into the application of force and cunning in the service of personal ambition.

The election was a beginning, a first step. Although this was only a constitutional assembly and the military government would still have the power of final approval, it would be hard for Thieu and Ky to reject its work. Little by little, the politics of democracy would take hold. The military government would have no alternative but to give way before it.

* * *

In the fall of 1966 it was evident that Saigon had, in fact, come a long way. For the first time in years we had a government that was not living in constant fear of the next coup or factional revolt, that could attend to the normal business of governing and to the conduct of war. We had made the first approach to transforming the political system into something worthy of the nation.

After so many years of frustration and despair, these achievements were as welcome in Washington as in Saigon. Angry about the growing, if still small, antiwar movement at home and the antagonism in Europe to his bombing policy, Lyndon Johnson decided to take advantage of the moment to demonstrate that the United States was not alone in its support for an embattled ally.

Over the previous months American diplomats had succeeded in shaping a de facto alliance of Asian and Pacific nations that had agreed to join the American effort. Thailand, the Philippines, South Korea, Australia, and New Zealand had sent either combat troops or support units to Vietnam. This diplomatic achievement coincided with the new spirit of optimism in South Vietnam, arising from the just completed constitutional assembly elections. Although the war was still lurching on inconclusively, President Johnson saw this as a good time to show the world that the United States had friends in the fight and that the struggle to protect South Vietnam's independence was bearing fruit.

At Johnson's urging, President Ferdinand Marcos of the Philippines agreed to host an international conference in Manila at the end of October, to which the governing heads of all the countries that had troops in Vietnam were invited. In fact, in his efforts to garner additional support, Johnson had already scheduled a tour of these nations, and Manila happened to be the halfway point on his seventeen-day itinerary. So it was a logical choice for the meeting.

Although the Seven Nations Manila Summit was clearly a public relations exercise on the grand Johnsonesque scale, for us it was also an important affair with its own significance, and we welcomed it. As a small nation whose existence was threatened, South Vietnam needed international recognition and guarantees. With Saigon's newfound stability and our recent progress toward free elections, the time was right for us to improve our diplomatic posture abroad. We were also eager to do whatever we could to further the international aspect of the fighting. Because we had had to accept the presence of so many foreign troops on our soil, we felt that an international force would be perceived as less of a threat to our sovereignty and dignity than troops from one power — a "lesser evil," as we called it.

Since shortly after the Honolulu conference, I had become more and more involved in foreign policy decisions. At that time there was a cabinet reshuffle that led to my appointment as deputy foreign minister, in addition to my job as special assistant to the prime minister. The move was one result of the constant friction in the Thieu-Ky government between the military and the few civilian officials. One of the civilians, my old friend Tran Van Do, was foreign minister. Do was a real gentleman, not nearly aggressive enough for the military circle, and in March they moved to have him replaced.

But Phil Habib (then minister-counselor at the embassy) had a high regard for Do, and when the Saigon rumor mill informed him of the impending dismissal, he rushed over to my office to ask about it. I told him that Ky and his group had asked me to consider taking over the foreign minister's portfolio, but that I had refused. Do was such a long-time colleague, a "big brother" of sorts, there was no way I would replace him.

As we talked, Habib became increasingly worried. Do enjoyed universal respect, and I was a known quantity with whom the Americans had dealt for years. But if neither of us was at the foreign ministry, then who would be? Someone, perhaps, who met all the requirements of the military people, but with whom the embassy would have real problems. Habib did not like the whole thing. In the end, all those involved were able to reach a compromise: Do stayed on as foreign minister, and I was appointed deputy foreign minister with substantial responsibilities. The hardline generals were not pleased, but because the U.S. embassy was, they found ways to accept it. For me it was a victory. I retained one of my few allies in the ongoing conflict with the military for influence on policymaking. In the drive to realize a constitutional government, it was a valuable win.

So, since the Honolulu summit, I had been working in the foreign ministry, trying to improve our relations with other states in the region and increase our visibility around the world. Preparation for the Manila conference thus fell naturally on my shoulders.

Ostensibly, four subjects would figure on the agenda: an overview of the current war situation, a review of the peace proposals that had so far been advanced, consideration of possible measures to end the war, and a plan for regional security. But during preparations for the conference, it quickly became clear that the national interests of seven countries were simply too diverse and the important issues too numerous to be covered in two days of talks, with their inevitable interruptions for meals, receptions, technical meetings, and other official functions. What was left, then, was the show of solidarity. And indeed, the mere fact that seven chiefs of state were able to meet and see eye to eye on the overriding issues did have its own significance.

As usual, Lyndon Johnson dominated the conference. He talked enthusiastically about U.S. commitments in Asia, his desire for peace, and his determination to fight communism. "For free men," he said, "for responsible men, for men of conscience, there just is no acceptable alternative but to resist aggression." The other participants agreed, although some of them were less than voluble. Thailand's white-haired Field Marshal Kittikachorn rarely opened his mouth. The icy Park Chung Hee of South Korea said even less. But Harold Holt, the Australian prime minister (whose policy of "LBJ all the way" was well known), was not at all reticent in pledging his country's backing, nor was Keith Holyoake of New Zealand. Meanwhile, Ferdinand Marcos obviously enjoyed his role as host, flitting from one leader to another, making himself as visible as possible.

When the two days were up, a final grandiloquent declaration was signed by all the participants. Critics of the war might say the declaration was long on platitudes and short on substance, but we, at least, were pleased by the renewed affirmations of support and by the promise that American and other allied forces would be withdrawn as soon as the aggression had ended.

The signing ceremony was followed by a procession from the Manila Hotel to Malacañan, the presidential palace. It was quite an event, the leaders walking together in a row, with Johnson towering above the others. Behind the heads of state paraded the foreign ministers, and behind them the rest of the delegations. The crowds lining the streets cheered, and hundreds of reporters and cameramen bustled around, turning the procession into an extravaganza. Our American friends obviously enjoyed it, and none of the other leaders seemed to complain about all the attention either.

At the lavish fiesta that crowned the evening, almost everyone was in a relaxed, festive mood. I was not, however. The previous day, the continuing friction between the regime's military advisers and me had surfaced in a nasty fashion. Thieu, Ky, and I were having dinner with Generals Co and Vien. In a light moment Co, one of the hard liners who had wanted to oust Foreign Minister Do, joked, "Well, this time when we get back to Saigon we ought to have Bui Diem's skin." I got angry and snapped back something about how "I work for the country, and nobody attacks me, even in fun." At this, Cao Van Vien, the chief of staff, put in, only half humorously, "If anyone wants to touch Diem, he'll have to go through my airborne troops." Co backed down, mumbling that it was only a joke. But I was really sore about it — a sign, I suppose, of the pressure I was feeling from the military.

By the time of the closing festivities, the rest of the South Vietnamese delegation had become quite nervous as well, but for a different reason. Earlier in the day, Phil Habib had come up to our quarters asking to talk to Thieu and Ky. President Johnson, he said, had decided to make a quick visit to the American base at Cam Ranh Bay directly following the conference. But for security reasons he would not be coming to Saigon.

We understood the security rationale all too well: with the not infrequent terrorist incidents in Saigon, there was good reason to exercise great caution. But we still felt humiliated by the way this was being handled. As it was, we wouldn't even have time to prepare a decent welcome for the president.* So, even as Marcos's fiesta was in full swing, our thoughts were focused on getting back home in time to arrange at least some kind of reception for Johnson the next day.

Although we tried to put the best face on it, Johnson's visit to Cam Ranh was like a slap in the face. The president of the United States was taking the time to tour six Asian capitals, and yet he would not visit Saigon, the capital of an allied country where more than 300,000 of his countrymen were fighting. Of course we understood that there was a war on and that no chances could be taken with the president's personal safety. Still, the open lack of confidence in our ability to protect him was humiliating. The South Vietnamese swallowed this bitter pill, not knowing that in ensuing years there would be more to come — part of the price we would pay for our overdependence on the United States.

So it was that President Johnson came to Cam Ranh on October 26, 1966. He spent just half a day there. Addressing the welcoming crowd of GIs, he declared, "I give you my pledge. We shall never let you down, not your fighting comrades, not the fifteen million people of South Vietnam, nor the hundreds of millions of Asians who are counting on us to show here — here in Vietnam — that aggression cannot succeed."

* Habib told me later that the American security people had been uncomfortable about informing Thieu and Ky at all, but he had insisted that Johnson simply could not visit without giving the Vietnamese at least some advance warning.

Chapter 21

Ambassador to Washington

I RETURNED FROM MANILA in bad shape. A severe case of flu I had picked up there kept me in bed for almost a week, which gave me plenty of time to just lie still and think. I realized I was very tired, not just physically but mentally too. I was especially tired of the low-level war the military circle had been carrying on against me for several months now, in which General Co's remark about getting rid of me was only the latest irritation.

In fact, the generals were becoming increasingly unhappy with some of Prime Minister Ky's policies, particularly his "precipitate" move toward constitutionality. His efforts to clean out some of the more egregiously corrupt and incompetent among them was also creating a strong backlash. Because the hard liners were unable to attack Ky directly, they focused their displeasure on me, since I was evidently the man behind Ky in these things.

Ky was under criticism from the southernists as well, who were accusing him of relying too heavily on northerners, and here too I was the most visible. In response, Ky was preparing to reshuffle his cabinet, and although I felt secure enough in my position, I was bothered by the fact that the sniping was bound to get worse.

I reflected too that I had already achieved at least something of what I had set out to do. There was some satisfaction in knowing that the road to civilian government was now prepared and that the constitutional assembly would be finished with its work before too long. As I mused about the situation I found myself more and more attracted by the idea of retiring. In part I was angry about taking so much criticism — unfounded, in my opinion. But I also began to think that it is important to know when to leave, to be able to bow out gracefully instead of waiting until your position is so undermined that you are forced out.

When I finally got well and went back to work, I took the matter up with Ky. Informally, without any dramatics, I mentioned to him in the middle of one of our meetings that perhaps the time was right for me to go. I told him that I knew he was under a lot of pressure from the southerners about the excessive number of northerners in the government, and that he was being criticized by some of the military people as well. Since I was one of the objects of all the pressure, this would seem an ideal moment for my departure. He could take advantage of the opportunity I was giving him and he could, of course, continue to count on my help from the outside.

Ky did not say a word. After a brief silence, he simply went on with what we had been talking about previously. But I had obviously presented the idea at the right moment, just as he was thinking hard about changing his cabinet. Several days later I brought the subject up again, asking him what he thought about my suggestion. It was then that he told me it would be better perhaps if I did not leave the government but took an ambassadorial post instead.

On reflection, that didn't sound bad at all. I especially liked Tokyo, where I had visited frequently as deputy foreign minister. Word even began to get around the foreign ministry that I had been given the ambassador's job there. But the prospect was short lived. Several days later Ky called me in and said, "Well, if you do take a post abroad, it should be Washington, not Tokyo." It took a number of weeks to make the necessary arrangements, but shortly after Christmas 1966, my family and I were boarding a plane at Tan Son Nhut on the first leg of the flight to the United States.

Although I was looking forward to the new job in Washington, my anticipation was tempered by more than just passing feelings of inadequacy. My hopes about making an unhurried, low-key start evaporated quickly, however, when my arrival in Washington was announced prominently by both the *New York Times* and the *Washington Post*. According to the *Post,* I was one of Prime Minister Ky's "most influential advisers"; the *Times* declared that I had "an important role in the formation of both foreign and domestic policy and in the conduct of press relations." Because Vietnam was news, apparently that meant I was news too. The two articles propelled me into the foreground, an area in which I was not used to operating and where at first I felt quite uncomfortable.

My initiation proceeded two days later when I went to the White House to formally present my credentials. White House protocol for such occasions did not include horse-drawn carriages *à la* the Court of St. James's, but it had its own, more democratic kind of majesty. The marines at the outer door saluted, and inside the Oval Office a fire crackled in the hearth, its warmth contrasting agreeably with the icy weather and snow-covered grounds outside the window. As I looked around the room, it passed fleetingly through my mind that this was a long way from the time I had waited in line to meet Major Patti and General Gallagher at the Vietnamese-American Friendship Society in Hanoi, half a lifetime ago.

When he greeted me, President Johnson was as warm as the fire. Although this was not the time for a substantive talk, he inquired about the situation in Vietnam as if it preoccupied him. Then, after a brief discussion, he presented me to the White House press corps, who had their own brand of questioning for me.

A week and a half later my acclimatization to the media continued with an appearance on *Meet the Press*. This was an event I looked forward to with all the eagerness of a lamb on its way to the slaughter, which was the delicate way one of my American friends referred to the occasion. Of course I had had experience with Western journalists in South Vietnam, but that was on my own turf, where the ground rules were mine rather than theirs. Here, Lawrence Spivak, Max Frankel, Peter Lisagore, Carl Rowan, and Ron Nessen would be interrogating me with no holds barred for half an hour. Spivak, the moderator, talked to me at length beforehand, trying to judge if my English was adequate for the ordeal. In the end neither of us was sure, so we had Dang Duc Khoi, from our embassy, sit in as an interpreter in case he was needed.

Dang Duc Khoi was not only a fluent English speaker but also a keen observer of American culture who had lived in Washington for many years. He briefed me about what to expect from the press, emphasizing their typically skeptical and adversarial orientation. During our preparation session in the small apartment I had rented near the embassy, he threw all the tough questions at me — about corruption, official optimism, Ky's flamboyance, peace negotiations — everything he could think of.

My tactic for all of them was to take the bull by the horns. I could not, for example, deny that corruption existed. It did, to a shameful degree. But I could explain why it existed and describe measures the government was taking against it. As I prepared for the show, my confidence grew. I had, after all, been dealing with these problems for two years. So I had at my fingertips all the knowledge I needed to answer any question.

As it turned out, I did not need Khoi's help as an interpreter; my English was up to it, although I did not know at first that on television you had to give brief, incisive answers. The panel asked intelligent questions, but when I tried to qualify my statements and convey the complexity of the situation, Spivak would interrupt me and move on. After two or three instances like this, I realized I would just have to plunge in and take risks. These people wanted really short, specific answers regardless of the intricacy of the issue they were asking about.

They wanted to know, for example, whether Saigon would negotiate with the Vietcong's National Liberation Front. I told them we would not, because the Front was controlled by Hanoi. On the other hand, we would be willing to sit down with the North Vietnamese at any time. Well, they said, the Front has soldiers in the field, they are full participants in the fighting, why won't you negotiate with them? It was difficult to compress into a three-word answer my experience of Vietminh-controlled front organizations from the French war; or the fact that the NLF was founded only in 1960, after the Third Party Congress in Hanoi had resolved to liberate South Vietnam and forcibly reunify the country; or that Liberation Army troops had been infiltrating from North to South Vietnam since 1959 while entire North Vietnamese divisions had been operating in our country since 1964; or that COSVN, the revolution's headquarters for South Vietnam, was the politburo's branch office, established and completely controlled by the party leaders in Hanoi. All of these facts were well known by both the Saigon and Washington governments at the time. (Since 1975, they have also been acknowledged in the Communist party's official accounts of the war.) But how was one to communicate all this in a phrase to journalists who assumed that none of it was true?

Despite the rush and the antagonistic tone of the questions, when it was all over I did not consider it a bad performance. I was surprised by the intensity of the debate, and I obviously had a lot to learn — especially about the way Americans liked their information. But I had successfully avoided being eaten by the wolves. I even found afterward that some of the journalists were decent, friendly people, in spite of their professional enmity toward anyone who worked for a government.

I spent the better part of my first few weeks in Washington making the de rigueur calls in the diplomatic community and initial contacts with key administration officials, congressmen, and senators. It snowed on and off during those weeks, the white flakes and bracing air giving my daughters their first taste of winter, a dramatic contrast to Saigon's torpid humidity.

Even more striking than the change in weather was the difference in outlook. In Saigon the war was part of daily life, and because it was, people tended to take it for granted. It even seemed somehow remote, at times almost an abstraction. But in Washington, ten thousand miles from danger, the war seemed strangely close. Each morning I woke up to it on the front page of the *Times* and the *Post;* I spent my days talking about it; then ended the evening watching it on the news. I did not realize then that I was experiencing the Vietnam War's special power to invade the consciousness of people distant from the fighting via their television screens. Much less did it occur to me that this revolutionary dimension of the war would slowly erode the patience of the American people and would eventually force an end to United States involvement in it.

The pace of life in Washington was different too. As Ky's special assistant, I had spent my days in Saigon dealing with seemingly endless crises, a profusion of urgent problems regarding the war or politics or the Americans or foreign policy, each one demanding immediate attention. For an adrenaline addict it would have been heaven. For me it was not, and though I coped well enough, it was only at a substantial personal cost. But in Washington I woke up, read the morning papers thoroughly, then embarked on my schedule of appointments. There were few sudden developments and no urgent crises; the workday progressed in an orderly fashion. Outside the snow fell gently, adding to the reigning serenity. After three years of constant pressure, it was a welcome change.

Washington was also a vast challenge. For someone from a country the size of South Vietnam, Congress alone was a huge and marvelously complex institution. With its 435 representatives, 100 senators, hundreds and hundreds of aides, and dozens of committees and subcommittees, even charting who was who and who did what was a little like exploring some dense virgin forest.

But I quickly got help from a number of people in finding my way around. My first meeting with Everett Dirksen, the Senate minority leader, was facilitated by an instant rapport. His advice gave me an excellent start on understanding how the system worked. Among other things, he suggested that I concentrate on meeting key members of important committees like Foreign Relations and Armed Services, and he often took the lead in arranging the introductions for me.

My early contacts and meetings were extremely useful, but I had not expected them to grow into friendships that I would enjoy long after my tenure as ambassador was over. George Aiken, the senior senator from Vermont, was one such friend. "The governor," as his wife, Lola, called him, took me under his wing, treating me as if I were a younger brother. We often met for long talks in his office or in the embassy when he and his wife came for dinner, and he would offer his advice.

A close friend of Mike Mansfield's, Aiken would often interpret for me the Senate majority leader's views. He also frequently helped convey my feelings to Mansfield and to many of his other friends in Congress, both

Republicans and Democrats. A simple and immensely decent New England, Aiken also had an ironic sense of humor. While taking pains to assure me that he did not favor what he called a "bug out" from Vietnam, he would still push me for a reaction to his now famous formula: "declare victory and get out."

Aiken's advice was invariably to the point. He impressed on me the value of preparation, of knowing a congressman's voting record and orientation before going to see him. In Aiken's view it was a waste of time to talk to vehement opponents; far better to concentrate on those who had not yet committed themselves. It was also a rule of thumb with him never to take friends for granted, but to make every effort to keep up and improve good relations.

All of this might have been elementary to Washington hands, but for a man who had lived all his life in a country with no tradition of popular government it was fascinating. I recognized, not without some awe, that I was right at the heart of a functioning democracy, elegant and robust but also strikingly complicated. All these congressmen and senators had their own constituencies and their own distinct problems. Whether or not you could get their support depended largely on how it would go over in their districts, where Vietnam was merely one concern among many. That in itself came as a surprise to me. I had assumed that Vietnam would be *the* problem for many of them. But in 1967 that was not the case.

Another revelation was that although some of the people I was meeting were men of the highest intellect and stature, others, even a number of the biggest names, clearly were not. It was a shock to find naked ignorance where I had expected erudition and brilliance, and at times I was startled by the bizarre questions I was asked. In a way it was natural that congressmen would know intimately the concerns of their constituents but be completely uninformed about international issues. But encounters with these congressmen always left me with an uncomfortable, edgy feeling. I had difficulty adjusting to the fact that someone who had not the vaguest idea that Vietnam had once been a French colony would be voting on questions essential to my country's survival.

I also had trouble comprehending the more dogmatic doves in Congress, like Senators McGovern, Fulbright, and Church. Although Aiken more than once offered to introduce me, I wanted nothing whatsoever to do with them. It was not that I had any hesitance about confronting their ideas, but I found their posturing insulting. Some of those who opposed the war were clearly sincere and decent people. Senator Mansfield, for example, was a strong opponent. But he was also a rational and civil human being who respected the war's complexity and understood that

Above: The Bui family in 1935.
Front row: fourth from right,
my father; fifth from right,
my mother. Back row: far right,
Bui Diem; fifth from right, my
brother.

Left: As a mathematics student
and political activist at Hanoi
University

Above: My wife and I shortly after our marriage in 1951

Left: With my uncle Tran Trong Kim, Vietnam's first modern prime minister, shortly before his death

Above: In Nice during a break in the 1954 Élysée negotiations

Right: With Dr. Phan Huy Quat after my uncle's funeral. At the time Quat was Vietnam's defense minister.

Right: Following the 1954 Geneva peace conference, I was in Cannes lobbying Emperor Bao Dai.

Below: With Barry Zorthian, director of the U.S. Information Service, who invited me to visit the U.S. as part of the USIS Leadership Program.

A press conference shortly after the Quat government took office. Defense Minister Nguyen Van Thieu is second from left, Quat is third from left, and Foreign Minister Tran Van Do is fourth. Bui Diem is at far right.

Above: An informal gathering at the home of Prime Minister Phan Huy Quat soon after Henry Cabot Lodge took Maxwell Taylor's place as ambassador. From left: Quat, Bui Diem, Tran Van Do, Lodge, U. Alexis Johnson (back to camera).

Right: Saying goodbye to departing ambassador Maxwell Taylor, July 1965. Under my arm is a copy of the *Saigon Post*, of which I was owner, publisher, and editor.

Prime Minister Nguyen Cao Ky holding forth in a press conference during the 1966 Honolulu Summit. Bui Diem is seated at center next to Stanley Karnow (in white suit).

At a Vietnamese embassy reception with Secretary of State Dean Rusk

Conferring with National Security Adviser Walt Rostow at the
LBJ Ranch (*Official White House Photograph*)

OPPOSITE PAGE

Top: President Johnson introducing ambassador Bui Diem to
the White House press corps on January 19, 1967 (*Official
White House Photograph*)

Bottom: With Lawrence Spivak on *Meet the Press* (*NBC
News, "Meet the Press"*)

Before reviewing the war situation at the Pentagon, I struck a ceremonial pose with Army Chief of Staff William Westmoreland. (*Official Department of Defense Photograph*)

My wife and I with Undersecretary of State U. Alexis Johnson and Mrs. Johnson at a Vietnamese embassy reception (*de Kun, International News*)

The 1967 Guam Summit. The Vietnamese side, from left: Bui Diem, Nguyen Cao Ky, Nguyen Van Thieu. The American side includes, from left: William Westmoreland, Earle Wheeler, Ellsworth Bunker, Robert Komer, Dean Rusk, Lyndon Johnson, Robert McNamara. (*Official White House Photograph*)

Southeast Asian and Pacific ambassadors at a luncheon meeting with President Johnson in the White House Fish Room. From left: Assistant Secretary of State William Bundy; ambassadors of Laos, Indonesia, and Malaysia; presidential assistant Richard Goodwin; President Johnson. Bui Diem is on right in middle. (*Official White House Photograph*)

OPPOSITE PAGE

Top: With President Johnson in the Oval Office shortly before he announced he would not seek re-election (*Official White House Photograph*)

Bottom: In Paris in 1968 during the first year of negotiations. From left: Cyrus Vance, Averell Harriman, Bui Diem, Nguyen Cao Ky (*Wide World Photos*)

Announcing the South Vietnamese government's offer of direct
talks at a press conference in
Paris, July 1968

Shortly after the funeral of former president Eisenhower.
From left: Nguyen Cao Ky, Ellsworth Bunker, Richard Nixon,
Bui Diem. (*Official White House Photograph*)

OPPOSITE PAGE

With Congressman George Bush and visiting
Vietnamese senator Huynh Van Cao

Top: My wife and I with Henry Kissinger at an embassy dinner in late 1970

Middle: A visit to the LBJ Ranch. William Jorden, Nguyen Cao Ky, Bui Diem, LBJ. (*Frank Wolfe, LBJ Library*)

Right: A farewell meeting with President Nixon and Alexander Haig in June 1972 (*Official White House Photograph*)

its outcome would determine the fate of fifteen million South Vietnamese and their descendants.

People like McGovern and Fulbright certainly had a right to express their opinions about the advisability of helping South Vietnam, but they habitually loaded their arguments with insults to Vietnam's leaders which I found unfair and exceptionally distasteful. McGovern would call Thieu "that corrupt general" and said that Ky did not deserve "a penny of American aid." Well, I had my own reservations about Thieu and Ky. But what did McGovern know about the struggle for a civilian constitutional government in Vietnam? Could he, from his seat in the Senate, determine exactly where Ky or Thieu stood in the effort to gently remove political power from the generals' hands? Could he not grasp that if there was ever to be a chance for humane and democratic government in South Vietnam, it would come only by nurturing the fragile growth that had already shot out its first few roots, and that giving the nation over to the totalitarian North Vietnamese meant the extirpation of every value he himself supposedly held dear?

But instead of informed arguments I heard the facile language of demagogues who reduced the situation to a matter of aiding corrupt generals, or some other blithely categorical formula. It was arrogant, and it was an affront. At times I would react in the press to some especially insulting remark, and once I called for a public apology. It was the only interaction I had with this group.

At the same time I was finding my way around Congress, I was also establishing contacts in the administration. William Bundy, assistant secretary of state for East Asian and Pacific affairs, became a regular companion. We knew each other from having worked together at various conferences, so our relationship was more a continuation than something new. Bundy was a man of Washington's inner circle who enjoyed the administration's full confidence. He quickly became my primary contact, the person I dealt with on a day-to-day basis. As our friendship developed, I felt I could be completely candid in presenting the Vietnamese point of view to him. Although a born gentleman, he never hesitated to convey American thinking to me without any of the diplomatic niceties that so often obscure the hard facts.

My relations with Secretary of State Dean Rusk were more formal, though also quite cordial. A forceful, self-possessed man, Rusk seemed the very symbol of quiet determination and strict adherence to the concept of American steadfastness in foreign policy. In his view, the United States must continue to be perceived as an ally that keeps its commitments and its word. Vietnam to him was first and foremost a test of America's international integrity. With his expressionless Buddha face, he seemed unflappable, an impression that was reinforced when I saw him in his own environment, the vast, severely furnished office on the seventh floor of the State Department building.

Two good friends I made at the White House were Bill Jorden, assistant to national security adviser Walt Rostow, and Robert Komer, special assistant to the president for economic affairs in South Vietnam. Through them I could feel almost directly the pressures from a president who was by now desperately trying to reconcile the needs of the war with his problems at home, especially with the increasingly vocal opposition to the war. Often we talked over lunch at the South Vietnamese embassy, where we could be assured of uninterrupted privacy. Over good food, away from the formal official atmosphere, it was easier to speak freely, easier for me to get the pulse of the administration.

Both Komer and Jorden were unusual characters. Komer was tall and thin, one of the most energetic, irrepressible individuals I had ever come across. As far as he was concerned, there was a solution to every problem, and if he did not find it, it would not be for lack of trying. His method of attacking each situation head on earned him the nickname Blowtorch. Komer was articulate and forceful in relaying the White House's concerns about various aspects of the war, and of course these concerns were conveyed in my own cables to Saigon.

Jorden was a very different sort of person: quiet, unassuming, almost shy. But in providing an understanding of Washington's perspective, he possessed a special sensitivity. A journalist by training, Jorden had a close understanding of our difficulties and helped me frame Saigon's problems in the context of White House concerns. This was a tremendous help in my efforts to formulate suggestions and proposals for Thieu and Ky. In a sense, he narrowed the gap between the perspectives of the two governments, and it was no surprise to me when later, as ambassador to Panama, he contributed to the successful renegotiation of the canal agreement.

It was through Jorden that I met Walt Rostow. In those days the national security adviser's office was still located in a modest corner of the White House basement. There Rostow welcomed me with a beaming smile, as if I were an old university colleague who had just stopped down to discuss some academic matter. Indeed, talking with him always seemed more an intellectual exercise than a diplomatic exchange. His views on political and economic development in Third World nations resonated with many of my own, although certain of his ideas did not strike me as appropriate for the special nature of the Vietnam War. Still, it was reassuring to find a man in the corridors of power who had such a profound knowledge of the Communist world and its methodology.

Rostow's critics called him a hard liner, too eager to advocate strong measures, such as an amphibious landing in North Vietnam. But his consistent rationale for intervention — to help postcolonial nations achieve political and economic stability — was in fact centered on the concept of mutual aid. To my mind, that was far more attractive than the dominant strain of American foreign policy thinking in which geopolitical and containment considerations were all that counted.

I was right in the middle of getting acquainted and establishing ties in Washington when, at the end of February 1967, I was called back to Saigon for consultations. Given my close connections with the Saigon government and the importance of "the American factor" in any significant political situation there, it was no surprise they were asking me to come home: the constitutional assembly had just completed its work. Now the military government would be forced to decide whether to promulgate the newly written constitution and, in effect, remove itself from office, or reject it and renege on the explicit and implicit promises that had been made first at Honolulu and reiterated in other forums since. To liven up the action, there were also hints that a new American-Vietnamese summit might be in the works.

Chapter 22

A Democratic Constitution

THE CONSTITUTIONAL ASSEMBLY had been a long time at its task. Its broad make-up had guaranteed that deliberations would be protracted and full of controversy. But finally, after six months, the delegates had reached agreement. The constitution they drafted called for a bicameral legislature and a presidential system, with the addition of a prime minister. Those who knew South Vietnam's experience with chaotic one-man regimes could see what the delegates were trying to do. With a president, vice president, prime minister, and legislature, the potential for dictatorship would be substantially diminished. The assembly had done its best to load the system with redundancies and checks. The question now was, would the South Vietnamese military men approve it? That was what they wanted me in Saigon for, to report on where Washington stood.

I did not need to go far for that information. I had known for a long time what the Americans thought of Vietnam's move toward democracy, and I had been gratified by their firmness about it since Honolulu. Nevertheless, on the eve of my departure I had a long meeting with Walt Rostow to review the recent developments in Saigon. What Rostow said convinced me that the administration favored unequivocal approval of the draft constitution and that its promulgation had great importance to President Johnson himself. Johnson saw it not only as the fulfillment of a pledge given to him by Thieu and Ky at Honolulu but also as a public justification of the American war effort.

American support for the war was already slipping at the beginning of 1967, and no one could see an end to the military struggle despite the presence of almost 400,000 U.S. soldiers. With little evident progress in the fighting, it had become especially important to demonstrate to Americans that the South Vietnamese were taking visible steps toward constitutionality and democratization. "We see no immediate military victory," the administration could say, "but there are great achievements elsewhere."

The need to highlight this dimension of the struggle meant that the United States would push hard for approval of the constitution. For the same reason, as Bob Komer told me shortly before I left, a new summit was definitely in the works, this time set for Guam.

I returned to Saigon on March 6 to find the city in an optimistic mood. One reason was that no matter how inconclusive the war was, it was still distant from the capital and still being fought with the help of a powerful American army, which seemed to preclude an enemy victory. But the optimism was also due to the completion of the new constitution, which for half a year had been the major preoccupation of the capital's various political groups.

Critics of the war dismissed the progress toward democracy in Saigon at that time — the constitutional assembly elections, the new constitution, and the general elections the constitution called for — as window dressing, imposed on the South Vietnamese by an American administration eager to provide its protégé with a façade of legitimacy. It was certainly true that the Johnson administration encouraged these political events and that it did so for its own purposes as well as for their inherent value to the South Vietnamese people.

But it was also true that the Vietnamese had their own ideas about democracy. In their more than seventy years of cohabitation with the French, they had picked up a great deal, not the least of which was the French passion for politics and their addiction to vehement political discussion. Politics had made its way into the Vietnamese bloodstream, and if circumstances had allowed it, democracy could have flourished in Vietnam despite all the fractious politicking and bickering *à la française*. In this regard, Vietnamese are no different from people elsewhere. When they have the opportunity to understand democracy and adopt it, they learn quickly. And once the process starts, it develops its own momentum.

Consequently, Saigon was now filled not just with optimism but also with heated discussions over the constitution. The political factions were in the midst of their own debates, but these did not begin to equal the vehemence of the arguments taking place among the generals. For the ball was now in their court. The constitution had been voted by the assembly, and now the military leadership was going to have to accept it or reject it in front of the entire world.

Many of the generals were not happy about accepting it. This was particularly true of the powerful commanders in the four major military regions. They stood to lose a great deal in the transition to civilian government. Were that to happen, instead of being important elements of the ruling clique, they would find themselves subordinate to political leaders with whom they carried no special influence. That was the real basis of their opposition. What they argued, though, was that they had a war to fight and could see no point in wasting time with disruptive complications of the kind sure to follow approval of a constitution. Their attitude dripped with contempt for the very idea that a civilian government could rule effectively.

Almost from the moment of my arrival I was plunged into these discussions in both military and civilian circles. Everywhere I went the first question was, "What do the Americans think of it?" My answer was always the same. "Of course the Americans are strongly in favor of the constitution. But that's not the most important issue. What we have to ask ourselves is whether the constitution can give us a stronger basis in fighting the Communists. Can it give the government greater legitimacy and can we expect it to rally support? My own answer is unequivocally yes."

I spent most of my time, though, lobbying Thieu, Ky, and a few of the most influential generals. To them I made the point that we had to be absolutely consistent with what we had said last year in Honolulu. There was no way to go back on that. On the contrary, we had to keep moving ahead without delay or deviation.

As far as Thieu and Ky were concerned, I got the distinct impression I was preaching to the converted. Although they were not committing themselves to approval beforehand, I believe they had already accepted the idea of a constitution and elections. In the first place, they had a good sense of the American position, and they knew how important it was for them to get out in front of this issue. Second, deep down they must have understood that the constitution would still leave them in control. Specifically, there was no question that they themselves would be in a dominant position in the proposed presidential elections. So for them, as opposed to some of the other generals, there was little reason to oppose the constitution and were very good reasons to claim credit for the march toward democracy. From my point of view this was all to the good. The more personal reasons they had for approving the constitution the better. The primary objective now was to get the system up and running.

On March 10 Thieu and Ky finally convened a formal meeting of the Council of Ministers and the important military commanders. After a full debate that covered the broad principles and the specifics of the proposed constitution, Thieu urged me to speak. There was a touch of malice in his voice when he half-jokingly introduced me as "the man who just returned from Washington," as if he could not completely suppress a certain resentment that Washington, in my person, was going to have the last word.

I made my presentation as brief as possible, pointing out that I had favored a gradual return to constitutional government from the beginning. More importantly, I said, my experience abroad convinced me that South Vietnam had to be perceived as making serious efforts to achieve democracy, that there was simply no practical alternative to it. When I was finished, the council voted, approving the constitution unanimously.

A few days after the constitution was promulgated, Bill Bundy visited Saigon, bringing formal word that President Johnson wanted to schedule a summit conference for March 20 in Guam. Because I had coordinated the Vietnamese side at the Honolulu and Manila conferences, I was chosen to plan this one as well. We had all become used to the procedures, so it was not as frenetic a task as it had been in the past. But preparations were suddenly complicated by a surprise development that took place at the United Nations on March 14.

Secretary-General U Thant was a determined opponent of the war who also possessed a remarkably naïve view of Hanoi's willingness to make peace. After some preliminary talks on the subject with the North Vietnamese, Thant sent an *aide-mémoire* to Arthur Goldberg, U.S. ambassador to the UN, formally proposing a truce and peace talks between the two countries.

In general the Americans had a low opinion of U Thant, and they were skeptical about this initiative. But to the conspiratorial-minded South Vietnamese public, the coincidence in timing of Thant's proposal and the Guam meeting suggested that the Americans were behind the secretary-general's efforts. Word began to spread that the real purpose of Guam was to pressure Thieu and Ky into a negotiated settlement that would be in the United States' best interest but would leave South Vietnam weakened and compromised. The result of all this was that we had to spend days carefully coordinating the U.S. and Vietnamese replies to Thant and doing what we could to dissipate rumors and calm down the hypersensitive Vietnamese public.

The Guam summit was the third between American and South Vietnamese leaders, and this time around, both sides were intent on reducing protocol to a minimum and using the occasion for substantive business. President Johnson was accompanied by the usual star-studded cast, including Rusk, McNamara, Rostow, and the top military commanders. Thieu and Ky too were surrounded by their top ministers.

The working session began on Monday, March 20. Apart from a thorough review of the war, three major items figured on the agenda: U Thant's peace proposal, political developments in South Vietnam, and the pacification effort. But as soon as everyone had settled down, President Johnson added a new element to the conference, introducing to us a new American team that would be coming to Saigon. Ellsworth Bunker would be replacing Henry Cabot Lodge as ambassador, and Robert Komer would be coming in to handle both the military and civilian sides of pacification.

We had known about the appointments in advance, but all the Vietnamese were curious, to say the least, about the new ambassador, who, especially now, could greatly influence not just the conduct of the war but also the balance of Vietnam's internal affairs. With presidential elections scheduled for the fall, the next few months would be a critical time in the country's political life. And just at this moment a new, untested man was coming aboard.

Ellsworth Bunker sat at the table without saying much. A thin old man, but erect and obviously energetic, he stretched his long neck at us as if he wanted to size up in a glance all these Vietnamese faces. There was an air of impenetrability about him, a shield of dignity that marked him instantly as an aristocrat. Before long, the cool demeanor had earned him the nickname Old Man Refrigerator among the Vietnamese. None of us suspected that we had in Bunker a dedicated friend whose aloof manner belied his warm heart.

When the introductions were over, the conference got on with its set agenda, and Lyndon Johnson dominated the meeting as he always did. The president seemed his usual energetic self; if he was already beginning to feel anxious and depressed about the war, nobody at the table was aware of it. Turning to the advisers and aides who surrounded him, he threw out questions, asked for clarifications and details, and issued instructions as only a commander in chief in full control of a situation could do. Though this time he did not ask to see the coonskins on the wall, he left absolutely no doubt that he wanted concrete results and he wanted them soon.

The only one at the table who seemed unaffected by Johnson's forcefulness was Robert McNamara. He was strangely silent that day, even neglecting his furious note taking on the ubiquitous yellow pad. He seemed unusually withdrawn, though I did not think anything of it at the time. No one in our party had an inkling that, as we later learned, for several months already the secretary of defense had begun to have serious doubts about the war.

In Guam Thieu and Ky were more confident and at ease with the Americans than I had ever seen them. They had been in power two years now, and had, to some degree at least, grown in office. Moreover, their standing was firmer than ever, certainly better than it had been in Honolulu when they were struggling to make a case for their own legitimacy. Now, a year later, they were able to announce that they had fulfilled their promises to promulgate a new constitution and prepare for national elections. It was a proud moment for them and for the South Vietnamese government as a whole.

President Johnson responded warmly to these accomplishments. As usual, he seemed at least as motivated by the human dimension of the situation in front of him as by the strictly geopolitical concerns that preoccupied people like Rusk and McNamara. It seemed to me that, at bottom, the personal interactions interested him most. In Honolulu he had for the first time seen Thieu and Ky as individuals and had subsequently become enthusiastic about the human side of the struggle, with its emphasis on helping the Vietnamese people achieve a better way of life.

That dimension of his character was in strong evidence at Guam, where his personal relationship with Thieu and Ky grew. I, too, received an unlikely bit of presidential attention when at lunch one day Johnson asked me if I was related to Bui Vien, the special envoy sent to the United States in 1873 by Emperor Tu Duc to seek help against the French. At first I could not understand just who the president was talking about; it was hard to cut through his thick Texas drawl. On the third or fourth try I finally recognized the name and had to tell him that I was unfortunately not related to Bui Vien, who was given a friendly welcome but no assistance by President Ulysses S. Grant. I did have a great-granduncle, though, by the name of Bui Dy, who was Emperor Tu Duc's special envoy to China at about the same time. Johnson seemed disappointed and even came back to the matter in his address to the conference, saying that he was sure I would have more luck with the United States than my predecessor Bui Vien had.

What was remarkable to me about this incident was that Johnson had taken the trouble to have his staff research the backgrounds of even Thieu's and Ky's aides and had made a point of using the information to help establish personal contacts. It was a mark of the man. I always knew that with Johnson I was dealing with someone who instinctively saw problems in human terms. Whatever his failings, he was always involved personally, and was tortured when decisions he made, however necessary he believed them to be, resulted in suffering. As I came to understand this, I developed a deep sympathy for him, and kept up our relationship even after he left the White House.

The only bad news at Guam concerned the faltering pacification program — the effort to keep the countryside under government control and strengthen the allegiance of the peasants. In the northern part of the country, the same hostility toward Saigon that the Buddhists had drawn on had also become fertile ground for the Vietcong. They had expanded their influence there, and had managed to pretty much hold their own elsewhere, despite the drubbing they took whenever they came out in the open.

In part this situation was due to the ineffectiveness of the South Vietnamese army, which had expanded rapidly in the last year and had not done a good job of integrating the large number of newly trained soldiers. Another, perhaps more important factor was the lack of a clear delineation of responsibility between the regular army and the local forces, and especially between the Vietnamese and the Americans. When it came to deciding who was responsible for what, confusion reigned, aggravated by what Robert Komer later called "a proliferation of overlapping programs and a competition for scarce resources to the point that everybody is getting in everybody else's way."

"Everybody getting in everybody else's way" was a good explanation of what was going on. Vietnamese officials, often unsure of how their own duties were defined, were told by their superiors to coordinate their activities with the Americans. But which ones? So many American agencies were involved in the countryside: MACV, USAID, JUSPAO, CIA, DIA, to name just a few. The programs often overlapped and duplicated one another, and the agencies spent much of their time playing out their traditional rivalries and bureaucratic games. Pacification was everyone's business and no one's, and the results were predictably deplorable.

The Guam summit tried to remedy this problem by bringing in Robert Komer to oversee the entire pacification effort. He and General Nguyen Duc Thang were charged with streamlining the numerous, diverse programs and getting them under central control. When combined with the orderly transition to an elected government, an efficient pacification program would greatly strengthen South Vietnam so it could eventually face the threat to its existence on its own — with American aid, of course, but without the need for American troops.

In this sense, the Guam conference initiated the policy of "Vietnamization," which was formally put in effect by Richard Nixon two years later. No one used the term in March 1967; then the name of the game was still "war of attrition" and "light at the end of the tunnel." But precisely because no one could predict how and when the war would end, the American orientation perceptibly shifted toward bolstering South Vietnam politically and economically as well as militarily. This change of emphasis derived in part from a slowly ripening frustration with the lack of military progress.

At Guam we talked about these things among ourselves too. Although there was certainly no solid indication that the Americans would eventually move out, I tried to impress on Thieu and Ky the need to act quickly on the whole political and social program that was being outlined. Developments in these areas would not happen overnight, and building internal coherence was the only line of defense we would have were the American shield ever to be lifted.

But it would be inaccurate to say that real anxieties about such an eventuality surfaced at Guam. Our thinking — mine at any rate — was based solely on what I considered reasonable prudence. There was no doubt that the mood at the conference's conclusion was upbeat, though perhaps somewhat more so for the Vietnamese than for the Americans. We were reassured that American support would continue and that we would be consulted fully about any developments that might grow out of U Thant's peace proposal. We were also pleased about the new emphasis on pacification. If we were concerned about anything, it was the upcoming national elections, which were now only five months down the road. For the first time in its history, South Vietnam would be freely voting for a president. As the Guam meeting ended, Thieu and Ky were already planning their campaigns.

Accustomed to my presence for many years now, the two gentlemen from Saigon almost forgot that I was no longer part of their administration and asked me to join them on their way home. I had just received another offer, though, to accompany President Johnson back to Washington on his plane. It was a friendly gesture, so on March 21 I parted company with my fellow Vietnamese and joined the presidential party for the flight eastward.

Air Force One was impressive in its appointments, and also amusing in certain ways. The presidential seal, for example, seemed to be embossed on everything in sight, including the ashtrays, napkins, and cutlery. I was just settling in for the flight when an aide invited me to join the president in his small private cabin to see a film. When I walked in, Johnson was sprawled in a huge swivel chair, with Rusk, McNamara, and Rostow seated on a sofa that followed the cabin's contour. I joined them on the sofa, and together we watched a short documentary.

The film was an absorbing portrait of China's emergence as a nuclear power, but I found myself paying less attention to the screen than to the men watching it. Johnson sat there pensively throughout the film, saying little. I wondered what was running through his mind, and I guessed that if he was considering the Chinese factor in the Vietnam equation, he would not dismiss it lightly. I also thought about the limits Johnson had placed on the air war against North Vietnam, measures meant to reduce the possibility of provoking the Chinese to intervene. None of us in the cabin could have predicted that within a few years the two Socialist allies, "teeth and lips" as they called themselves at the time, would be adversaries.

Nine hours later the plane landed at Andrews Air Force Base, outside Washington. From there we took a helicopter that set us down on the White House lawn. At the embassy the next day, I received an unexpected reminder of the American penchant for memorabilia: a framed certificate attesting to the fact that I had indeed flown the Pacific on Air Force One with the president.

Chapter 23

Behind the Scenes

THE RELATIVE POLITICAL CALM that prevailed in Washington at the end of March 1967 suited the serious but optimistic mood we brought back from Guam. True, there were signs of discontent. Antiwar sentiment was growing, especially on college campuses, and a number of Democratic senators — Morse, Church, McGovern, and Fulbright — were already outspoken opponents. Nevertheless, the 1966 congressional elections had left the Democrats in solid control of both the House and Senate, and the next presidential campaign was far down the road. No one was yet challenging Johnson's leadership. If the previous strong support for the war was declining toward tolerance, it was still substantial enough for the president to approve another increase in the number of American troops, this time to 470,000.

The assessments of the American political situation that I began sending back to Saigon during this period were based as much on my contacts with journalists as on government sources. Hardly a day passed when I did not have lunch or a long talk with one or another of Washington's veteran correspondents and columnists, men like Joseph Kraft and Murray Marder of the *Washington Post;* Tom Wicker, Hedrick Smith, and Neil Sheehan of the *New York Times;* Crosby Noyes of the *Washington Star;* and the brothers Kalb, then working for CBS. Their views reflected a wide range of political opinions, and though we often were far apart on issues, I found their company amiable and stimulating. Some of the old hands were frequently accused of being out of touch with the world outside the capital, but their observations were always valuable to me.

In fact, no matter what their opinions, if you were alert enough not to be swayed by their biases, you could always distill from these conversations a hard core of substantial information. Moreover, their political antennae were so finely tuned that their questions in many cases put me on the trail of developments I had not been aware of, or sent me to double-check information I had thought was firm.

As far as those who were vehemently prejudiced against South Vietnam — Anthony Lewis and Mary McGrory, for example — I considered them an important part of the political landscape, but I saw no reason to spend time with them. Of course not all the journalists were systematically antiwar. But many of them seemed carried away by an ingrained cynicism toward anything that came from the government, American or Vietnamese. As a result, they tended to look at each issue and event through their own prism, discarding evidence that did not fit in with what they regarded as the truth. In some cases they even seemed to consider themselves as oracles of the truth about Vietnam. I would often walk away wondering how they had managed to convince themselves they knew so much.

Most foreign ambassadors in Washington get to see the president only on rare occasions, usually once or twice a year at state functions, and then only to shake hands. Most often they carry on their regular business with assistant secretaries of state. But because of the prominence of the war on Lyndon Johnson's agenda, I was in a somewhat different position. Already I had talked with him at the Guam summit and had even had an opportunity to get to know him a bit during the flight back to Washington.

On April 19, just four weeks after Guam, I met him again. During a SEATO conference, attended by the foreign ministers and ambassadors of Australia, New Zealand, Pakistan, Thailand, the Philippines, Great Britain, and South Vietnam, we were all invited to the White House for an off-the-record session with the president. I understood that this invitation was strictly symbolic, intended to underline Johnson's personal interest in the problems of Southeast Asia, so I did not attach any particular importance to the session.

In the cabinet room of the White House, Johnson was in an exuberant mood. He had just returned from a trip to Latin America, which had obviously encouraged him, and he spoke strongly about the strategic importance of Southeast Asia. Though he did not specifically mention Vietnam, there was no doubt where his thoughts were. But as Johnson gathered speed, I found myself getting impatient. I had scheduled a reception at my embassy that afternoon and was eager to get back as soon as I could.

As the meeting wound to a close, an aide passed me a note saying that the president would like to see Foreign Minister Tran Van Do and me in private immediately afterward. In the few moments it took to walk from the cabinet room to the Oval Office, Do and I were in a fluster of curiosity mixed with some apprehension. Surely something unusual was up. When Do asked me what I thought it might be, I told him, "You're the one who should know. You've just gotten here from Saigon. Is something going on there? Or maybe it's something more about this U Thant business?"

Inside the office we found Dean Rusk and Johnson talking together. But as soon as we came in, Rusk took Do aside and Johnson walked me toward his desk, putting his arm around my shoulder as if I were an old friend to whom he was about to give some brotherly advice. To lessen the distance between his six foot three inches and my five foot four, he leaned down and, in a voice that was little more than a whisper, told me that he had been getting reports about the upcoming presidential election in Saigon and about Thieu and Ky. "Look," he said, "it's not my place to say which one of them ought to be the candidate. They both deserve to be candidates. But do tell them, will you, that whatever they do, they should make sure it doesn't upset the stability of the government. That's important to us."

Johnson's message about Thieu and Ky's rivalry was crystal clear, yet his manner was gentle. The Old Man (*Ong Gia*, our nickname for Johnson, combined respect and affection) had so many burdens on his shoulders, and here was another one, rightly not his at all. I felt embarrassed he even had to mention it to me, but I told him that I shared his concern and would do everything I could to convey his feelings to Saigon.

In the car on our way back to the embassy, Do and I compared notes. When I asked him whether the political situation in Saigon really warranted this much anxiety, he said he believed it did not. There were plenty of rumors about which one of the generals would be the presidential candidate, and it was possible that some of these had aroused American fears of a possible coup. But it was his firm opinion that, despite the rivalry between Thieu and Ky, they both had a strong sense of responsibility, and a return to a period of upheavals was improbable.

I was not completely reassured by Do's assessment. Johnson would have felt it necessary to raise this issue with me only if he had received disquieting reports through his own channels. But whatever the validity of what he might have heard, all we could do was impress on Thieu and Ky the seriousness of the president's concern. Do and I agreed that he would report in general terms my conversation with the president when he returned home. Given my closer relationship with the two leaders, I would take up the matter personally on my next trip to Saigon.

* * *

Several days later Do was back in Saigon. Apparently, his report had an immediate effect, because directly after his return, I received a cable from Prime Minister Ky asking me home for consultations. But I was right in the middle of establishing my contacts in Washington (the process had been interrupted by my previous trip), and I decided not to go immediately. I sensed that there was nothing else urgent in Ky's summons, and I considered it not a bad idea if he and Thieu had a chance to reflect for a while on President Johnson's message. In the meantime, General Westmoreland had arrived in Washington to report to Congress, and this event gave me a good reason to stay a while longer. I told Saigon it was necessary for me to be on hand to evaluate the congressional reaction to Westmoreland's report and the public response. I also wanted to see what the Pentagon would have to say about Westmoreland's new request for yet another troop increase.

By the time I did get back to Saigon it was late May, and already everyone had heard that Thieu and Ky both would be running for president. With the deadline for filing still a month away, the race was already provoking close attention, not just among South Vietnam's politicians but among the general public. Various civilian candidates had already announced their intention to run, and with Thieu and Ky both in it, it was certainly possible that one of the civilians would come out victorious. So avid was the interest that military developments were typically treated as completely separate from the election. In Saigon, at least, the bloody fighting just then raging in the northern part of the country was receiving far less attention than the presidential race.

Everywhere the chief topic of conversation seemed to be the military-civilian conflict. The civilian presidential candidates included Phan Khac Suu, the former chief of state, and Tran Van Huong, who had been prime minister during part of General Nguyen Khanh's regime. (Dr. Quat was not a candidate; as a northerner with no indigenous power base, he felt he had no chance.) Together with a number of lesser-known politicians, they represented a respectable alternative to either Thieu or Ky, although the still raw spectacle of their squabbles and failures several years back gave the civilians a formidable handicap. In addition, the idea of electing a general as president had little appeal to many, though the fact that the country had enjoyed two years of stable government under these men could hardly be ignored. On the other hand, a bitter fight was brewing among the military people themselves over how to deal with the separate Thieu and Ky candidacies. I arrived in Saigon just in time to get into the middle of it.

By the end of May, the Thieu and Ky factions were at each other's throats, though on the surface it did not appear that Thieu would be able to come close to matching Ky's power. Ky, the younger man, was backed by an active group of young generals, most of whom, like Ky himself, were northerners. Moreover, as prime minister, he held in his hands all the obvious reins of power. He controlled, for example, all the government agencies that would run the election. He also controlled the ministry of interior and the ministry of information, which ran the radio and television stations, as well as the police and security apparatus, the army units around the capital, and the air force, of which he was still titular head.

Thieu's assets, on the other hand, were mostly intangible. He projected a serious, mature image, in distinct contrast to Ky's unpredictable cockiness. And he was from central Vietnam, able to capitalize on southern resentment of northern influence in the government and military, of which Ky was now the leading example. But these advantages were perceptual; few believed they could balance Ky's hold on the machinery of government.

To a certain extent, my return from Washington was considered an advantage to Ky. I was a northerner too, which in most people's minds made us colleagues in this fight. Beyond that, it was Ky who had brought me into the government in the first place, and for a year and a half I had worked closely with him as his special assistant. To the superheated imaginations of Saigon's political cognoscenti, the fact that I had returned at this particular moment was an undeniable indication that, though I was South Vietnam's ambassador, I was also Ky's own man in Washington, and now I was bringing the prime minister advice and support from our American connections.

In fact, the Vietnamese were incapable of believing that in this race the United States was remaining strictly neutral. They were convinced that the Americans must be energetically maneuvering behind the scenes for the candidate of their choice (the "hairy hands of the CIA" theory again), and my presence in Saigon left little doubt about who that candidate was.*

As for me, I kept my preference strictly to myself. The fact was that I did hope Ky would emerge the victor in this battle, but for reasons quite different from those which popular opinion ascribed to me. Since my period of close collaboration with Ky on the daily affairs of government, I had harbored the conviction that the man was, to some degree, malleable. He was young, impetuous, impressionable, and naïve about govern-

---

* After the war I asked Ellsworth Bunker about the American stance in the election. He told me then that personally he felt more comfortable with Thieu (Westmoreland said the same thing in his memoirs), but that Ky would have been quite acceptable. There was, he said, no American attempt to influence events one way or the other.

ment in many ways, but he was also quick to learn and enthusiastic about new ideas. And he had a certain fearlessness about him; he was cast in the heroic mold. The Vietnamese say that only deaf people don't hear the guns, and in a sense Ky was deaf. He was capable of taking tremendous risks without thinking much about the consequences of failure. It was Ky who had embraced the concepts of constitutionality and social amelioration that had informed the Honolulu speech, while Thieu had objected and qualified and hedged at every turn.

Thieu was a much tougher nut. He was secretive and suspicious and calculating, a harder man to trust and to work with. What people like Bunker and Westmoreland saw as maturity, I felt as hesitancy and indecisiveness. He was the kind of man who could say yes but mean no, who could commit and not commit at the same time. He was a hard worker and had great patience. But he was not, I thought, a man of ideas or vision, nor was he ever likely to become one. By nature he was too careful, too aware of all the angles, too convoluted in his thinking and indirect in his methods.

It was for these reasons that in my heart I supported Ky, despite my fear of his rashness and mercurial nature. But outwardly I said nothing, content to let people think whatever they wanted to think.

On the day I arrived in Saigon, I briefed Ky on my conversation with President Johnson and on the mood in Washington. Among other things, I reported to him that support for the war had reached a plateau. I described the demonstrations, the polls, and the academic opposition, as well as my talks on the subject with military and State Department people. I tried to impress him with the very real possibility that if the war dragged on, serious domestic opposition in the United States would grow. On the subject of elections, I made it as clear as I could that the overriding concern in Washington was about the possibility of a coup or some other negative development that might result from an army split into two hostile factions.

That evening Ky took me to his headquarters at the Bien Hoa air base. There we had dinner with several of his strong supporters: General Nguyen Duc Thang, the minister who ran the pacification program; General Nguyen Bao Tri, minister of information; and General Le Nguyen Khang, commander of troops in the Saigon region. I learned that Ky was absolutely determined to proceed with his candidacy, and that as far as he and his circle were concerned, the only remaining question was how to get Thieu to renounce his own.

I also learned that after some inconclusive preliminary talks between the two camps, a few days earlier General Thang had been delegated to pressure Thieu into giving up the campaign. Thang had been considered the right man for the job because he was a favorite of the Americans, particularly of Lansdale and Bob Komer, who was his American pacification counterpart, so Thang's words were likely to carry more weight. Moreover, Thang had the American ability for putting things in blunt, explicit terms, something Vietnamese are congenitally reluctant to do.

So in his iciest manner Thang had told Thieu that he had no choice, that he would simply have to remove himself from the race. Apparently, it had been a stormy session. At the end of it, for all Thang's strong tone and leverage, Thieu's only answer had been an emphatic no. Since then, communication between the two camps had been cut off, and none of Ky's people had any idea how to proceed with their recalcitrant rival. That was one of the reasons they were talking to me. They were not precisely asking me to serve as an intermediary, but as the ambassador who just returned from Washington, I clearly ought to be talking to Thieu anyway. Perhaps I could just sound him out on this business at the same time.

A few days later, on May 25, I went to have a talk with Nguyen Van Thieu in his modest office at the headquarters of the Joint General Staff — a lonely place, I thought, considering that most of his colleagues there had already sided with Ky. I reported to him, as I had to Ky, my conversation with President Johnson and my assessment of Washington's perspective on the war, especially after General Westmoreland's address to Congress in late April. But Thieu no doubt sensed that I was going to take up other matters as well, so when I had finished the general briefing, he anticipated me and began talking about his candidacy. He told me he had given a great deal of thought to it, that he had consulted all his friends, and that he had decided to run. It was a firm decision. He was fully aware of all the difficulties, he said, but he was a patriot. Like every other patriot, he had a right to be a candidate, a right he was determined to exercise even if he got only two votes, his own and his wife's. That was all there was to it.

When it was clear there was nothing more to say, I got up to leave. Thieu shook my hand and thanked me for my visit. "At least," he said, "you're not like the rest of those guys," a none too oblique reference to the plain-spoken General Thang and the rest of Ky's entourage.

I stayed in Saigon a few more days, touching base with the various political groups to try to round out my evaluation of the race now that it was certain both Thieu and Ky would be running. It was a confusing scene, to put it mildly. In addition to the two generals, there were seven civilian candidates. Encouraged by the military split, they were furiously trying to work out deals among themselves to strengthen their own candidacies. There was even one peace candidate, a lawyer named Truong Dinh Dzu, who was running on a vague platform of reconciliation with the Vietcong. This Dzu was a maverick, a Saigon wheeler-dealer and influence peddler who had never been a candidate for anything before. But though not a professional politician, he was nevertheless an accomplished opportunist who apparently saw a bloc of peace votes that were there for the taking.

Ky, for his part, was already vigorously pushing his unofficial campaign (candidacies could not be formally declared until July 1), which was being managed by Nguyen Ngoc Loan, the director of police. Everywhere one turned, Ky's slogan was painted on a wall: "The government of Nguyen Cao Ky is the government of the poor." Thieu, on the other hand, remained secluded, surrounded by his advisers. It seemed as if he was waiting for Ky to destroy himself by some horrible gaffe or other.

As far as I was concerned, it was not an encouraging picture. One of the ideas I had picked up in my travels around Saigon was that a combined Thieu-Ky candidacy would be the surest path to electing a stable government. So before I left for Washington, I saw Ky again and asked him point blank if he would consider the possibility of making a joint run. No, he said, that was out of the question. But he did want me to take back to the United States his personal pledge that no matter what the outcome of the elections, there would be no military coup, and the transition from the present government to its successor would take place without problems.

I returned to Washington convinced of Ky's sincerity; he had made the strongest personal commitment to respect the elections and maintain the integrity of the armed forces. However, I was not at all sure he could stick to these intentions if he and Thieu were really flailing at each other for the next three months. So it was with crossed fingers that I relayed Ky's assurances to the State Department and the White House. I was certain that Johnson and Rusk were glad to have them, but given the recent history of Saigon governments, I knew they would not be considered as the definitive word on what the next period might hold in store. Personally I was just hoping, or, more accurately, praying, for the best.

Chapter 24

The 1967 Elections

FORTUNATELY, June and July of 1967 were months of relative quiet in the war. For a change, headlines were taken up with news of other events, particularly the Six-Day War in the Middle East and the surprise meeting between President Johnson and Soviet Premier Alexei Kosygin in Glassboro, New Jersey. The lull allowed me to begin living the normal life of an ambassador in Washington, to the extent such a life can be considered normal.

My family had moved from our crowded apartment into a new home behind Washington's Rock Creek Park. With our improved domestic circumstances, my wife and I began playing the social role so important to conducting business in the capital. At the embassy we started hosting simple luncheons and small dinners, with occasional receptions thrown in. Though the war was controversial, we quickly discovered that the Vietnamese cuisine attracted liberals and conservatives equally, and our chef was called on regularly to expand his repertoire to please the Democrats and Republicans who found their way to our tables.

The guest lists were ordinarily made up of senators and representatives and their wives, along with administration officials and members of the news media and the diplomatic corps. Congressmen were the most unpredictable; debates and roll calls often meant they would unexpectedly show up late or leave early. But as we became familiar with their odd schedules, we learned to accommodate ourselves to them, though sometimes it meant serving meals at unconventional hours. At other times dinners would be interrupted by some surprise international development, as happened in August 1968, when William Westmoreland, Bill

Bundy, and several other administration officials had to rush back to their posts when the Czechoslovakia crisis broke just before dessert.

These affairs were often a mixture of socializing and politics, with the accent on socializing. They helped people who were commonly engaged in very serious business, often as adversaries, to leaven their relationships with friendship or, at the very least, civility. On occasion the chemistry would even produce something memorable, like the night when Tom Corcoran, the New Deal lawyer and adviser to Franklin Roosevelt, played piano and sang Irish duets with William Sullivan, who later became ambassador to Iran. At such moments the war receded from our minds, and we could feel almost free of its constant weight.

With the embassy's social schedule picking up and with all the required appearances at other diplomatic luncheons and affairs, my life became unbelievably hectic. I felt as if I were spending all my time either smiling or talking, or doing both at once. But it was necessary. I began to see that it was precisely the multitude of casual conversations with people engaged in the affairs of state that formed the background of understanding, without which one could not function in the American capital.

Relevant pieces of information, whether picked up formally or informally, I included in my daily cables home. On occasion, though, these reports did not satisfy, especially when the febrile imaginations in South Vietnam saw hints of American peace plans that at some point might be imposed on us without adequate consultation. The Glassboro summit stirred intense interest along these lines. In spite of my reports that the meeting was primarily on global issues between the two superpowers, the foreign ministry sent persistent inquiries about the possible fallout for Vietnam.

I discovered later that these inquiries were motivated by the super-heated political atmosphere in Saigon, where the presidential campaigns were just reaching their peak in the week prior to the official filing deadline for candidates. The civilian hopefuls were all trying to assess the real intentions at Glassboro and to adjust their campaigns accordingly. At the same time, the suspense over the Thieu-Ky clash was building, with more and more rumors about what was going on between the two, some asserting that there would be a total breakdown and chaos, others that they would soon join forces on a unified ticket.

The Johnson-Kosygin meeting was concluded on June 25. I was in the middle of answering a flurry of questions from Saigon about surreptitious American peace plans when suddenly I was assaulted by another batch of pointed inquiries, this time from Washington. The White House and the State Department had both picked up reports of an imminent coup attempt, and they wanted me to try to verify their information through my own channels.

The rumors had their origin in a meeting in Saigon of the top South Vietnamese army (ARVN) commanders which had been called by General Cao Van Vien, the defense minister and chief of the Joint General Staff, apparently to settle the conflict between Thieu and Ky once and for all. Calling Saigon directly, I managed to get through to Ky just as he was preparing for the second day of this marathon meeting. When I told him about the American fears, he assured me that there was no coup, adding, "The armed forces have confidence in me. We have the situation completely under control, and I am going ahead with my candidacy."

I made the call at 8:00 P.M. Washington time on June 29 (8:00 A.M. on June 30 in Saigon). Then I passed the word along to my friends in the administration and shortly afterward went to sleep. Though I knew none of the details of General Vien's meeting, Ky's confident tone had suggested that he was prevailing over his rival and would emerge as the single candidate from the military.

Early on the morning of June 30, a friend woke me up with a phone call, suggesting I have a look at the morning news. I switched on the small TV set next to our bed and heard that what the French call a coup de théâtre had taken place in Saigon. The Armed Forces Council, under General Vien, had apparently forced Thieu and Ky to accept a combined ticket, with Thieu as presidential candidate and Ky in the vice-presidential slot. Given the determination to run that Thieu had expressed to me a month earlier, I was not completely surprised that the generals had not been able to force him to back down. But what was really intriguing was that Thieu had managed to outmaneuver Ky for the presidential nomination.

I did not have to wait long to find out how it had happened. Just three days later I received a cable asking me to return to Saigon again for consultations. This would be my third trip back in six months (my second in little over a month), each of them involving twenty hours' flying time, one way. It was beginning to seem like a new definition for the word "shuttle."

The general assumption among the Americans, as among many South Vietnamese, had been that in the end Ky would be the sole candidate and that he would then be elected president. But as I found out at the U.S. embassy in Saigon, the recent surprise had not been an unpleasant one. There was little question that the combined Thieu-Ky ticket would prevail, and the two generals would surely maintain the stability that was so desired. Moreover, the two men were known quantities with whom the Americans were sure they could work. In addition, the somewhat erratic reputation that Ky and some members of his entourage had acquired — especially the pistol-toting police general Loan — would now be diluted under the leadership of the cautious and conservative Thieu.

It was, of course, foreordained that Vietnamese public opinion would attribute the surprise outcome to CIA manipulations. The Saigonese were convinced that many of the generals at the meeting had been suborned or at least influenced by the supposedly ubiquitous American intelligence agency. The truth — that the Americans had been just as surprised as anyone else and had been faced with a fait accompli — was just too logical to accept.

As the press reported it, there was little drama at General Vien's Armed Forces Council meeting. According to the newspapers, Thieu and Ky presented their cases, then awaited the decision — although several papers reported that Thieu's emotions got the best of him at one point and he broke into tears. The actual story, recounted to me by Cao Van Vien himself, was somewhat different. The consensus among the generals was that two separate candidacies would split the armed forces and lead to the victory of one of the civilians. This, in turn, would ensure an eventual reversion to the bad old days of chaos and paralysis. Because both Thieu and Ky were adamant about running, the council realized that the only alternative was a combined candidacy.

To enforce their will, the council decided to ostracize whichever of the two generals refused to go along. So they first made it clear that whoever did not abide by their ruling would be excluded from any role in the military leadership. Then they pressured the two into a joint ticket. At one particularly tense point in the proceedings, Thieu and Ky were asked to leave the room. At another, the commander of Military Region One, General Hoang Xuan Lam, took off his stars and put them on the table. Looking from Thieu to Ky, he told them that if they refused to get together, every last general in the meeting would do the same. They had no choice.

Once a combined ticket had been agreed to, the matter of who would lead it was settled in a strictly military fashion, that is, according to the generals' undeviating sense of hierarchy. As the senior man (older and with three stars as opposed to Ky's two), Thieu would have the top spot. To make it easier for Ky and his Young Turks to swallow this very bitter pill, the generals created Quan Uy Hoi, a secret military committee, with Ky as secretary-general and his closest colleagues in leading positions, the idea being that this committee would serve as a kind of shadow government, keeping a tight leash on Thieu's independence.

But even with his secret committee leadership, Ky was furious about the whole thing. As angry as he was, though, he refused to renege on his commitment to Johnson or create a schism in the armed forces. As it turned out, rather than restraining Thieu, in a short time Thieu (by this point dubbed the Sly Fox) was able to outmaneuver the committee and force its dissolution. But that was still in the future.

Shortly after my return to Saigon on July 7, I decided to make my own appraisal of the country's mood. Although I had been back in South Vietnam four times since January, each visit had been brief and filled with activity. Now I wanted to get back in touch with Vietnamese attitudes and developments myself, rather than receive all my information through the filter of government and military officials. The result was an extended tour, which I started by making the usual rounds among Saigon's political and intellectual circles, then continued in the provinces, traveling incognito whenever it was feasible.

It was a flying trip that took me to eight provinces in a little under two weeks. Given the timing, there was no possibility of looking at conditions in depth, but everywhere I went, I asked questions and got involved in discussions, trying to gauge what people were thinking and how they viewed the forthcoming elections. Among the politicians and intellectuals, the first question to me was always, "What are the Americans really up to?" Businessmen and other ordinary city people tended to have less political concerns, in particular the rising cost of living and the pervasive corruption, especially among provincial authorities. For peasants and villagers, the gut issues were even more concrete. They needed better protection from both their own government's troops and the Vietcong, and they wanted more fertilizer at a lower price.

The progress of the election campaigns was nothing short of amazing. Already the get-out-the-vote movement was shifting into high gear. Building on the success of the constitutional assembly elections the previous year, the Ministry of Information had again mobilized the country's entertainers to exhort and cajole and amuse the people into voting. In many areas the campaigns generated their own fiery enthusiasm. Particularly in the cities, where assembly nominees could gather easily and debate, it hardly seemed there was a war going on, so vehement and outspoken were the attacks on government policies. In more remote areas people were calmer about it, and more careful. Deep in the countryside there was always the threat of Vietcong sabotage and at least some danger in being too visibly enthusiastic about the elections. But even there interest was lively, and it appeared we would have a high level of participation.

There were some obvious problems as well. The government oversaw the machinery of the election — establishing polling places and voting procedures and counting the ballots — and it was already evident that the opposition would not have enough people to serve on all the committees that would supervise the elections around the country. So there was plenty of room for abuse. In addition, the sizable portion of the rural population under Communist control would, of course, be prevented from voting. But all in all, I finished the tour in an optimistic mood. As far as I was concerned, the pros far outweighed the cons, if only because in the final analysis political reforms — even when initiated by reluctant politicians — create a momentum that no politician can easily stop. The road to a free democracy on the American model might be long and tortuous, but I anticipated that these elections would give us a good start along the way.

At the end of July I returned to Washington in time to help prepare for the visit by an American delegation that would observe the elections, which were scheduled for September 3. While in Saigon, I consulted at length with Thieu and Ky on this subject. Subsequently, we had suggested to the Americans that we should take the lead in this matter. The administration could help our Washington embassy prepare the visit, but we firmly believed that this should be a Vietnamese affair, not an American one.

The idea had been accepted by Bunker, and back in Washington I had gone over it with Bill Bundy at State and Bill Jorden at the White House. Nevertheless, as if by sheer habit, the White House staff took the business into their own hands, neglecting to even inform me of the delegation's members as they were chosen. My intention had been to send each of these people a formal invitation on behalf of the South Vietnamese government, and it was an embarrassment to me when the news media announced the list of delegates — which included many congressmen, senators, and clergy — before I had a chance to get the letters prepared and sent. It was a small thing, perhaps, but typical of how the Americans' enthusiasm and eagerness to do everything their way could sometimes become overbearing.

I spent the last part of August organizing briefings for the observers, in addition to carrying on the usual work of the embassy. By that time there was no doubt in my mind about what the election results would be; the sheer abundance of civilian candidates was enough to ensure that the Thieu-Ky ticket would win handily. Still, I was anxious about how the observers, whose own standards of democracy derived from the two-century-old American tradition, would view what was about to take place in South Vietnam.

More damaging than any incidental irregularities they might see was the attitude toward the elections that was already being spread by the increasingly antiwar press. By this time it was apparent that any event in

Vietnam that did not fit the antiwar bias would be distorted or dismissed by many in the media and in academic circles. The elections were no exception, and so I had the distinctly unpleasant experience of watching the American media vilify the process, which I and others had been working toward since before Honolulu and hoping for since 1954. To the critics, the elections were nothing more than a prefabricated farce arranged through the collusion of the military dictators and the American embassy. Given this kind of atmospheric poisoning, I was sure that many of the observers would approach their job in a less than objective frame of mind.

I must also say that these concerns were compounded by a persistent nervousness that the voting might in fact not go well. I had talked at length with Thieu and Ky about the need for a clean election. Not only was it unnecessary for them to try to manipulate the voting, given the likelihood of their success; blatant improprieties would be disastrous. But these were not individuals who came from a democratic background, and because I was not there to see what was happening, I was more than a little anxious.

September 3, voting day, was declared a national holiday throughout South Vietnam. On that day people dressed in their holiday clothes and went to the polls en masse. Of the six-million-plus registered voters, more than five million cast ballots, a turnout of over 80 percent. Two days later the vote count was completed, and the final tally brought some real surprises. The Thieu-Ky ticket had won, as expected, but despite the advantages of their incumbency, they had polled only 35 percent of the total vote. In second place, with 17 percent, was the maverick peace candidate Truong Dinh Dzu.

The same general pattern prevailed in the senatorial elections, which were held at the same time. Of the sixty newly elected senators, more than one-third were either self-proclaimed independents or confirmed opponents of the government.

Thieu and Ky were badly disappointed that they had been elected with such a low percentage. But as Ky was quick to point out, at least the results demonstrated that there had been no attempt to prevent people from voting as they wished.* "Had we rigged the election," he said, "we certainly would have gotten a more respectable percentage of the vote."

---

* Ky told me later that the government had given no formal instructions to provincial authorities about influencing voters in any way. On the other hand, he said, there was of course a tacit understanding about the kind of vote he and Thieu would like to see. As a result, there was no doubt that some pressure had been applied where local authorities were especially zealous and well organized. But the result showed a very uneven pattern and consequently a relatively clean election.

Ky's assertions were largely seconded by American and international election observers, and their positive comments reinforced the U.S. embassy's evaluation of the overall fairness of the process. Washington was extremely pleased. Although by itself the voting would not alter the course of the war, I regarded it as an extremely important step. We had managed to achieve a real democratic election for the first time in South Vietnam's history. And this in the middle of the war, with the Communists on one side and two career military men on the other. I considered it a signal accomplishment for the nation.

Chapter 25

A Change in Mood

THE ELECTIONS, HOWEVER, were only part of the overall picture. Although the country was now enjoying a degree of political normalcy undreamed of two years before and the threat of a Communist military victory was no longer palpable, still, deep under the surface, feelings of discontent were widespread. Many Vietnamese resented the growing dependence on the Americans and their increasing visibility in every aspect of life. It was obvious to everyone that they were fundamentally unlike the inveterate French colonialists, but that did not prevent people from wondering out loud how South Vietnam could maintain its own identity if the Americans were dominating everything, from the country's economy to the manner of waging war.

These worries were reinforced by the Americans' characteristic "take charge" attitude. In the provinces, for example, they were eager to get their programs implemented quickly, and that usually meant doing it all themselves, often with only the most perfunctory contact with the Vietnamese province chiefs. On the war front, American officers rarely informed the Vietnamese of the details of even major operations. The majority of the Vietnamese General Staff had no idea from day to day of what it was that the American forces were doing.

General strategy, too, was a bone of contention. To a man, the Vietnamese generals were convinced that the only effective strategy would be to "march north," to strike hard at the source of their ills or at least to pose a credible threat above the seventeenth parallel. But the Americans maintained that it was simply impossible to accept that kind of thinking. They suggested, politely of course, that the South Vietnamese must be crazy. They couldn't even keep their own house in order, so how could they want to invade North Vietnam? In fact, this approach was largely a rationalization; with their unpleasant experience in Korea in the background, the Americans were primarily concerned to avoid provoking the apparently militant Chinese.

But whatever the feasibility of such a move, I thought it made no sense at all to announce to the enemy what you would and would not do. Every action the Americans took had to be confined to the framework of a "limited war," as if North Vietnam would bind itself to the same ground rules. True, the United States was a global power that had to take into account such factors as the Soviet reaction and the possibility of Chinese intervention. But for the South Vietnamese it was a different story. They were at war already, and their existence was being threatened. It was they who had been invaded. And although they were told it was their war, the Americans tended to elbow them aside at every turn.

There were good reasons for this, of course, ranging from the disparity in size between the two allies, to the ingrained passivity of many Vietnamese, to the traditional Asian tendency to avoid direct confrontation — to acquiesce instead, or to seem to acquiesce. There was also a feeling among the Americans that Vietnamese civilian and military officials were ineffective and often corrupt. For their part, Vietnamese resented American attitudes that were too often based on ignorance of Vietnamese customs and values. As a result, productive cooperation between Americans and South Vietnamese seldom materialized.

In Washington, too, the mood was getting edgy. The summer of 1967 was relatively quiet on the war front, but in Congress, as one of my journalist friends put it, "On the surface it might look like calm waters, but watch out for the undercurrents." The combination of continuing American casualties and no decisive results was stirring a restlessness that had not been apparent earlier.

I already knew the views of the doves, so I now concentrated my attention on the hawks, to try to determine just what changes were taking place. I particularly sought the voices of John Stennis of Mississippi, Henry Jackson of Washington, and Strom Thurmond of South Carolina, senators whose influence on the Armed Services Committee was well known. Although they maintained their long-time support, I did sense an increased frustration with the administration's "no-win," limited strategy.

These three, as well as others I spoke with, had also become concerned about the cost of the war and its impact on domestic programs. (On August 10 President Johnson had proposed a 10 percent tax surcharge on individual and corporate incomes.) Before, my administration contacts had always assured me that Congress would approve the president's budget requests. But now they were beginning to worry about it. As one State Department expert on congressional affairs told me, "It's the beginning of the [fiscal] year and we had better watch out."

As I continued my explorations with senators and congressmen (and as often as not with their staff, who frequently had a closer view of the situation than their bosses), I began to realize as never before how complex this task was that I had so easily assumed. Neither Washington nor Saigon ever remained the same, and as the middleman between them, I had to strive to interpret and reconcile not only their different perspectives but also the shifting realities and how these realities were perceived in the two capitals. There was a never-ending need to assess and reassess. The job was daunting, and more than once I questioned my own adequacy to perform it.

President Johnson, too, felt the sand beginning to shift under his feet. As the news media continued to proclaim the war a stalemate and antiwar sentiment expanded its beachhead in Congress, Johnson decided to take the offensive. To show he was ready to "go the extra mile" for peace, he declared on September 29 in a nationally televised speech from San Antonio that the United States was "willing to stop all air strikes when this will lead promptly to discussions." This carefully worded formula was slightly more flexible than his earlier proposals. It was part of a delicate flirtation with negotiations (of which we were not informed) between the Americans and North Vietnamese which were begun in June by two French go-betweens, Raymond Aubrac and Herbert Marcovich. But despite indications from the French that Hanoi would now be more accommodating, Johnson's new offer was not taken up. The air war intensified.

As the air assault on North Vietnam stepped up, so did U.S. opposition to the war. In October there was a massive protest at the Pentagon, with many nationally known figures, including Norman Mailer and Arthur Miller, participating. At almost the same time, *Life* magazine, which until then had staunchly supported the president's policies, condemned the war in an editorial. These two events greeted congressmen as they returned to Washington from the summer recess and set a very uneasy mood for the fall session.

I spent a good part of that fall attempting to gauge the extent of the transformation that was clearly taking place. I tried to take comfort in the opinion of many of my American friends who said that the media's bias and the protests reflected only a part of overall public sentiment. I even began accepting speaking engagements in the Midwest and deep South to try to judge for myself if they were right. For the same reason I expanded my college speaking schedule.

The results were not always happy. At one college in central Massachusetts I stepped up to the podium and faced an angry crowd screaming epithets and chanting, "Ho Chi Minh, Ho Chi Minh." When they began throwing eggs, the people who invited me said they thought we should leave. But I decided to stay. I just stood at the podium for about ten minutes, until there was a lull in the shouting. Then I took the microphone. With a big NLF flag waving in the audience, I told them as calmly as I could, "Listen, I came here in good faith. I believe the tradition among Americans is for anyone to be able to present his point of view. That's the only thing I am asking." Little by little it quieted down and I began to talk. It was not easy to accept the insults, but I swallowed them, and on that occasion I finally did get my chance. That was still possible in 1967 and 1968. By 1970 it no longer was.

On September 17 I took advantage of a trip back to Vietnam (for consultations on the new government) to bring Thieu and Ky up to date on developments in the United States. I had previously talked to Ky about eroding domestic support for Johnson's policies, but this time I hit the issue as hard as I could. I distilled for them what was happening in Congress and in the media and told them about the increasingly frequent protests on the streets and campuses. I presented an analysis of my talks with various high-ranking military people. The Americans, I said, will not be around after another five years. We have got to organize ourselves to deal with that.

I was not happy with the reception these comments got. Thieu and Ky seemed to treat what I was saying in an offhand way. Although I was out of touch with South Vietnam's domestic situation, it was evident that they were preoccupied with their own problems and that much of this had to do with their continuing rivalry for power. But that wasn't all. The fact was that they simply found it difficult to grasp the nuances of the American system and how its many interest groups inevitably affected and even determined national policies. Although each time I returned to Vietnam I made a point of trying to convey to them the texture of the Washington political scene, I never felt I was more than partially successful.

The Johnson administration, on the other hand, was taking the changing national attitude very seriously indeed. The president kept a very high profile regarding the war, a clear sign of its importance to him. In every way he could, he tried to promote an atmosphere of normalcy, if not progress and optimism. On November 2 he took time to invite me, along with the ambassadors of Australia, Indonesia, Malaysia, Taiwan, and Laos, to a White House luncheon, at which he reiterated his San Antonio formula for a bombing halt and insisted on his determination to bring peace to the area. A week later he took the unusual step of inviting rectors and professors from various South Vietnamese universities to the White House in order to highlight his commitment to the "nation-building" dimension of the American effort. One of these was a Buddhist monk named Thich Minh Chau, who was the head of Van Hanh Buddhist University. I had to admit that in his saffron-colored robes he provided a colorful reminder that not everything in Vietnam was tainted by war.*

Ambassador Bunker and General Westmoreland were also called back to Washington for the president's public relations campaign. The fact that they were both able to leave the country at the same time was another public indication that the situation in Vietnam was not as gloomy as the press was making it out to be. Westmoreland even said, during a *Meet the Press* appearance, that conceivably "within two years or less the enemy will be so weakened that we will be able to phase out our military effort and withdraw some troops." (In fact, Richard Nixon ordered the first withdrawal of U.S. troops little more than a year and a half after Westmoreland's comments.)

But all President Johnson's efforts to reinforce a sense of confidence were shattered at the end of November when, in a surprise statement, the White House announced that Robert McNamara was resigning as secretary of defense and would be appointed head of the World Bank. Somehow, for all their finely tuned antennae, the Washington press corps had not picked up a hint of this bombshell in advance. Though a few of the old hands had speculated over the summer about McNamara's disenchantment with the war, no one had predicted he might leave the administration. The announcement had the impact of a small revolution in political Washington.

My own contacts with Secretary McNamara had been strictly formal. In general the Vietnamese regarded him as a computer man, more interested in facts and data than in understanding the human dimensions of the situation, certainly not much concerned to develop relationships with Vietnamese. In a culture that prized personal relationships in all aspects of life, often at the expense of the kind of data McNamara constantly sought, his attitude was especially abrasive. The common appraisal of him may, in fact, have been wrong. But since the time he had met with a group of South Vietnamese generals shortly after the Ngo Dinh Diem coup and had somewhat contemptuously asked, "Who's the boss here?" most Vietnamese had considered him a cold and arrogant man.

Nevertheless, McNamara was known as the proconsul of the war. So his sudden departure provoked a decidedly mixed reaction in Saigon.

---

* Ironically, after the war Thich Minh Chau publicly declared that he had for many years supported the Communist cause.

Under ordinary circumstances, a change of personnel in Washington, even at a high level, would not have created much excitement. But in McNamara's case it raised a multitude of questions. Rightly or wrongly, for many years he had personified the American war effort, so many South Vietnamese wondered whether the rumors in the press concerning his disenchantment actually reflected his feelings. And if they did, to what extent did others in Washington's inner circle share them? Specifically, did McNamara's departure indicate an imminent change in the administration's overall policy?

I was reassured on this issue by friends in the White House and State Department, and I relayed the message to Saigon. But deep inside I could not help wondering how long support for the war could be sustained if even a man like McNamara had decided not to stay the course. And I knew, too, that primaries for the next American presidential election were only a few months away.

In the meantime, the war continued, but not at the leisurely pace it had assumed during the summer. As Washington began its shake-out over the American commitment to Vietnam, evidence was mounting that a new enemy military offensive was in the making. During one of his November press conferences in Washington, General Westmoreland had said, "I hope they try something, because we are looking for a fight." By the end of the month, it was clear he would not have to wait long to find what he was looking for.

In fact, as early as October enemy activity had begun to increase ominously. The quiet of the summer was broken by a campaign combining guerrilla and conventional warfare. The usual guerrilla harassments were picking up, but in addition, Communist forces also started launching large-unit assaults on carefully chosen targets. On October 29 two regiments of the Vietcong's well-known Ninth Division attacked the provincial city of Loc Ninh, just a few miles from the Cambodian border. Loc Ninh was defended only by South Vietnamese regional and popular forces. But although inexperienced and poorly equipped, they fought courageously, and with reinforcements from regular ARVN units and elements of the U.S. First Division, they beat back the attack, forcing the Vietcong to break off after sustaining heavy losses.

A month later four North Vietnamese and Vietcong regiments attacked the remote district of Dakto, on the Laotian border. The fighting in this difficult terrain was ferocious, and the elite American 173rd Airborne Brigade suffered over five hundred casualties. Ultimately, the enemy was overwhelmed by the firepower massed against them and had to retreat to their Laotian sanctuaries. But their tenacity and ability to fight large-unit encounters was a grim augury.

These two attacks, together with indications of intense southbound traffic on the Ho Chi Minh Trail, led intelligence analysts in Saigon and Washington to conclude that a large offensive was brewing. The heavy North Vietnamese build-up in the demilitarized zone and around the Khe Sanh Valley suggested to Westmoreland that the attack would come in northern South Vietnam. As a result, he began to shift U.S. army units upcountry while the marines busily reinforced their base at Khe Sanh.

With conclusions drawn as to where the offensive would strike, military planners decided to disregard a set of captured documents that detailed a large-scale attack of a very different nature. These plans outlined a nationwide general offensive of "very strong attacks in coordination with the uprising of the population to take over towns and cities." The strategy described in these documents was so audacious, so unthinkable, that no one accepted its validity. It was only with the dawning of Tet, the lunar new year, that analysts realized what they had had in their hands.

Chapter 26

Tet Mau Than

AS THE FALL OF 1967 merged into winter, I continued to assess American opinion on the war, watching intently the impact of Lyndon Johnson's Vietnam public relations campaign. Meanwhile, in Saigon the new government was off to an auspicious start. Nguyen Van Thieu had been as good as his word. As part of the deal he had cut with his disappointed vice president, Thieu had agreed to allow Ky to choose the prime minister, and consequently to name the cabinet. With the real power firmly in his own hands, Thieu could afford to be magnanimous.

As a result, after the elections Ky and the new prime minister had been busy negotiating with the various political, religious, and regional groups whose participation in the new government was considered crucial. It was to assist in putting together this balancing act that I had been called home in September.

On October 17, when I was still in Saigon, I received a cable from Washington. My wife had gone into George Washington University Hospital, where she had given birth to our third child, a healthy baby boy. Because the due date was not for another two weeks or so, the news came as a surprise. The next day I was on a plane back to the States, where the relative quiet of the next couple of months allowed me to enjoy our newest addition. I traveled, gave speeches, and worried about the McNamara resignation and the quickened pace of fighting, but I also had more time at home than I was used to, and I vowed to make the most of it.

Tet Mau Than, the Vietnamese new year, is more than a holiday; it is a symbol of hope and peace and new beginnings. For years Tet had been honored by both sides with a three- or four-day truce, allowing soldiers to return to their homes, celebrate the ingathering of their families, and venerate their ancestors — also giving a brief respite to the warring governments. Always, Tet is an occasion for feasting and visiting, an exceptionally busy time for all Vietnamese, even those living in foreign places. It was an excellent time, I thought, for our newly enlarged family to get away from it all.

In this spirit, at the end of January my wife and I decided to take a short ski vacation with the children to Camelback, Pennsylvania, not that distant from Washington but far enough to enjoy a feeling of isolation from the usual tension. By that time, my daughters had become fairly good skiers, and I had been surprised to find that I, too, liked the challenge of trying to stay on my feet in the snow, that strange element I had first wondered at in Switzerland back in 1952.

Early in the afternoon of our first day at Camelback, I was paged on the bunny slope with a message to call the embassy. When I did, my staff assistant told me excitedly that Saigon was under attack by Communist forces, that I was needed back in Washington immediately. Within an hour we had gotten everyone off the slopes and packed, and had trundled the whole family into the car for an anxious drive back to the city.

By the time I got to our embassy on Sheridan Circle, it was already six or seven in the evening of January 31. My staff was ready with a full status report gathered largely from Pentagon and State Department sources. It was evident that Saigon was undergoing a major assault in which enemy commando units had managed to penetrate the American embassy compound, though not the embassy itself, and to briefly seize the radio station. This was apparently part of a coordinated countrywide offensive that had caught both the Americans and South Vietnamese off guard. At the White House there was real consternation at first, which did not begin to diminish until it was clear Ambassador Bunker was safe. Even then, Rostow, Bill Jorden, and the National Security Council staff were quite concerned about whether the South Vietnamese would be able to hold.

The attack had caught President Thieu at his wife's family home in the Mekong Delta, but Ky was handling things in the capital. By the time I managed to get a call through to him, the situation had already improved substantially. He told me that we were in control of the situation, that the Vietcong had already been wiped out at the U.S. embassy compound, and that security precautions at the government radio station had prevented the enemy from going on the air with their call for a popular uprising. It would take some time to clear them out of the city altogether, he said, but already there was no question that the attack had failed. From the provinces there were still only scattered reports, but from what he could tell, it looked as if the same general pattern was taking shape: initial surprise followed by strong military response and heavy Vietcong losses.

Meanwhile, even as I was taking stock, events in Saigon were being played out on American TV screens. The film clips were dramatic, electric. We saw Bunker inspecting the embassy, where the Vietcong dead were still sprawled on the ground. Elsewhere in the city, Vietcong and American soldiers were shooting at each other while officers and sergeants screamed orders that were picked up clearly by the mikes of the reporters who were huddling behind cover just yards from the action. Even veteran TV war viewers had not seen anything quite like this before.

During the next two days our political affairs officers worked around the clock, as did our military and press attachés. Between their reports and my own contacts with the White House and Saigon, I was able to piece together a decent picture of what had happened. Vietcong and North Vietnamese forces had launched a countrywide offensive the object of which was to take cities and start a widespread popular rebellion that would bring chaos to the population centers and precipitate defections by South Vietnamese army units.

With the traditional Tet fireworks sputtering in the streets, at first most people had not even realized that fighting had broken out. Moreover, the very idea of frontal assaults against the cities in the face of South Vietnamese and American firepower was so preposterous that early reports of attacks were taken as jokes. But it was no joke at all. In Saigon and some of the provincial capitals, Vietcong commandos had succeeded in infiltrating prior to the offensive, even bringing heavy weapons in with them. Under cover of the chaotic pre-Tet traffic and the usual holiday excitement, they had slipped units into the city using a variety of ingenious subterfuges. Afterward, people recalled an unusual number of funerals wending their way through Saigon's streets, and prisoner interrogations later confirmed that some of these had been staged: the mourners were Vietcong guerrillas, the caskets loaded with weapons and explosives.

On the night of January 31, the commandos struck at selected targets in the capital: the presidential palace, police and navy headquarters, the radio station, and the Joint General Staff compound, in addition to the U.S. embassy. At dawn these attacks were reinforced by main-force assaults in the northern and southern suburbs. The results were spectacular. The city that until then had been almost impervious to the war suddenly found itself in the midst of ferocious street fighting. In many cases the enemy initially succeeded in penetrating the inner defenses of their targets, but nowhere could they hang on. At the U.S. embassy the Vietcong assault unit that had breached the compound wall was eliminated by early morning. By noon the last guerrilla at the radio station had been killed.

Although the enemy commandos had achieved almost complete surprise, the vigorous reaction of Saigon's military police, under Ky's volatile supporter General Nguyen Ngoc Loan, prevented any major disasters. Then, quickly marshaled South Vietnamese and American army reinforcements stopped the Communists' main-force units and began driving them back from their objectives. After several days of confused and vicious fighting, the back of the offensive had been broken.

The same was true in the provincial capitals that had been attacked simultaneously with Saigon. In Cantho, Bentre, Vinh Long, Chau Doc, Mytho, and other cities, early Vietcong and North Vietnamese successes were quickly reversed and enemy units suffered devastating losses from concentrated American and South Vietnamese firepower.

The only exception to the pattern was Hue, the lovely imperial capital in the center. There the enemy took most of the city and held on for three blood-drenched weeks. Casualties among soldiers on both sides were exceptionally heavy, as the Communists retreated slowly before the South Vietnamese infantry and U.S. marines, then made a determined last stand in the citadel, an old fortress in the middle of town. It was in Hue, too, that the most severe civilian suffering occurred. As soon as the city was occupied by Communist troops, people's committees and special military units began instituting revolutionary justice. Before it was over, almost three thousand people had been murdered, including Catholic priests, foreign doctors, newsmen, and people from every walk of life who had somehow made it onto the execution lists. Some had been clubbed to death, some shot, and many were buried alive in the war's most dramatic example of barbarism.* But, fortunately, Hue was the only place the Communists held long enough to assert their authority.

Although the optimistic account I had gotten from Vice President Ky over the phone during the first day of the offensive was borne out within the next thirty-six hours, American media coverage that first week was conveying quite a different story. Especially on television, the scenes of war communicated a feeling of impending disaster. Drawn to the most

---

*The true extent of the Hue massacres became evident only slowly. As late as nineteen months after the battle, U.S. troops from the 101st Airborne Brigade discovered a mass grave with the remains of over four hundred Catholics, who had been led from Hue's Phu Cam Cathedral, where they had taken refuge. In the aftershock of the Tet offensive, news of the killings in Hue was diluted, never entering the American public's awareness as did, for example, the far less extensive incident at My Lai. (Dan Oberdorfer's *Tet* is the most authoritative Western account of the slaughter in Hue.)

vivid and dramatic fighting, the network's cameras presented, night after night, ferocious battles in which it was difficult to distinguish winners from losers. Even when the commentary was more accurate, the lingering impression was of hard-pressed government troops and GIs fighting desperately to stem the tide.

Although there was no possibility of competing with the media, at the embassy in Washington we put together background briefings for the press and for the staffs of congressional committees with jurisdiction over the war. As often as I could during the week of Tet, I organized press luncheons at which I attempted to convey reliable information and put the offensive in perspective. Among other things, I pointed out that the battlefield reports were all positive, that the Vietcong was suffering crippling losses, and that the war would certainly not end with this battle. The real question, I told reporters, was not the outcome of the offensive, but whether or not it would lead the United States to change course.

I was especially anxious about the effect the offensive would have on American public opinion. At the beginning, of course, I shared some of the dismay evident at the White House. But even when I was sure that the offensive was becoming a military disaster for the Communists, I was still concerned. It was just impossible to tell what effect the reporting and photographs would have. Pictures like *Life* photographer Eddie Adams's shot of General Loan shooting a captured Vietcong in the head were extraordinarily powerful. They crystallized the war's brutality without providing a context within which to understand the events they depicted. No one looking at Adams's picture, for example, could know that the man Loan was executing was a member of a Vietcong assassination team that had just murdered the wives and children of several police officers. As a result, the immediate reaction to such scenes was a gut revulsion to the barbarity of the war which tended to supersede more rational, long-term considerations. What the eventual consequences would be in regard to U.S. support were impossible to predict. But it was a worrisome subject.

At least in the immediate aftermath of the Tet offensive, Congress and the administration were not badly affected. If anything, policymakers seemed upbeat and reassured. South Vietnam had defeated a carefully planned and executed assault that struck without warning throughout the country. Not just defeated it but crushed it. When the analyses were done, it appeared that the Vietcong had lost between 35,000 and 40,000 men, fully half of their effective fighting strength.* Although the enemy

*Afterward there was a good deal of conjecture about how the Communists could have miscalculated so badly. Some have even speculated that the North Vietnamese politburo set up the southern Vietcong guerrillas, who were on the front lines and suffered accordingly. Certainly it is true that after Tet the war became mainly a North Vietnamese army

had billed Tet as a "general offensive and general uprising," there had not been a single uprising. Whatever claim the revolution might have had to controlling the South Vietnamese people's hearts had been revealed as baseless. Whatever hopes they had had for precipitating mutinies within the South Vietnamese army had evaporated. On the contrary, ARVN had shown itself capable of quick retaliation and effective fighting.

But despite the military victory, little by little the implications of the offensive began to exert a different effect. In particular, Americans were struck by the contrast between the enthusiasm of President Johnson's public relations campaign and the reality of enemy capabilities. Westmoreland and Bunker had been so optimistic during their recent U.S. tours, but now it seemed as if all the talk about progress and being "in control" had been either blatantly mistaken or intentionally deceptive. In Congress and among the press, people started asking questions. How could American intelligence estimates have been so woefully inaccurate? Why was it that with half a million American soldiers in the country, the Vietcong was still able to penetrate the major cities in force, even to attack the American embassy?

Slowly it became clear that whatever the military results, psychologically the offensive undermined the Johnson administration's credibility. It made people distrust the government's assessments, its judgment. And in so doing it cast doubt on the entire war policy.

Officially, in the executive branch at least, there was no sign of an imminent policy change. On the contrary, in the weeks following Tet, President Johnson reaffirmed the American commitment to Vietnam in unequivocal terms. Nevertheless, I began to pick up grumbling and new skepticism from various quarters. It was said that Clark Clifford, who had taken Robert McNamara's place as secretary of defense and who was one of Johnson's closest advisers, was turning away from the war. Military friends told me that the civilian aides McNamara had left behind at the Pentagon — Paul Warnke, Leslie Gelb, Morton Halperin, and others — were now explicitly, though not yet publicly, favoring a policy of disengagement.

I was most alarmed, however, by a conversation I had with Hedrick Smith of the *New York Times* somewhere near the end of February.

---

affair, and when it was all over, the South Vietnamese revolutionaries had almost no leverage with their North Vietnamese cousins. This *cui bono* reasoning is augmented by the fact that during the offensive Vietcong units were ordered to hold against the South Vietnamese and the Americans long beyond any reasonable hope of success, and by the fact that they never received the North Vietnamese reinforcements their commanders were expecting. On balance, it is still not likely that there was any conscious design of this sort. But it could not have escaped the politburo planners that if the offensive was to fail, almost all the losses would be borne by their southern allies.

Investigating a story about a new request by General Westmoreland for even more American troops, he asked if I could use my own channels to confirm for him the nature and extent of what Westmoreland wanted. I told Smith candidly that I could not be of much help, because South Vietnamese officials rarely knew what was happening on the American side, particularly about such matters as force levels.

But that was hardly the end of it. Smith's questions alerted me that something was up. Before long I was able to learn that Westmoreland's new request had indeed stirred intense wrangling between hawks and doves in both the administration and Congress. This was a mortifying development. With the government's credibility coming under increasingly heavy attack in the aftermath of Tet, and with the New Hampshire primary only weeks away, I sensed that a conflict about additional troops would quickly turn into a widespread debate on the Johnson administration's overall conduct of the war. Politically and psychologically, such a request could not have been more poorly timed.

Truly apprehensive that we were approaching a watershed in American policy, I alerted Saigon and tried to ascertain exactly what was happening in the heart of the American administration. The first step was to ask Thieu and Ky to call me back for consultations. With that done, I requested meetings with Rusk, Clark Clifford, and several other key government and congressional figures. It was just as I began making my rounds that Hedrick Smith's story broke in the *New York Times*. The front-page headline for March 10 blared out: "Westmoreland Requests 206,000 More Men, Stirring Debate in the Administration."

The reaction came hard and fast, fulfilling my grimmest expectations. Denunciations roared in from Fulbright, Mansfield, Robert Kennedy, and others, all of them from the president's own party. Rusk was called to testify before a hostile Senate Foreign Relations Committee, the spectacle carried live on national television. Under aggressive, accusatory questioning, he seemed as determined as ever but was not, I thought, particularly convincing. When it was finally over, what remained was the painful impression of a hard clash between Congress and the administration.

At just the same time, the New Hampshire primary began making news, the race there providing a forum for Senator Eugene McCarthy to blast Johnson's war policies, again with full media exposure. On March 14 the primary's startling results came in. McCarthy had missed beating Johnson by a scarce three hundred votes.

It was against this backdrop that I went about gauging the mood in Congress. First I called on George Aiken, as sympathetic and astute a friend as I had on Capitol Hill. It was a cold morning in March when we sat down to breakfast in the Senate cafeteria, and Aiken's comments did nothing to dispel the chill. My notes on the meeting record that, among other things, Aiken said, "The president sincerely believes in his policy, but he no longer has the support of people in his own party. I'm not talking about the dove senators; you know them already. I'm talking about the people who have supported him up to now, like Stennis and Jackson. He can't even count on them anymore. A few years back you could talk about a consensus on Vietnam. But even if it did exist, right now it's disintegrating fast." A bit later he added prophetically, "My guess is that Bobby Kennedy will get into the race soon. Then everything will break loose."

In the time I had known him, I had always found Aiken's judgments to be not just candid but accurate. Certainly, I could not have gotten a clearer indication of what to expect in Congress. With his information in mind, I turned my attention to the White House. From Aiken and others I had learned that in every administration, at the moment of an important decision, there is always a fight for the mind of the president. Given the developing policy crisis, it occurred to me that I ought to try to see Johnson himself, as well as Rusk and Clifford. I did not harbor any illusions about being able to influence the president, but I did think that even a brief discussion would give me a chance to understand where he stood. During a meeting with Walt Rostow and Bill Jorden, I raised the question of seeing the president. Their reaction was positive, and on the morning of March 18 Jorden called to say that Johnson would meet with me at the end of the day.

Late that afternoon I went to see Jorden (to deflect the press), then walked with him over to the Oval Office. There Johnson greeted me with all his usual warmth. But as I sat down on the couch, facing him in his rocking chair, I recognized that he was a changed man. This most forceful and energetic of leaders looked drawn and exhausted. There was an air of lassitude about him that was dramatically different from anything I had ever seen before. He seemed to bear on his shoulders the entire weight of a war that had simply become too heavy a burden. Not for the first time, I felt a flood of sympathy for him.

I began the meeting by reviewing the situation from Saigon's perspective. I told him that although there were, of course, tremendous difficulties, we believed we had all the important aspects of the war well in hand. We had just won a resounding military victory that had put the enemy at a substantial disadvantage. We were making good progress restoring normal life in the countryside and gaining the confidence of the people. The victory had engendered a widespread feeling that the Communists could be beaten, and building on the new enthusiasm, we had announced a complete mobilization of manpower, starting with eighteen-year-olds, something we had never before felt able to do. As far as additional U.S. troops were concerned, I advised him that we were ready to increase our own share of the fighting. Our army, however, was suffering from a shortage of modern weapons, assault rifles in particular. Very few of our units were equipped with M-16s, while our North Vietnamese adversaries were all armed with Chinese-made AK-47s.

This last point seemed to surprise the president, who looked over at Jorden, the only other person there, and asked him to make a note of it. Other than that, Johnson sat silently in his chair throughout my presentation, his chin resting heavily in his hand. Occasionally, he raised his eyebrows over the rim of his glasses, as if to get a better look at me, but I had the impression as I spoke that for the most part he was absorbed in his own thoughts.

When I was finished, Johnson just sat there silently for a minute or two. Then, slowly, he picked up the conversation. "If we don't win," he said, "we are in deep trouble. I've tried my best, but I can't hold alone." I made an attempt not to show my surprise at this admission from a man with Johnson's pride. As I ran over its implications, I decided that, without telling me so directly, he wanted me to convey to Thieu and Ky that he was not going to be able to sustain his commitment. But he did not elaborate further, changing the discussion instead to the business of the M-16s, which he said would be given serious consideration.

All in all, I did not spend more than forty minutes with Johnson. Yet at the end, I realized that a major change in policy had already been decided on, that in the fight for the president's mind, those who advocated a new direction had now prevailed. Leaving the Oval Office, I passed through corridors that, at the end of the working day, were almost deserted. I walked slowly, awash in a sea of grim reflections about the future.

Two days later I kept my appointment with Clark Clifford at the Pentagon. I knew Clifford from meetings in Saigon, where he had visited several times while on special missions. A close friend of Johnson's and a consistent backer of his policies, Clifford impressed me as an affable man who expressed himself naturally in the careful and precise language of an experienced international lawyer, more diplomatic than the diplomats themselves.

That, at least, had been my previous impression. But when I saw him on March 20, he had traded his normal reserve for an obvious impatience. He told me that he had received word from the president about our request for M-16s and that he would do his best. Then he launched into a blunt, emotional description of the administration's new mood. Again, the notes I made directly after the meeting convey the flavor of

Clifford's remarks. "We have run out of time for diplomatic niceties," he said. Then, alluding to the on-again, off-again jockeying between Thieu and Ky, "We are sick to death of their feuding. Our people are discouraged and our support is limited."* As we concluded this very uncomfortable talk, Clifford rang a note of despair that paralleled the words Johnson had used. "We must find a solution for this," he told me, "or we will be facing a disaster."

My final meeting prior to flying home was with Dean Rusk. Talking with him, I got the distinct impression that the three of them — Johnson, Rusk, and Clifford — had coordinated their messages to me. For his part, the secretary of state, the man who just a year and a half ago had told me, "When Americans decide to do something, they do it," now said, "We have no choice. Now we have to win not a military victory but an honorable peace." It was the first time I had heard that particular combination of words: "an honorable peace." They were to stay with me on the long flight back to Saigon, and I was to remember them later, in October 1972, when Henry Kissinger announced that the United States had gained for itself "peace with honor."

*Tet had caught Thieu away from Saigon, leaving the vice president to oversee the successful South Vietnamese counterattack. As a result, there was something of a push from the American mission to give Ky more authority, which had led to a renewed round of bickering between the two leaders.

Chapter 27

The Talks Begin

SEVERAL HOURS after I left Rusk, I was on the plane to Saigon, carrying the message that the American will to continue the war had begun to collapse. The next day I gave a full report to Thieu and Ky, emphasizing that we were now looking directly at an American disengagement. Although I had not heard this explicitly, my meetings with Johnson, Clifford, and Rusk left no room to doubt that U.S. policy was undergoing a radical alteration. The inevitable result, I told them, would be the withdrawal of American troops — not right away, of course (over half a million GIs were in South Vietnam), but gradually, over an extended period.

Thieu and Ky reacted with a kind of diffuse worry. For them this was a serious problem but not an immediate one; there was still plenty of time to deal with it. At the moment, they were busy attending to the more pressing business of getting the second, smaller wave of the Communist offensive fully under control. Although they asked my impressions of the American political campaigns, it was obvious I had not been successful in conveying the implications of the administration's new frame of mind. I left the briefing feeling that, despite my efforts, neither Thieu nor Ky really grasped what it meant. Perhaps, I thought, it was necessary to live in Washington to measure the impact of such things on the complex American political process.

It was neither the first nor the last time that my inadequacy in translating the realities of my two worlds to each other bore home on me. Living in the American capital, I began to realize, too, that the perceptions and nuances that governed its political landscape were insinuating themselves more and more into my own outlook.

The aftermath of Tet was a telling example. Preoccupied and perhaps conditioned by the depressing mood in Washington, I was surprised to find that Saigon had emerged from the offensive invigorated and optimistic. It was impossible not to feel the enthusiastic spirit that had replaced the usual doom and gloom about the war. True, sporadic fighting was still going on not too far from the capital, and Hue was only slowly recovering from the bloodbath it had been subjected to. But everywhere I saw and heard indications that, far from collapsing, the government and army had been strengthened by the experience.

The initial shock of the massive assault had been severe but the end result was that the enemy had finally come out in the open and had been destroyed. Government and military officials, and ordinary people, too, had had a chance to see the Vietcong up close and realized that the feared guerrillas were not ten feet tall. Besides the substantial if intangible lift in morale, concrete results were also evident, among them an increase in the number of South Vietnamese army recruits and the formation of volunteer block committees to monitor neighborhoods for Vietcong infiltration and activity. The turnaround was evident for anyone to see. Ironically, it had come at precisely the moment when Washington had begun to lose heart.

On March 31 the extent of the American malaise was driven home as Lyndon Johnson gave a televised speech (broadcast in Saigon as well) that ended with the explosive declaration that he would not be a candidate for re-election. I was watching the speech that evening with Vice President Ky. We both knew exactly what it meant. Johnson, South Vietnam's staunchest friend, would be gone from the political scene in a matter of months. Imponderable forces would come into play; there would be a new president and a new policy. Whatever they were, we would now be traveling a slippery and dangerous road into the future.

That evening President Johnson also announced another in the sporadic series of American bombing halts. Each one of these halts had been calculated to tempt the North Vietnamese to the bargaining table, but until now none of them had drawn more than scorn. This time, however, the politburo responded. Three days later word came from Hanoi that they were ready to begin discussions. In the wake of this announcement, Westmoreland and Bunker returned to Washington for consultations. So it was that, in a matter of a few days, the Saigon government was faced with an entirely new situation.

During my years in Washington I often heard critics say that the Saigon regime's raison d'être was the war itself, and that for this reason alone Saigon systematically opposed any peace talks. The truth of the matter was that in peace, as in war, the South Vietnamese never had the chance to make a free choice. In 1965 the United States took over the fighting and, to serve its own interests, employed the strategy of limited warfare to try to defeat a wholly committed enemy waging total war. By the same token, we feared that American peace initiatives were meant to serve the purposes of the United States, without much regard for the desires or needs of South Vietnam, the only nation whose existence was at stake. Motivated partly by increasingly vocal domestic opinion and partly by a genuine if naïve optimism, the Americans were desperate for talks at any cost. Out of these negotiations, so they believed, would come the acceptable compromises that would allow them to put an end to their military involvement.

It is no exaggeration to say that every South Vietnamese with a working knowledge of Communist tactics and strategy was convinced there was not a single chance for serious negotiations at this stage of the war. We understood that for the North Vietnamese politburo, these talks would simply constitute another method of fighting, that the war had now entered what Communist theoreticians called "*danh va dam, dam va danh,*" the phase of "fighting and talking, talking and fighting."

Basically, "fighting and talking" was a strategy to be used against a stronger opponent once the opponent had begun to show signs of fatigue and internal stress — that is, when time was clearly on your side. At that point talking becomes desirable not in order to reach a compromise resolution (the American concept of negotiations) but to feed the enemy with hope and consequently heighten divisions within the enemy camp. The idea was, again in Communist terms, to "stimulate and nurture the enemy's internal contradictions." Far from moderating the armed struggle, talking was to be accompanied by fighting, to continue the pressure that brought the enemy to the table in the first place.

There was no great secret to any of this. Hanoi's military and political planners even discussed *danh va dam* openly in their serious journals. As I watched the Americans race to Paris, it was evident that they had less than a full understanding of the people with whom they were so eager to begin compromising. Equally disturbing was the fact that, as usual, we had not been consulted about these talks and were not to be formally included in them. The meetings would be strictly an American–North Vietnamese affair, which on the one hand fueled our fears about American intentions, and on the other gave credence to Communist claims that their war was against the "American aggressors," thus undermining the legitimacy of the South Vietnamese government.

But in spite of all this, there was little we could do. Theoretically, we could have vigorously objected to the talks. But that would have further alienated opinion in the United States. (Public opinion in South Vietnam was another matter. There we were hard pressed to explain why it was that the Americans were talking to the North Vietnamese. We emphasized that these were just preliminary talks, that nothing substantial would be discussed, that only technical matters would be dealt with. It was at best a confused and difficult situation.) In fact, because this was an American initiative that had been answered by the North Vietnamese, the talks would go ahead regardless of what we might say. For lack of an alternative, then, we put on our best face and acquiesced with as much grace as we could muster.

The American political scene was becoming increasingly intense and complex. Primaries were in full swing. The candidates (now including Robert Kennedy) were making their moves and outlining, or at least hinting at, their positions. The whole changing-of-the-guard process was unfolding even while the lame duck administration was attempting to move ahead in Paris. Under these circumstances, it seemed to me that just keeping up with developments in Washington would be a full-time job, but Thieu and Ky felt otherwise. Thinking more of my access to and rapport with the Americans than of my physical limitations, they now appointed me South Vietnam's "official observer" to the peace talks, in addition to my job in Washington.

With no choice in the matter, I stayed a few more days in Saigon to develop my plan of action, then flew to Washington to meet with the newly designated American negotiators: Averell Harriman and Cyrus Vance, former deputy secretary of defense. On my arrival I was delighted to learn that my two old friends William Jorden and Philip Habib would be rounding out the American team.

Harriman, nicknamed the Old Crocodile, was no stranger to me either. Because he was the senior Democratic diplomat, I had made it a point to pay my respects at his Georgetown home when I first arrived in Washington. Since then, our relationship had been cordial, and each time he was sent abroad on a mission related to Vietnam, we had gotten together for an exchange of views.

Cyrus Vance I had not met before. I did, however, know him by reputation, having heard nothing but praise for him in Washington's political circles. The day I returned from Saigon, I arranged to have lunch with him, eager to size up the delegation's number-two man. I soon found it a real pleasure to work with this immensely decent person. Vance had a crisp, analytical mind, typical of the breed of international lawyer–public servant who seemed born to deal with complicated world issues. Before the lunch was over, we had succeeded in working out a method for coordinating our activities at the upcoming talks.

* * *

In May Paris was magnificent. My own presence there as an observer was more than a little awkward, though, an obvious patch-up job to save the appearance of American–South Vietnamese unity. Certainly, it could not conceal the fact that the future of South Vietnam was now on the table, at which the Americans sat on one side and the North Vietnamese on the other, while I hovered somewhere on the sidelines. The whole arrangement shouted, "This is an American war."

But uncomfortable as it was, Paris also offered opportunities, and I intended to make the most of them. I was convinced that nothing of substance would happen in the talks, that the North Vietnamese had come not with peace in mind but only to further their strategy of playing for time and exacerbating American political divisiveness. Consequently, I thought that since we were engaged in a pure propaganda gambit, there was no reason to let the North Vietnamese monopolize the stage. With hundreds of reporters covering the conference, there was a chance to make a significant impact on the international press, if matters were handled properly.

As I began making my contacts, the first negotiating sessions were held at the Majestic Hotel. They produced nothing. The North Vietnamese came encased in rigid armor, refusing to do anything more than reiterate their unswerving propaganda line: the United States was responsible for everything; the United States had to completely cease its bombing (Johnson's halt had not included the area below the twentieth parallel); the United States had to withdraw all its troops from the country. For their part, the Americans were more serious; they had, after all, come to Paris to negotiate. They avoided invective, listened patiently, and probed, hoping to find a hook with which to pull the North Vietnamese toward substantive talks. They seemed hopeful. For them, the mere fact that the two sides were sitting in the same room was by itself something of an accomplishment. There was plenty of time for exploration and maneuvering; the breakthrough could come later.

The glacial movement — if it could be called movement — of the early sessions fit my own plans perfectly. As an observer, I had no definite responsibilities. Two or three times a week I drove from the Hotel Claridge on the Champs-Élysée over to the U.S. embassy, to be briefed on a session just completed or to help prepare for an upcoming one. In either case it was routine, a friendly exchange of ideas rather than a discussion of pertinent developments, because there were no pertinent developments to discuss. My daily reports to Saigon contained little of interest and nothing at all of substance. As a result, I was able to devote practically my entire time to a political and public relations counteroffensive of sorts.

Having a horde of journalists in one place was a bonanza for someone who wanted to make a public point. For starters, I accepted all the interviews I could possibly fit in. One day I met with André Fontaine and Claude Julien of *Le Monde*, the next with Roger Massif, Nicholas Chatelain, and Max Clos from *Le Figaro*. I did interviews for the *Times* of London, German and Italian newspapers and television, and what seemed almost daily background briefings with American journalists, of whom I remember especially Stanley Karnow, Marvin Kalb, Peter Kallisher, James Wilde, Takashi Oka, and Jessie Cook.

With all of these people I had to answer embarrassing questions about why we were in Paris as observers and why the United States was talking for us. But I was also able to clearly state our position. South Vietnam, I said, desired peace. We were in favor of any talks that explored avenues toward that end, even bilateral talks between North Vietnam and the United States. Nothing could demonstrate our good faith more forcefully than the evident fact that we would not block these meetings. However, South Vietnam absolutely reserved to itself the right to determine its own fate in any substantive talks pertaining to the future of our country. I then called for direct negotiations between South and North Vietnam as the shortest and most direct route to peace.

This call was rebuffed by the North Vietnamese, as I knew it would be. When questioned about the proposal by reporters, they simply answered that it had no meaning. Undoubtedly, as long as the Americans had agreed to talk to them, there was not a chance in the world they would meet with us.

A few days after my public proposal for direct talks, I met with the papal legate, a man known to have contacts in every corner. I suggested to him in my most diplomatic French (a language wonderful for conveying layers of allusive nuance) that if there was an opening on the other side, my government would of course be interested to learn of it. This probe, too, was stopped cold. From time to time, the legate and I would meet and I would inquire; the response never changed. In private as well as in public, our enemies would have none of it, confirming (had I needed any confirmation) that Hanoi was there to match patience with the eager Americans, not to move toward someone else's idea of peace.

At any rate, my public overtures had served their purpose. They had gained South Vietnam a measure of sympathy in the world press. They had also provided me an opening into the highly politicized and largely hostile Vietnamese community in France.

The Vietnamese émigrés in France had a long history of support for political movements in their native land. Vietnamese political figures, from Phan Chu Trinh (whom my father had lived with in the early twenties) to Ho Chi Minh, had found a home among them and support for their causes. During the anti-French war the overseas Vietnamese were effectively organized; they provided financial support for the Vietminh and played an important role in turning French public opinion slowly against what became known as "the dirty war."

The most vocal part of this community still had pro-Communist sympathies, but there were also active nationalist groups, some of them associated with the various Vietnamese nationalist parties. But even these people had very strong reservations about the Thieu-Ky government, and one of my aims in Paris was to change their hostility into support.

Toward this end, I invited many of the prominent activists to a meeting, knowing they would come but expecting a confrontation. As usual, my approach was to take the bull by the horns. "I know you have reservations about this government," I said. "But I can tell you that I was once a student activist myself. So I think I understand your feelings. For a moment I'd like you to forget that I am an ambassador and to think of me as a kind of older student. At least all of us here are nationalists, so let's talk about that, and about Thieu and Ky. I know you have problems with them. But I'd like to know explicitly, from your own mouths, what the problems are. What exactly do you have against the Saigon government?"

Their answers were as direct as my questions. They told me point blank that there were two things they did not like at all. They were disgusted by the corruption they were hearing about, and they hated the fact that Thieu and Ky were puppets of the Americans.

My answer to this was very simple. I told them that even though I was part of the government, that didn't mean I talked to Thieu and Ky about everything, and it didn't mean that I myself didn't have problems with the regime. "You can look at Thieu and Ky," I told them, "and say that these people are corrupt and that we won't have anything to do with them. In that case, you can wait until you yourselves are in power, and then you can clean the entire house, do things exactly the way you want.

"But I would say to you that if you keep waiting for that moment, you will never live to see it. The Communists will come in and you will be forever and eternally in the outer darkness. With the totalitarian side, you do not have a single chance. With this side, you do. Of course you want to keep your hands perfectly clean. But you know, in politics there is hardly such a thing. If you want the Saigon government to be clean, you have got to get involved in it. You have a chance to do this. Everybody knows the saying that only the one under the blanket knows what goes on in the bed. Well, I am under the blanket, so I know what goes on. And I have serious reservations about these people. But I can tell you that there is a chance of working with Thieu and Ky. With the other side there is no chance to do anything.

"I don't know, perhaps there are some among you who will report what I am saying back to Thieu or Ky, and I don't care about it. We are all nationalists. We have common ideals. We have no choice but to get together. But it depends on you to see that."

The meeting lasted the entire day, and slowly my approach succeeded in dispelling the antagonism. But really, these were easy things for me to say. I actually did have a great deal in common with these young activists, at least in terms of my basic outlook. Our differences were primarily in the philosophy I had adopted over the years, I suppose as a reaction to the painful stripping away of my own political illusions. Rightly or wrongly, I had come to believe that you have to put your hand to what is possible. If you want to strive to avoid the worst, that is the only path to take. You cannot afford to wait for the perfect time — which means that circumstances can force you to ally yourself with the relatively bad. Under these conditions, you can work toward what you see as the good, or at least the better, while accepting the limitations on your hopes and goals and methods. On this path, I believed, you can, with luck and some help, make progress. If you only wait on the sidelines roaring your anger, you are sure to be lost.

This is the message I tried to get across that afternoon. As the meeting drew to a close — in a far friendlier atmosphere than it had started — I said that I had not asked them there to support Thieu and Ky, but only to talk about how we nationalists could best get together to oppose the Communists. I was asking for no promises, no resolutions, nothing like that. I did not want to know what they would decide to do afterward, but whatever it was, I would consider it a personal understanding between us, and they should know that I stood ready to help.

This lengthy affair was only one of many heated discussions I had with the overseas activists. Such meetings, together with the interviews, briefings, radio and TV appearances, the regular discussions with the American team and the French diplomatic circle, filled out my daily schedule, from Tuesday to Friday, throughout the summer of 1968. On Friday afternoon I would make my way to Orly Airport to catch the 4:30 TWA flight to Washington. There I would work with my staff until Monday or Tuesday, trying to bring myself up to date on intervening events and chart the course of the presidential campaigns that were now at their peak. Then it was back to Paris aboard the Air France Washington–Paris shuttle, whose cabin crews soon came to know my habits by heart.

This transatlantic commute would have been exhausting under any ordinary circumstances, but that summer was anything but ordinary. In France and the United States the streets were raging with marches, demonstrations, and, on occasion, pitched battles between demonstrators and police. In the United States students were protesting against the war, but in Europe the anger was focused on "the establishment," in all its ostensibly grisly manifestations. In Paris, where we were supposed to be talking about peace, the atmosphere was so volatile it seemed almost like the first stage of a revolution. One day, strikers prevented us from landing at Orly and forced the plane to divert to the Bretigny military airport. Another day, I was not able to get out of Paris at all, but was forced to leave for Washington from Brussels. I remember that trip particularly well. I was on my way to the funeral of Robert Kennedy, senselessly gunned down a few days earlier, right after the California primary.

It was during this extremely hectic period that I made a special trip to New York City to meet with Richard Nixon, who had by then become the Republican candidate for president. This meeting (had I only been able to foresee its consequences) would eventually lead to a considerable political imbroglio, in whose aftermath I was to be charged with improperly influencing the outcome of the American presidential election. The agent through whom this was said to have taken place was the elegant and intriguing Madame Anna Chennault.

Chapter 28

The Anna Chennault Affair

AFTER THE TRAGIC ASSASSINATION of Robert Kennedy, the American presidential race developed into a contest between Hubert Humphrey and Richard Nixon. I had known Humphrey for quite a number of years, both as senator and vice president, and we maintained an easy, friendly relationship. As vice president, he had, of course, supported Lyndon Johnson's war policies, and he was especially enthusiastic about the rural development programs, which accorded with his own brand of democratic liberalism. Now, with Johnson having opted out of the race, Humphrey was in an awkward position. The gathering tide of antiwar sentiment suggested that he should divorce himself from Johnson on the Vietnam issue, and this was probably in line with his own wishes. But with Johnson still head of the party and still president, this was delicate ground, and Humphrey was having considerable difficulty negotiating it.

Nixon I had met in 1953, when he visited Vietnam as vice president. But all I really knew of him was what I had heard during his 1960 campaign against John F. Kennedy, when I was quite taken with the energetic, appealing young senator, whose election I had first rooted for, then rejoiced over. But now, with the Democrats distancing themselves from Vietnam, I began to view Nixon more sympathetically.

In the middle of June Anna Chennault suggested I might like to meet with Nixon. Chennault was the widow of air force hero Claire Chennault, who commanded the famed Flying Tigers in Burma during World War II. Born of Chinese parents, after the war she became one of the most visible Asian-Americans, close to the China lobby and active in certain Washington political circles.

She was also quite interested in Vietnam and visited the country often.

She had a sister living in Saigon, and the Flying Tigers air freight company, which her husband had founded after the war, did a substantial amount of hauling for the Defense Department between South Vietnam and the United States. I met her first in Saigon in 1965, when I was special assistant to then Prime Minister Ky, with whom Chennault was already on friendly terms. Eager then to know as much as possible about Washington, I saw her frequently and we became friends. Later, when I was a novice ambassador, she helped me find my way around the American capital. Among the people she introduced me to was Tom Corcoran, the New Dealer who was known as Mr. Democrat. Corcoran had provided Chennault's entrée into the world of Washington politics, and eventually he became a close friend and invaluable counselor to me as well. It was Anna Chennault, too, who introduced me to Everett Dirksen, telling him that I was her "good friend from Vietnam." Dirksen responded warmly, saying in his husky baritone, "Listen, good friend, you come to me if you need help." It was an offer I had taken prompt and repeated advantage of.

It was one night in June when I was having dinner at the Georgetown Club with Corcoran, Republican Senator John Tower, and Chennault that Anna suggested I get together with the Republican presidential candidate. She was at that time working on the Nixon campaign committee and indicated that she had direct access to the nominee. It was an intriguing idea, and I told her I would think it over. For some time my staff had been monitoring the development of both the Democratic and Republican platforms, and through friends in the parties, I had tried my best to influence the planks on Vietnam. Now I had an opportunity to discuss the issues with one of the candidates in person.

That was an enticing prospect, but also a dangerous one. Any meeting with Nixon would carry the inevitable implication that I was somehow dealing behind the Democrats' backs, an impression I wanted to avoid. Johnson had been a great friend, and Humphrey might yet win. I certainly did not want to jeopardize South Vietnam's relations with the Democrats. Yet how could I turn down a meeting with the Republican front-runner? On balance, I decided that if Anna was actually able to arrange it, I would have to meet with Nixon. But I would do it independently, without reporting to Saigon, so that Thieu could later repudiate the move if necessary.

On one of my weekly return trips from Paris in early July, I learned that the meeting was on and had been scheduled for July 12. A book that discusses this period, *The Man Who Kept the Secrets,* by Thomas Powers, affirms that by this time I was being watched by the CIA and that the National Security Agency was intercepting my cables to Saigon. If they were, I was completely unaware of it. But all the same, I realized that eventually the Johnson administration was bound to learn of the meeting, so it seemed the wisest course would be to inform them in advance.

At that point, I was conferring almost daily with Bill Bundy and Walt Rostow about the Paris negotiations and also about arrangements for an upcoming meeting between Johnson and Thieu. Accordingly, several days before seeing Nixon, I brought up the subject with Bundy. As a friend and an experienced diplomat himself, Bundy understood my position and accepted my assurances that I would limit myself to a general discussion with Nixon and would not go into details about the peace talks.

Believing I had found a way through the mine field of this meeting with Nixon, on the twelfth I flew up to New York to see him at his Hotel Pierre headquarters. Waiting for me in the lobby was Anna Chennault. A few minutes later I was being introduced to Nixon and John Mitchell, his law partner and adviser. Although Nixon had been described to me as an odd and difficult man, that day he could not have been more gracious. He did his best to put me at ease and listened attentively as I gave him an overview of the war and described the various military problems, especially the need to furnish South Vietnam's army with M-16s and other modern infantry weapons. During the discussion he inquired about North Vietnam's dependence on the Soviet Union and China and conjectured about the extent to which Hanoi could be pressured through her two major allies.

Toward the end of our talk, I raised the subject of the increasing unpopularity of the war in the United States. I told him directly that I anticipated an eventual withdrawal of American troops, and I mentioned that I would like to see an intensive training program to enable the South Vietnamese to take over the burden of their own defense. Nixon's immediate response to my suggestions was positive, though I had no sense that he was already thinking along the dual lines of Vietnamization and negotiations, which within a year would form the pillars of his Vietnam policy. Finally, Nixon thanked me for my visit and added that his staff would be in touch with me through John Mitchell and Anna Chennault. I left the hotel quite pleased with the encounter, happy to have made contact with the Republicans and happy, too, that I had been candid about it with the Democrats.

In the rush of flying back and forth between Paris and Washington, with side trips to Saigon to prepare for the Johnson-Thieu summit, I soon forgot the Nixon meeting. Within a couple of months, though, it would come back to haunt me.

* * *

On July 18 Johnson and Thieu met in Honolulu, where I witnessed nothing other than pro forma mutual reaffirmations of solidarity and devotion to peace. Nothing was happening in Paris either, where the talks continued without a single sign of progress. Back in Washington from Hawaii, I was rushing out to keep some speaking engagement when my wife stopped me and asked if I knew where I was going and what I was going to say. I knew that my chauffeur knew where I was supposed to be, but I myself did not have the slightest idea. I realized that I had finally reached the end of my rope. I was physically unable to continue the frenzied globetrotting of the past several months. So I insisted that Saigon find a replacement for me in Paris, and on August 28 I made a last trip there to introduce the new man, Ambassador Pham Dang Lam, to Governor Harriman and the rest of the American negotiating team.

Immediately afterward, I returned to my permanent post in Washington, where the presidential race was now in full cry, and the Vietnam War was the dominant issue. Nixon was claiming that he had a secret plan to end the war, and Humphrey was desperately maneuvering to distance himself from his own past as vice president in an administration that was under violent attack from antiwar critics. As far as I was concerned, this was the time to pull out all stops in laying South Vietnam's case before as many influential people as I could reach. Consequently, I plunged head first into the overheated Washington political world, seeing senators and congressmen of both parties, newsmen, and political commentators — everyone I could get my hands on. As the Democrats steered with all due haste away from the Indochinese involvement they had engineered, I was increasingly attracted to the Republican side. As far as courting Republicans went, there were few places in Washington like Anna Chennault's penthouse apartment at the Watergate. Obviously wealthy, she gave frequent cocktail parties and receptions, attended by a good part of the capital's political society. By October I was back in touch with Anna, who was now co-chairman of Nixon's fundraising committee, and Senator John Tower, chairman of the Republican Key Issues Committee. I also got together with George Bush and other Republicans from whom I was trying to elicit support for a strong Vietnam policy. Politically, it was a tense time, a period when the polls showed Hubert Humphrey cutting deeply into the lead with which Nixon had opened the campaign.

On October 15 Phil Habib, back in Washington for consultations, came to see me with news that the North Vietnamese had responded favorably to an American offer to stop all bombing and shelling north of the seventeenth parallel. (Johnson's bombing halt of March 31 had not included the southern part of North Vietnam, from where the Communists staged their attacks on American and South Vietnamese troops in the I Corps region.) In exchange, the politburo was willing to expand the Paris talks to include the South Vietnamese — whom they habitually referred to as American "puppets" and "lackeys" — as well as the National Liberation Front, whom they called "the sole legitimate representatives of the South Vietnamese people."

I already knew about this development, having just been informed of it by wire from Saigon. As I understood him at the time, Thieu believed the North Vietnamese offer was nothing but a ploy to influence the presidential race in favor of Humphrey, whom they much preferred to Nixon, with his cold war background. By accepting the American offer, the North Vietnamese were achieving both a bombing halt and this potentially vital ability to affect the election. In return, they were agreeing merely to begin another round of talks, which would be only as substantial as they themselves desired. In other words, it was costing them nothing.

Thieu was furious, but his anger, as I learned later, was not wholly justified. In fact, he had been informed privately of the American position several months earlier. He knew that the United States was ready to accept expanded talks that would include the NLF within a vague our-side, your-side formula. Feeling pressured by the Americans, Thieu had acquiesced to these conditions back in July, but with profound inner reservations. He hoped — and believed — that the North Vietnamese would never agree to such an offer. But now they had, and at the worst possible moment: just before the elections, a time when the Democrats would have every incentive to move fast rather than to insist on spelling out the details of the expanded talks.

I shared Thieu's concerns fully. I wanted the strictest assurances that the inclusion of the NLF in these talks would not lead eventually to some form of American recognition. I also wanted assurances that the North Vietnamese would enter into direct, substantive talks with us. If they did not, we would remain outsiders, watching as our fate was decided by others.

Already we had watched for five months as the North Vietnamese persistently demanded that the United States stop all its bombing, withdraw all its troops, and depose Nguyen Van Thieu. We had watched the American negotiators become increasingly impatient to find some reciprocity on the Communist side. They seemed to think the Communists should act like normal negotiators and say something like, "If you do this, we will do that." But instead they had been treated to a propaganda campaign from which they were prevented from withdrawing by their own hopes.

In my opinion, there was every likelihood the campaign would go on.

As long as the Americans were assailed by increasing domestic divisiveness over the war, the Communists would just wait patiently, without budging from their most militant demands. That was what the "fighting and talking" strategy was all about. Their adversaries would be under growing political and popular pressure to make concessions, while they themselves were subject to no equivalent compulsion. And while all this unfolded, we would be relegated to the sidelines. These were the reasons we needed the firmest assurances that we would be intimately involved and that any new talks would be substantive.

We were going to face tremendous pressure on this, so I buckled down to make a real fight of it. Saigon bombarded me with cables informing me of what was happening between Bunker and Thieu and with instructions for my *démarches* for the White House and State Department. I spent my days closeted with Bundy and Rostow and a good part of each night reporting by cable to Saigon.

Finally, after a cascade of memos, explanations, and clarifications between Washington, Saigon, and Paris, a resolution of sorts was reached between Thieu and Bunker. The essential elements of the agreement were an unambiguous American pledge not to recognize the NLF as a separate entity and a guarantee that North Vietnam would engage in "serious and direct talks with the Republic of Vietnam." With this done, a declaration was produced in which President Johnson and a still unhappy President Thieu were to announce a total bombing halt and the beginning of newly expanded talks in Paris.

I received a draft of the agreement by cable on October 29, seven days before the election. It read in part, "The first meeting of direct talks will be convening in Paris as of [time and date]. Delegations of the Republic of Vietnam and the United States will attend that meeting." After laying out the terms of the agreement, the cable continued, "I draw your attention to the words 'serious and direct talks with the Republic of Vietnam.' "* By this time, Humphrey had closed to within several percentage points of Nixon, well within the pollsters' margin of error. Among the Democrats there were high hopes that this announcement would tip the scales.

Suddenly it all came to a halt. At about 4 A.M. on October 30, I was awakened by a phone call from Hoang Duc Nha, Thieu's cousin and personal secretary. Thieu had reconsidered his position and would not agree to the joint declaration after all. Subsequent to the agreement, Ambassador Lam cabled Thieu from Paris that he had just been told by Harriman and Vance that the United States was in fact not going to insist

* Strictly confidential cable #449CMAE, from the Ministry of Foreign Affairs in Saigon (now in the Indochina Institute Collection, George Mason University).

on some of the procedures that were included in the draft agreement. In particular, Harriman had told Lam it would be impossible for the United States to force the North Vietnamese into "serious and direct talks" with South Vietnam. Consequently, no such guarantee would be forthcoming. With this development, Thieu had decided to withdraw his commitment to send a delegation. Lam had already been recalled to Saigon for urgent consultations.*

Early that morning, on specific instructions from Saigon, I went over to the State Department to request a clarification from Bill Bundy. I was under no illusions about how upset the American administration would be about this last-minute monkey wrench Thieu had thrown in their works, and I was prepared for a difficult meeting. But I was not ready for the reception I got when I arrived in Bundy's office.

Bundy, whom I considered a good friend and colleague, did not even ask me to sit down. In a frigid tone I had never heard from him before, he informed me bluntly that the U.S. presidential election had nothing whatsoever to do with the negotiations in Paris. With that, he stood up at his desk and turned his back to me, as if he could not say what had to be said face to face. Looking at his back, I heard a mumbled growl of words, among which I distinctly made out "improper," "unethical," and "unacceptable." Then, still with his back turned, he started making allusions to my connections with the Nixon camp.

I was dumbfounded by the whole performance, but hardly in the mood to sit still for an attack like this, friend or not. Obviously, Bundy was laboring under a serious misapprehension about what had gone on between Nixon and me. So, once I caught my breath, I told him firmly that I had done nothing that could be construed as detrimental to the good relations between our two countries. I reminded him that in July I had given my assurance that my discussions with Nixon would not touch on any specifics of the Paris negotiations. I had done nothing contrary to that pledge. My relations with the Republicans consisted only of normal contacts I could be expected to maintain. I categorically rejected the suggestion that I had done anything improper.

For his part, Bundy did not make an outright attack. He could hardly say that the administration inferred something was going on between the South Vietnamese and the Republicans from having studied my secret cables. Nor was I willing to push this argument to the edge — for example, by asking him directly what he thought had transpired between me and the Republicans and on what basis he came to think so. As a

* The same day as Nha's call, Thieu cabled me to confirm the telephone message. Strictly confidential cable #3222-PTT-VPM, from the president's office in Saigon (now in the Indochina Institute Collection, George Mason University).

result, mutual restraint prevailed, and once we had both calmed down, we were able to start exploring ways of resolving the new impasse.

Although we tried our best (Bunker and Thieu were meeting at the same time in Saigon), the issue was too complicated and it was too late. The next day, October 31, Johnson dropped his political bomb in a televised address. "We have reached a stage," he said, "where productive talks can begin." There would be a complete bombing halt and expanded talks in Paris. Representatives of the government of South Vietnam were free to participate. Representatives of the National Liberation Front would also be invited, though that did not in any way indicate American recognition.

A day later Thieu announced that although South Vietnam did not object to the bombing halt, no South Vietnamese negotiating team would at present be going to Paris. For the first time in the war, the two governments acknowledged openly that they were at odds. As far as the election went, the pollsters said that Humphrey had gained significant support subsequent to the president's announcement of the bombing halt but had lost it after Thieu's refusal to go along with the new peace talks.

As luck and Murphy's Law would have it, the breakdown between the two governments came out in the open on Vietnam's national day, November 1. This meant that in the middle of frantic negotiations with the Americans and complicated press briefings, our embassy was on the verge of hosting a major reception, with more than a thousand guests from Congress, the administration, the diplomatic corps, and the public.

Nevertheless, the affair went off on schedule, and by Washington standards for such things it was a resounding success. It was also the scene of a fine display of graciousness on the part of the Johnson administration. All of South Vietnam's friends were there, including Rusk, Rostow, Bundy, and other top government officials — in plain view of the media, as if to show that the rift between Americans and South Vietnamese was in essence a family affair that would soon pass.

The week just ended had been extraordinarily busy and difficult. I had spent the best part of Monday and Tuesday in strenuous discussions with Bundy and Rostow. Johnson's speech had come on Wednesday, and Thieu's refusal to participate on Friday. On Thursday there had been a large reception at the embassy, then on Friday the thousand-guest gala. I badly needed a day off. But it was not to be.

The next morning, November 2, was a cool, sunny Saturday, just three days before the elections. I was awakened early by a call from the embassy decoding officer telling me that two urgent messages had come in from President Thieu. I rushed through the streets, nearly deserted at that hour, thinking that perhaps another new crisis was in the works. But the cables proved not so urgent after all. Certainly, they contained nothing that would help resolve the tense confrontation we were still involved in. I was on the verge of going back home when a call came in from Saville Davis, the *Christian Science Monitor*'s Washington correspondent, who wanted to see me on what he said was an extremely important matter. Davis was one of the press people I had lunch with from time to time, and I could hardly turn down a request like this, even on a Saturday morning.

A few minutes later Davis was sitting in my office, showing me a long teletype he had received from Beverly Deepe, the *Monitor*'s correspondent in Saigon. According to Deepe's sources, Ambassador Bui Diem had sent a telegram to President Thieu urging him not to send a delegation to the Paris peace talks. She then noted rumors circulating among journalists that the South Vietnamese had made a deal with Richard Nixon. The essence of the deal, she wrote, was that Saigon would drag its feet on the Paris talks in order to sabotage the political momentum Humphrey might otherwise have gained, thus turning the election in favor of the Republicans. As president, Nixon, of course, would show his gratitude by providing stronger support for South Vietnam than what the Democrats could have been expected to provide.

I was flabbergasted. Silently, I raced through a second reading, realizing that exactly this information must have been behind Bill Bundy's angry reception a few days earlier. I knew for sure that there was no secret deal, but I could not imagine how such a misunderstanding could have started. I had no idea what to say to Saville Davis, who was now asking me if I could confirm the story. He and I both realized that if this was published, it would cause a political scandal that could seriously affect the outcome of the election.

I knew this would not be easy to clarify in a brief discussion, even if I knew all the answers. And any statement I made would be dangerous. Even a flat denial would create undesirable repercussions once the story broke, leaving me with the onus of having intruded unconscionably into a very close race, where only a slight shift in opinion could decide who would be the next American president. (In the end Nixon beat Humphrey by less than 1 percent of the popular vote.) I could, of course, hide behind the infamous, hypocritical "backgrounder" rule and say anything I wanted, though not for attribution. But my main concern was to be honest with myself. I also did not want anyone grilling me until I had had a chance to sort it all out. To Davis I said, "I can neither confirm nor deny anything. As the representative of my country, my job is to be in touch with all segments of American society and inform my government about what is happening here. As far as my personal recommendations to President Thieu are concerned, those matters are strictly confidential, and I would not wish to comment one way or another."

Davis left the embassy perplexed, not knowing what to do with the cable. It was the last time I saw him. To my knowledge, the *Monitor* never printed the story. Unable to establish whether the information in the cable was true or false but well aware of its volatile nature, they did the ethical thing. Whether Nixon would have won had the charge been aired that he had sabotaged the peace talks is impossible to say. But William Safire, a speech writer for Nixon at that time, opined in his book *Before the Fall* that, as it turned out, "Nixon would probably not be president were it not for Thieu." This assigns Vietnam and the Paris talks too much weight, perhaps, but in an election as close as that of 1968, anything could have happened.

When I had seen Davis off, I sat down and tried to figure out what was behind the *Monitor* story. Since Beverly Deepe mentioned that I had urged Saigon not to send a delegation, I began reviewing the cables I had written to Thieu during the intense two weeks since the subject of expanded talks came up. Among them, I found a cable from October 23 — six days before the October 29 cable from Saigon informing me that agreement on South Vietnamese participation had been reached on the twenty-eighth — in which I had said, "Many Republican friends have contacted me and encouraged us to stand firm. They were alarmed by press reports to the effect that you had already softened your position." In another cable, from October 27, I wrote, "I am regularly in touch with the Nixon entourage," by which I meant Anna Chennault, John Mitchell, and Senator Tower.

These were the only relevant messages I had sent back to Saigon.* They certainly did not mean that I had arranged a deal with the Republicans. But putting the two together and looking at them in the context of the charged pre-election atmosphere, I saw that they constituted circumstantial evidence for anybody ready to assume the worst. (I did not know how my cables could have leaked to the American administration — or to Beverly Deepe, for that matter — but I had the uneasy feeling they knew everything). On the other hand, it was well known that Thieu had had plenty of reasons to oppose the expanded talks without

---

* In *The Man Who Kept the Secrets*, Thomas Powers wrote, "During the week which ended Sunday, October 27, the National Security Agency intercepted a radio message from the South Vietnamese Embassy to Saigon explicitly urging Thieu to stand fast against an agreement until after the election. As soon as Johnson learned of the cable, he ordered the FBI to place Madame Chennault under surveillance and to install a phone tap on the South Vietnamese Embassy."

making any deals with anyone. After all, the South Vietnamese president had agreed to sign a joint declaration on October 28, which he had overturned only after Phan Dang Lam's report pointed to the serious inconsistencies in the American position. He would hardly have come to an agreement at that late date only to step away from it a day later.

Although I knew I had not been involved in a deal, there were still some uncomfortable ambiguities in the situation, especially concerning the role played by Anna Chennault. My impression was that she may well have played her own game in encouraging both the South Vietnamese and the Republicans. She was in touch with John Mitchell and Richard Allen (Nixon's foreign policy adviser and, years later, Ronald Reagan's national security adviser), she was in touch with me, and she also had other avenues to Thieu, primarily through his brother, Nguyen Van Kieu, South Vietnamese ambassador to Taiwan. What messages went to what people during that hectic and confused time are certainly beyond recovery at this point, and the so-called Anna Chennault affair will doubtless remain a mysterious footnote to history, though one that could easily have had greater consequences.

In any case, three days later, on November 5, Richard Nixon was elected thirty-seventh president of the United States. With that event I consigned the whole unpleasant episode to the past, or so I thought. The next Saturday, November 9, I was working alone in the chancery when the doorbell rang. With no staff there that day, I looked out the window and saw an old man on the doorstep, huddled against the wind. I went down to ask what he wanted and was taken aback when I found myself face to face with Everett Dirksen, the Senate minority leader. I ushered him in, and he apologized for having intruded unannounced. He had come over himself, he said, because he had a message of "utmost import" to deliver to me.

As soon as we sat down in my office, he said in his low, husky voice, "I am here on behalf of two presidents, President Johnson and President-elect Nixon." Awed, I listened to him in silence. The message was simple: "South Vietnam has got to send a delegation to Paris before it's too late." Before I could even ask why it might be "too late," Dirksen pressed on. "I can also give you firm and unequivocal assurances that under no circumstances will the United States recognize the National Liberation Front as a separate entity. I absolutely affirm that the United States does not contemplate a coalition government between the two sides in Vietnam."

Dirksen had been so helpful to me and I had so much esteem for him that it was impossible for me to doubt his word. The unusual manner of his arrival only redoubled that feeling. Still slightly in shock, I thanked him for coming and told him I would convey the message to President Thieu immediately. A few moments after saying goodbye to Dirksen, I was back in my office. The telephone rang. It was Joseph Alsop, the well-known syndicated columnist, on the line, asking if he could possibly stop over to see me. He had, he said, an important message to convey. Wondering what in the world was going to happen now, I sat there in my chair and waited for Alsop to make his way over from his nearby Georgetown home.

Joe Alsop was another old friend, a man I had known since the early sixties, when he had made frequent visits to South Vietnam and had been close to Dr. Phan Huy Quat. We had been in frequent contact since my arrival in Washington, and I'd even become his private supplier of *nuoc mam,* the famous Vietnamese fish sauce and hot pepper condiment. He and Dirksen were among my most trusted friends in Washington. It was as if somebody was making a concerted effort to impress me with the seriousness of the situation by using the most effective possible messengers.

Fifteen minutes later Alsop was occupying the same chair Dirksen had recently vacated. I had started some small talk about Nixon when he abruptly interrupted me, saying, "You know, my friend, your president, Mr. Thieu, is playing a deadly game. I saw the old man yesterday, and he is really furious." For a moment I did not catch whom he meant by "the old man," but then I realized he was talking about President Johnson. Remembering what Dirksen had said just half an hour before, I looked at Joe and asked, "Did he ask you to come and see me?"

"Not exactly," Alsop said. More precisely, he had talked with Johnson the previous day, and it was clear the president was losing patience with Thieu. He was so agitated that Joe had felt compelled to convey his anger to me. Nervously smoking and punching out one cigarette after another, Joe strongly advised me to return to Saigon and talk to Thieu in person.

Later that day I received yet another unexpected call, this time from the State Department, inquiring whether Senator Dirksen had seen me. By dinnertime a department official had come to my house to arrange a direct hook-up to President Thieu, using secure Pentagon telephone channels. The next day, Sunday, I met with Bundy for a final review of the situation, and on Monday I was on a flight back to Saigon. It was the first time in almost four weeks that I had had a moment to reflect on the significance of the events that had taken place. I thought, too, about the advent of a new president and a different Vietnam policy and, perhaps, a secret plan.

Chapter 29

New President, New Policy

WHEN I ARRIVED in Saigon on November 13, I immediately told Thieu and Ky about my encounters with Bundy, as well as about Dirksen's and Alsop's visits at the embassy. I tried to convey the anger and impatience impressed on me by Dirksen "on behalf of two presidents." On the fourteenth I briefed South Vietnam's National Security Council, and on the fifteenth the Vietnamese Senate's Foreign Relations Committee.

On November 16 I tackled the problem directly with Ellsworth Bunker. A little over a week later, after numerous proposals and counterproposals and seven drafts, we agreed on formulas that would be acceptable to both sides. At the same time, I told Bunker that we now had a golden opportunity to promote real cooperation between the two governments. This was the ideal moment, before there was a newly defined Vietnam policy, for the allies to begin working toward mutually acceptable positions that would govern the coming negotiations with the men from Hanoi. I had, in fact, been thinking along these lines for several months now, and had recommended as much in my cables and reports from Washington.

Bunker's stature as ambassador to South Vietnam was in part due to the fact that while he was every inch a professional diplomat, at the same time he harbored a deep sympathy for the Vietnamese people and strove within the bounds of his office to work for what he saw as their interests. Our friendship was in part based on this and also on the fact that our concepts of Vietnamese interests often overlapped, if they did not always coincide. He was enthusiastic about my suggestion for an agreement on policy before new talks began, and encouraged me to pursue it. With Bunker's reaction as an extra stimulus, I took the matter up with Thieu shortly before I returned to Washington on December 5. But confronting him in person brought him no closer to a decision than had the written recommendations in my cables and reports. The man had an uncanny way of deflecting those who wanted something from him, putting them off with smiles and promises while drawing the issue into some dark interior corner where he could turn it over and over until it seemed to dissolve away. Only rarely did an actual decision emerge from his anxious and irresolute mind.

To the majority of South Vietnamese, from Thieu and Ky on down, Richard Nixon's election was a reassuring event; they saw the new president as a hard-line anti-Communist. After the uncertainties of the last few months, there was a surge of confidence that Vietnam's cause was now in good hands.

I was considerably less optimistic. Much closer to the Washington political scene than were South Vietnam's leaders, I believed that the momentum for change was now irreversible. Nixon's administration might well prove less susceptible to pressure from the antiwar movement, but the Republicans' long-range eyesight was just as good as the Democrats'. There was little question that the die had been cast. It was no longer a question of whether the Americans would withdraw, but of how the withdrawal would take place. On September 23, more than a month before the election, I had written the following confidential report to President Thieu:

Public opinion here in the U.S. is increasingly impatient about the war in Vietnam and wants an end to it. The reasons for this are to be found both in the mistakes of the U.S. administration and in our own shortcomings. But whatever these reasons are, public opinion is the most crucial factor. We cannot expect to have another Johnson administration with a strong policy on Vietnam, and whether it is Humphrey or Nixon, the situation will change drastically after the election and the focus of U.S. policy will be on how to gradually disengage from Vietnam and end the war.

But although I thought disengagement inevitable, I also came to believe, in the fall of 1968, that Nixon's so-called secret plan to end the war was a fiction, created out of whole cloth to enhance his candidacy. All my observations and contacts at the State Department, the Pentagon, the CIA, and within the Republican party convinced me that in fact there was no plan at all. It was much more likely that directly after his inauguration, Nixon would review the American position on Vietnam and would, within several months, give birth to a firm policy. And it was just as clear that once that policy was in place, it would thereafter guide events.

As I saw it, this meant we had a brief window of time in which to grasp the initiative ourselves. Thieu would have to accept the inevitable, make a virtue of it, and do everything possible to ensure that the American disengagement took place on our terms. All our experience with the Americans indicated that once they had decided on a policy, they would move ahead on it, leaving us with no alternative but to accept their decisions. But if we took a strong, well-thought-out position now, we would have leverage as American policy developed. If we failed to act, we were likely to end up once again as passive witnesses.

On January 13, 1969, a week before the inauguration, I spelled out these thoughts in another long confidential report to Thieu, following up the points I had tried to make during our discussion in early December:*

1. While U.S. policy is not yet defined, I urge you to undertake a complete review of the situation so that we may develop within the next few weeks a rational set of concrete proposals on military, diplomatic, political, and economic matters.

2. Within a short period of time (by mid-February at the latest) after we have completed these reviews, we must provoke discussions with the Americans on the basis of our proposals. Experience has shown that in the past, although the interests of the two allies have coincided in many areas, still mistakes on both sides have been enormous. In the future it will not be so certain that the interests of the two countries will remain identical. Consequently, if we do not present our views candidly now, we will regret it later. . . .

I then moved on to the specific problem of American disengagement.

Particularly on the issue of American withdrawal, I do not know how many troops will be involved, or the time frame, or the conditions, but I know that we cannot avoid this problem. Sooner or later the U.S. government will be forced to take this decision. Consequently, it will be better for us to take the initiative. In so doing we will favorably influence public opinion here [in the United States] and in the world. And public opinion is what counts in a democratic society like the United States. . . .

I never received a response. I referred to this report in subsequent cables. I asked to be called home for consultations. I discussed the matter at length by telephone with Hoang Duc Nha, Thieu's cousin and close adviser. At each step I met only silence.

To me this seemed an urgent, even vital, business. I was sure that get-

* My usual procedure was to compose nightly cables to apprise Thieu of events that day. For ease in coding, these were written in French or English. At two- or three-week intervals, I would write a report in Vietnamese, summarizing the period since my previous report. These were generally twenty to thirty pages long and were sent to Saigon by diplomatic pouch.

ting out in front of the Americans was the only way we were going to have any influence on the disengagement process. I also believed that taking the initiative would be invaluable in conveying the image of South Vietnam as an independent government using American assistance, rather than as a satellite regime being used by the Americans for their own purposes. If the Americanization of the war that began in 1965 had made the Saigon government appear to be an American puppet, U.S. disengagement could be used to help overturn that image.

By this time, I was closely attuned to the powerful, even decisive role of public opinion in the United States. But I was finding that communicating my understanding of the American system to the Vietnamese was a lot like preaching in a desert. There was little receptivity to instruction on such themes as the role of public opinion, the limitations on presidential power, or the importance of Congress. Perhaps because we had lived so long under regimes where public opinion did not count for much, and where the National Assembly could often be controlled or subverted, the ingrained idea seemed to be that in the United States it must be essentially the same. It appeared to me that at heart Thieu and the other military people believed that, however the American government tricked itself out, in the last analysis it was the president's will that counted. All one really had to do was convey matters appropriately to the president. What was the use, then, of the kind of maneuvers the ambassador to Washington was suggesting?

Meanwhile, the Paris talks would reconvene under the our-side, your-side formula, which we had arrived at under American pressure to circumvent the problems that had derailed expanded talks in November. Although the Nixon administration was now busily preparing for inauguration day, secretary of state designate William Rogers called me to say that the outgoing and incoming administrations were on absolutely the same wavelength as far as the negotiations went. Rogers told me that Ellsworth Bunker had received precisely the same instructions from Rusk and himself, as if to confirm that this time there would be no discrepancies in the American position and to breathe a warning to me against another Saigon reversal.

Whatever continuity there might have been between the new and old administrations regarding the Paris talks, everything else in January spoke of endings and beginnings. The melancholy round of farewell receptions for the departing Democrats contrasted sharply with the joyful inaugural parties for the victorious Republicans. It was impossible not to feel that the old era had passed while the new one was eagerly bursting into life.

For me it was a time of mixed feelings, anxiety foremost among them. Assurances notwithstanding, the United States had reached a crucial point in its approach to Vietnam. A new team was coming in, headed by Nixon and Henry Kissinger, strong, intelligent men, but men with whom we had no experience and with whom we had yet to establish a relationship of trust. It was they who would be designing and carrying out the new American strategy in their own style, whatever that proved to be.

Nixon had been Eisenhower's vice president when that Republican administration put an end to the Korean War, where American involvement had also been started by Democrats. Would the new Republican administration likewise succeed in putting an end to the Vietnam War, and could they do it without sacrificing a non-Communist South Vietnam? Such somber questions colored my mood as my wife and I attended the swearing in, parades, and balls that marked the transition. I admired the smooth, peaceful manner with which the Americans handled this changing of the guard — exactly the way I thought this kind of thing should work in a democracy. I felt, too, a touch of sadness as Lyndon Johnson departed almost unnoticed for his ranch, a proud man who, until yesterday, had held in his hands the reins of ultimate power.

Once the inauguration was completed, I set out to explore the new Washington environment, to determine what we could expect from the Nixon administration and to see if I had been right about the heralded secret plan. My first meeting, four days later, was with Henry Kissinger, installed now as national security adviser in Walt Rostow's old office in the White House basement.

I came to this appointment armed with memories of the first time I met Kissinger, in my Saigon apartment back in 1966. He had been in the country on a fact-finding trip for Henry Cabot Lodge, and I had given a dinner for the visiting Harvard professor and a group of South Vietnamese politicians and opposition leaders. Afterward, a number of guests had wondered what he was doing in the country, asking as many questions as he had in his strange-sounding English. Whatever his reasons, my own opinion, gained at the dinner and at a meeting between Kissinger and Ky that I had sat in on, was that the man was brilliant. For someone relatively ignorant of Vietnamese affairs, his questions had been practical and acute, not at all what I expected from an academic.

Now the professor was launched on a meteoric rise indeed, though just how meteoric perhaps neither of us guessed as we renewed our acquaintance in the crowded basement office. In an effort to get an early reading of the new administration's sense of the alliance, I almost immediately brought up one of Clark Clifford's last official statements, to the effect that if South Vietnam did not want to go along with the Paris talks, then the United States would "go it alone." This kind of thing, I told Kissinger, was counterproductive; unless the two governments could see eye to eye on such matters, we would all find ourselves in an impossible situation, not just in terms of immediate problems but also in terms of long-term developments. According to my notes on the meeting, Kissinger's answer was "Well, it won't be like that anymore. The president has said that if there are differences between the two governments, the two governments will work them out. We want very close cooperation."

At this first official meeting, barely a few days after the inauguration, I was reluctant to push Kissinger on issues of substance. What I did pick up was that although the new administration was treating Vietnam with the utmost seriousness, there was, in fact, no secret plan and no definite policy or strategy. Nixon had, though, already given thought to limiting divisiveness between the two governments. As a result, I came out of the meeting quite satisfied, reassured that my intuition about American planning was on target and convinced that there was still time for us to formulate our own approach to disengagement. In a cable to Thieu the next day, I reported the following:

In first contact with Kissinger yesterday I insisted on the necessity of close cooperation between the two governments, not only for immediate problems, but also for problems of strategy regarding the future. I have also insisted on the necessity of avoiding giving an impression of impatience [e.g., toward Saigon,] which can only benefit the enemy. Kissinger assured me that President Nixon had just issued strict instructions for stopping controversy with Saigon and for avoiding public statements to this effect. Kissinger made allusions to atmosphere of suspicion between Saigon and Washington during past few weeks and asked me to come to see him regularly for better co-ordination. Finally he said he does not see any basic difference between the positions of the two governments, but that probably the U.S. would like some flexibility for diplomatic maneuvering.

What I somehow failed to catch was what Kissinger meant by "flexibility" (he used the word twice), which I repeated to Thieu. During our meeting the word suggested to me that though the national security adviser wanted agreement between Saigon and Washington on broad principles, he did not want to be completely tied down by a weak ally. It was, I mistakenly believed, a harmless and natural reservation. A few years later, I had ample opportunity to reflect that the concept was not innocuous after all but held tragic implications for South Vietnam.

In the following days, I completed my rounds of the Nixon administration's appointees. Above all, I was eager to evaluate the officials whose voices would mean most in formulating Vietnam policy. I had been in Washington long enough to understand the pervasiveness of bureaucratic infighting among government departments and agencies, the bosses of which were always looking to enlarge their turf. Kissinger, I knew, would be a powerful influence. How Secretary of State Rogers would stand in the hierarchy I did not know. Nor did I suspect that a sharp struggle would develop between them. My Washington friends told me that the new secretary was better known as a tough negotiator than as a man with a clear vision of U.S. policy.

When I visited him in his vast State Department office, Rogers was congenial and relaxed, certainly a less austere man than his predecessor, Dean Rusk. Rogers had been attorney general under Eisenhower and represented the eastern establishment tradition, courteous and pleasant to deal with. At first blush, though, he seemed to be a man of general ideas rather than sharp intellect. He did not come across as a strong, dynamic personality.

This impression was confirmed in the following months, as the rivalry between Rogers and Kissinger emerged. For historians, the course of their struggle sheds an interesting light on the style of Nixon's administration. For foreigners with policy matters that demanded urgent attention, it was less than helpful. As an ambassador, I was accredited to Rogers's State Department and so had to maintain the best of relations there. But I also had to know where the power was and to create the most advantageous channels of communication. As the conflict between the national security adviser and the secretary sharpened, these two tasks became increasingly more difficult to balance.

Just how difficult was brought home dramatically toward the end of 1969, when I met separately with Rogers and Kissinger prior to a trip back to Saigon for consultations. Rogers suggested to me then that a prolonged Christmas truce might be a good idea, a spur, perhaps, to the still bogged down peace process. When I saw Kissinger the following day, I mentioned that I had met with Rogers and that he had seemed quite interested in a truce. "A truce?" Kissinger interrupted. "No, it's too early for any truce." He paused for a moment, then continued in his most commanding guttural, "I also want you to understand that policy is made right here, *not* in the State Department!"

In addition to Kissinger and Rogers, I also visited Secretary of Defense Melvin Laird, whom I had known as one of the most influential of the House Republicans. As a representative, Laird had been a strong and consistent advocate of support for South Vietnam, and my object in meeting with him was simply to get a feeling for how this skillful career congressman would operate among the Pentagon brass. He seemed right at home in the office previously inhabited by Robert McNamara and Clark Clifford. If there was some doubt in my mind about who would be making foreign policy, there was none at all as to who would be running the military side of things. My gentle probing about new policies, however, elicited from Laird little but smiles and noncommittal generalities.

John Mitchell was another new appointee I wanted to see. Though in theory the attorney general had almost nothing to do with Vietnam, power and influence being what they were, Mitchell was sure to be a crucial figure in the administration. A close friend of the president's, Mitchell, I knew, had been asked to attend National Security Council meetings, though he was not a statutory member. I also knew that he was one of Nixon's few political confidants. Mitchell and I had met on occasion prior to the election, and now he greeted me like an old friend. In the new attorney general I found a useful contact for communication outside ordinary channels, one that I took advantage of several times during the ensuing years.

Finally, I made a quick trip to Paris to confer with the new American team of negotiators. Henry Cabot Lodge and Lawrence Walsh had replaced Averell Harriman and Cyrus Vance, though my old friend Phil Habib was staying on as the permanent member and, by now, vital cog in the American negotiating effort.

From this series of meetings with the new policymakers, I concluded that the Nixon administration's thinking at this point — it could not by any definition be regarded as a "plan" — was based primarily on the vague hope that somehow the Soviets would help convince Hanoi of the necessity for serious negotiations, and on the as yet untested supposition that Saigon would not stand in the way of a gradual withdrawal of American troops. In general terms, the idea seemed to be that strong diplomatic pressure could be applied to Hanoi through their Russian friends, and that the growing burden of domestic opposition to the war could be alleviated as American troops were brought home.

During February and March I was in contact with Saigon almost daily by cable, reporting whatever information I was able to glean about American policy as it developed. As often as I could, I arranged to meet with Kissinger, attempting to probe him for answers. I learned to appreciate the subtle play of his intelligence, but I also found him secretive and evasive. I would, for example, ask about negotiations, only to have him answer, "Well, your president knows about it. He understands the situation completely." In that evening's cable I would double-check to make sure that Thieu was in fact aware of developments, indicating my doubts about Kissinger's forthrightness.

Meanwhile, unknown to us, Kissinger was busily exploring new avenues to a solution with Hanoi: on December 20 through Jean Sainteny, the former French diplomat, and again in mid-March through an attempted overture to the Soviets involving Cyrus Vance. Although Sainteny was involved only as a conduit for messages between Nixon and Ho

Chi Minh, the Vance plan was part of a more carefully worked out strategy. Kissinger had hoped to bring substantial Soviet pressure to bear on Hanoi by linking progress in the SALT talks to progress with the North Vietnamese. Vance was to be sent to Moscow with broad powers to carry on both sets of talks simultaneously. On Vietnam, he would be empowered to reach both military and political settlements with Hanoi, "compatible" (in Kissinger's view) with Saigon's survival.* Neither of these approaches came to anything; the North Vietnamese treated them with calculated scorn. When I learned about them later, they provided a new and disturbing dimension of Kissinger's concept of "close cooperation" between the two governments which he had been so forward in declaring during our first meeting.

Interestingly enough, it was while Kissinger was incubating the Vance plan that the first direct, high-level talks took place between the Saigon government and the new American administration. In France, as part of his first presidential tour of Europe, Nixon scheduled a meeting with Vice President Ky, who at that point was supervising our Paris delegation. Ky asked me to fly out from Washington for it, and in early March, Pham Dang Lam (our permanent representative at the talks), Ky, and I sat down with Nixon, Kissinger, Lodge, and Phil Habib to review the situation. It was a long, friendly session, at which it was decided that Lodge would continue to try to engage the Communists in private talks, because the public sessions at the Majestic Hotel had proved hopeless. Other than this direction to Lodge, neither Kissinger nor Nixon said anything at all about possible alternatives to the official "negotiations," at which the North Vietnamese had done nothing more than reiterate, for nine months now, that the United States must unilaterally withdraw all its troops and that the South Vietnamese government must be dismantled.

Immediately after the Paris meeting, I returned to Washington determined to keep the pressure on Thieu for our own comprehensive review and strategy formulation, the absolute prerequisite, I felt, for arriving at a joint policy with the Americans. But still there was no reply. I knew Nixon would be forced to go public with his own peace proposal before too long, and I could see our grace period coming to an end. It was an immensely frustrating time. In my mind I attributed the silence from Saigon to Thieu's indecisiveness. I could also easily imagine Bunker reinforcing Thieu's natural reluctance to act, urging him not to do anything at this delicate juncture, while the new American administration was still feeling its way among the pieces of the complex situation it had inherited. I had by this time developed the fixed idea that Kissinger was playing

---

* Henry Kissinger, *The White House Years* (Boston: Little, Brown, 1979), p. 267.

things very close to the vest, and that despite what they were telling us, the Americans would do everything they could to keep the initiative firmly in their own hands.

My equanimity was not improved during this period by what seemed a sudden deluge of delegations visiting Washington from South Vietnam. Somehow Vietnamese assemblymen, senators, judges, and members of an astonishing number of government agencies had discovered the concept of "fact-finding" junkets. Where better, after all, to learn first hand about the nuances of the democratic process than in the heart of the world's leading democracy? By the dozen these groups assaulted the embassy with their often unfathomable demands. As often as possible, I would arrange lunches and dinners for them with their American counterparts. But they were also interested in sightseeing and shopping tours, all of which the embassy staff was called on to organize. We learned quickly how to arrange trips to Niagara Falls and other well-known spots, but a request to visit a place like Salem would leave us tearing our hair out. Our atlases listed dozens of Salems, and nobody was quite well enough versed in American history to know which of them might be a tourist attraction, or why. Other times, embassy personnel would get calls complaining that members of one delegation or another were wandering around some first-class hotel in their pajamas, oblivious to the distinctions between Vietnamese and American ideas of sartorial propriety.

In the midst of these distractions, the State Department advised me that Xuan Thuy, Hanoi's representative in Paris, had agreed to private talks with Henry Cabot Lodge, and that the first of these would take place on March 22. Because there had been no coordination between Washington and Saigon on the parameters for such discussions, there was a flurry of concern in Saigon about just what might happen. But any anxiety we may have had about a peace initiative undertaken with no South Vietnamese input was rapidly allayed. Whatever Xuan Thuy's reasons for agreeing to private talks, when he finally met with Lodge, all he did was repeat the same undeviating demands he was making in public.

Former President Dwight D. Eisenhower died at Walter Reed Hospital on March 28 after a long illness. That night I heard from Saigon that my old boss, Nguyen Cao Ky, would come to Washington to represent the South Vietnamese government at the funeral. Ky was, of course, just one of many world leaders who came to pay their final respects to the great World War II leader, among them Charles de Gaulle. Vietnam, though, was significant enough that I was able to use the occasion to arrange meetings for Ky with sympathetic members of Congress and with military colleagues of his at the Pentagon. Private talks were also scheduled with Rogers, Kissinger, and President Nixon.

On April 1 I accompanied Ky to the White House, where it turned out that Nixon had also invited Kissinger and Ellsworth Bunker. Once again, neither Nixon nor Kissinger revealed anything substantial about American strategy. Instead, Nixon expressed his satisfaction with the close cooperation between our two governments. Speaking of his own vision for the future, the president noted that it would be of no use to achieve a settlement that "would not bring peace, but merely an interlude between two wars." He asked us to "have faith in America."

A separate meeting with Kissinger brought no additional enlightenment. But when Secretary of State Rogers arrived at the South Vietnamese embassy for lunch the next day, he was in a more communicative mood. Rogers got right to the point. He said that there was no alternative to the withdrawal of at least some American troops. What, he asked, were the most important practical measures that could be taken for accelerating the South Vietnamese army's capacity to take up the slack? On the political side, Rogers inquired about formulas that might be developed to allow the NLF to participate in government once it had renounced violence and accepted the ground rules of peaceful political competition.

Neither Ky nor I was impressed with an analysis of the NLF that dismissed its existence as a front for the Hanoi politburo and theorized that it might forgo the total, relentless war to which the politburo was committed. Nevertheless, since we were still unaware of the secretary of state's losing battle for dominance in foreign policymaking, this seemed to us a serious proposal.

In early April I learned, through various Washington sources, that Kissinger had ordered the Pentagon to undertake studies regarding the withdrawal of troops. With this, I warned Saigon that the problem had come to a head, that we could now expect the new American initiative to rapidly unfold. The basic elements, at any rate, were now in place: a two-pronged policy that would couple American withdrawal (shortly to be dubbed Vietnamization) with secret negotiations. Exactly how the two would be coordinated, and what the American negotiating positions would be, we did not know. It was to clarify these questions that I asked for a meeting with Henry Kissinger.

On May 6 the two of us took up these issues in Kissinger's office. Contrary to my expectations, by the time we were finished talking, I began to feel optimistic. In the first place, Kissinger had assured me that despite the existence of several "power centers" in Washington, in fact the White House was keeping tight control of overall strategy. (This was not quite the "policy is made right here" outburst I was to hear later on, but it did go some way toward clearing up the ambiguities that clouded American signals at this period.) He then discussed the prospects for U.S.

disengagement, assuring me that the withdrawal of troops would depend more on the ability of South Vietnam's army to sustain the balance of forces than on pressure from American public opinion. Even after the bulk of the American army was out of Vietnam, a residual force would remain. Finally, Kissinger reiterated that President Nixon attached great importance to close cooperation between the two governments, and that consequently nothing would be decided without Saigon's knowledge and agreement. Specifically, we should understand clearly that the gradual transfer of military responsibilities would in no way serve as camouflage for an American policy of abandonment. As far as negotiations were concerned, I knew the nature of Xuan Thuy's private talks with Lodge. Prospects for progress in the near future were not bright.

Almost immediately after this meeting, the pace of action picked up. On May 8 in Paris, the Communists announced a ten-point proposal that in their view would bring a just conclusion to the war. The points included the by now soporific demands for total, unreciprocated U.S. withdrawal and for the abolition of the South Vietnamese government.

This proposal was answered by President Nixon in a nationally televised speech on May 14 in which he outlined an eight-point plan that constituted the most comprehensive peace proposal yet advanced by the Americans. It included an offer for simultaneous withdrawal of American and North Vietnamese troops from South Vietnam (until then, the American position had been that Hanoi must withdraw six months prior to an American pullout). Nixon also declared that the United States was ready to accept the participation of the NLF in the political life of South Vietnam and would commit itself to free elections in the country under international supervision. Right after the speech, in a background session with the press, Kissinger emphasized the "flexible" aspects of the proposal and mentioned, too, that the speech had been "cleared" with Saigon.

The whole process was something of a shock. There had been some informal exchanges on these subjects, but there was no real consultation or agreement, certainly nothing that had ever been "cleared" with Saigon. Instead, only two days before the speech, I was told that Bunker would present the text to Thieu. My cable informing Thieu to expect it went out on May 12. There was no time for the Saigon government to object to any of Nixon's proposals, only to accept them. The game of imposition and attempted finesse that would become the Nixon administration's trademark in dealing with its ally had begun with a bang.

Chapter 30

Buying Time

EXACTLY ONE WEEK after the May 14 speech, I was instructed by Thieu to contact the State Department in order to prepare a summit meeting between himself and Nixon, this time on a desert island in the middle of the Pacific called Midway.

Scheduled for June 8, this meeting had been a long time coming. Even before the November elections, Anna Chennault had intimated to me that if Nixon was elected, he would make a trip to South Vietnam or at least send a special delegation. When Nixon did win, Thieu sent him a long congratulatory telegram. Perhaps because of the conjectures about South Vietnamese interference in the elections, Thieu channeled the message through the Washington embassy rather than sending it directly to the White House. I, in turn, had it delivered through the State Department, feeling a bit awkward about the excessive protocol. Following the telegram came a series of signals from Thieu, some not terribly subtle, that he would be amenable to a meeting. But until May these had not met with a positive response.

Now, five months after Nixon's inauguration, the president's honeymoon with the American public was nearing the end of its run. Consequently, this was a good time for him to formally announce the first withdrawals of American troops. If Thieu was not happy about the move toward Vietnamization, he had by that point accepted the inevitable. Besides, it was he who had wanted the meeting originally, and by now it had become especially important to have an opportunity to discuss the new American policies that had been taking shape over the preceding months.

In the process of setting up the summit in late May, I had a series of meetings with Kissinger and Assistant Secretary of State for East Asian and Pacific Affairs Marshall Green (who had taken Bill Bundy's place). The major problem that emerged from these talks was the American reluctance to issue a joint communiqué. It became clear to me that they wanted to use Midway for one purpose only: to get Thieu's formal consent on troop withdrawals. Other than that, their objective was to minimize the meeting's importance. It would be the briefest of talks (five hours all told) at an obscure place, meant solely as a ceremonial gesture of agreement on one issue. From the American perspective, a joint communiqué would accomplish nothing except to give the South Vietnamese an opportunity to raise other issues and insist on other agreements.

Of course, Kissinger and Green were correct. From our viewpoint, a joint communiqué was necessary for a variety of reasons. Most importantly, we wanted to nail down the Nixon administration's new strategy. If there were to be troop withdrawals, we wanted them handled in the most positive way, that is, in the context of an agreement on compensatory support for South Vietnamese forces. We also wanted it phrased properly, as a step made possible by the ongoing development of South Vietnamese capabilities. Additionally, we wanted official assurance that we would be kept completely informed of the substance of any private negotiations between the United States and North Vietnam. Finally, we wanted a public statement to the effect that the United States would not agree to a coalition government that included the Vietcong — a statement that would formalize the understanding reached the previous December, before we agreed to send a delegation to Paris.

For us, all these points were important, both in themselves and as a way of calming public opinion in South Vietnam. The American troop withdrawal, coupled with a new negotiating policy, was sure to cause real anxiety among the South Vietnamese, and we wanted to counter the demoralization as best we could. After a good deal of back and forth with the two Americans, they saw their way to accepting our position. The joint communiqué affirmed the "common resolve" to reject the imposition of a coalition, hailed the "replacement of certain American units by Vietnamese forces," and agreed that the replacement program would take place "in consonance with the security situation prevailing at the moment."

Even after the communiqué had been agreed to, the Americans continued to worry that the troop withdrawal announcement would not go smoothly. Vietnamization had now emerged as one of the two prongs of American strategy (the second was negotiations) and the essential element in the administration's effort to buy time from the onslaught of domestic antiwar sentiment. With so much invested in the concept, they were anxious that it proceed without the South Vietnamese creating problems.

Their fears on this score were caused by the indirect manner in which they had eased the South Vietnamese into tacit acquiescence. Through general discussions and press reports, the idea of troop withdrawals had been floating around for some time. The result was that everyone involved knew that the withdrawals would take place, creating a kind of conceptual fait accompli. But in what was to become the usual fashion, the idea had never been officially submitted to the South Vietnamese for their approval or for some counterproposal. Consequently, both Nixon and Kissinger were somewhat unsure of what Thieu's reaction would be at Midway. As Kissinger put it in his memoirs, they were "concerned that the projected troop withdrawal would produce an awkward scene."

In the event, the South Vietnamese president did what he could to put the best face on the situation, even taking the initiative in proposing a "redeployment" of American troops. He also agreed to the idea of private talks between the Americans and the North Vietnamese, provided that he would be fully briefed on the proceedings.

Although Thieu avoided a confrontation with the Americans at Midway, inside he was not happy. Perhaps most of all he rankled at having been compelled to meet with Nixon in this desolate and gooney bird–ridden place. As did we all. It was impossible not to reflect on the difference between the treatment we were receiving and that accorded the North Vietnamese by the Russians. We knew that in private the Soviets referred to the northerners as "those stubborn bastards," but in public, at least, Moscow rolled out the red carpet for visitors from Hanoi. Yet our own meetings were relegated to such places as Guam and Midway, almost as if we were regarded as lepers by those in whom we had placed our security and with whom we had shed so much blood. Circumstances forced us to swallow such things, but we did not forget them. With a continuous history of two thousand years, Vietnamese — whether Communist or non-Communist — have a low tolerance for humiliation, and such indignities created permanent scars. Thieu especially did not forget, and if Kissinger was enraged by the scornful treatment Thieu gave him during their crucial October 1972 talks in Saigon, he should at least have understood the cause.

With these fresh scars, we left Midway at five in the afternoon (we had arrived at ten that morning) for an overnight stop in Taiwan, then proceeded to Saigon. On the plane Thieu and I prepared for the press conference he would give on arrival in Vietnam. Our chief object was to provide public reassurance, which we tried to do by focusing on the positive side of the meeting: the United States had now unambiguously rejected the imposition of a coalition government. As far as the troop with-drawal went, that too had its pluses. We had accepted it, even welcomed it, because we felt comfortable with our own strength. All South Viet-namese should feel proud of that. We emphasized, too, that it was benefi-cial for the Vietnamese people to rely less on the Americans and more on themselves.

After another week and a half in Saigon, briefing people on Vietnamiza-tion and making a tour of the general staff to review the concept, I re-turned to Washington. I brought with me a new idea of Thieu's, which he termed "long haul/low cost." Broadly speaking, Thieu suggested re-ducing the level of American involvement so it would be far less costly in terms of lives and resources, which would better allow for a sustained American presence.

On June 24 I met with Rogers at the State Department for a general review of the situation and also to float the "long haul/low cost" idea. Rogers's reaction was intriguing. Such a policy, he said, was not a bad idea. But reducing American costs in Vietnam would not by itself ensure long-term U.S. support. The flaw in "long haul/low cost," according to Rogers, was that nobody could predict what level of involvement, no matter how low, the American public would accept. Consequently, to give any policy of support the public backing it needed, it would be nec-essary for Vietnam to build what Rogers called "a broad-based govern-ment." "The United States government," he said, "doesn't want to create obstacles, doesn't want to force you to cooperate with those who are trying to destroy you. *But you have to somehow do what you can to create the impression that you are not a negative regime, not an exclusive regime. . . . Am I clear enough?"* (Italics added.)

In a follow-up discussion the next day, William Sullivan, now head of the State Department working group on Vietnam, returned to this theme. He noted that Rogers had given him instructions to review all the points presented up to now by both the South Vietnamese and the Americans with a view toward arriving at a common strategy. He referred to meet-ings between Thieu and Rogers in Saigon during Rogers's March visit and to the private talks between Thieu and Nixon at Midway. He summed up by saying that it seemed the two sides agreed that the best solution would be for South Vietnam to hold elections that would be open to everybody, except that the NLF would not be permitted to participate as an entity. "The idea of elections," Sullivan said, "is dramatic."

I told Sullivan that we had always considered the complete withdrawal of North Vietnamese troops a prerequisite for elections. The South Viet-nam government could not possibly hold open elections of the sort he was describing while its life was being threatened by an enemy army operating on its territory. Nor was it technically possible to organize elections in areas under Communist control. Then Sullivan asked if Thieu had his own proposal to make. I told him that we would probably favor a general package combining military and political aspects, that is, open elections in South Vietnam in conjunction with the withdrawal of North Vietnamese troops. Finally, Sullivan said that Henry Cabot Lodge in Paris was awaiting new initiatives, so that he could press the North Vietnamese for private talks among all four parties.

In these discussions the Americans were carefully probing our reactions to the possibility of an open election, which might include individuals associated with the NLF and would definitely include all elements of the non-Communist opposition. They felt that without some dramatic measure — what Rogers had called a "broad-based government" — there would be little chance of generating sufficient American public sympathy to sustain a long-term military presence. Beyond this, they believed that an open election combined with a North Vietnamese troop withdrawal might well form the basis for a new American proposal in Paris.

Although by this time I was aware that Henry Kissinger was the dominant voice in foreign affairs, I could hardly imagine that American policy was being formulated in a truly secretive fashion, and that the State Department was being kept ignorant of the substance of Kissinger's approach. Consequently, I treated Rogers's and Sullivan's discussions very seriously and described them in detail to Thieu in my long report of July 1.

Three days after my talk with Sullivan, I took up the same subjects with Henry Kissinger. In part I was doing my own probing, attempting to determine how far Kissinger's and Rogers's thinking coincided and what the divergences were. Some of the difficulty of working in Washington during that period is conveyed in the beginning of the cable I sent to Thieu on June 28, 1969, immediately after this meeting.

Before attempting to report fully about my conversation with Kissinger, I must tell you that in Washington the opinion is that there are many differences between him and Rogers. I confess that I do not see it clearly yet. But it is a delicate situation for me as ambassador. Despite knowing both of them, I must be very careful.

I went on to describe my discussion with Kissinger. I started by bringing up the "long haul/low cost" concept, exactly as I had done with Rogers. Kissinger answered that he was "aware of [your] difficulties," alluding to the problems we would face were the American presence simply to wind down and vanish. The current state of negotiations was unsatisfactory to both Nixon and himself, he said, and there had to be some alternative. What that might be he could not afford to speculate on, but Nixon "is not going to be the first president to lose a war." Then he asked, "What would be the alternative from your point of view?"

My answer was that the minimum would be some variation of "long haul/low cost," that is, a formula which would allow the Americans to maintain a long-term presence in Vietnam despite whatever stalemate or breakdown there might be on the negotiating front. "As far as I am concerned," I told him, "the idea of a general election is the last line. Beyond that is surrender and the end of survival."

Kissinger agreed with this, but also remarked that the idea of a general election was "appealing and dramatic." At this I told him that general elections were just one idea among many others that we were currently looking at. As he knew, there were obvious problems with it, especially in terms of uncertainties for the Vietnamese government. He then asked if it might not be possible to tie down the idea of general elections to some other conditions, so that we might avoid these problems. I was unwilling to speculate along these lines, especially since I had no instructions regarding the details of any open elections. But Kissinger was not deflected by my silence.

"For example," he said, "regarding the withdrawal of North Vietnamese troops, is that a prerequisite for you?"

"Yes," I answered, "it is a prerequisite."

"Well, if a proposal is tied down by too many corollaries," he went on, hinting that a North Vietnamese withdrawal might be one of these excessive conditions, "the proposal would lose its appeal. Is there any possibility for general elections while North Vietnamese troops are still in South Vietnam?"

"No," I insisted, "there is no possibility."

Kissinger, like Rogers, was trying to find a common ground on which a negotiating strategy could be based. He even mentioned that he was studying how the United States could help Thieu with his domestic situation, for example, by making it possible for "all the nationalists to get together." At the end of the discussion, Kissinger told me that he knew I had had talks with Rogers and Sullivan, but if I had something to say to either Nixon or himself, "please feel free to knock on my door."

At this point in my relationship with Kissinger, I had developed a standard technique to help me focus and check on the substance of our talks. Shortly after a meeting I would invite some of Kissinger's staff to the embassy for lunch, always separately of course — people like John Negroponte, Richard Smyser, and John Holdridge. In the course of conversation, I would mention in passing points from my discussions with

Kissinger, to try to determine which of their chief's themes had been substantial, which peripheral, and which, perhaps, deflective. These were careful and intelligent people, but with enough talk and lunches I was usually able to find out what I wanted to know.

One of the points in our June 28 meeting that I was eager to cross-check was Kissinger's suggestion that he would like to help "get all the Vietnamese nationalists together." With a certain degree of hope, I pursued the subject with each of my luncheon partners. But the consensus was that for Kissinger this was not a serious issue and if it was, it certainly had a low priority.

This, I believed, was unfortunate. My own thinking about the problems of South Vietnamese democracy had evolved during the two and a half years since I had been away from domestic politics. Through 1967 I had worked to accomplish a transition from military rule to a democratic government. With the constitutional assembly of 1966, the promulgation of the constitution in 1967, and the first presidential and assembly elections in that same year, this transition had been largely accomplished. Not perfectly, by any means; intimidation and suppression of the opposition and cronyism at the top were all too common. But there was no question that a generally workable system was in place, and for all their faults, the National Assembly and Senate were functioning in a basically acceptable manner.

Nevertheless, as ambassador I was sensitive to the continuous and strident criticism from the American press, attacking Thieu as a repressive authoritarian and his regime as a government without national support. The effect this was having on American public opinion and, consequently, on Congress was considerable, and I had silently concurred with Rogers's assessment that it would be difficult to sustain American involvement without a substantial change in the Saigon government's image. As a result, one of the constant themes of my cables and reports to Thieu was the need to understand the role of public opinion in the United States and the corollary need to create a national unity government that could muster the broadest possible support in South Vietnam. In addition, I believed we had to develop a pool of technocrats — professional administrators and technicians — who could take the daily task of running the country out of the hands of the regime's incompetent and all too often corrupt political appointees.

My ability to work for such changes, however, was severely limited. First of all, I was out of domestic affairs, ten thousand miles from developments in Saigon. Second, I knew Thieu viewed me with suspicion, as someone whom Ky had brought into the government and whose deep-down loyalty might still be with his rival. Third, my intimate contacts with the Americans also gave him reason to question the objectivity and accuracy of my views. Perhaps I had grown too close to them or was allowing myself to be unduly influenced by their charms and persuasions (Thieu had once called me "the man from Washington"). Most important of all, in the final analysis, helping to build a more effective democratic government in South Vietnam was simply not one of the dominant themes of American strategy. Bunker agreed with the need and would always lend a sympathetic ear, but he was neither a forceful advocate nor a prime policymaker. Rogers and Sullivan made sporadic gestures of impatience, but little more. Kissinger, meanwhile, was too fascinated by the complex interplay of negotiations, triangular diplomacy with the Russians and Chinese, and the exercise of military force to have much energy left for this subject. The end result was that there was little effective pressure from the Nixon administration to move Thieu off the mark. And Thieu was not the man to grasp the significance of such things by himself.

This state of affairs is dramatically displayed by the closing paragraphs of my June 28 cable to Thieu and his handwritten reply of July 5, which responded both to this cable and my cable of July 1, in which I described my meetings with Rogers and Sullivan.

From the June 28 cable to Thieu:

From the day I came back to Washington, I have been in contact with many members of Congress and the press. My overall assessment is that in spite of six months of Nixon administration efforts, public opinion is still very impatient. There are still many attacks on the Vietnamese government. If I can sum up my impressions in a phrase, I should say that for those people who oppose the war in Vietnam — still a minority, but still very vocal — Vietnam is finished. As far as their opinion goes, there is no way to resurrect it. But for the majority of public opinion, and for the Nixon administration itself, there is still some support left, although no one can tell exactly how much. *But one thing I am sure of is that whether we can keep this support intact depends right now more on the Vietnamese than on the Americans* [italics added].

Finally, I request from you the following:

1. Instructions on what to do (I cannot continue discussing these [domestic political] problems without instruction).

2. In case you decide in favor of some sort of initiative [a combined general election and North Vietnamese withdrawal proposal for the Paris talks], it is important to give thought to its presentation in the international press. The mode of its presentation is as important as the substance.

From Thieu's response:

Dear Brother Diem:

Leave this initiative alone for the time being. Restrict yourself to talking about Vietnamization. I will inform you of the opportune moment to raise this subject.

. . . Do not let Rogers pre-empt me on this either. It annoys me. He should respect me on this.

August and September of 1969 were relatively slow months. Unknown to me, Kissinger and North Vietnam's representative Xuan Thuy met secretly for the first time on August 4 at Jean Sainteny's apartment in Paris. But it was a purely symbolic meeting; neither side did more than repeat its previous positions. On September 7 Senator Everett Dirksen died while still in office. Though he had been ill, his death came unexpectedly. A good and close friend had now gone, in a Senate where I was finding it increasingly difficult to find friends of any description. Two days later came news of another death, this time in Hanoi. After a long, debilitating illness Ho Chi Minh died at the age of seventy-nine. Along with other observers I found myself speculating on his possible successors and on the effect his passing would have on the course of the war. In the end, it had none.

My time during those months was taken up with visiting the various Vietnamese communities around the country, hosting more junketing South Vietnamese assemblymen, and speaking at conferences and universities, where I was able to keep an eye on antiwar activity, just beginning to percolate again with the start of the academic year. One event that stands out from the daily round was an invitation from President Nixon for my family to attend a worship service at the White House, to be led that Sunday by Billy Graham. My wife and I were equally nonplused by it. The invitation was clearly meant as a token of friendship, but I was unsure exactly why someone of my Taoist background or of my wife's deeply felt Buddhism would be accorded such an honor. My daughters, however, knew exactly how to view it; they were scared to death. It meant wearing the unfamiliar traditional *ao dai* dresses with the accompanying silken pants, in which one could easily slide off a chair, and high heels, which made it hard for one to walk.

Despite the misgivings, we were all there at the specified time, four among forty or so invited worshipers, including the president and his family, Attorney General Mitchell and his wife, Martha, and other presidential friends, colleagues, and their families. It was a short service; Graham spoke for about fifteen minutes on a subject I no longer can recall. I spent most of the time glancing out of the side of my eye at my younger daughter, Giao, who kept fidgeting on her chair, and at the rest of the congregation to determine when we should be bowing our heads. It was a strange interlude in an unusually quiet time.

In October, though, things started to pick up. The New Mobilization Committee had begun an energetic and well-organized campaign to coordinate the dozens of antiwar groups and plan for a countrywide event called the Moratorium, to be held on October 15. Congress, too, had returned from its vacation ready to escalate the drive to end American involvement in the war. I cabled Thieu on October 5:

Anti-war elements in Congress and universities are starting on a larger scale. . . . It is clear the scene is heating up again. We can expect debate shortly on the following:

1. Senator Goodell has a proposal that would force U.S. withdrawal of troops by 1970. It is considered unlikely to pass, but it gives the Foreign Relations Committee a chance to debate Vietnam.
2. A number of senators have declared their support for the new student organization "The Moratorium."
3. A review of the Tonkin Resolution.
4. Mansfield's proposal for the withdrawal of troops, cease-fire, pressure on GVN [government of Vietnam] for elections including participation of NLF.

We have to anticipate a lot of criticism, especially between October 15 and November 15, the so-called "moratorium period." A "New Mobilization Committee," which has been organized by students, religious groups, and youth, includes the Women's Strike for Peace, Business Executives for Peace, Fifth Avenue Parade Committee, Clergy and Laity Concerned, Lawyers' Committee Against the War, Quakers, SDS, and others. Co-ordinating everything is the "Vietnam Moratorium Committee," composed primarily of students who worked for McCarthy. They have taken October 15 as the date when all universities around the country will have a day off to oppose the war. . . . On November 15 they propose a great march, the "March Against Death."

The crescendo of demonstrations in mid-October absorbed my attention. I thought, well, these hundreds of thousands of demonstrators in fact know almost nothing. But how is it possible to convince them that their knowledge is limited and that what they are advocating is surrender to ruthless totalitarians?

But the phenomenon also seemed to go beyond the war. I had already witnessed the mass student demonstrations in France and Germany, and I wondered to what extent the anger was a reflection of mood and culture, not really about the war, but for which the war served as an opportunity, a vehicle. If the war did not exist, would such demonstrations happen anyway? Was Western society going through some sort of cultural revolution of its own?

The thought tortured me. I knew beyond any doubt that South Vietnam's cause was right, and I could not fathom how so many could protest against it while understanding so little about it. In October and November I was in a state of continual mental turbulence on this subject. I knew that most South Vietnamese dismissed the demonstrators as dupes inspired by Communists or leftists who infiltrated their movements. But it seemed to me a much broader question than that. I could understand people not wanting to go to war or to have their sons go to war. I believed, of course, that they were wrong, that this was a war worth fighting. But that, at least, was a motive I understood. What I could not grasp was the roots of the anger, which I was beginning to see as a protest by Americans against their own society as much as against the war. It was a baffling and tragic predicament: the future of Vietnam was being affected by social forces we could not block and that only partly had to do with us.

On the night before the March Against Death, there was a demonstration in front of the embassy itself. It was like a military siege. Hundreds of police were doing their best to bar the protesters from attacking the building. From the windows, my staff and I looked out on the helmets, the police cars, the flashing lights. From the chanting crowd came a rain of stones and bottles. Not until late that night did the demonstrators begin to disperse, in order to gird themselves for the next day's activities.

Richard Nixon, I knew, was big on "hanging tough." John Mitchell had told me that the president would not be influenced by protests. But watching the demonstrators in front of the embassy, I did not believe it. Deep in my mind I thought that the pressure would eventually prove too much; in the long run it could not help but have its effect. The most Nixon could do was buy time. So in the end it would come down to South Vietnam, to what we could do by ourselves and for ourselves.

Chapter 31

Losing Time

ON NOVEMBER 3, in the middle of the Moratorium period, President Nixon gave a major address on Vietnam that was carried live by the networks. It was a powerful performance. He presented clearly his two-track approach to peace — Vietnamization and negotiations — and stressed that he would not be moved by demonstrations and protests. He appealed instead for support from "the great silent majority" of Americans.

The speech had a remarkable effect, drawing out latent backing from the public and even from Congress. It came at a volatile time. The New Mobilization Committee and its March Against Death arrived on schedule in Washington on November 15 (its vanguard had attacked the embassy on the fourteenth), 250,000 protesters who, in effect, took over parts of the capital, smashing windows and attacking government buildings, the Vietcong flag waving above their ranks. But once the initial fury was spent, it was clear that Nixon's address had struck a chord. His ratings in the polls rose, and by December an unaccustomed calm settled on the antiwar movement.

Although opposition had been dampened, I was too obsessed with the problem to believe we were experiencing anything more than a temporary respite. Reviewing this period several months later, I wrote to Thieu that "the U.S. administration can create conditions to calm down public opinion. But the administration cannot go contrary to it. And that makes public opinion here the most important factor of all. Temporarily we have a relative calm . . . but this does not mean it is over."

I told Thieu, in a long report home on March 12, that friends as well as enemies in the United States were raising the hard political questions:

"Is the Vietnamese government solid? Or does the lack of unity among the various political groups mean that the government will be progressively isolated? In a word, the problem for Vietnam is public opinion in the United States. In this regard, support for the Vietnamese government is quite fragile. Opposition can be stirred up again very easily, especially this coming fall when the American midterm elections come up."

Despite Nixon's convincing public performance and his ringing declaration that the United States would continue fighting until either the North Vietnamese negotiated a fair peace or the South Vietnamese became capable of defending themselves, from my point of view the course of American disengagement was set. Nineteen seventy would bring us another step closer to total withdrawal. Domestic opinion, fueled by the antiwar movement and the media, would only gain momentum. Congress would undoubtedly become less and less tractable.

This pessimism was based on the judgments I solicited from my most realistic friends. A discussion I had with General William Depuy, formerly Westmoreland's assistant in South Vietnam, stands out in this regard. I included an account of it in my March 12 report to Thieu. "I am not President Nixon, and I am not representing the United States government," Depuy told me at a military base in North Carolina, where I was attending a ceremony.

But I believe the policy is as follows. For many reasons — international and domestic — we have concluded we have to solve the problem of Vietnam within the next four or five years. We will do our best to help Vietnam within the limitations of our means. As long as our forces are there, they will fight. But Vietnam has to understand that we can do no more than that. I don't believe the Paris talks will lead to any results. If it happens, so much the better. If within five years Vietnam can stand alone, well, that is what we hope for. But if afterwards, for reasons of your own — corruption, disunity, lack of cohesiveness — Vietnam cannot stand alone, there will be nothing we can do about it.

Looking back on my cables and reports to Saigon from that period, I have no doubt that I was doing everything I could to get Thieu to see events in Vietnam through the prism of the great debate rocking American society. For that reason I larded my accounts with references to the centrality of public opinion in America's political life, descriptions of demonstrations, and verbatim conversations pointing out the need for reform in South Vietnam's government. For our American friends, I told him, the basic attitude was *tant mieux* or *tant pis,* so much the better, or so much the worse. They had done what they could, and now we would either stand or fall. If we stood, so much the better. If we fell, so much the worse.

* * *

On March 17 my attention was diverted by the coup d'état that overthrew Prince Norodom Sihanouk of Cambodia. The palace revolution was engineered while the prince was on vacation in France by Sihanouk's defense minister, Lon Nol, and his deputy premier, Sirik Matak. Whatever the internal stresses that had led to the coup, in the resulting instability, Cambodians began a series of bloody massacres against the Vietnamese civilian population living in Phnom Penh and in the eastern regions of the country. Sporadic racial friction between the two groups had been a fact of life for many generations, but nothing on this scale had ever taken place. As the news began coming in, I met with Marshall Green and William Sullivan to try to arrange American help in stopping the carnage.

Before long the flight of ethnic Vietnamese refugees across the border into South Vietnam made it clear that a massive disaster was in the making. I told Marshall Green at one point that we would shortly be forced to do something to protect our own people over there. But in all fairness, the State Department needed little urging. The Americans soon became intermediaries between us and the Cambodians, eventually getting assurances from Lon Nol and Sirik Matak that they were doing their best to get the situation under control. In Green's opinion, Lon Nol and Matak were serious people, but as everyone knew, they could not exert authority in their eastern provinces, where thirty-five to forty thousand Vietcong and North Vietnamese troops had established their camps and staging areas.

Beyond the immediate problem of civilian violence, the new order in Cambodia created a dangerous instability among forces that Sihanouk's delicate maneuvering had kept in balance. Under the prince, Cambodia had maintained official neutrality among the warring armies of Communists, South Vietnamese, and Americans. Too weak to take action against the virtual annexation of his eastern provinces by the North Vietnamese and Vietcong, he had, on the surface at least, ignored it. But his true feelings were evident in the tacit permission he gave the Americans for B-52 raids against the Communist sanctuaries.

With Sihanouk gone, the Cambodian government now took a hard line against those who had invaded their country. Allowing valor to triumph over wisdom, at the end of March Lon Nol launched the overmatched Royal Cambodian army toward the Communist sanctuaries. Shortly afterward, South Vietnamese forces began their own series of attacks on the Vietcong bases that straddled the Cambodian border. In response, COSVN (the Hanoi politburo's Central Office for South Vietnam) and the NLF headquarters units moved their operations deep into northeastern Cambodia, from where they initiated a fierce offensive against

Lon Nol's hapless army. They also stepped up their training of the Khmer Rouge, the small but vicious Communist guerrilla movement operating under North Vietnamese tutelage. Green and Sullivan were not concerned about an immediate threat to Phnom Penh, but there was no doubt that Cambodian storm clouds were gathering fast. Already it was evident that the new Cambodian government would need aid. And given the mood in Congress, it would not come easily.

As the weeks passed, Cambodia began to slide toward the abyss. Unable to contain the onslaught of the combined Communist armies operating on its territory, the government of Phnom Penh was increasingly desperate for American help. On April 30 Nixon gave his answer, announcing a joint American–South Vietnamese offensive to destroy the enemy bases and supply lines woven along the Cambodian border regions. In his speech Nixon pointed out that the concentrations of North Vietnamese now threatened to expand into "a vast enemy staging area and springboard for attacks on South Vietnam." He described the potential consequences of a Communist victory over the Cambodian government, emphasizing the extreme danger this would create for the remaining American forces in Vietnam (ten days earlier he had announced the withdrawal of 150,000 troops, scheduled for the coming year). The American action, he said, was indispensable "to protect our men and to guarantee the success of our withdrawal and Vietnamization programs." The United States could not act "like a pitiful, helpless giant" before "the forces of totalitarianism and anarchy."

Despite the purple rhetoric, Nixon's analysis was correct on every count. The prospect of a Communist-ruled Cambodia creating an in-depth, six-hundred-mile-long military front against South Vietnam was enough to bring visions of quick and comprehensive disaster to even the most optimistic. There was no alternative but to do whatever was necessary to preclude that development. Nor was there any doubt that an effective operation against the Cambodian bases would substantially damage North Vietnamese offensive capabilities for an extended period.

For many South Vietnamese as well as American planners, this option should have been pursued much earlier. Such an incursion had long been justified by the Communist occupation of strategic regions of neutral Cambodia. For years the existence of inviolate staging areas and supply routes adjacent to the battlefield had seriously weakened the allies' military posture.* It was a sign of my growing preoccupation with the American domestic arena as the most crucial battlefield of the war that my first

---

* "Inviolate" is perhaps too strong a word. For almost a year, secret B-52 strikes had been pounding these areas. But reports indicated that the bombing had relatively little effect on the flow of men and materiel.

thoughts after Nixon's speech were not about the military consequences of the incursion but of its impact on the antiwar movement.

The combined American–South Vietnamese incursion was launched on April 30. On May 2 I cabled my initial observations to Thieu.

Primo. President Nixon's decision has provoked a very strong reaction here among liberal circles and it is still difficult to predict to what extent this new situation is going to tie the president's hands. Students are beginning again their demonstrations and it is expected that the next few weeks will see many of them.

Secundo. While the reaction is mixed around the country, the two leading liberal papers strongly oppose the decision. The New York Times calls it a "military hallucination," while the Washington Post calls it "erratic, irrational and incomprehensible."

Tertio. Observers here are of the opinion that it was a major political and military gamble by President Nixon. . . . On the internal political scene it is obvious that he is running a lot of risk because the decision has not only provoked a split among the Republicans, it can also rekindle the blaring national debate that seemed to have faded.

The "blaring national debate" now exploded in earnest on the streets and campuses as well as in the newspapers and in Congress. Marches, strikes, and denunciations filled the news alongside detailed accounts from reporters covering the military operation. Riots and fire bombings on campuses moved the domestic conflict toward darker realms than it had yet explored. In Ohio the National Guard was called out to maintain order in the face of protests. At Kent State University, on May 4, they fired into a crowd of students. Four young people were killed. During the ensuing days it seemed as if the fabric of the country was coming undone. "The atmosphere here," I cabled Thieu on May 7, "is dominated by passionate debates in Congress, by preparations for the Saturday demonstrations in Washington by antiwar groups, and by demonstrations by students around the country. All day long the TV, radio and press have nothing but news about the war in Cambodia and the very vocal outbreak of protests. It is difficult not to be influenced by this highly emotional atmosphere."

On Saturday, May 9, a hundred thousand protesters gathered in a park behind the White House. Police barricaded the White House grounds with rows of buses; now the president himself was under siege. Members of my staff, whom I sent out for a firsthand look, were astonished by the number and vehemence of the demonstrators.

At just this moment Ellsworth Bunker returned to Washington for consultations. As protests rocked the capital, he, Sullivan, and Phil Habib briefed me on the battles in Cambodia, on American military objectives, and how long they expected the operation to last. But despite their positive accounts, I could not help considering events in the context of the demonstrations and protests I heard outside my office window and saw each night on television. It seemed to me that all Nixon's efforts to calm American opinion — withdrawals, Vietnamization, the masterly "silent majority" speech — had become irrelevant. He had cast aside his carefully arranged tactics of buying time from the American public and Congress in order to build up South Vietnam's army and attempt a negotiated settlement with North Vietnam. Now the administration was looking elsewhere. And there was no question that with the destruction of many of the enemy's Cambodian staging areas, Nixon and Kissinger had gained time on the military side. (It would take the North Vietnamese a year or more to rebuild their infrastructure.) But by precipitating an onslaught of public outrage, they had lost the time that really mattered, the time measured in the patience and support of the American people. I recorded these views in my daily cables, and as soon as the fervor in Washington had subsided, I asked to return to South Vietnam to brief the government in person.

I arrived in Saigon on July 1. Immediately, I became involved in briefings with various executive and legislative committees and in a series of long private meetings with Thieu. In these discussions I followed up the theme of my reporting from Washington, emphasizing the overall impact of the antiwar movement and striving to convey my understanding of the vital role of public opinion in the United States — and consequently the requirement for highly visible reforms in South Vietnam's government. I knew I was becoming repetitive on these issues, but I saw no alternative. Again I explained that, in the short and even in the long term, I could not foresee the survival of the nation without American assistance. Support for that assistance could only come through Congress, and congressmen were, in essence, creatures of opinion in their constituencies. Public backing in the United States right now was marginal. Nixon's policies had won the administration several battles on that front, but the Cambodian operation was a setback from which it would be difficult if not impossible to recover. South Vietnam had to do what it could, to broaden the government and remove the incompetence and corruption that stigmatized it in American eyes. We needed to do this to disarm critics abroad and reshape South Vietnam's image. But we also needed these things for our own health. Corruption and nepotism debilitated the armed forces and the government equally. Without the inclusion of moderate and competent opposition people, the domestic base of support would narrow; eventually it might crumble altogether.

As always, Ellsworth Bunker was my chief ally. The two of us had discussed exactly these subjects for years now, and our views coincided almost exactly. Bunker regularly urged me to take up the issues with Thieu. "You should tell him," he would say, "that he needs reforms badly, both for strengthening your defensive posture and for improving the atmosphere in Washington. It's a precondition for continued support." What Bunker and I did not agree on was the approach to making the proper impression on the suspicious and resistant mind of South Vietnam's president.

One discussion I had with Bunker during this period illustrated both the problem and my frustrations. In response to a steady barrage of complaints about South Vietnamese corruption from the press and from middle-level American civilian and military advisers, Bunker had ordered a discreet investigation of South Vietnam's provincial administrators. He had gathered evidence against a large number of officials, implicating them in a variety of illegal schemes. As we talked, he showed me the dossiers. He had already spoken to Thieu about it, Bunker told me. Now he wanted me to do the same.

It was one of the few times I became truly upset with Bunker. "Ellsworth," I said, "I'll certainly raise the subject with Thieu, as I have many times already. I've pointed out to him the bad image we have abroad. But in terms of influencing him, you are the only one who can do it. You are the one who can be really forceful about it. You have the power for it, the clout." I knew Bunker for the gentle, soft-spoken aristocrat he was. I had no trouble at all imagining his talk with Thieu, carried on in his elegant and understated manner. By nature the American ambassador would be reluctant to use the influence of his office in a blunt, explicit fashion. Even in this sort of discussion, Bunker would maintain his respect for Thieu's sensibilities.

What really disturbed me about Bunker's approach was the fact that he and Thieu were quite close, and that Thieu regarded him with far more trust and esteem than he ever had for any of the other American ambassadors with whom he dealt. (Thieu had all sorts of suspicions about Henry Cabot Lodge, and after Bunker left, he never did get to know Graham Martin well. But the South Vietnamese president was grateful to Bunker for supporting him during the difficult early days of his presidency.) With this easy relationship and access to the presidential palace, Bunker was able to bring up the most sensitive problems. But his manner of intervening, at least from my point of view, was altogether too dignified and polite to be effective.

For his part, of course, Thieu never refused anything. His usual way was to agree, to acquiesce and make promises, then to wait and see what would happen. As long as he sensed that the American position was not being pressed with great force or energy, as was the case most of the time, he would procrastinate, waiting for the issues to disappear by themselves or to lose their urgency as other, more demanding matters piled up. Thieu's dilatory instincts were thus a perfect foil to Bunker's low-key, almost British personal style. I sometimes thought of Clark Clifford's parting words to me just before I returned home after the Tet offensive. "Look" — he had bitten the words out — "we are sick to death. . . . Our people are discouraged and our support is limited!" No diplomatic niceties about it. I had been quite uncomfortable listening to that short speech, and it had had its effect. More than once I found myself wishing that Bunker would take a similar approach with Thieu.

But the real problem was not Bunker's style. Gentleman that he was, Bunker was also a polished, professional diplomat, quite capable of presenting his government's views in appropriate terms. The real problem was that South Vietnamese corruption and political reforms were simply not high on the American list of priorities. This was as true during Kissinger's tenure as it had been before him. Left on his own in these things, Bunker pursued them in his own way, according to his own instincts, as had Lodge before him and as would Graham Martin after him.

It was not as if the problems were ignored. Rogers and Sullivan were concerned about these issues and sporadically brought them up. From time to time, Henry Kissinger thought about them too. But the emphasis was always elsewhere, on negotiations and military moves and big-power diplomacy. The dominant Washington attitude toward Saigon's domestic affairs was governed by regard for a stability that in the end proved all too superficial. Having watched a status quo of sorts emerge with the ascendancy of Nguyen Van Thieu, the Americans were reluctant to probe too deeply or pressure too forcefully. Perhaps they thought it unnecessary, or of questionable value. But as they pursued their larger ends, neither Kissinger nor Nixon nor the other American policymakers realized that the stability they thought they saw was only a deceptive appearance, that beneath the surface its substance was brittle. At the highest levels they failed to detect the unsound heart of their ally, or detecting it, they neglected to act. And that was to make all the difference when the days of reckoning finally arrived in the spring of 1975.

On July 4, three days after I returned to Saigon, Secretary of State Rogers and Ambassador Sullivan arrived for a round of meetings. Their main topic was negotiations. It was time, Rogers thought, for a new initiative; some way should be found to open up the talks and get them moving. Just then, David K. E. Bruce had been appointed chief American negotiator in Paris, replacing Henry Cabot Lodge (who had resigned the previous November and had not been replaced). Bruce was a senior diplomat, an old man by that time, aristocratic, highly respected, and very independent. Because he had accepted the position, people had reason to expect that something new might be in the works.

Nothing was, though I had no way of knowing at the time. Unknown to all but a very small circle (which at first excluded Secretary Rogers), Henry Kissinger had already met a number of times with North Vietnamese representatives in Paris in an attempt to establish more productive negotiations outside the public glare that bathed the four-sided meetings taking place on avenue Kléber, which had been stalemated ever since the North Vietnamese first accepted President Johnson's invitation back in 1968. But the secret talks, like the open sessions, had gone nowhere. In the summer of 1970 they were in abeyance while the two sides assessed the balance of forces that was emerging after the American thrust into Cambodia. They would be resumed in September, still secret from all but those who had to know. Thieu, of course, knew about them. But as he revealed much later, he already suspected that he was not being kept fully informed of what was passing between Kissinger and his North Vietnamese counterparts, Xuan Thuy and Le Duc Tho.

Blissfully ignorant of the secret talks, on July 30 I left Saigon for Washington, with a stop in Paris to see Nguyen Cao Ky, who was now supervising South Vietnam's delegation to the official negotiations. With nothing to do in Saigon, Ky had been sent to Paris by Thieu, the idea being that it would be better for him to do nothing in France than in Vietnam. On the other hand, if something actually were to happen in Paris, Ky would be on the spot to take the blame for it. Thieu's maneuvering here could not exactly be called silken, but Ky, in his forthright way, didn't seem to care about it, and so he went. While in Paris, I took the opportunity to have lunch with Phil Habib, who was staying on as David Bruce's associate. But it seemed to me that Habib knew little more than anybody else about what was really going on.

Without anything of interest happening, or likely to happen, in the public talks, by September Ky was finding Paris tiresome. On the second he sent a telegram instructing me to make arrangements for him to visit the United States in early October. He had received an invitation, he said, from a Reverend Carl McIntire, who had organized something called the March for Victory, and he was planning to attend.

McIntire's name was not familiar to me, but when I started checking around, I discovered that he was an extremist preacher who headed the far-right organization that was putting this parade together. Almost immediately, I began hearing from people. First Kissinger, then Rogers, then Sullivan and Marshall Green, then everybody else who had heard about the visit. They were all adamant that such a thing could not be allowed to happen. If Ky came to the United States under McIntire's sponsorship, it would stir the opposition into a frenzy. Nor would it be at all helpful (they did not say this directly) to the administration's supporters who were running for office in November's elections.

I had no idea what might have given Ky the notion to accept McIntire's invitation. I was sure he hadn't the slightest idea who the man was. But there was no doubt that identifying ourselves with the extreme right was the last thing we wanted to do. I wrote to Ky, tactfully but firmly advising him that it would not be "appropriate" to accept this particular sponsorship for a visit.

In return, Ky asked me to come back to Paris for talks he would be having with Kissinger and David Bruce in late September. I went, harboring slightly disloyal but still unavoidable thoughts about how much happier I was going to Paris than I would have been hosting Ky in Washington. On the twenty-sixth Ky and I met with Kissinger, Bruce, Habib, and Dick Smyser, one of Kissinger's top aides, in Ky's residence near the Bois de Boulogne. It was a meeting without consequence, during which we discussed, in general terms, a range of possible new peace initiatives. It seemed odd at the time that I would be called to Paris for this kind of desultory exploration. Later, when I discovered that Kissinger had scheduled a secret meeting with Xuan Thuy the next day to discuss specific proposals that the Americans had put on the table several weeks earlier, the strangeness was cleared up. I was simply part of the cover. But even in retrospect, I am amazed that Kissinger could carry off this kind of subterfuge, holding meaningless talks with South Vietnam's vice president and using them as a blind for the real negotiations he was simultaneously holding in secret with the North Vietnamese. No doubt it was a virtuoso performance, what the French would call a *théâtre de fantôme*. But it was not calculated to instill trust in either colleagues or allies once the secret negotiations became known.

The one positive result of the September 26 meeting was that, by the end of it, Ky had at least tacitly agreed not to come to the United States for McIntire's March for Victory. But as it turned out, even that was not the end of the story. After I returned to Washington on the twenty-seventh, Ky was in touch with me by phone. Apparently his dignity had been bruised by the affair. (Had he only known about the secret talks!) Then on October 2 I got the news that though Ky would not be coming himself, he had now decided to send his wife to represent him. The whole business had now stretched my patience beyond the breaking point. During my next conversation with him, I heard myself yelling into the receiver, "It's not possible! It's just not possible!" The next day the press reported that because of "engine trouble," Mrs. Ky would not be able to make it to Washington for the March for Victory after all.

If September's events in Washington and Paris were not particularly edifying, in Saigon it was a different story. That month, senatorial elections were held for the National Assembly. They were marked by fiercely fought races between the many different candidates and slates. Most interesting was the emergence of several coherent blocs of candidates: one rallying behind Tran Van Don, a leading general in the Diem coup who subsequently had quit the military and embarked on a political career; another behind Vo Van Mau, a former foreign minister under Diem; even a separate Buddhist slate. Among the candidates were many opposition figures, and one could even see the old nationalist parties beginning to realign themselves with these new groupings. On the whole, the elections were fair and judged a success by everyone.

Although these elections got little play in the American press, I thought they constituted a landmark of sorts; they brought Vietnam another step toward solidifying the system established under the constitution of 1967. To measure the progress, it was only necessary to recall the combined Buddhist and central Vietnamese rebellion against Ky and Thieu in the spring of 1966. At that time, the two generals were military strongmen ruling without benefit of constitutionality. Followers of the militant Buddhist leader Thich Tri Quang and the Military Region One warlord Nguyen Chanh Thi had no compunctions about challenging their rule through armed insurrection. Now Thieu, for all his faults, was a duly elected president, against whose followers the Buddhists and central Vietnamese were running their own slates. If this was not exactly American-style democracy in full bloom, it was at least a notable advance over what had come before. Compared to it, the government of North Vietnam — which seemed a preferable alternative to many of the protesters and doves in Congress — resembled nothing so much as some especially repressive medieval theocracy.

On October 7 President Nixon gave another major address on Vietnam. If his previous speech announcing the Cambodia incursion had drawn down the wrath of his critics, now he seemed to bend over backward to be conciliatory. The heart of it was a new peace proposal, which included a standstill cease-fire throughout Indochina, a comprehensive peace conference on the region, a complete withdrawal of American forces, and a political settlement in South Vietnam that reflected the "existing relationship of political forces."

The last item made me leery, hinting as it did that for the sake of a settlement the Americans might be willing to dismantle the South Vietnamese government. But the truly significant aspect of this proposal was that, for the first time, the Americans were talking publicly about a complete, unilateral withdrawal. They had given up, at least implicitly, their consistent demand that if American forces were to withdraw, North Vietnamese troops would have to leave also. It was a disquieting development and suggested that the North Vietnamese strategy of fighting and talking was beginning to bear fruit in terms of American concessions.

Several days after the speech, I received yet another phone call from Ky, informing me that he would be coming to the United States after all, on November 15. This time there was no connection with Reverend McIntire, and with congressional elections over, mid-November would be a safer period. I got to work immediately with the State Department, and before long an agenda had been arranged that included meetings with Nixon and Kissinger, an appearance before the National Press Club, and another in front of the Senate Foreign Relations Committee. The social schedule would be highlighted by a visit to the LBJ Ranch, a black-tie dinner hosted by Vice President Spiro Agnew, and on the way home, a meeting with Governor Ronald Reagan in California.

The Nixon meeting came first, a two-hour session over breakfast on the twenty-fourth, with Kissinger, Sullivan, and Holdridge in attendance. Most of the time was devoted to a general review, in which Ky concentrated on the economic difficulties created by the American withdrawal. He spoke with special intensity about the hardships faced by soldiers and civil servants, outlining a problem that was to become increasingly severe in the coming years.

Moving to political topics, Ky mentioned that he and Thieu had been discussing the possibility of a constitutional assembly, to rework the present system of government. Nixon sat up when he heard this (as did I), a look of concern on his face. "But what about the 'seventy-one elections?" he asked, referring to the presidential and assembly elections scheduled for the following September. He would welcome, he said, any move that would push the enemy to the wall. But certainly nothing should happen that might upset the stability of South Vietnam's government. Continuing on this subject, though with considerable tact, Nixon said that, as a politician himself, he realized that different candidates would no doubt come forward in 1971. But he hoped this would happen in such a way that opinion in the United States would not be upset. Then, turning to me, he went on, "Ambassador Diem here would agree that if we were to have the same situation now that we had a few years back, with no stability, it simply would make support of Vietnam an impossibility." Taking the hint, Ky answered that he was sure the elections would go smoothly.

If necessary, he would even give up his own interests to ensure that they would.

On that note the breakfast broke up, and as it did, Kissinger invited Ky and me to his office, where we would have a chance to continue the discussion. Like Nixon, Kissinger was obviously concerned by the idea of a South Vietnamese initiative that would involve a new constitution. Such a move, he thought, would only delay elections and might "sap the legal basis of the regime." Somewhat bemused that he had stirred up such a hornet's nest with what he considered an offhand remark, Ky said, "Well, at this point it's just an idea. Thieu and I have not agreed to do anything about it yet." With rather more tranquility, Kissinger indicated his satisfaction and reiterated that while we must continue looking for new formulas for peace, we should also do our best to keep everything under control. In particular, we should avoid anything that could undermine stability in South Vietnam.

In effect, nothing of substance had come out of the meetings with Nixon and Kissinger; I had certainly expected nothing. But the reaction to Ky's chance remark heightened my awareness that the Americans were very nervous about any hint that South Vietnam would begin to determine events rather than be content to follow the American lead. What Kissinger and Nixon wanted most was a South Vietnam that would remain stable (in one form or another the word had come up a dozen times) while they did their best to extricate the United States from its Indochinese quagmire.

The day after the meeting, Ky and I flew to Texas for a brief visit with Lyndon Johnson at his ranch on the Pedernales River. Walt Rostow and Bill Jorden were also there, making it feel like a reunion. Johnson was as warm as ever but seemed rather subdued even as he drove us around the ranch in his Jeep, pointing out the sights. He told me that he followed the situation in Vietnam constantly, and asked Ky what he thought the Communists' annual dry-season offensive might bring this time around.

The day before, Kissinger had asked the same question. It seemed to be in the back of everyone's mind. Not that anything unusual appeared to be afoot, but by now some 200,000 American troops had left the battlefield, and the remaining forces were increasingly assuming defensive posture. Nineteen seventy-one was likely to see the first test of Vietnamization. The real question, then, was not so much what the enemy would do, but how South Vietnam's army would respond.

A watershed was approaching. In the coming months, such interrelated elements as the effectiveness of South Vietnamese forces, the level of American public support, the balance of congressional factions, and the strength of South Vietnamese and American leadership would determine the shape of the future.

The remainder of Ky's visit rushed by against the background of these larger forces. Vice President Agnew's dinner went smoothly, memorable only for Agnew's off-the-cuff question to Ky about "what we can do to infiltrate North Vietnam." Startled, I experienced a sudden anxiety about where this line of thought might lead the two vice presidents, neither of whom was famous for circumspection. But Ky was as surprised as I, and to my relief he let the moment pass.

Next came lunch with the Senate Foreign Relations Committee, which might have been an explosive affair. But although most of the leading doves attended — Church, Cooper, Mansfield, Fulbright, Kennedy — everyone was exceedingly polite. Ky was at his most diplomatic, and the war critics had obviously decided to forgo confrontation on this occasion, perhaps out of deference to George Aiken, who had arranged the meeting.

By the time I accompanied Ky out to the West Coast on the first leg of his trip home, I was in excellent spirits. The visit had gone unexpectedly well, and as Washington's lights faded beneath our plane's wings, I felt a weight lifting from my shoulders. Looking at these events seventeen years afterward, it seems odd that I had been so apprehensive about what was, really, nothing more than a symbolic state visit of one ally to another. But it was symptomatic of those delicate times that we thought it a triumph to have accomplished such a thing without jeopardizing the goals for which our two governments worked so hard.

Chapter 32

The One-Man Election

THE FIRST TEST of South Vietnamese capabilities under Vietnamization came in February 1971, approximately six weeks after Ky had returned home. Contrary to my expectations, it did not take the form of an ARVN response to a new Communist offensive. Rather, ARVN itself took the initiative.

My first inkling of what was in the works came on February 1, when I received a cable from Thieu's office informing me that military news from Cambodia and Laos would be embargoed until further notice. Several days later came a coded message that an attack would shortly be launched against the Ho Chi Minh Trail in Laos, in conjunction with a similar raid into Cambodia. South Vietnamese forces would undertake these operations themselves, with American air support but without even American advisers in the field. (Through the Cooper-Church amendment, passed at the end of 1970, Congress had prohibited U.S. ground combat missions outside South Vietnam.) Then on February 7 Hoang Duc Nha, Thieu's assistant, called me with instructions about how to handle press releases on the imminent operation, code-named Lam Son 719.

All this communication suggested the optimism of Thieu and his generals for this venture. Although I was not close to the operational side of the military situation, their enthusiasm came as no particular surprise. The previous July, during my month-long visit to South Vietnam, I had taken one of my usual tours, checking in at a number of military installations to try to get a firsthand impression of the fighting. I had found the soldiers' mood upbeat. Psychologically, at least, they were handling the American withdrawal well. My impression was that they had begun to feel that the physical presence of the Americans was perhaps not a necessity after all. The Cambodia operation had been quite an encouragement. Of course, the Americans had been along, but the ARVN units had acquitted themselves ably; they had come out of it with the feeling that they did not match up at all badly. They had returned home from Cambodia as conquerors.

As a result of this tour, I had gotten the idea that ARVN morale was up to the new operation. But whether their training and equipment were sufficient, I was not so sure. Since Midway, I had been serving as the lone South Vietnamese representative on the ad hoc Washington committee charged with overseeing the Vietnamization program. Made up of representatives from the White House, the Pentagon, the CIA, and the State Department, this committee operated in a somewhat desultory fashion. It met every couple of weeks, but there was little in the way of planning or organization. As important as Vietnamization was, no one really had the responsibility for it. The Defense Department was supposed to implement the program, but part of the work was handled in Saigon by General Creighton Abrams, who had replaced Westmoreland in 1968, ARVN Chief of Staff Cao Van Vien, and Thieu himself; the rest was done in Washington. This scattered operation had no specific goals and no overall control. As a result, nobody really knew much about the effectiveness of what was taking place. True, training was going on and equipment was being transferred. But beyond these general observations, it was difficult to ascertain much.

On February 8 Lam Son 719 kicked off. The next day I went over to the Pentagon for a complete briefing, in part to check on the accounts I was getting from Saigon, in part to pick up the mood among the American military. There I was relieved to find the Americans optimistic. South Vietnamese forces were making decent if somewhat slow progress toward their objectives, though it appeared that they had not yet encountered any substantial opposition.

For the next day or two reports from Saigon remained positive. Then a quiet descended on the cable lines. Though each day I requested details, I received no responses. The contrast between the earlier glut of information and the silence now was, to say the least, troubling. Reports from the Pentagon indicated that the advance had run into trouble short of the town of Tchepone, the Communist base that was its objective. But even the Pentagon seemed unsure of exactly what was happening on the ground.

Slowly, from Pentagon reports, media accounts, and driblets of information from Saigon, a picture emerged. North Vietnamese reinforcements had inflicted heavy casualties on ARVN forces. Nevertheless, by March 8 South Vietnamese troops had managed to occupy Tchepone before beginning their withdrawal to the border. Under constant North Vietnamese pressure, the retreat in some places had gone badly. In others, South Vietnamese units had conducted themselves well, covering their retreat courageously. A few television pictures of ARVN soldiers clinging to the skids of evacuation helicopters provided another one of those indelible images that oversimplified and distorted the truth of events. But it was also true that although results of Lam Son 719 were mixed, there was quite enough confusion to enable everyone involved to blame someone else. American commanders accused the South Vietnamese of insufficient aggressiveness, and ARVN commanders accused Americans of providing inadequate and haphazard air support.

By the middle of March Lam Son was over, leaving military analysts to try to figure out the balance between ARVN losses of men, materiel, and morale on the one hand and the disruption of the North Vietnamese supply system on the other.

However ambiguous the military results, though, the repercussions in the United States were all too clear: Lam Son rekindled the furies. Protests began almost as soon as news of the operation broke and grew to an intensity that was still building weeks after the fighting ended. On April 24 close to 200,000 demonstrators gathered in Washington, initiating a week of anger in the streets. Nguyen Van Huyen, the ascetic, independent president of Saigon's senate, was in Washington at the time, along with Foreign Minister Tran Van Lam. I took advantage of the opportunity to show them around, allowing them to see for themselves the flood of hatred and rage that had regularly washed the capital over the past several years. We drove through the streets in my unobtrusive beige Buick, skirting the main crowds but getting good close-up views of the ragged clothes and bitter faces of demonstrators and the stolid rows of police and national guardsmen. Huyen and Lam were profoundly shocked. As longtime friends of mine and important political figures, neither had been spared my briefings and reports over the years. But apparently, my words had not adequately conveyed the emotion loose on America's streets or the pressure under which the American government struggled to cope with its obligations.

On May 3 ten thousand national guardsmen and police lined Washington's streets. Hundreds of protesters were arrested. The next day, during a march on the Capitol, there were more arrests. On May 6 police surrounded the South Vietnamese embassy to forestall a threatened siege. That action fizzled, but its failure gave none of us much comfort. When some of the protesters turned to disruptive and violent tactics, a backlash of sorts developed, and careful observers of these phenomena thought the polls showed a momentary respite for an embattled President Nixon.

But that, too, was short lived. In my long report covering this period, dated May 14, 1971, I wrote to Thieu:

The view is of thousands of students carrying the VC flag in the streets of Washington, and of ten thousand troops. All these images coalesce on the TV screen every night. These things undoubtedly provoke reflections from the American people who ask the question, more than ever — when will the war end? These reflections will perhaps push the ordinary man into a situation where he thinks it is better to give up than continue. And this situation is like a mirror staring back at Richard Nixon when he looks at the future of the war. . . . In the meantime, the antiwar elements have tried their best to put forward the idea that it is past time to think about such things as a schedule for withdrawing troops. Now it is simply — when will this war be ended? That is to say, the attitude is — we don't care about the consequences.

In fact, as the demonstrations of April and early May subsided, a new and particularly insidious element had been injected into the public consciousness. Irrespective of whatever justice American foreign policy goals might embody, regardless of the desire or right of the South Vietnamese to live lives free of North Vietnamese totalitarianism, heedless of any argument or reason whatever, to many ordinary Americans the war now seemed purely and simply immoral.

To me this new perception was hallucinatory. From a historical standpoint it was something like the revulsion against war that swept Western Europe in the thirties, just as Hitler's Germany was preparing to devour her neighbors. The crucial difference was that then French and English pacifism was suicidal. Now American antiwar emotion threatened not America's survival but only South Vietnam's. The horrible irony of the parallel was that during World War II the Europeans had a strong and resourceful America to rescue them from the darkness. But who would there be to rescue us?

Inevitably, the shift in the moral climate accelerated antiwar action in Congress. I cabled to Thieu on May 15, "Critics of the war are now trying to single out that the issue is no longer how to end the war, but when to end it. In this regard it is to be noticed that the leftist organizations have this year adopted very shrewd tactics and focused their attention mainly on the growing impatience of public opinion and on the humanitarian and moral aspects of the war."

Antiwar elements were putting pressure not only on Nixon but on Congress. Their efforts, I warned Thieu in my May 14 report, "will create difficulties for the administration, because in the end it is the Congress that has the last say on the budget. . . . In brief, the Nixon administration will have to confront in the next period many difficulties in the face of public opinion, which constitutes a springboard for the antiwar movement, operating with a well-planned, long-term strategy and careful tactics."

There was nothing hypothetical about this warning. The spring of 1971 saw a deluge of congressional initiatives aimed at destroying the administration's capacity to carry on the fight: resolutions for limiting combat expenditures for Laos and Cambodia, for forbidding them altogether, and for mandating the withdrawal of American forces. I was heavily involved in each of these battles, lobbying and providing arguments, memos, and position papers in an attempt to stem the tide. But as time passed, the climate grew harsher and the numbers on our side dwindled. On February 22 the Democratic caucus voted for a resolution demanding the withdrawal of all U.S. forces by the end of 1972. It was not binding, I told Thieu in my nightly cable, but it would turn the war into a partisan issue. Four hectic months later the Senate itself passed a resolution demanding a withdrawal of troops "at the earliest practicable date." Each day I lived with the constant erosion of support, and each night I attempted to translate the experience into a cogent message to Saigon.

When I wrote my long report on May 14, another dimension of the problem was on the horizon: the South Vietnamese presidential elections scheduled for the coming September.

With the approach of the political season here, attention is on our own presidential elections. In this regard there are two schools of opinion taking shape: One wants to send delegations of observers with the unstated purpose of preventing the U.S. administration from supporting your own candidacy. This is being called the Vietnam Election Project. The second — neutral — school says in effect that what happens is up to the Vietnamese. They have formed the Committee for a Political Settlement. Sullivan and Holdridge have promised me that the U.S. will co-ordinate with us before making a decision on what formula to adhere to regarding our elections.

The administration had in fact been focusing its attention on the elections since around the beginning of April. To an extent, the raging anti-war movement and the simultaneous congressional assault had deflected this interest, but in another way it had sharpened it. With the tide flowing so strongly against the war, Vietnam's image in the United States had become a correspondingly greater concern, at least among some government officials. In my May 14 report I put it this way:

In conclusion, many people in the White House and State Department hope you will give attention to the following issues, which they believe will greatly influence public opinion in this country.
  1. The ability of ARVN forces.

2. What kind of elections we will have.
3. Corruption.
4. Drugs.
5. Increasing efforts to improve relations between GVN [Government of Vietnam] and international press, to deflect criticism and bring out positive elements.

All these issues were significant, but all of them were also ongoing, except for the approaching elections, which would undoubtedly provide a focal point for reaction in the United States. In my role as lobbyist and public relations man, I considered that, in one way or another, the elections would be crucial to the image of South Vietnam's government. American perceptions of the Saigon regime habitually fastened on the negatives: the corruption that was all too obvious and the repressiveness that was actually relatively moderate.* The other side of it was hardly noticed by a critical and sensationalist American press: the slow but visible progress of South Vietnamese democracy under wartime conditions.

From my perch on the other side of the world, it seemed to me that political development in South Vietnam was proceeding along a dual track. On the one hand, the forms of constitutional and democratic government were all in place. Most recently, they had demonstrated their viability in the previous fall's senatorial elections. Both the Senate and Assembly were alive with people who opposed Thieu (foremost among them was Tran Van Tuyen, who, along with Vo Nguyen Giap, had been one of my teachers at Thang Long High School). Since 1966, there had been a steady progression of events that indicated South Vietnam was on a track toward eventually becoming a decent, functioning democracy.

But on the other hand, regressive forces were also at work. Their prime mover was Nguyen Van Thieu's strongman instinct: his attachment to personal power and his reflex suspicions about any attempt to limit his authority. Although he was the elected president of a democratic republic, his predilections, and consequently his methods, were anything but democratic. He surrounded himself with weak and incompetent people who were often corrupt and incapable of challenging him. Among them, they gave South Vietnam a government of "immobilists" and paralytics which showed the outside world a furtive and acquisitive face. Among the military, too, Thieu sought loyalty above ability. As a result, the skill

---

*The regime that attracted such scathing notices in fact tolerated a wide latitude of opinion and a vocal opposition press. Politicians who stepped over the line might find themselves in jail for several months, but they weren't murdered nor did they disappear. In terms of basic freedoms, there was, of course, no comparison between South and North Vietnam, nor even between South Vietnam and such authoritarian regimes as Park Chung Hee's South Korea.

of junior officers and the courage of common soldiers were too often wasted, as were their lives, at the hands of unable and dishonest generals.

To an America sacrificing its own treasure and its own sons, the negative face was conspicuous, the positive one indistinct. Working the congressmen and their staffs — in whose hands lay South Vietnam's lifeline — I thought that the 1971 elections would be a crucial event, an opportunity to dramatically display the upbeat dimension of Vietnam's political life. A fair and decently run election would give eloquent testimony for the moral claim South Vietnam had on continued American support.

In April I learned that Ky was planning to run against Thieu. By May it was clear that Big Minh, the popular general from the Diem coup, had also decided to be a candidate. Then on June 2 debate began in the National Assembly about a law governing electoral procedures. The 1967 constitution had stipulated presidential elections every four years, but it had not spelled out the details. Now the Assembly was arguing about how the elections should take place. On June 22 an electoral law was passed that required all presidential candidates to obtain signatures from either forty members of the Assembly or one hundred members of the provincial councils. The law was a body blow to chances for a fair election, an obvious attempt by Thieu to keep his opponents out of the running. It was unclear whether Ky or Big Minh would be able to fulfill the signature requirements, and it put everybody on notice that Thieu intended a no-holds-barred pursuit of re-election. Reports multiplied about the tactics of intimidation and bribery the president's people had brought to bear on the legislators.

As it turned out, despite the exclusionary election law, Big Minh was able to obtain the requisite number of signatures. Ky, however, was not. Angry, he challenged the law in the supreme court. With these uninspiring developments, Big Minh now began to have second thoughts about running. Although it was still too early to tell what the outcome of all this might be, I watched events with a sinking heart. I had hoped the elections would enhance South Vietnam's stature and provide at least some margin of added leverage in dealing with the U.S. Congress. Instead, it seemed likely we were going to see even more international opprobrium heaped on us as a result of Thieu's unsubtle manipulations.

On July 12 Hoang Duc Nha, Thieu's adviser and secretary, arrived in Washington to evaluate American attitudes. He stayed for a week, and I brought him to see people in the administration and in Congress. Nha spoke English fluently and had a quick intelligence. He had gone to college in the United States and understood a good deal more about the American system than did most Vietnamese. Despite the occasionally flip manner that impressed some as arrogance, I liked him and found him easy to talk to. I was confident he would grasp the importance of handling the elections properly, and I felt he would convey the message clearly.

Nha was a conduit to Thieu, and I was close enough to him to judge that it was a job he handled with tact. But I knew that personally I was in a delicate position. Given my long-term friendship with Ky and what I knew were Thieu's permanent suspicions about me, my judgments about the election were almost sure to be discounted in advance. I was also eager to avoid getting involved in an embarrassing entanglement between Thieu and Ky. I had been there before, and I was not eager to repeat the experience. The fact was that I had no private preference for either one, and had not had for many years. In my time away from Saigon politics, I had become uninterested in the personal battles and preoccupied with the relationship of my country to the United States and with the bearing this relationship had on our survival. So after Nha left, I sat back and watched, saying little for a change, and conspicuously (or so it seemed to me) not asking to be called back for consultations. As Ky's challenge proceeded in court, I even took the family for a week's vacation in Haiti.

When I got back, Vietnam's supreme court had upheld the election law, thus excluding Ky from the race. After this decision, Ellsworth Bunker returned to Washington for consultations. Ordinarily on these occasions, Bunker and I would meet for lunch and a long, informal discussion of events. This time I was especially eager to talk with him, to discover what the real state of affairs was in Saigon. On August 13 I went to see Bunker and William Sullivan at the State Department. The following day Bunker and I met in private. I found both men as disturbed as I about the prospect of a one-man election. I described the meetings in a cable to Thieu on August 14.

I had these days two consecutive conversations with Ambassadors Sullivan and Bunker. During these conversations both expressed their concern about the eventual prospect of a one man race. . . . Their arguments are that in such an eventuality Congress and public opinion will be extremely critical and that we will have the greatest difficulties getting the aid program approved. They pointed out the fact that the administration can have its policy, but money comes from the Congress and that particularly in the present circumstances the mood in Congress is really unpredictable. In fact recently the House went along with the Senate to refuse military aid to Pakistan and Greece. One year ago such an attitude from the House would have been out of the question. It is within this context that the administration is extremely cautious about sending a delegation to observe the elections and the present attitude is rather toward no delegation . . .*

*Ellsworth Bunker has been accused by some people of attempting to undermine Ky's candidacy. In fact, as this cable indicates, he was seriously disturbed by Thieu's manipulations and feared that they would do irreparable damage in Congress to the cause of aid for South Vietnam. Bunker was sure that Thieu would win a legitimate election handily, and

But Sullivan's and Bunker's strong views on the elections did not, unfortunately, reflect a unanimous opinion within the U.S. administration. This, at least, was my feeling when I met with Kissinger's assistant John Holdridge on the eighteenth. From Holdridge I got the distinct impression that the national security adviser was less concerned with the course of the elections than he was with maintaining "stability" in Saigon. Years later, Kissinger reinforced my sense of what his priorities had been, writing in his memoirs that while Thieu's methods were "unwise . . . neither Nixon nor I was prepared to toss Thieu to the wolves; indeed, short of cutting off all military and economic aid and thus doing Hanoi's work for it, there was no practical way to do so. We considered support for the political structure in Saigon not a favor done to Thieu but an imperative of our national interest."*

I thought Kissinger's position was unwise then, and I continue to think so. Enmeshed in the flow of his diplomacy (he was just then engaged in secret meetings with the North Vietnamese and was preparing another trip to Peking), he wanted nothing so much as quiet from the unruly South Vietnamese. From his standpoint, the elections were, in essence, an unfortunate disruption, "a new source of turmoil and uncertainty," as he called them later. But in opting to permit Thieu his methods, rather than unambiguously facing him with American requirements for reform and straightforward procedures, Kissinger invited the blossoming of one-man rule. Eventually, this would prove the most destructive and destabilizing factor of all.

The day after I met with Holdridge, August 19, news came from Saigon that Big Minh had decided to withdraw his candidacy. Then, on the twenty-first, the supreme court reversed itself and ruled that Ky was eligible after all. But two days afterward Ky announced that he would not be running either. Faced with Thieu's clear determination to control the election, neither man considered that the race would amount to anything more than an exercise in futility. On September 2 Thieu declared that he would carry on with the elections, despite the lack of opponents.

At this point, the dual track of South Vietnamese political development halted abruptly. In these pre-election events the democratic process, even in its roisterous and imperfect Vietnamese mode, received the kiss of death. With the prospect (soon to be the reality) of unchecked one-man rule, people naturally lost interest in the concept of liberal democracy as a feasible ideal. From then on they considered political matters a foregone

---

that his stature would be substantially enhanced in the process. Any illegality, he thought, would be self-destructive to Thieu and harmful to the country.
*Kissinger, *White House Years*, p. 1035.

conclusion. That, they seemed to say, was the nature of government. Outside South Vietnam, as well as inside, the image of the Thieu regime as a corrupt and repressive dictatorship got a rousing confirmation.

The destructive consequences of a progressively narrowing domestic base of support would take time to emerge, as would the fatal attrition in the ranks of American congressmen who believed South Vietnam was a cause worth sustaining. And these eventualities were not solely due to 1971's one-man show. But in South Vietnam's brief history, the election was a point of no return, at which the search for a vivifying national purpose was finally discarded in favor of the chimerical strength of an autocrat.

In the fall of 1971 I had no inkling of what the future held, certainly no premonitions of national disaster. But I felt fatigued and disheartened. And when, on October 2, I heard the formal reports of Thieu's re-election, I also realized that I was facing a certain practical dilemma. I was, after all, the ambassador of a nation whose president had just been re-elected. Officially, it was an occasion for rejoicing. Courtesy and protocol required that I send a telegram of congratulations. But such a message would hardly reflect my true feelings. It was perhaps a minor thing; nevertheless I racked my brain to try to find a way to assuage my conscience without insulting Thieu, who was, like it or not, the president.

After spending a day and a night thinking about this, I arrived at a conclusion that would perhaps have been evident from the start to a more practical man. Unhappily, there were only two options: to send the telegram or not to send it. If I did not send it, there would be a lot of conjecture; the rumor mongers would have a field day. But with all the ruminating, it also seemed that sending a telegram would be unworthy of what I had tried to stand for all my life. In the end, I decided not to send anything except a coldly factual report on the American reaction to the election.

With this done, I somewhat unexpectedly found myself beginning to think about resigning my post. I knew Thieu, and knew that whether or not he would ever mention this obstinate omission of mine, he would keep it in his heart. He understood all too well how I felt about the one-man show, and he probably suspected that I had been conniving with Bunker to pressure him. I thought, too, that as he consolidated his strength, he would begin looking to replace me anyway.

The more my thoughts on this subject fell into place, the more it seemed that now would be a good time to leave. I had been in Washington for almost five years already; perhaps that was long enough. I would enjoy getting back to the *Saigon Post* finally. I had even been thinking sporadically over the last year about starting up a new literary magazine, a cultural weekly, a genre that did not yet exist in Vietnam. During my long visit to Saigon the previous summer, I had made it a point to talk to a fair number of well-known Vietnamese writers, all of whom had naturally considered it a wonderful idea. At that time it had been only a thought, a possibility for the undefined future. Now I began to wonder if the time had not come.

With this idea running through my mind, I decided that a quick trip to Saigon might be worthwhile, to talk the whole matter over with friends and try to get a perspective on taking this step. But when I cabled my request to be called home, it was ignored. Clearly this was a sign of some sort. Up to this point, I only had to announce that I was coming in order to receive the formal request. On the phone, Nha said briefly that we would "talk about it soon." Now I had the feeling that something was really going on, and it reinforced my decision to resign.

I recognized by now that I had put myself in an awkward position. Certainly, it would be better to leave of my own volition rather than wait for Thieu to remove me. That would hardly be the elegant way. I thought briefly about my father. All his life he had conducted himself as an artist, unconcerned about money or position. Whatever he did he wanted to do "correctly," "aesthetically" — by which he meant freely, unconstrained by vulgar obligations. I had, perhaps, not inherited all of his fine disregard for the world. But I did have a full measure of his antipathy for acting under compulsion. Whether that was a character flaw or a virtue I could never quite determine. But it had often guided me in making decisions, and it did here as well. This was clearly the time for me to put my own closure on my life in the affairs of state.

With this in mind, at the beginning of December I wrote an especially comprehensive report to Thieu, reviewing the recent past and attempting to outline the future as I saw it. Using a recent Harris survey, I described in detail the withering American public support for any kind of involvement in Vietnam, not even for residual forces or continuing economic aid. I made my by now ritual explanation that although Nixon had stood fast until now ("a president with less determination could not have done it"), in the end aid and even troop withdrawals were up to Congress. "We have to remember that in spite of the tremendous powers the president of the United States has in his hands, political realities constantly tie him down and it is not true that he can do anything that he wants." My report went on:

During the past years, due to reasons stemming from our own mistakes as well as the American government's mistakes, sympathy for our cause has gradually diminished up to the point where now there is just a drop left. If we argue that the Americans are on their way out and that Vietnam does not need their help anymore, then the problem of sustaining their support is not relevant.

But on the contrary, if we think that at least for a period of time Vietnam still depends on help from the United States, then the problem of sustaining support is important. Whether Vietnam agrees or disagrees with the conclusions of public opinion or of the U.S. administration (e.g., on the one man election, corruption, lack of unity), the problem for Vietnam is to face these political realities, realities that even the president of the United States cannot ignore. . . .

We have to start on a new basis a campaign aimed at public opinion and the political circles to demonstrate that Vietnam today does not need any more "blood" from the United States, but only aid on the military and economic fronts, and this only for a short period of time. In spite of the unavoidable shortcomings of an underdeveloped society in wartime, the Vietnamese people are a people which deserves help from the United States. And one of the vital factors in this campaign is still, in my opinion, the image of a Vietnam united, free from corruption, ready to take its destiny in its own hands.

As the concluding flourish suggests, with this report I was putting my own house in order rather than saying anything I thought would be taken seriously in Saigon. Looking back at it, I can see that an undercurrent of personal frustration cuts through the words, with their transparent allusions to "our mistakes" and their explicit references to the "one man election," "corruption," and "lack of unity." In any event, it would be the last speech I launched into the void, and I wanted to put myself on record. In essence, though, my final advice to Nguyen Van Thieu was a simple reiteration of a truth I had learned about Washington and he had not. The American president does not stand alone. Those dependent on U.S. aid must look beyond him to the Congress, and beyond Congress to the media and to the people. In one way or another, I had spent nearly five years saying this. I had not, up to and including this final report, learned to say it so that I would be heard.

Not long after writing, I called Nha in Saigon, telling him that if Thieu was thinking of reshuffling ambassadors or changing the government, "I think it is fair to give him every freedom to make whatever choice he wants." After a month of silence on the issue, I received a phone call from Foreign Minister Tran Van Lam, who told me that the government was indeed planning to move some of the ambassadors around. He did not say whether I was personally involved in this, but he did want to have my opinion about it.

Regarding Lam's call as a signal, I immediately sat down and wrote out a formal resignation and sent it off to Thieu's office. Within several days Nha was on the phone, telling me he would shortly be coming to Washington to see me. When he arrived, he said that President Thieu understood my position, and he would agree with me if I thought I needed a rest. With the various ambassadorial changes going on, several other positions were open, including London and Canberra. Might I be interested in taking either of these? That evening I wrote back to Thieu, expressing my appreciation for his generous offer, but confirming my resignation. It was past time, I told him, for me to come home.

Chapter 33

Two Showdowns

ON JANUARY 25, 1972, as I was making my final decision to leave Washington, Richard Nixon gave a televised speech from the Oval Office that startled almost everyone who heard it, myself included. Henry Kissinger, he said, had been meeting secretly with the North Vietnamese since August 1969. Over that period, twelve sessions had been held, the last one on September 13, 1971. Subsequent to the last meeting, the United States had submitted a written peace proposal to the North Vietnamese to which it had never received an answer. Now Nixon reaffirmed that proposal. He offered a complete American withdrawal within six months and an internationally supervised presidential election in South Vietnam, open to candidates of "all political forces in Vietnam." One month prior to the election, Thieu would step down as president.

The speech was a spectacular coup, on the same order as the revelation of Kissinger's secret trip to China the previous year. Suddenly, the war critics found themselves on the defensive, discovering to their chagrin that many of the concessions they had been advocating so stridently and with so much recrimination had in fact been offered already by their supposedly immoral government, and had been turned down by the North Vietnamese.

My own reaction was not chagrin but apprehension. It was unsettling to learn that Kissinger was negotiating alone and in secret on behalf of both the United States and South Vietnam. No one knew better than I that Washington's interests and priorities were no longer identical with Saigon's, and had not been since the early days of the Nixon administration. American withdrawal and South Vietnamese survival were not necessarily incompatible goals, but it was a matter of deep concern that the formulation of negotiating strategy and the negotiations themselves were being treated as a wholly private American affair. Vacillating and indecisive, Thieu in early 1969 had sidestepped the opportunity for a partnership, so since then Kissinger and Nixon had maintained tight control over talks with North Vietnam. For three years the salient features of their attitude toward South Vietnam had been their desire for stability and their nervousness about any hint of an independent South Vietnamese initiative. I knew Thieu had had no hand in developing the positions that Kissinger was arguing, and I had no idea of the extent to which South Vietnam's president was even being kept informed. Kissinger's penchant for secrecy and Thieu's distaste for confrontation suggested that there was less than an open dialogue between them.

I did not want to put in a cable my questions about Thieu's familiarity with the substance of Kissinger's talks (the Anna Chennault affair had taught me that my cables were far from secure), so instead I called Nha. But he was not eager to discuss the subject. He refused to say whether Thieu was satisfied with Kissinger's conduct of the secret meetings, telling me simply, "We'll talk about it later." It was not a reassuring response.

Shortly after Nixon's speech, Ellsworth Bunker returned to Washington for consultations and, as usual, I made arrangements to meet with him at the embassy. Bunker was the primary channel through which Kissinger conveyed information to Thieu, and I was especially eager to learn what Thieu's reactions had been to the secret negotiations as they developed. "As you well know," Bunker told me, "it is always difficult to measure Thieu's response." Whatever Kissinger conveyed to him, he relayed to Thieu. But whether or not Thieu approved of what Kissinger was doing, Bunker found it impossible to say.

When Nha arrived in the United States at the end of February, he filled in some of the background. Thieu was briefed about the negotiations, he said, but sketchily. Typically, Kissinger would send a laconic report to Bunker, and Bunker would simply pass it along. Thieu was consulted to a certain extent on the outlines of major negotiating positions, but not in a way he was happy with; certainly, he had little opportunity to offer his own views. He had acquiesced with great reluctance, for example, to heavy American pressure for internationally supervised elections and for relinquishing his office beforehand. But he had done so, in the first place out of a belief that the Communists would never accept the offer and in the second place because he was unwilling to get into a potentially unnecessary controversy with Nixon. It was, in other words, a continuation of the syndrome I had been watching since 1965. The United States was making decisions that bore on the very existence of South Vietnam, and it was making them on the basis of its own geopolitical and domestic interests, with only the slightest nod to those whose protection it had gravely undertaken.

The arrogance that led to what I considered by this time an institutionalized American moral failure was complemented on the South Vietnamese side by an abject failure of leadership, passive and dilatory and incapable of assuming the burden of responsibility for the nation. Doubtless there were national characteristics, ingrained in the psychology and history of the two peoples, that contributed to this ill-fated symbiosis. But the personal styles of their leaders played no insignificant role: Kissinger's secretiveness, his habit of finesse and manipulation; Thieu's evasiveness and indirection, his chronic irresolution.

Close to both sides, I had watched this particular relationship develop for three years, with an increasing awareness of my own inability to affect it. With my resignation submitted, I thought I would at least separate myself from the frustrations of the job. But strangely, nothing happened. Saigon sent no word about a replacement date or even a formal acknowledgment of my resignation.

As a result, in March I was still at work, pursuing inquiries along two lines. With the revelation of the secret talks, I became even more disturbed by Kissinger's personal approach, by the direction we might expect him to take, and by the timing of the next developments. To divine what I could of these things, I met with Kissinger staffers Holdridge and Negroponte, as well as with Marvin Kalb, the long-time CBS diplomatic correspondent, who had an unusual sensitivity to the national security adviser's modus operandi. Most of all, I wanted to understand Kissinger's concept of "flexibility," a term I had first heard him use during our initial meeting in 1969 and that had now taken on a vastly more ominous coloring.

But beyond the secret talks, something even more dangerous was in the air. The North Vietnamese had broken off the talks in November, though in fact the last face-to-face discussion had taken place on September 13. Now we were in 1972, a presidential election year, and there was no question that the North Vietnamese had been impressed by the results of their previous election year offensive, during Tet of 1968. Sir Robert Thompson, the British antiguerrilla expert, was sure that a large-scale offensive would take place, sufficiently in advance of November to have an impact on the nationwide political debates the U.S. election would bring with it. Beyond these considerations, the dry season was well along now, and all intelligence reports indicated that a massive North Vietnamese build-up had been under way for months. Since the good dry fighting weather ended in July, something would have to happen by June at the latest. Already it was mid-March. My schedule became cluttered with meetings with State Department and military people — Sullivan, West-moreland, Laird, and many of the generals who were involved with the Vietnamization program. With American combat forces in Vietnam re-duced to a negligible level and no longer taking an active role in the fighting, the expected eruption would now pit the North and South Viet-namese armies against each other. The first prong of American strategy, negotiations, had yielded nothing. The second prong, Vietnamization, was about to receive its baptism of fire. Something big was in the works. The only questions were when it would happen, and where.

The North Vietnamese wave broke across the demilitarized zone and into Quang Tri province on March 30. At first it was not altogether clear if this was part of the major assault everyone was expecting or simply a large-scale probe. But within a week two other attacks followed, one from the Laotian sanctuaries toward South Vietnam's central highlands, the other from the Cambodian border toward the provincial capital of An Loc, north of Saigon. The besieged Saigon government soon appealed for help.

On the phone almost continuously with Saigon and my aides stationed at the Pentagon and State Department, I watched the battle expand across the map. Though the offensive itself had come as no surprise, I had not expected anything quite of this magnitude and intensity, nor, it seemed, had my friends at the State Department and the Pentagon. By the second week in April, twelve enemy divisions were engaged. South Vietnam had been invaded by the bulk of North Vietnam's army.

As the offensive grew, it was apparent that we were nearing a crisis point. If South Vietnam's troops were unable to hold, a disaster would ensue. On the one hand, I had great confidence in ARVN's elite units, the airborne, marines, and rangers. On the other hand, the protective Amer-ican shield was gone. I hung on the briefings, watching the slow destruc-tion of ARVN's Third Division in Quang Tri province and the North Vietnamese advance toward the provincial capital. It was also evident, however, that though Richard Nixon wanted to wind down the war, he was not going to allow this challenge to go unanswered. By April 5 American bombers were attacking staging areas and supply targets north of the demilitarized zone, while navy and air force reinforcements were readied for battle.

On April 15, with the offensive still gathering force, B-52s hit targets in Hanoi and Haiphong, the first time in four years that these cities had been attacked. For Nixon and Kissinger, these strikes were a demonstra-tion of courage and will. The reaction to them was inevitable and im-mediate. Student demonstrations surged around the country; a general campus strike was called and hundreds of protesters were arrested. In the

Senate, William Fulbright's Foreign Relations Committee called Secretary of Defense Laird and Secretary of State Rogers into the dock. The televised hearings were loaded with hostility, marked by angry interchanges between the secretaries and dove senators.

At this point, the battle was fully joined. The North Vietnamese pulled out all the stops, throwing into this offensive all the forces they were able to marshal. Against this, Nixon was unleashing the full fury of American air and sea power. There would be no buckling under to either domestic protest or congressional pressure. Amidst these developments, the fighting on the ground became a magnet, drawing the attention of every observer. The question was simple: Would South Vietnamese forces, with American air support, be able to defend their country, or would American policy of almost twenty years crumble to dust on this battlefield, and with it the existence of a free Vietnam?

By the third week in April the issue was still unclear. On the twenty-first Alexander Haig returned from Vietnam with a firsthand report. That night I cabled Thieu: "Haig said he detected a general feeling of confidence. Apart from some isolated cases, ARVN has fought well. He agreed with our analysis of the situation, that the fighting will continue for some time. But he appeared somewhat concerned about the extent of our losses, which in the long run will have effects on morale. The general opinion here is that everything depends on the ground fighting and on the behavior of our troops."

On May 1 the northern provincial capital of Quang Tri fell to elements of the North Vietnamese army's 304th and 308th divisions, supported by two tank regiments. ARVN's Third Infantry Division disintegrated under the attack. With Quang Tri occupied, columns of refugees and fleeing troops took to the roads and were pounded as they went by North Vietnamese artillery. Hue was threatened, as was Kontum, in the central highlands. Sixty miles from Saigon, near the Cambodian border, An Loc had now been surrounded.

The day after Quang Tri fell, Kissinger and Le Duc Tho met in Paris, the first private meeting in eight months. As Kissinger described it later, the session was brutal, marked by Le Duc Tho's arrogant assurance that North Vietnam's invading army would prevail. But in the days that followed, it became apparent that Tho's confidence was premature. Although South Vietnamese units had been shocked at first by the scale of the attack and by the unprecedented artillery and tank forces arrayed against them, now they had begun to dig in, fighting desperately to hold ground. On each of the three battlefronts, North Vietnamese advances were grinding to a halt, caught between vicious air attacks and a grim South Vietnamese determination to resist.

Among the battles raging along the different fronts, An Loc was one of the bloodiest and certainly the most dramatic. In a sense, it was the model for the pattern of fighting that was developing throughout the country. Located only fifteen miles from the Communists' old Cambodian border strongholds, the city of An Loc sat astride National Route 13, which led directly to Saigon, two days' march to the south. Set in a small valley, surrounded by forested hills and vast rubber plantations, between April 7 and June 9 the city underwent a siege that turned it into a small, Vietnamese version of Stalingrad.

In An Loc, ARVN General Le Van Hung had a garrison of approximately 6,000 men, composed primarily of local provincial troops and soldiers from the Fifth Division. Against him, moving out of their sanctuaries in Cambodia, were the Vietcong's Fifth, Seventh, and Ninth divisions, the North Vietnamese Seventy-fifth Artillery Division, and three North Vietnamese tank battalions, a total of approximately 28,000 troops, including blocking units. By April 11 enemy forces had eliminated the forward defense positions protecting An Loc. On the twelfth they sealed off the city.

The following day, after a massive artillery barrage, the first Vietcong assault was launched against the trapped defenders. It was not stopped until almost a third of the town was lost. Two days later the second mass assault began. This time the attackers penetrated farther into the city, in vicious house-to-house fighting, until finally being driven off with the help of murderous close-quarter bombing and strafing.

An Loc's defenders and hapless civilians were being kept alive now exclusively by high-altitude parachute drops of food, medicine, and ammunition, more than two-thirds of which fell behind enemy lines as the C-130s dodged the barrage of antiaircraft fire. For weeks the outmanned and outgunned South Vietnamese fought off repeated infantry probes and tank assaults through the city's ruined streets while their defense perimeter slowly contracted.

Two days short of a month after the initial attack on the city, elements of the enemy's Fifth and Ninth divisions massed to attack simultaneously from the north, northeast, south, and west. From 3 to 6 A.M. on May 11, artillery pounded the defenders nonstop. Then, through An Loc's western gate, the Vietcong 272nd Regiment boiled through the defenses. By 10 A.M. they had occupied the public works building and were only 150 meters from General Hung's command headquarters. In the north, too, the attack broke through ARVN lines and neared the city's center. Vietcong forces in the south were also making headway against the exhausted and shell-shocked South Vietnamese.

On May 12 dawn broke on battle lines that had been consolidated during the night. Once again the Vietcong's Fifth and Ninth divisions struck toward the heart of the city, covered by the North Vietnamese tank regiments. But the defenders were ready, as were the South Vietnamese and American flyers. Between the withering fire of the ARVN fighters and the effective, close-range air support, each of the Vietcong assaults during the day was thrown back. By late in the day it had become apparent that the attackers had lost their momentum and their spirit. The last assault on An Loc had run out of steam.

In the following days, the enemy Fifth Division was withdrawn from the battlefield to recover from the mauling it had received. But still the Vietcong Ninth Division retained its positions around the city, enforcing the siege with shelling and small-unit activity, though by now An Loc was clearly a losing proposition for them. At the end of May, with most of the antiaircraft positions destroyed, helicopters and transports were again able to use the airfield. Finally, on June 9 the relieving forces of ARVN's Twenty-first Division and its attached units penetrated the battle zone along highway 13 and linked up with the city's defenders. The relieving forces had waged a two-month-long moving battle with the enemy's Seventh Division, which had been used to block reinforcements. After fifty-eight days of continuous combat, the siege of An Loc was over. ARVN had lost over 4,000 men, either killed or missing in action; the enemy dead counted over 6,000.

In the final analysis, An Loc was far more than a tactical victory for South Vietnam's army. It was a symbol, a crystallization of the lesson both sides had learned from what was now being called the Great Spring Offensive. Vietnamization, for all its flaws in planning and implementation, was a success. South Vietnamese troops were capable of fighting magnificently in extended actions against superior forces. In conjunction with American and South Vietnamese air power, they were capable of stopping and destroying the best their enemies could throw at them. As long as that air power was available for support, there was excellent reason to believe that ARVN could succeed in the role it had been designed to play.

The last assault on An Loc was turned back on May 12. Below the demilitarized zone, although Quang Tri had fallen, the North Vietnamese had not been able to develop their thrust toward Hue. Nor had the enemy sweep into the central highlands borne fruit. With the anxiety of the Great Spring Offensive's early successes completely dissipated, I started making serious plans to turn over my post. At the end of May I made the rounds of my fellow diplomats, and in early June I stopped at the White House to pay my respects to President Nixon. My wife and I had a goodbye lunch with Averell Harriman and his wife, then another with George and Lola Aiken. I saw all of my colleagues at State and the Pentagon, people I had worked with closely, sometimes for many years: Rogers, Westmoreland, Laird, William Sullivan, Alexis Johnson, Alexander Haig, Kissinger staffers John Holdridge and John Negroponte, and close congressional friends John Tower and Clement Zablocki.

With many of these people, the farewells were touched by an undercurrent of emotion. I felt as if I had known Washington all my life, as if I was leaving a place that had become a second home. Of course, I had chosen to go. And because I had deliberately taken this path, I thought I would be well prepared to leave. But the last-minute rush of friends, the meeting with my superb staff, who had shared so much with me over the previous five and a half years, the sendoff from Washington's Vietnamese community — all of this brought me face to face with the fact that I had created roots in this place, attachments that went far deeper than the professional liaisons that came with the position I had tried to fill.

From Dulles International Airport we flew to Paris, my wife and I, our two daughters, twenty-one and seventeen now, and our five-year-old son, Han. There we stayed with friends for a week, then packed everyone into a rented Peugeot and headed down the *route Napoléon* toward Nice, Cannes, and Grenoble, then to the little border town of St. Gervais, where we had spent an idyllic year during my wife's convalescence, far from the political turmoil of those days. There we stopped to see the people who had taken such good care of her twenty years before, then drove southward toward Italy.

The farther we went, the farther behind we left the war that had dominated my life almost as far back as I could remember. It was an exquisite luxury, driving that Peugeot through Geneva, then across the Italian Alps to the fairy tale city of Venice, then down to the glowing churches of Florence. We were entirely on our own, tourists struggling to get along with the few words of Italian we knew, staring at the gardens and palaces along with the rest of the admiring foreigners. The privacy was uncanny, on occasion even disorienting. It seemed to me that we blended in with the hordes of visitors, Asians, of course — we couldn't very well hide that. Perhaps, I thought, we looked like a family of touring Japanese.

Two delicious months later we were back in Paris, embarking on the Air France flight to Saigon. It was mid-August. I did not know yet that Henry Kissinger and Le Duc Tho had started up the secret talks again, that the dust of the spring offensive had settled sufficiently, that the two sides had taken stock of the new realities and had begun to glimpse the outline of a settlement.

For the moment these developments, earth shaking as they were, remained outside my field of vision. Although back in the steamy political world of Saigon, I was very much a private man. I began showing up in my office at the *Saigon Post,* working out the best way to reintegrate myself into the newspaper's daily affairs. I also began setting up the cultural magazine I had been mulling over. I arranged the financing, hired editors and writers, and commissioned the first articles for what we had decided to call *Gio Moi (The New Wind).*

Of course, Saigon being what it was — and I being what I was — I found myself listening attentively to the mood of the city. With the fighting winding down, my old friends in the military seemed, if not enthusiastic, at least confident. There was a lot of talk about the heroic defense of An Loc, a feeling that the North Vietnamese could be beaten on the battlefield. I sensed as well a general, underlying concern about the renewed negotiations. Henry Kissinger had just visited Saigon, so it was clear that with the military spasm almost over, the diplomatic front was heating up again. People took for granted that Kissinger would get on with Le Duc Tho, that they would move toward a conclusion, though what the conclusion might be, nobody could yet say.

Sometime in early September I went to the palace to pay my respects to Thieu. It was a friendly encounter, complete with smiles and handshakes and small talk. Both of us kept the discussion away from politics. Over the next month Thieu invited my wife and me to dinner several times, social occasions but political too — a kind of re-establishment of a relationship that had, through all its years, been assaulted by suspicion on one side and frustration on the other.

In mid-October my successor in Washington, Tran Kim Phuong, returned to Saigon to assist with a new round of meetings between Thieu and Kissinger, who arrived on the nineteenth after still another series of talks in Paris with Le Duc Tho. Phuong and I saw each other regularly during this period, and he brought me up to date on the negotiations. From Phuong I learned that Kissinger and Le Duc Tho had in fact reached agreement during their last sessions, and that Kissinger was in Saigon to elicit Thieu's approval of the terms.

Phuong's own opinion of these negotiations coincided with mine. The United States was under an irremediable compulsion to get out of Vietnam. Essentially, their problem was how to arrange this with the other side. It appeared as if the men in Hanoi had now given Kissinger and Nixon the minimum they required, a return of prisoners and a basic recognition of the Saigon government. On the other side, the Americans had agreed to withdraw entirely, leaving no residual forces behind — as they had, for example, in Korea. North Vietnamese forces in South Vietnam, though, would be allowed to stay where they were. One way or another, Phuong and I thought, the Americans would now accept. Thieu would undoubtedly be hostile to the terms of the agreement, and this might prove an embarrassment and an obstacle, but in the long run there would be no way for us to escape from the enormous American pressure.

As it turned out, Thieu was not merely hostile to the terms; he was outraged. Word began to spread that he had not been informed when the talks had entered this final stage, and he was certainly not expecting Kissinger to present him with a fait accompli, an agreement so full of holes and discrepancies as this one. (Among other objectionable points, the pact referred to the "three nations" of Indochina, i.e., Laos, Cambodia, and only one — not two — Vietnams.) By October 23, the day Kissinger left Saigon, the news had already leaked out that Thieu had rejected the American–North Vietnamese agreement. On the twenty-fourth Thieu went on the radio to announce that he would not accept. He would agree neither to any form of coalition government (Kissinger affirmed there would be none, but the agreement was ambiguous) nor to the continued presence of the North Vietnamese army in South Vietnam. He proposed direct negotiations between Saigon and Hanoi and also direct negotiations between Saigon and the Vietcong's Provisional Revolutionary Government.

With this speech, speculation flared in Saigon about the kind of pressure the Americans would now apply to Thieu and to what extent he would be able to stand up to it. There was a wave of public support for him, a visceral response from a small nation that resented the treatment it was receiving from its giant ally. But this was merely a first reaction. Soon it began to sink in that Thieu would be unable to sustain his opposition, that he would have to reach a compromise. South Vietnam could simply not afford the loss of support that a real rupture with the Americans would mean.

During November Hoang Duc Nha and I began to see each other more frequently. It was a difficult period for him and for his cousin Thieu. The South Vietnamese had presented Kissinger with a list of sixty-nine changes in the draft peace agreement which they insisted he take up with Hanoi. Although Kissinger had, of course, agreed to do what he could, everyone knew there was little chance that Le Duc Tho would agree to the major points, in particular the demand that North Vietnamese troops be withdrawn from South Vietnam. It was, then, a period of high-stakes testing, with Thieu attempting to push the Americans as far as he was able, and the Americans warning Thieu that if he did not ultimately go along with the agreement, he would be cut off entirely from the support he needed to survive. In one particularly disgraceful letter, written on October 6, Nixon even reminded Thieu of what had befallen his predecessor Ngo Dinh Diem in 1963.[*]

* Quoted in Hung and Schecter, *The Palace File* (New York: Harper & Row, 1986), p. 376.

For Kissinger, these developments constituted a bitter and somewhat surprising dénouement. From the outset he had chosen to treat the South Vietnamese as secondary players in the negotiating game. He and Nixon had formulated their strategies without us and had pursued their objectives with the least possible reference to us. In finding their way out of the war, America's leaders were not deviating in the least from the peculiar arrogance with which they found their way into it and with which they afterward conducted it. Yielding and essentially insecure, Thieu had gone along with the role assigned him, acquiescing to American policies and proposals — or so it had seemed. In reality, the South Vietnamese president harbored a fierce resentment at the way he had been treated, a resentment alleviated only by his conviction that, in any case, the various American efforts at compromise would be scornfully rejected by the fanatical North Vietnamese.

But now that Le Duc Tho had unexpectedly dropped the intransigence of four years, everyone's chickens were coming home to roost. Never having viewed Thieu as a partner, Kissinger was completely unprepared for the rejection and personal animosity that greeted him now that he had an agreement in hand.* Thieu, for his part, was suddenly presented with the bill for having declined to take a strong, decisive stance with the Americans when the opportunity was his. All the years of deflection and false accommodation had now brought him an agreement that he considered a death knell for South Vietnam.

Negotiations between Kissinger and Le Duc Tho resumed in Paris on November 20. On that day, Kissinger presented his North Vietnamese interlocutors with gifts: a picture book of Harvard for Le Duc Tho, a crystal horse's head for Xuan Thuy. Then he presented them the sixty-nine proposed amendments and additions that he had been given by the South Vietnamese. Although a number of days of serious negotiations followed, before long it became clear to the Americans that the North Vietnamese strategy was neither to settle nor to break off the talks; they had decided to play for time. Perhaps they realized that with Congress's return after Christmas vacation, a cutoff of funding for the war was likely. No doubt they were also eager to exacerbate the explosive differences between Washington and Saigon, hoping to precipitate the threatened break between their enemies.

After more than three weeks of unproductive talk, on December 13

---

* On October 21 Thieu kept Kissinger and Bunker waiting for six hours before informing them that he would not see them until the next day. "No ally," Kissinger fumed, "had a right to treat an emissary of the President of the United States this way. . . . We felt the impotent rage so cunningly seeded in foreigners by the Vietnamese" (*White House Years*, p. 1379).

Le Duc Tho returned to Hanoi for consultations. Before leaving, he and Kissinger agreed to be in contact regarding the next session, perhaps after the Christmas holidays. But in an Oval Office meeting on the morning of the fourteenth with Kissinger and Haig, Nixon decided that the North Vietnamese were simply stalling for time, that they were indeed pushing the administration up against the threatened congressional cutoff even while they were exploring the possibility of a real rupture between Washington and Saigon.

All three participants in the meeting thought that only a powerful demonstration of force would convince the North Vietnamese of the need to settle quickly. Three days later, the port of Haiphong was seeded with aerial mines. The day after that, 129 B-52s struck targets in Haiphong and Hanoi. The Christmas bombing had begun.

The bombing was a dual signal. To the politburo in Hanoi it sent a message that they would find agreement preferable to further stalling. Nixon would not sit by while Hanoi used the element of time against him. To Saigon Nixon was saying that he could be trusted as a party to this agreement, that he was not afraid to take unpopular measures if circumstances required. Together with a massive airlift of military supplies (code-named Enhance Plus), the bombing was a gesture of assurance, a demonstration of American reliability.

Early in December, Thieu had invited me to the palace for a general exchange of ideas. When the bombing was over, he asked me back, this time with a request that I undertake a mission to Washington. For all the pressure the Americans had brought to bear on him, he still wanted to try to push them a bit further. "It's late in the day," he told me, "but we still have to do everything we can. I'm asking you to explain to the gentlemen there that the problem of North Vietnamese troops in the South is a problem of life or death for us. Maybe it's too late to influence them on this. I don't know. But you know the saying: As long as there is any water left, we have to scoop it."

For all my problems with Thieu, I had felt a good deal of sympathy for him over the months of his battle with Kissinger and Nixon. I also thought he was right about the agreement. And though I knew as well as he that in the end the Americans would force the issue with us, it seemed worthwhile to make one last effort. Although we had no real leverage left, a small hope was visible nevertheless. The North Vietnamese had been surprised by the Christmas bombing and badly hurt. If Kissinger pushed them hard enough, perhaps they would show a new flexibility. Perhaps there was a moment here to exploit.

310 · In the Jaws of History

necessity for us to see who our real friends were — alluding
Nixon's defense of South Vietnam against those who for years
d to give the country over to the Communists. Given the mood
ss, he and the president had decided "in cold blood" that it was
o reach an agreement now, basically the one that had been
d. Moreover, he believed that this agreement would provide "a
for the continuation of aid to South Vietnam." Besides, he said,
came to worst, the United States would always be there. This
ration would never tolerate Communist violations of the agree-

ger's tone that morning was sharp, his mood defensive. He bris-
ut rumors from Paris alleging his contempt for the South Viet-
These, he said, were entirely false. (I had not mentioned them.)
equally irate about other rumors to the effect that he was cutting
vith the Soviets at South Vietnam's expense in order to restrain
nese. (Neither had I mentioned these.) When I told him that al-
the troop problem was perhaps not so important to the United
t was a matter of life and death for us, he answered again that he
ood, that he would put it on the table again and do what he
But this seemed to me a ritual response, uttered without any dis-
e conviction. The message behind the words was that he could
be expected to endanger the agreement by fighting over major
that had already been settled. It was a disheartening meeting, de-
f any sign that Kissinger felt strong enough after the Christmas
ng to open up a new area in the talks, scheduled to reconvene in
days.

next day Phuong, Do, and I were invited to lunch by Alexis John-
With Johnson were Marshall Green, John Holdridge, Ambassador-
rge Sam Berger, and Warren Nutter, assistant secretary of defense
ternational security. Once more Phuong and I argued our case, in-
g that the issue of North Vietnamese troops had not been satisfac-
y settled, and that now there was an opportunity to settle it. Alexis
son did not debate the issue. On the contrary, he agreed that we
right — in principle. But in practice, he said, given the extremely
y pressure from Congress and U.S. public opinion, and given the
ielding attitude of the North Vietnamese, what was the alternative?
fter lunch Johnson took me into a corner of the room. "This is a
rt to heart conversation between old friends," he said. "Your presi-
t, with his extremely skillful approach during the last months, has
ven beyond a doubt that he is nobody's puppet. If I am not mistaken,
has achieved a high point in his political career. Now he should take
vantage of what he has accomplished. Now it is time for him to rec-
nize that the United States has not changed its policy in the least. If we

The Paris Ag

I LANDED IN WASHINGTON on the m
afternoon Tran Van Do, Tran Kim Phuong
ton), and I were sitting down with Kissing
were there to argue, but Do's and my pre
former foreign minister and a former amba
as moderates who had demonstrated over
derstand American views and requirements. If
that afternoon, it was a signal from Thieu to
port he had on the North Vietnamese troop i

In the years I had known Kissinger, his styl
create a relaxed, friendly atmosphere for even
ordinarily did this through a preliminary dis
and self-deprecatory joking that had a way of
ing conflict. But this time there were no jokes.
by saying that there was no need to elaborat
Washington. Then I launched directly into my t
able presence of North Vietnamese troops in S
the proposed agreement acquiesced.

Kissinger's answer was that their continued pr
ted tacitly for a long time already, that Thieu h
agreed to the principle of a cease-fire in place in
late to raise this again," he said. "But I will try my
he had no illusions about Hanoi's future intentions
he felt strongly that the future of America's over
"global strategy," depended on successfully conclu
was a necessity, he said, for Vietnamese and Ameri

and a vita
to his and
had want
in Congr
essential
negotiate
new basi
if worst
administ
ment.
    Kissin
tled abo
namese.
He was
a deal
the Chi
though
States,
unders
could.
cernib
hardly
points
void
bomb
three
    Th
son.
at-La
for i
sistir
toril
John
wer
hea
uny
    A
hea
der
pr
he
ad
og

have had to change tactics, it has simply been so that we could maintain the same policy. But if your president refuses to accept the agreement once Nixon has accepted it, it will be tragic, a total break between our two peoples. If that happens — I am saying this to you as a friend of Vietnam's for many years — I will have to give up my position of support. I believe that every last friend of Vietnam will have to do the same."

I remonstrated that the United States had forced Thieu into an exceptionally dangerous situation, and that now it was time for the United States to help him keep his responsibility to the Vietnamese people. But Johnson only turned the question around. "Will President Thieu be willing to let us help him do that?" (i.e., by signing the agreement).

Alexis Johnson was indeed a longtime friend of Vietnam's. In 1964 and 1965 he had served in Saigon as deputy ambassador under Maxwell Taylor. He was one of the few stalwarts who had argued against the precipitate American intervention in March of 1965, and he had been deeply disturbed by the fall of Dr. Phan Huy Quat's civilian government in June of that year. He was a man of principle and understanding, with whom I had worked closely. Yet here we were, carrying on a dialogue of the deaf. The two sides were simply at odds, with no room between them for compromise.

Yet this dialogue of the deaf went on. Alexis Johnson's luncheon was in the State Department building, and directly afterward Phuong, Do, and I took the elevator up to the seventh floor to meet with William Rogers. Elaborating on my theme, I told the secretary of state that we simply had to draw the American government's attention to the basic requirements for South Vietnam's survival. If he put himself in our shoes he would understand that we were not trying to be an obstacle to peace, but that our concerns were basic, vital. For the United States, I said, Vietnam is just one among many issues. If the United States loses in Vietnam, it is just the end of a chapter of American history. But for us, to agree or not to agree, or to agree on what conditions, that is the whole story, the only issue, the issue of existence.

Rogers insisted that President Nixon had never considered Vietnam a matter of secondary importance, and that, as far as the North Vietnamese troops went, he agreed with me "in principle" (as had Johnson just a few minutes earlier). "But," he said, "if we do not have the practical means for upholding the principle, then the principle becomes useless. Now there is no more time for principle. The problem is simply what to choose out of what is left to be chosen. What choices are left? What alternatives are left? With the international situation prevailing right now, and with the pressures from Congress and public opinion, President Nixon has taken too many risks for Vietnam already. He cannot go further."

In the few days remaining before I left for Paris, I sandwiched in all the meetings I could with senators, congressmen, and newspeople. I was determined to keep digging for traces of support. I set up meetings with several of my friends from the Senate: Hubert Humphrey, Jacob Javits, John Tower, and George Aiken. Among these four, I felt I would be able to get an accurate indication of the mood of the new Congress. It was no great surprise when each of them told me point blank that this Congress would be determined to put an end to the war. The Christmas bombing had raised too strong an emotional reaction. Even many Republican senators who had previously supported Nixon were now against him. He would get no further support in the Senate. The House, up to this point, had lagged behind the Senate in cutting the budget for Vietnam. Now that too had changed, and the House was taking the lead. Of course, nobody wanted to bear the responsibility for cutting everything off. But it would be easy enough to find ways to delay Vietnam business and to delay all of Nixon's other legislative business as well. At the moment, they said, the atmosphere for aid was really bad. However, if peace comes, it was quite possible we might see a psychological turnaround. Were there to be a signed agreement, they themselves would work hard for a continuation of aid.

At the end of the discussion, both Aiken and Tower — my two closest friends in the Senate — advised me that South Vietnam should now be "realistic" and understand that the United States could do nothing else.

In an attempt to see if there was some dimension of this situation I had missed, I also met with a number of friends from the press, concentrating on those who had had substantial contact with Kissinger. Among Joe Kraft, Marvin Kalb, Murray Marder, and Chalmers Roberts, all experienced and perceptive diplomatic hands, there was only unanimity. In one way or another, they all told me that there was simply nothing left to say. They seemed to feel that there was a tacit understanding among the major powers, that they had at least implicitly agreed on a cease-fire in place. According to this view, there had been a tradeoff of sorts: North Vietnam would no longer demand Thieu's removal (Hanoi's constant refrain for four years), and the United States would not press for the withdrawal of North Vietnamese forces from South Vietnam. As a result, they thought, no really serious bargaining would take place from this point on.

In an increasingly black mood, on the morning of January 9 I went to see Al Haig. Although Haig was now army vice chief of staff, over the previous four years he had served as assistant to both Henry Kissinger and Richard Nixon. He knew Vietnam, not just as a diplomat but as a soldier, having commanded an infantry battalion there in the mid-1960s. He understood Vietnam's people and its terrain, and, as a military man, he had a clear concept of the battlefield. During my last year as ambassador, I had spent a good deal of time with Haig. Ordinarily, I found him an easy person to talk to.

As soon as I arrived at his Pentagon office, Haig told me that he had had a long discussion with Nixon the previous night. The president, he said, was "extremely concerned" about the rift that he saw opening between the United States and South Vietnam, because that was precisely what the Communists were waiting for. Nixon was "very disturbed" about Thieu's attitude and had the impression that Thieu was drawing back from agreements he had already made. As a result, Thieu was making it impossible for Nixon to help him.

I stopped Haig to tell him that we were disturbed ourselves. When Dr. Kissinger and he brought the draft agreement to Saigon in October, we felt that we had not been consulted at all adequately about even its major provisions. To this Haig said, "Yes, it was a bad mistake, a bad error on our part." (The direct quotes here are from verbatim notes I made right after the discussion, the substance of which I included in my cable to Thieu that night.)

"You know," I said, "while I was ambassador, I frequently mentioned to you that from September 1971 through January 1972 there was nothing approaching adequate contact between the two governments."

"Yes," Haig replied, "it was a kind of mishandling. But your attitude toward Henry Kissinger is wrong. Your president misreads him, though part of that is Henry's fault. But all that is past now. Now what's the outlook? President Nixon has no flexibility. If the Communists agree to the DMZ language, to the modalities for controlling the cease-fire, and to the modalities for signing the agreement, President Nixon will proceed. I have no doubt about the determination of the president to proceed. President Nixon will call publicly on President Thieu to join him, and if Thieu rejects it, then that will mean the abandonment of Vietnam. I myself will be going to Vietnam soon, and at that point there will be a moment of truth."

It was with Haig's "moment of truth" ringing in my ears that I returned to the embassy to write a last report to Thieu and get my things together for the trip to France for the last round of negotiations.

Late that afternoon, Do and I took off for Paris, where Henry Kissinger had already been negotiating with Le Duc Tho for three days. Although we were unaware of it at the time, the breakthrough (from Kissinger's point of view) had already taken place. On January 8 Kissinger and Le Duc Tho had decided to focus on two major issues: the DMZ and the method of signing. If the presence of North Vietnamese troops in South

Vietnam was to be addressed at all, it would be only in the most perfunctory fashion. The following day, January 9, the DMZ issue was settled, strengthening, to a degree, the concept of the demilitarized zone as a firm barrier between North and South Vietnam. With this matter resolved, the only thorny problem left on Kissinger's agenda was how to sign the document so that the South Vietnamese foreign minister's signature would not have to appear together with that of the PRG* representative — a contentious point, no doubt, but a "theological" (Kissinger's term) rather than a substantive one.

On the evening of January 12, the five senior South Vietnamese diplomats in Paris met with Kissinger, William Sullivan, and several of their aides to discuss the progress of the talks.** Kissinger's first comments, as we all sat in the living room of the U.S. ambassador's residence in Faubourg Saint-Honoré, were addressed to Do and me, the two special envoys. Apparently unhappy with the number of South Vietnamese who were constantly badgering him with pointed questions about his negotiations, he suggested that because Do and I had met with so many people in the United States, did we not think that we should be getting back quickly to Saigon to inform Thieu of our findings? Thieu must be persuaded of the necessity to conclude an agreement prior to the expected congressional vote cutting off further funds, so speed was of the essence. At this, Do remarked that it was the easiest thing in the world to conclude an agreement with the Communists in the shortest time. All you had to do was concede to them everything they were really interested in having.

From here on, the discussion took a somewhat less abrasive tone, though on our side the mood was of unrelieved grimness. Kissinger summed up the current state of negotiations, indicating the various areas in which progress had been made. These included the strengthened DMZ provision, an improved provision on the continued supply of military assistance, an enlarged function for the inspection teams of the International Control Commission, and several other items.

When he had completed his review, there was silence for a moment, interrupted by Do (I believe), who said, "Dr. Kissinger, these improvements are not negligible. But the crux of the matter is still the presence

---

* In 1969 the National Liberation Front had established the Provisional Revolutionary Government. Subsequently, the Vietcong's diplomatic efforts were formally carried on by this new entity.
** In addition to Do and myself, the Vietnamese were Pham Dang Lam, head of the Paris delegation, and Vuong Van Bac, ambassador to London. Sullivan, at that point, was heading the American team of technical experts. The following account is from notes taken at the meeting by Vuong Van Bac.

of North Vietnamese troops in South Vietnam. What has been done about this fundamental question?"

Kissinger's reply might have had some meaning in the civilized world of courts and lawyers, but when applied to a war between implacable enemies, it seemed to all of us little more than metaphysical nonsense:

This week, I raised again the question of withdrawal of North Vietnamese troops for almost three hours, to no avail. However, if the provisions for the agreement relating to the DMZ, Laos, and Cambodia are respected, there is no legal way for North Vietnam to have troops in South Vietnam. My point of view is that to this point North Vietnam has not claimed any right to be there. On the other hand, there is no provision in the agreement granting them that right. And I can give you excerpts of the proceedings where North Vietnamese representatives stated that they have no troops over there. We can give you a note quoting what they said and deducing that they thus do not claim to have the right to be in South Vietnam.

It was, in my view, a disgraceful answer. One could only imagine what the American reaction would be to a third party's insistence on negotiating a peace treaty for the United States which left an enemy army spread out from California to New York, and then, through a series of deductions, concluding that the enemy had as good as admitted that it had no legal right to be there.

"Very soon," Kissinger went on, "your president will have to decide whether to go along with us. By refusing to sign last October, he has achieved many things: the protocols, one billion dollars' worth of arms, three months to prepare for the cease-fire, and a much improved situation. But we will come soon to the moment of truth. You will either conclude the agreement or be cut off from U.S. assistance."

Our meeting with Kissinger and Sullivan wound down around midnight. Back in my hotel room, I immediately began work on a report to Thieu summing up my impressions after seven days of attempts to search out options:

Through an accumulation of circumstances, international public opinion, especially public opinion in the United States, will not tolerate any more delay in the re-establishment of peace in Vietnam. Right or wrong does not matter anymore. The only problem left is: When will peace come back? Even if it is an artificial peace. Consequently, Vietnam has to avoid being placed in a position in which all the blame in the world is on our shoulders. Otherwise, we will be completely isolated.

As far as the attitude in the U.S. is concerned, I consider that Rogers, Kissinger, and Haig have, to a certain degree, deliberately threatened us. But at the same time, we have to recognize the difficult position of the Nixon administration. On the one side, they cannot afford not to solve this problem. On the other, they feel they cannot go further than they already have. My conclusion is that Mr. Nixon has no more margin for maneuvering. In Paris Kissinger said to me, "You know we would prefer a military victory, but we just could not do it. Now is the time to settle before we cannot do anything more."

It is within the context of the push for peace by American and international public opinion and the political realities in the United States that I have done my best [to look for alternatives], because "As long as there is still any water, etc." But frankly speaking, I find myself under the influence of a very depressing atmosphere. I have scarcely the serenity necessary to provide advice or suggestions. But I am certain of one thing. We are at a turning point in our history. The problem of making a choice is difficult, complicated, and dolorous. But it is unavoidable.

My opinion is that we should fight with all our strength until the last minute. Then and only then should we make a choice. That choice is between refusing to sign (and accepting all the consequences of our decision) and signing, with the hope that in spite of the agreement's imperfections, with unity between all the Vietnamese nationalists, and with the promised aid from the Americans, we can survive our difficulties. Obviously, in the middle of the two choices is a third choice, that is, accepting the agreement without putting our signature on it. But I have to add immediately that if in principle this third choice looks attractive, in practice it amounts to a refusal of the agreement. In such a case the consequences for our relations with the Americans would be the same [as not signing].

I finished writing this report by hand somewhere between four and five in the morning. It came to more than twenty-five pages. When I was finished, a personal messenger took it for immediate delivery to Saigon.

I had little doubt that, in the end, Thieu would have to sign the agreement. But regardless of the final outcome, I wanted to do what I could to reconfirm our ties with friends other than the Americans. I wanted, first of all, to impress on them that South Vietnam was not obstructing peace, and second, to begin building an independent base of support that we would need after the agreement was finalized, either with or without Thieu's cooperation.

Toward these ends, I met first with Robert Schumann, the French foreign minister. Schumann was cordial, even though current relations between France and South Vietnam were more than a little strained. His country, he said, would be in favor of participating in an international conference on Indochina to confirm and guarantee the agreement. As I knew, in a recent speech President Pompidou had spoken of the four states of Indochina. There was nothing inadvertent about this. France would continue to support South Vietnam's independence.

While in Paris, I also took the opportunity to meet with a number of influential French and Vietnamese intellectuals. Here I engaged in a bit of creative diplomacy, reporting back to Thieu their opinions of the forthcoming agreement, but emphasizing comments that were in accord with my own thinking, specifically on the subject of unity. "Even if we had a good agreement," I wrote to Thieu, "if there is no unity, it will come to nothing. On the other hand, although the agreement we have is far from perfect, if we have unity it is hardly hopeless. Up to now it has been a waste; far too many nationalists have stayed away from the fight."

On the seventeenth I left Paris for London and a gratifyingly friendly meeting with the foreign secretary, Sir Alec Douglas-Home, who told me that we should not hesitate to let the British know what they could do to help us. Home also introduced me to various members of Parliament, who were as warm in their support as the foreign secretary. James Callaghan, a Labourite who later became prime minister, mentioned that at the recent Socialist International meetings, the British and Israel's Golda Meir had voiced their backing for South Vietnam.

I was back in Paris on January 21 when word came that Nguyen Van Thieu had finally given up his long and tenacious battle to resist the agreement. He did not do so before exchanging a grueling series of last minute letters with Nixon and participating in not one but several "moments of truth" with Nixon's personal emissary, Alexander Haig. But in the end he accepted the inevitable. Nixon had solemnly assured him of his continued support if Thieu went along, and of an utter and irreversible American abandonment if he did not. Without U.S. support, Thieu knew that neither he nor the nation would survive; with it there was a fighting chance. As a result, on January 23, in Paris, the agreement was initialed by Kissinger and Le Duc Tho. Four days later it was signed by all the parties, Hanoi's and the PRG's representatives on one page, Saigon's and Washington's on another.

An added incentive for South Vietnam's signing the peace agreement was that afterward Thieu would be invited to the United States for a state visit with Nixon. Thieu attached a good deal of importance to this meeting. Part of it was that an American visit would enhance considerably his own prestige at home. But more importantly, having accepted Nixon's effusive, if general, promises of ongoing support made during the long haggle over the agreement, Thieu wanted to confirm and concretize the understanding at first hand. He needed to gauge the extent to which he could count on Nixon, and he considered that only a face-to-face meeting would allow him to do that. This would be Thieu's first trip to the States. "What are the Americans really up to?" had been a constant obsession throughout his political life, and now was his chance to find out.

With the visit scheduled for April 3, Thieu asked me at the end of

February to return to the United States to prepare the ground. My wife and I both went. Our daughter Lulu, who was now in her senior year at Georgetown University, was planning to get married at the end of April. So, while I was working on the Nixon-Thieu meeting, my wife would have her own arranging to take care of.

Laying the groundwork for this visit brought me back in touch with White House aides, congressmen, senators, newsmen — the whole Washington circle. As I began to sniff the new post-Paris air, I noticed some remarkable differences. I did not sense the same strident opposition to support that had been so oppressively present just two short months ago. With the American soldiers home now, with the POWs all either released or about to be released, America's fevered obsession with Vietnam seemed to be dissipating.

On April 2 I flew from Washington to Honolulu to meet Thieu's plane so I could accompany him to Los Angeles and from there south to Nixon's home in San Clemente. Needless to say, as a site for a presidential meeting, San Clemente was somewhat more satisfying than Midway, but it was still not Washington, and none of us was happy about the gesture. For someone noted for his attention to public relations, Nixon seemed astonishingly obtuse about what our press would make of the venue of this visit.

But though the setting was disappointing, Thieu managed to come away from his discussions with the American president in very good spirits. In private, Nixon had given him precisely what he had come to hear: the firm personal assurance of strong retaliatory action if the other side violated the agreement. "The United States will meet all the contingencies in case the agreement is grossly violated," Nixon had told him. "You can count on us." At first, my own talks with John Holdridge over our attempt to draw up the joint communiqué did not go well. I wanted to incorporate the strong and specific language of the private talks while he favored a fuzzier, more general statement. But in the end the arguments turned out to be of not much consequence, and by cocktail time the problems were resolved.

At dinner that evening I sat next to Graham Martin, whom I knew would soon be replacing Ellsworth Bunker as ambassador (after six years at his post, Bunker was retiring). Naturally, I had more than a polite interest in this table partner, and I spent much of the dinner trying to size him up. All I knew of Martin was that he was a former ambassador to Thailand and an old Asia hand. But the dinner conversation did little to enlighten me further. Like all diplomats, Martin was extremely polite. But he spoke little and seemed rather cold and standoffish. I got little indication of his personality and no sense of the characteristic lack of realism that he was to display during his tenure in Saigon.

Although in his memoirs Kissinger describes the shame he felt at the reception accorded Thieu — so much more private and constrained than was typical of affairs of this nature — in fact, the South Vietnamese were generally encouraged. Thieu, in particular, thought the meeting a success. He had received promises of economic and military support, and of the president's readiness to take military action in case of treaty violations. There is no doubt that his trust in Nixon's good faith was enhanced significantly. As we flew toward Washington for the second stop on our trip, Thieu celebrated his birthday with cake and champagne.

We would have been a great deal less jubilant had we known that for the past month Nixon had been drawn ever deeper into the morass of Watergate, that even as he hosted us at San Clemente he was struggling desperately to grasp the extent of his predicament and to limit the burgeoning damage. What we saw was different: a national leader at the height of his powers, one who already had historic foreign policy accomplishments to his credit and who had just been inaugurated to his second term after a landslide election victory. There was no hint that his administration would soon be in ruins and he himself unable to fulfill his most rudimentary duties, let alone promises to his Vietnamese ally which required an abundance of will and courage.

In Washington we were met by Spiro Agnew, who hosted a formal dinner in Thieu's honor. The following night Thieu gave a speech at the National Press Club. It went extremely well, but not without an all-night rewriting session by Nha and me to transform the long, grandiloquent remarks that had been prepared for him in Saigon into something more appropriate for the ravening skeptics at the press club. There was, of course, the usual inquisition, but none of the hostility I had feared. At the time, it seemed to me a sign of sorts.

Haig was in Washington, too, and we arranged a reception for him at the embassy to award him the National Order of Vietnam. Upstairs in my former office, we had a chance to talk privately; it was the first time we had seen each other since just before the final Paris negotiations. He told me that he would soon be off to Vietnam. Intelligence reports indicated significant Communist infiltration and supply build-ups, and the president had asked him to examine the situation first hand. The fact that Haig was being sent as Nixon's observer was also an encouraging sign. Haig was knowledgeable, perceptive, and tough. If Nixon was sending him, it meant that the American president was prepared to take action. (The violations turned out to be massive enough, but by the time Haig returned, Watergate was flaring up and had already impaired Nixon's ability to respond.)

Two days after the embassy affair, we took off for Europe. Again the champagne bottles were uncorked to celebrate what Thieu considered a highly successful trip. Warm feelings spread liberally around the plane, as did Thieu's thanks to all of us who had contributed to the American visit. Looking back at it, that flight was perhaps the high point of the ambivalent relationship I had shared with Thieu for almost a decade. For the moment at least, we enjoyed a feeling of relaxed good spirits, untroubled by the habitual undercurrents of suspicion on his part and anger and frustration on mine. As the chartered 707 jet raced across the Atlantic that night, our festivities were sustained by the blessed human inability to divine the future. I for one was not yet impressed by the omens already gathering in important places: the heavy traffic flowing unimpeded down the Ho Chi Minh Trail, or the opening salvos in Washington of Senator Sam Ervin's select committee on the Watergate affair.

In Rome Thieu (a converted Catholic) had an audience with the pope. Then the South Vietnamese Paris delegation came up to meet us for a review of the ongoing negotiations on implementing the peace accords. Pham Dang Lam's report on these talks was depressing enough. In Paris there was a three-way dialogue of the deaf going on between South Vietnam and the PRG, between South Vietnam and the United States, and between the United States and North Vietnam. But we had all discounted these talks in advance, and it is likely that had Lam reported progress, several of us at least would have experienced a serious shock. Whatever the euphoria might have been among Kissinger and his team when the accords were signed, all the South Vietnamese had known that their implementation relied not on any spirit of peace and good will among the parties, but on one thing and one thing only: the strength of America's military guarantee. And that — well, that we had just had confirmed at San Clemente.

From Europe I returned to Washington in time for my daughter's wedding to a young Vietnamese student who was finishing his degree in accounting at Georgetown. Then, leaving Lulu and her new husband in Washington, my wife and I flew home to Saigon.

Chapter 35

Last Things

THE LIFE I BEGAN TO LEAD from mid-1973 on was immensely enjoyable. I say this even though the problems both at home and abroad that eventually proved so catastrophic were already on the horizon. In common with most other South Vietnamese, I regarded the Middle East conflict, inflation, corruption, and domestic divisiveness as serious problems, but hardly terminal ones. At first, even Watergate did not reveal itself as the utter disaster it would soon prove to be. Besides, neither I nor anyone else of my generation could recall a time in South Vietnam's existence when we had not faced monumental difficulties, and always we had survived them.

In any event, I now found myself leading a kind of semiprivate, semipublic life. I was able to seriously get back to my work at the *Post* and the new magazine. But at the same time, Thieu began to use me more and more as his special envoy, sending me on a variety of missions in Asia, Europe, and the United States. I felt I had the best of both worlds. I was a free man and a private citizen, yet circumstances were keeping me close to the center of power, from where I could continue to feel I was making a contribution to the larger cause.

The fact was that I was especially happy that I had retained my access to Thieu and my ability to consult and propose, and perhaps even to influence him. As the negotiations over the Paris accords were running their course the previous January, I had begun to develop an approach to the direction of South Vietnamese affairs in the post-Paris period. By mid-1973 I was discussing these ideas with Nha and then more often with Thieu directly.

It seemed to me that any strategy for South Vietnam's future would necessarily have to start with the fact of the American withdrawal. As traumatic as that was, I did not by any means view it as an unmitigated evil. Throughout the war, I had been unhappy with the pervasive U.S. presence and influence. As Dr. Quat's cabinet secretary in 1965, I myself had participated in the whirlwind events that resulted in the arrival of an American land army. And, with Quat, I had had deep reservations about that development. Later, as Ky's assistant, I had acquiesced to American intervention as *le moindre mal,* the lesser evil. But like other Vietnamese nationalists, I had never been able to reconcile myself to the erosion of national identity that had inevitably followed.

Consequently, I viewed the Paris accords as a potential turning point in the life of South Vietnam. True, the Americans had presented us with a demoralizing and dangerous fait accompli. But in another way, there was opportunity in the event. With the Americans gone, we had at least regained a substantial part of our autonomy, and that we could take advantage of. Our task was now to retake and build on the national identity that had been consumed in the alliance.

Within this context I began to develop a diplomatic strategy that would carve out a legitimate, independent role for South Vietnam that would enable us to shed our image as an American puppet. Primarily, that meant creating a circle of friendly relations among Southeast Asian nations and other neighbors in the region. It meant diversifying our ties with the outside world.

Partly as a result of my talks with Thieu along these lines, in 1973 and 1974 I embarked on a series of diplomatic trips to Asian states — Indonesia, Malaysia, Singapore, India, and Japan — as well as to France and England, building contacts and looking for aid. In Indonesia and Malaysia I was able to establish especially cordial relations, and eventually I came to know well Abdul Rahman of Malaysia and Adam Malik, the Indonesian foreign minister. Among the more interesting aspects of my talks with Southeast Asian leaders were their constant concern about the solidity of the United States' commitment to South Vietnam and their persistent requests for an assessment of America's staying power. In the eyes of Indonesia's President Suharto, for example, a strong anti-Communist South Vietnam was a necessity, and for this the Americans played an irreplaceable role. In his view, Thieu was right to maintain a rigid stance. There was, after all, no way of managing a successful compromise.

This, at least, was how the talk went in private. In public it was a different story. "You know," Adam Malik would say, "in our public attitude we cannot afford to take the same approach. We are, after all, part of the nonaligned group, and at the very least we have to keep up appearances." I got along well with Malik, and the others too, but I was intrigued by the un-self-conscious ease of their hypocrisy. Twenty years earlier I might have been shocked by it, now I simply took note. I had seen enough by this time to know that it was no more than normal practice.

In New Delhi I found less hypocrisy, perhaps, but also a less pleasant atmosphere. At first my discussions there were with people from the foreign ministry, but I also had to deal with that difficult woman Indira Gandhi. India's international alliances had placed her with the Soviets, who supplied a great deal of her arms, and Gandhi herself had always sided with the Communists in Vietnam. As a result, we had never managed to establish full diplomatic relations with India, but we did maintain skeletal contacts through our consul general in the Indian capital. Between the shakiness of our existing ties and my hope to enlarge the scope of contacts, I was in India frequently. That vast country, I found, always affected me strangely. The endless humanity was daunting, and the misery seemed likewise out of scale, beyond the ability of man to address. By comparison, the solution to our own problems appeared, if not simple, at least within reach.

Thieu found it easy to espouse the concept of enlarging South Vietnam's sphere of foreign relations, but he was less than comfortable with the second item on what I considered the necessary agenda: the old idea of a national unity government. In one form or another, this concept had been a mainstay in the political thinking of the circle that had originally formed around my uncle Tran Trong Kim and had afterward been led by Dr. Quat. As one of the heirs of this political family, I had done what I could to nurture its spirit within the essentially alien environment of military leaders who succeeded Quat's government. The thrust toward democracy that was a fiber of the tradition had had its moments and had exhibited some of its potential before succumbing to the one-man election of 1971. But the idea of a national unity government, drawing from the political spectrum the most capable men, that was hardly a dead issue. On the contrary, as 1973 drifted into 1974, it seemed more and more a necessity for survival.

By then, South Vietnam's domestic situation was worsening steadily. The Arab oil embargo, instituted in the fall of 1973, had powered an inflation rate that was soon spiraling toward 50 percent. Under the combined blows of inflation and the decrease in American economic assistance, the economy was edging toward collapse; it was becoming increasingly difficult for many people to feed their families. On the military side, intelligence reports estimated that, by the end of 1973, steady infiltration from North Vietnam had swollen the Communist forces inside South Vietnam to thirteen full divisions. With increasing frequency these forces were launching battalion- and even regiment-size attacks on South Vietnamese positions, constantly probing for an American response. Cautious by nature, fearful of exposing themselves, and concerned about Nixon's unpredictability, the Communist leaders were evaluating the residual strength of the American administration's will. Each probe that went unanswered by the B-52s led inevitably to the next escalation. Gradually, systematically, the tempo on the battlefield picked up.

As the cracks in South Vietnam's social, economic, and military systems spread, the need for dramatic reforms became undeniable. Thieu knew he was sitting at the head of an administration and a military that were heavy with corruption and incompetence, and he was incapable of either eliciting loyalty or acting resolutely. He was achingly, frustratingly aware of the problems, yet he continually stepped back from resolving them. He clearly saw the need for an effective government that would pull together the nation's disparate political forces, but his suspicious, insecure, and inherently indecisive nature told him to retain what he had rather than take steps into the unknown. Perhaps he believed that, however incompetent his regime, the Americans would never let him fall; their investment in lives and treasure had been too great, their geopolitical requirements too compelling, their president's promises too solemn to allow a Communist victory.

For reasons that are still unclear to me, Thieu was willing to listen to my talk about the regime's weaknesses and my advocacy of immediate and thorough reform. My own great frustration was that he often appeared to agree. Frequently, he was unable to conceal his contempt for those with whom he had surrounded himself. I recall one meeting of his inner cabinet that he convened in early March 1974, on the eve of one of my trips abroad to solicit assistance. The idea was that the ministers would brief me on the economic and military situations, then afterward Thieu would give me my instructions in private. The meeting was a disaster, not unlike the regular inner cabinet sessions that often lasted an entire day without arriving at a single decision. The ministers spent the time arguing among themselves while Tran Thien Khiem, the prime minister, sat there silently, to all appearances oblivious to what was going on in front of him. Shaking with fury, Thieu finally put an end to the session himself. When we were alone, he burst out, "Now do you see what I have to put up with? Do you understand the conditions I am working under?"

But he was never sufficiently aroused to act. Instead, he would nod his agreement with my diatribes, then ask me to do my best on this or that mission. We could continue the discussion when I returned. He hinted that the best time to make a really clean sweep of all the deadwood would be when the U.S. Congress agreed to an increase in military and economic aid (he seemed not to grasp that the context of American politics made such an increase impossible). With this kind of clear indication of support for his policies, he would be able to act from a position of strength. At that moment, he would institute his reforms. And so, with one delaying tactic after another, time slipped away from him and from the nation.

From mid-1973 through 1974, I was in the United States often, monitoring developments in Washington and doing what I could to keep the supply pipeline open. I watched Watergate unfold with growing concern, astonished that Nixon's people had felt the necessity of doing what they had. At first I believed the damage would be controlled. How could a bizarre incident like this be allowed to strike at the heart of the administration? But by the fall of 1973 I began to realize how serious the situation was, and I began to worry about its consequences. Already, at the end of April, Nixon's closest domestic advisers, Bob Haldeman and John Ehrlichman, had resigned. On October 10 came the news of Vice President Spiro Agnew's resignation. Then, a week and a half later, Attorney General Elliot Richardson and his deputy, William Ruckelshaus, quit over the firing of Watergate special prosecutor Archibald Cox. It so happened I was in Washington at the time, making a plea for essential military supplies. Richardson's action hit Washington like a shock wave. For days the city seemed paralyzed; there was literally not a single person I could talk to about the Vietnam lifeline. Nixon's administration was hemorrhaging, and as it did, our own ability to withstand our enemy's assaults grew increasingly precarious.

In November Congress overrode a Nixon veto and passed the War Powers Act, dramatically limiting the president's power to use armed force. There was no question now of the severity of the damage Nixon had sustained. He no longer had the ability to fulfill all the obligations he had undertaken during the Paris negotiations and then confirmed at San Clemente. By the beginning of 1974 I was convinced that even if he were to survive, he would be in no position to do anything at all about Vietnam.

All of these chilling developments I discussed at length with Thieu. At first he could not believe that a third-rate burglary could jeopardize the president of the United States. But as the situation worsened, he became more alarmed. In March 1974, with the impeachment hearings under way, he sent me to Washington to assess the damage and gauge the administration's ability to continue support for us. During the visit I met with Vice President Gerald Ford as well as with many of my old contacts, but the meetings were hardly necessary. It took no genius to discover that, in the midst of Nixon's tragedy, Vietnam was not on anybody's agenda.

Returning to Vietnam, I found Thieu grim and uncommunicative. Though obviously troubled, he did his best to conceal his thoughts. I believe that inside he was deeply frightened by the enormity of the events in Washington and by an emerging vision of their consequences. I know that I was. On August 9 he was shaken by Nixon's resignation.

On the following day, though, Thieu received a letter from incoming president Ford. "I do not think I really need to inform you that American foreign policy has always been marked by its essential continuity and its essential bipartisan nature," Ford wrote. "This is even more true today, and the existing commitments this nation has made in the past are still valid and will be fully honored in my administration." In a state of high enthusiasm, Thieu showed the letter around, as if he held in his hand a guarantee of South Vietnam's survival. As I watched him, I could not decide if at heart he knew this was the most fragile of fragile reeds, or if perhaps the real nature of the American presidency, with all its checks and balances and hedges, escaped him even now.

While August brought its news of historic turmoil in Washington, Saigon retained an air of superficial calm. We knew that Communist forces had by this time established a military infrastructure in South Vietnam, the nature and extent of which were different from anything that preceded it. Oil pipelines had been laid from North to South Vietnam, a sophisticated military communications network was in place, thousands of tons of war materiel had been stockpiled near the battlefields. But, for all this, the politburo had not yet made the strategic decision to launch an all-out offensive.

Richard Nixon's resignation, however, moved that decision a step closer. In September Communist forces enlarged the scope of their attacks. It was evident that Hanoi's leaders believed Nixon's departure had minimized the chances of American retaliation, as of course it had. But still they tested. The dry season, the traditional time for major offensives, was now only months away. As if the situation were not grim enough, by mid-August we began to understand that despite President Ford's hopeful assurances, Congress was doing what it could to shut down military and economic aid. One of Nixon's last acts in office had been to sign a bill that allowed for a $1.1 billion aid package to South Vietnam. Several days later Congress chose to appropriate only $700 million of that amount. (In the end, because of various Defense Department fiscal procedures, only $400 million was actually received, and soaring world fuel and commodity prices consumed much of this.)

More significant still, only weeks after Nixon's fall, Nguyen Van Thieu found himself in a major political crisis of his own. The catalyst of this crisis was Tranh Huu Thanh, a Catholic priest who in earlier days had been close to President Ngo Dinh Diem. For a variety of reasons, some sincere and some political, in August Father Thanh launched what he called the People's Anticorruption Movement. By September the campaign had tapped into a running tide of popular emotion. Father Thanh's attack on President Thieu, Thieu's wife, and many of his associates came at a time of economic collapse and galloping inflation. Soldiers, junior officers, and government functionaries, as well as peasants and workers, were by this time suffering terribly. Perhaps 95 percent of the country's breadwinners worried each day about how to get enough food. Whatever the root causes of their predicament, Father Thanh's scathing indictments of corruption galvanized an outpouring of rage. People who were suffering real deprivation could no longer restrain themselves when Father Thanh and the politicians who quickly flocked to him began pointing to the looting that was going on at the highest levels.

Personally, I did not feel that corruption, as bad as it was, constituted the whole story. I had traveled extensively through Southeast Asia and had seen, not just the same level of corruption elsewhere, but corruption far more extensive and far more blatant. Nevertheless, the regimes that nurtured it did not fall, nor were they threatened by campaigns such as Father Thanh's. But neither, of course, were these countries at war. None of them faced the task of motivating people to die for them.

In a short time Father Thanh's People's Anticorruption Movement became an outlet not just for popular hostility but for the long-suppressed anger of Thieu's political opponents as well. The authoritarian controls through which Thieu had arrogated power to himself since the one-man election of 1971 had spawned many adversaries. Leftists, neutralists, Buddhists, Catholics, even rightists — almost every sect, movement, and party had been denied a reasonable voice in the government, and now their frustration came boiling over. All of them, it seemed, joined forces under Father Thanh's banner, transforming the anticorruption campaign into a vast antigovernment crusade. The NLF, too, got involved, and no one could tell which of the daily demonstrations owed its origin to a legitimate group and which were precipitated by one of the covert Communist cells. A glance at the newspapers each morning conveyed the impression that the entire country was in flames.

By this time Hoang Duc Nha had left the government, forced out by direct pressure from the Americans, who hated him for his abrasive manner and, in their opinion, his obstructionist influence. (In his memoirs, Kissinger immortalized him as "the egregious Nha.") But regardless of the Americans, Nha and Thieu were cousins and had continued to stay in close touch with each other. By late September, Nha and I were talking regularly about the turmoil in the streets, and together we came up with the idea that perhaps we could help Thieu dampen the conflagration. Specifically, I could draft a speech Thieu might use in his scheduled television address to the nation.

I was glad to help. I thought I understood as well as anyone the harm Thieu had brought on himself by alienating the strong, effective people who might well have become allies or at least part of the loyal opposition. As for his entourage, between their corruption and incompetence there was not a good word to say about them. And yet this explosion of hostility and anarchy showed an astounding disregard for the fragility of the country's existence, at the exact moment the Communists were preparing a dry-season offensive on a scale beyond anything we had previously faced. In my own mind, it was clear that the civil discord had to be ended quickly, that Thieu had to dissipate the anger and focus attention on the danger that was so close to breaking on us.

His speech could be the first step in that direction. I would be happy to write it, but only if there was a good chance that Thieu would use it. Nha thought I could be sure of it, but he also suggested I talk with Thieu's chief of staff, Colonel Vo Van Cam. When I asked Cam about it, I got the impression that the effort would be worthwhile. He, at least, would do his best.

That evening I began to work on Thieu's speech, actually a variation of a speech I had given over and over in one form or another for years, sometimes in public and sometimes to myself, adapted now to the circumstances of the anticorruption campaign.

Although I do not admit the veracity of all the specific allegations made by Father Thanh and the opposition, I do recognize the existence of corruption, and I do recognize the necessity of dealing with it. I am willing to sit down and discuss with you ways and means of dealing with it. But corruption is not the main issue facing us. The issue facing us is far more serious than corruption. It is the survival of our people as a nation. So let us sit down together, but not as government and opposition. Let us sit down together as patriots who temporarily disagree among themselves, but who can surmount their personal feelings for the sake of the country in this dangerous hour.

This would be an opening, I thought; nothing concrete, but a necessary step toward calming the atmosphere and opening up the urgently needed dialogue.

The evening of Thieu's speech, I was having dinner at the home of a friend of mine. A few days earlier I had handed Colonel Cam the draft. Since then I had heard nothing. I turned on the television during dinner to listen. Thieu was talking to the nation, but not with any of the words I had prepared for him, or anything like them. Instead of taking a conciliatory approach, acknowledging the problem and then moving on from there, he was ignoring it. Instead of addressing the opposition, he was talking about Communists, the Communists who opposed him, the Communists who were behind all the trouble. Rather than accepting a share of responsibility and moving to rally the nation, Thieu had decided to try to sidestep the problem.

As I watched the speech, I could not keep myself from thinking that this man must think he is the center of the universe, that he must believe he has the mandate of heaven on him. He seemed to have no sense that he was involved in an interaction with his people. It seemed to me that somewhere along the way he must have lost his balance, that his years in power had obscured from him the basis of his own survival. He could not seem to really grasp what had happened in the United States, and I was right then watching as he failed to grasp what was happening to him in his own country. Seeing him on that television screen, I was oppressed by the recognition that Thieu could not summon the stature to look beyond himself, even in this extremity. His view of life was essentially that of the politician, the power seeker and power holder. Even with the enemy waiting to devour us all, the man who led the nation was unable to reach toward the requisite accommodation and compromise and acceptance that might have enabled his leadership. Perhaps he recognized he was not capable of sustaining the role these things demanded. Or perhaps his vision refused to encompass the possibility.

From September through January, Saigon was consumed by infighting that drained the government's energies and distracted the inhabitants from the dangers that were thrusting in on them. The government was too stubborn to look for avenues of compromise, the opposition too blind to notice the approaching disaster. Most of the city's people were too busy trying to find two meals a day to think about anything beyond that. In reality, Saigon was on the verge of collapsing under its own internal pressures.

It was against this exhausted enemy that Communist forces unleashed their offensive in mid-December. After three weeks of hard fighting, the provincial capital of Phuoc Binh was taken. There were no counterattacks by South Vietnamese forces. From Washington, the Ford administration gave no indication that it would help. As the fighting spread, I began to suspect I was living on two levels. On one, I saw and understood precisely what was happening. On another, I refused to accept it. I thought that now, like so many times in the past, somehow we would come out all right. We had, after all, seen it already. We had seen Tet Mau Than. We had lost Hue and then retaken it. We had held on for our lives at An Loc. We had lost Quang Tri and regained that. In the most desperate circumstances, we had always managed to survive. Why should this be different?

Tet in 1975 fell in January. Just before the holiday Thieu asked me to go on another fence-mending visit to India. I can no longer recall what fences needed mending on that occasion, but whatever they were, my wife was dead set against my going anywhere on the first day of the holiday. She argued that it was my obligation to be home with the family. Besides, she said, I knew perfectly well that the first day of Tet determined a person's luck for the rest of the year. If the first people I was to meet on the new year were foreigners, who could say what consequences might not follow?

In the end, I informed Thieu that the Indian fences would have to wait for a while; I would make the trip after the holiday. I did not leave Saigon until the middle of February. By the time I got back, it was a new month. The second phase of the Communist offensive had already triggered off with a multidivision assault on the central highlands city of Banmethuot. The city had been taken by surprise and had fallen after only two days of fighting. South Vietnamese troops were being pulled away from the battlefield, unsure of whether to counterattack or withdraw. A more perceptive observer than I might have guessed that the countdown to South Vietnam's final debacle was now under way. It was a few days later that Thieu called me in to talk over a last mission to Washington.

*   *   *   *   *

My final abortive mission to Washington was finished when, on April 11, Congress voted against sending any emergency funds to South Vietnam. Three days later Bob Shaplen had called, and on the seventeenth I arrived back in Saigon, still sick with the flu and still shocked by the events of the previous weeks. When I called Thieu at his office, I was told he could not see me. He was too distraught by the loss that day of Phan Rang, his native province. Instead, the inner cabinet had been called together to hear my report.

The meeting was a brief, stressful affair. A few of the ministers spoke about the possibility of continuing the fight, perhaps withdrawing to the Mekong Delta and making a stand there. Given a large enough redoubt and a reasonable chance to defend it, might the Americans then send help? I did not know the situation here in Vietnam, I told them. "I've just gotten back. But as far as the situation over there is concerned, it's over. No one is going to help." There would be no more aid, no supplies, no ammunition, no marines, nothing. They sat there, caught in the silence of their own thoughts, no one able to muster the will to break the room's stillness.

From there, I called the American embassy and spoke with Graham Martin, who invited me to come over immediately. On my way there, I wondered what he would say. As ambassador, Martin had religiously maintained a determined optimism about the situation both in Vietnam and in Congress. Even in the worst moments he had seemed supremely confident in the ultimate success of his mission. Despite his cool personal relationship with Thieu, Martin had supported him strongly and consistently; one got the feeling that Martin was a zealot in the cause of South Vietnam. It would be difficult to understand his unswervingly positive assessments otherwise.

But with half the country already lost, and with no apparent way to stop the advancing tide, Martin was a changed man. Pale and worried, he asked me, "Have you seen Thieu yet?" He himself had not seen the president recently. "The situation is precarious, grave. No one in Saigon, including the military, thinks that Thieu can stay on as president." Whatever Martin's fears might have been, it was evident he did not want to discuss anything relating to defeat. He had no assessment and no plans for action during this final period. What he wanted to talk about was Thieu. Thieu was finished — he had to be told that. Even now, Martin seemed to think, there might still be some way of negotiating a settlement with the Communists. "You have to tell Thieu the truth," he said to me. If necessary, he would go himself, but could I possibly get to see the president and tell him, then get back to Martin about it?

I left the embassy blinking my eyes, wondering how Martin could believe at this stage that a political solution could be achieved, even in the form of a disguised surrender. Over the next few days, however, I found that if Martin was deluded on this score, he was hardly alone. Others, from South Vietnamese politicians to foreign officials (especially the French) were indulging the same thoughts. The superheated atmosphere seemed to lend substance to the airiest notions. Having opposed Thieu and advocated compromise with the other side, some "third-force" politicians sincerely believed they could serve as a bridge between the Communists and the South Vietnamese. Human nature being what it is, others grasped at a chance for a moment of fame, as a minister, or perhaps something more, in a "transitional" government.

In the Saigon diplomatic community, the French were the superstars of the "negotiated settlement." Partly to regain their lost prestige at the expense of the Americans, partly to position themselves favorably in the postwar configuration (and partly, too, because they received encouragement from Hanoi), the French ambassador publicly espoused the political solution as a way of ending hostilities. But in his effort to assume the role of an "honest broker," Ambassador Jean-Marie Merrillon was playing a game designed in Hanoi by helping to paralyze the South Vietnamese as they searched around for an acceptable alternative to Thieu, and to delude the Americans.

That the French might wish to enhance their diplomatic position with this farce I could appreciate, but how Graham Martin could give it credence I did not know. I saw the American ambassador again on Friday, April 18, then talked to him by phone on Saturday. He wanted to know if I had seen Thieu yet. I hadn't. I had sent word through Colonel Cam and also through General Tran Van Don, a leader of the Diem coup and a politician, who had just been appointed minister of defense. But Thieu had not responded. "Well," I heard Martin say, "I'll have to go and see him myself."

The next days I spent in my apartment, doing what I could to tie up my affairs. Somehow, a giant automated printing system for the newspaper was delivered; I had ordered it over a year ago. The time raced, most of it consumed in talking with relatives and friends who crowded the apartment, anxious for news or advice. Again and again I repeated the same story. For Washington the war was over. For us the war was over. Each time I said it, the reaction seemed the same. At first disbelief would spread over these faces — some of which I knew so well — as if they could not swallow the sharp cruelty of the words. Without speaking, eventually they would leave with heads bowed, deep in thought about their families and themselves. During free moments and late into the nights, I pored over my papers, the collection of a lifetime, burning some and deciding that I would take others with me.

On the twenty-first Thieu resigned. I expected it; I knew Martin had spoken with him and had left him no choice. But watching Thieu say it on television was still a shock, or perhaps it just seemed so because I was so physically and mentally exhausted. I listened as he rambled on about Kissinger and the Americans and possible negotiations, crying and smiling at the same time. For a moment, I could not help thinking about the power vacuum this would create and the chaos as others moved to fill it. But the moment quickly passed. As Thieu's image disappeared from the screen, all I could think of was that the end had now come.

It was time to leave. The Communist armies were dangerously close to

Saigon, and I had arrangements to make if I was going to evacuate my mother and sister. Subconsciously, I had resisted the idea, suppressing the realization that the longer I stayed the more difficult it would be to get out. To get a breather from the cramped apartment and its steady stream of visitors, I took a walk outside. Also, I think, to fix the city on my mind one last time. I walked down Nguyen Hue Street into the downtown area. I saw people buying flowers at an outdoor stand and wondered how they had the peace of mind for such a luxury. Children were still playing in the parks, oblivious to the decisions that at that very moment were rocking their parents' minds. I breathed the air in like a tourist, trying to sense the uniqueness of the place, as if later I might be able to summon it back.

I owed my departure to Graham Martin. The first day I saw him, he had offered his help. Now I called to say I was ready. He acted immediately, making arrangements to fly my mother, my sister, and me out to Bangkok in a navy plane, then from Bangkok to Washington on commercial flights. That day, I made my last calls to friends, most of whom I was sure I would never see again. I took another slow look around the house, then gave the key to the maid. The last night was sleepless, most of it spent trying to persuade my ninety-year-old mother that she had to leave her home and all the things she had lived among for so many years. I also had a last look through my papers, burning some more and packing the rest into a large suitcase. A smaller bag I filled with stacks of family and official photographs.

The next day, at noon, Joe Bennet, the political counselor at the American embassy, arrived to drive us to Tan Son Nhut, where a small plane was waiting for us on the runway. My mother, sister, and I got in with our suitcases, then waited an excruciating hour before the pilot was cleared to take off. Finally, he began to taxi, and a moment later we were in the air, watching Saigon and its suburbs pass below us.

As the shifting greens of the Mekong Delta appeared below, I strained to make out the rice paddies and the canals cutting silver patterns across the plain. Without warning, the grief welled up. My vision blurred with tears for this lovely, lovely land rushing so quickly by beneath the plane.

Epilogue

EXCEPT FOR THE SPECIAL circumstances that put me close to the center stage of the war in Vietnam, and except for the sheer luck that spared me much of the suffering endured by others, I am not different from other Vietnamese of my generation. In terms of dreams and aspirations, frustrations and disappointments, my life story is essentially theirs.

Vietnamese of my generation came of age in the early forties with the hope that after almost a century as second-class citizens in their own country, they would have a chance to recover their dignity and achieve their independence from France. They dreamed also of peace and a decent life for themselves and their children. It was their misfortune that instead of independence, peace, and a decent life, they saw only revolution, war, and destruction. For three decades they existed in the maelstrom. And even now, when Vietnam no longer has to deal with foreign invaders, their misery continues. Theirs has been a tragedy of historic proportions.

In an interview with Walter Cronkite in 1963, President John Kennedy said, "In the final analysis, it's their war and they are the ones who will either win it or lose it." Much as we might like to, there is no getting away from Kennedy's judgment. The South Vietnamese people, and especially the South Vietnamese leaders, myself among them, bear the ultimate responsibility for the fate of their nation, and to be honest, they have much to regret and much to be ashamed of. But it is also true that the war's cast of characters operated within a matrix of larger forces that stood outside the common human inadequacies and failings. And it was these forces that shaped the landscape on which we all moved.

First among these root causes was the obduracy of France, which in the late forties insisted on retaining control of its former colony rather than conceding independence in good time to a people who hungered for it. Second was the ideological obsession of Vietnam's Communists. Not content with fighting to slough off a dying colonialism, they relentlessly sought to impose on the Vietnamese people their dogma of class warfare and proletarian dictatorship. Finally came the massive intervention by the United States, inserting into our struggle for independence and freedom its own overpowering dynamic. These three forces combined to distort the basic nature of Vietnam's emergence from colonialism, ensuring that the struggle would be more complex and bloodier than that of so many other colonies which achieved nationhood during mid-century.

Caught in the midst of these powerful forces, Vietnam's nationalists found themselves in a succession of precarious situations. In most cases they were forced to choose among unpalatable alternatives; often, indeed, they saw no choice at all. With their survival at stake, they were forced to take refuge in a series of uneasy and uncomfortable compromises that little by little eroded their legitimacy. From one experience to another — first with the French and Bao Dai, then with Ngo Dinh Diem, then with the Americans and the military — they tried to carve out a role for themselves and establish their influence. But always they were pushed to the periphery, and the influence they wielded was never enough to affect the ultimate course of events. To myself and others, for a time it seemed we might be able to develop the nation's economy and build a functioning democracy, even while waging war. But eventually the room to make this kind of contribution diminished, and in the end, against a mechanized North Vietnamese invasion army equipped by the Soviets, all that remained was an alley fight for survival. By then Vietnam's nationalists had been forced to take their place alongside all the other Vietnamese who could only stand by and watch their fate unfold in front of them.

As I look back on the external forces that shaped our lives, it is the American intervention that stands out. French colonialism, after all, is dead and gone, a subject for historians who prefer the inert remains of the past to the passions of the present. As for Vietnamese communism, no one but the fervid or the blind any longer argues the merits of a system that has brought in its wake only war and deprivation and mass flight. (Not that having been right comforts us as we house our refugees and send what sustenance we can back to our families.) But American intervention is a living issue. In the train of failure in Vietnam, and in the face of hard choices elsewhere, the questions of its correctness and its morality still inform American foreign policy debates. Americans still seek to learn the lessons of intervention, and so do America's smaller allies, who cannot help but see in the fate of Vietnam intimations of their own possible futures.

For critics of the Vietnam War, the original decision to intervene was wrong, a result, as one of them put it, of a "steady string of misjudgments." It was wrong because American policymakers in the sixties failed to assess correctly the vital interests of the United States, because they exaggerated the geopolitical importance of Vietnam, and because they had an inflated concept of American capabilities.

Although it is neither my business nor within my competence to pass judgment on how the United States defined its interests at that time, it is my impression that such arguments are made on a distinctly *a posteriori* basis. I remember vividly the political atmosphere in the United States in the summer of 1964, the summer of the Tonkin resolution and Barry Goldwater's nomination, when I first visited this country. At that time the Johnson administration and practically the entire Congress were in favor of the commitment to defend Vietnam (the resolution passed in the Senate, 98 to 2, and in the House, 416 to 0). And so, *mirabile dictu*, were the national news media.

Moreover, the context of international affairs in that period provided good reasons for this nearly unanimous opinion, reasons that went beyond the specific perception of North Vietnamese aggressiveness. It was then the aftermath of the Communist attack in Korea, and China's Communist leaders were broadcasting the most belligerent and expansionistic views, even as they attempted to establish a Peking-Jakarta axis with Indonesia's pro-Communist President Sukarno. For the fragile governments of Southeast Asia the situation seemed serious indeed. Although twenty-five years later it became fashionable among some Americans to belittle Communist threats to the region's stability, among the responsible governments at the time there was deep anxiety.

Even for those South Vietnamese who thought they saw the inherent dangers in American intervention, there was still nothing illogical about it. The American interest in Vietnam, even its land intervention, seemed a natural extension of U.S. policies in Europe (the Marshall Plan, the Berlin airlift, Greece) and Asia (Korea) aimed at preventing the expansion of combined Soviet and Chinese power (at least until the early 1960s, no one could imagine that the two Communist giants would become antagonists). And for the Europeans who were able to rebuild their countries and save their democratic institutions, for the Germans in Berlin, for the Greeks, and for the South Koreans, those policies were not wrong. Nor were they based on misjudgments of geopolitical realities. In Vietnam the policy failed. But that is not to say that it was wrong there either. The disastrous mistakes that were made were mistakes in implementation rather than intention. But the thrust of the policy of containment and protection, that I do not think can be faulted. It is, on the contrary, something for Americans to be proud of.

The more vocal critics of the war in the sixties and seventies characterized the intervention, not just as wrong, but also as immoral. Their charge was based primarily on the theory that the war in Vietnam was a civil war, and that consequently American intervention was an act of aggression against people who were fighting to free themselves from an oppressive regime and unify their country in accord with the aspirations of the great majority of decent-minded Vietnamese.

It is my own belief that this theory held the field for so long primarily because it was a powerful attraction to the many Americans who were angry at their own government and society and were looking for issues to hang their anger on. Certainly, the facts that refuted it were readily available. From early on, both Saigon and Washington knew beyond a doubt that the National Liberation Front — the Vietcong — was a creation of the Communist party, and that without North Vietnamese organization, leadership, supplies, and, starting in 1964, without the North Vietnamese regular army, there would have been no revolution to speak of and no war. It was one of my greatest frustrations that our firm knowledge of this — both from widespread and incontrovertible evidence and also from personal experience among many of us of communist "front" techniques — made no impact on popular understanding in the West. Regardless of what was there to be seen, people saw only what they wished.

After the war, when propaganda no longer mattered, the party dropped its pretense. "Our Party," said Le Duan in his 1975 victory speech, "is the unique and single leader that organized, controlled, and governed the entire struggle of the Vietnamese people from the first day of the revolution." During the war, the North Vietnamese never openly admitted they had troops in South Vietnam. (Le Duc Tho even kept up the pretense with Henry Kissinger, although Kissinger knew the situation as well as he knew his own name, and Tho, of course, knew that he knew it.) But afterward the party treated this subterfuge simply as an excellent piece of public relations and its own role as a matter of intense pride. As the North Vietnamese general Vo Ban told French television interviewers in 1983, "In May 1959 I had the privilege of being designated by the Vietnamese Communist Party to unleash a military attack on the South in order to liberate the South and reunify the fatherland."

During the heyday of the antiwar movement, I marveled at the innocence of its spokesmen in believing something different from this. I wonder even now if they ever feel shame for their gullibility and for their contribution to the tragedy. But they are not heard from. It was, after all, only one chapter in their lives, as it was only a chapter in the book of American history.

The issue of morality, then, comes down to whether it was moral for the United States to have supported an admittedly flawed South Vietnamese regime in its attempt to survive against a totalitarian antagonist. Here, too, the answer seems to me self-evident. However unpalatable leaders like Nguyen Van Thieu might have been, South Vietnam was full of pluralistic ferment and possibilities for change and development. It was a place where good people could hope for something better to evolve, where they could even fight for it, as so many strong-minded opposition politicians, intellectuals, and writers did. None but ideologues can compare such a place with the chilling police state that destroyed it. And none, I think, can fairly question the morality of the effort to prevent its destruction.

To my mind, the lessons of American intervention in Vietnam have to do not so much with the geopolitical or moral underpinning of the war, but rather with the way the intervention was implemented. The real question was not whether to intervene, but how to intervene effectively.

In this book I have described in some detail the process by which the Johnson administration decided to bring an American land army to Vietnam. The salient feature of that confused and unclear process (as Bill Bundy characterized it) was not that it was ill planned and based on no comprehensive strategy. It was the startling attitude of American decision makers toward their ally. At the top levels of the administration, the State Department, and the Pentagon, there is no evidence to suggest that anyone considered the South Vietnamese as partners in the venture to save South Vietnam. In a mood that seemed mixed of idealism and naïveté, impatience and overconfidence, the Americans simply came in and took over. It was an attitude that would endure throughout the remainder of the conflict. The message seemed to be that this was an American war, and the best thing the South Vietnamese could do was to keep from rocking the boat and let the Americans get on with their business.

The military consequences of this orientation were that the United States took the entire burden on itself instead of searching for ways to make a decisive impact while limiting its exposure. Had the South Vietnamese been consulted in early 1965, it is likely they would have preferred either no intervention or a limited effort sufficient to stabilize the military situation and block the infiltration routes from North Vietnam. An agreement among the United States, South Vietnam, and Laos, allowing U.S. troops to be stationed along the seventeenth parallel as a barrier, would have been quite feasible at the time. With that done, an immediate Vietnamization program could have been undertaken to strengthen and up-grade the South Vietnamese army.

Could such a simple strategy have worked? That is one of the "what if" questions with which the Vietnam War abounds. Colonel Harry Summers, in *On Strategy,* his uncompromising review of American military planning, concludes that it would have, that in fact, isolating the South Vietnamese battlefield from North Vietnamese reinforcement and resupply was the only logical objective for American arms. Whatever the imponderables of war, this approach would at least have had the virtue of establishing the United States as a peace-keeping force protecting South Vietnam from outside aggression. It would have reduced American casualties and precluded the involvement of American firepower in the disconcerting people's war that was such a nightmare for the GIs to fight and that created such powerful antagonism in the arena of international public opinion.

On the political level, too, this American failure to regard the South Vietnamese as people worthy of partnership had destructive results. It meant that the United States never pursued a consistent policy aimed at encouraging the development of a viable democracy in South Vietnam. Certainly, such a thing was possible. Between 1965 and 1967 the South Vietnamese drafted and adopted a constitution, elected a president, vice president, and legislature, and successfully held many local elections — all of this in the middle of a war. It was a substantial achievement, but it would not have happened except that during those years the impulse toward democracy in South Vietnam and the objectives of the Johnson administration coincided.

Unfortunately, thereafter "stability" became the American watchword. As long as the Saigon government demonstrated a modicum of equilibrium, that was all that was asked of it. Several years of progress toward decent government might erode, corruption and autocracy might swell, but these things were not a primary American concern. By 1969 Henry Kissinger and Richard Nixon had embarked on a complex chess game, manipulating big-power diplomacy, military force, and secret negotiations in an attempt to extricate the United States from its quagmire. Amidst this constellation of variables, they needed a government in Saigon that was stable and predictable. If Thieu provided them with that, then whatever else he might do was essentially irrelevant.

It was a fatal error on two counts. First, stigmatized as undemocratic and corrupt, South Vietnam was deemed unworthy of support by an ever-increasing percentage of the American public and Congress. Second, within South Vietnam itself, the unpopular nature of the regime produced apathy, cynicism, and finally, in the anticorruption movement, outrage. Charles Mohr, veteran correspondent of the *New York Times*, summed it up succinctly in a seminar at the American Enterprise Institute. "We lost the war in Vietnam," he said, "not because we did not bring enough pressure to bear on our enemy, but because we did not bring sufficient pressure on our ally." Admittedly, bringing pressure for reform and democracy is a delicate business. But in situations where the United States has significant leverage, the role of catalyst for change, of prodding contending factions toward consensus, beckons to American diplomacy.

To successfully play such a role, there are two prerequisites. One is the will to carry out a strong and consistent advocacy. The other is the determination to accept the consequences if in the end American pressure proves unavailing. The United States must find a way to say to a Ngo Dinh Diem or a Nguyen Van Thieu (or a Ferdinand Marcos or an Augusto Pinochet), "We have no alternative but to stand by our own values. If for your own reasons you find you cannot bring yourselves toward conforming with them, then we are very sorry, but we will have no choice but to leave you to your own devices." With all its power and prestige, the United States simply cannot allow itself to yield to the tyranny of the weak, to authoritarians who believe their importance is so vast that the United States cannot help but support them. If Vietnam has one single lesson to teach, it is that people cannot be saved in spite of themselves. Far better to get out and cut losses before ensnaring treasure, lives, prestige, and all in the service of those whose rule means violent discord and social breakdown.

In Vietnam I always believed that among decent and reasonable people there could be no disagreement about things like corruption, economic and social reforms, and democratic procedures. I believe the same is true elsewhere. Another *New York Times* man, A. M. Rosenthal, in reflecting on his decades of covering American diplomacy, had this to say: "What should our policy be? Simply to act in our belief and interest. Our belief is political freedom and our interest is political freedom. We will not be able to achieve them for others all of the time or even much of the time. But what we can do is stand up for what we believe in, all of the time. . . . That requires two things: vision and constancy. Haitians, Filipinos, Koreans, Afghans seem to have no great confusion about what they really seek from us. Neither do the Czechoslovaks or the Poles." Neither, he might have added, did the South Vietnamese.

The experience of Vietnam suggests that a policy such as Rosenthal recommends would not be simple idealism. After Vietnam it is natural to question the extent to which the United States can sustain any major commitment to a foreign nation unless that nation is capable of eliciting moral support from an idealistic and essentially antimilitaristic American public. The suggestion is that geopolitical considerations by themselves constitute an insufficient grounding for stable, long-term policy. From this perspective, a democratic commitment in foreign policy is not mere idealism; it is also pragmatic self-interest.

From 1965 through 1967, Lyndon Johnson's administration acted according to this concept of idealistic pragmatism. From time to time other administrations did too, but never consistently and never strongly. For all the rhetoric, the American commitment to democracy in South Vietnam was a timid and wavering and sometime thing. That is another way of saying that in South Vietnam American policy neglected the human dimension. It did not accord its allies their requisite dignity as human beings. (I am not speaking here of the thousands of Americans who worked devotedly alongside the Vietnamese.) At the decision-making level, Vietnam was regarded primarily as a geopolitical abstraction, a factor in the play of American global interests. That was true about the way the United States intervened in the war with its land army. It was true about the way the United States conducted the war. And it was especially true about how the United States left the war.

Of all the successive phases of U.S. involvement — the intervention of 1965, the Americanization of the war, then its Vietnamization, and finally the disengagement — it is the disengagement that will stick longest in the minds of the South Vietnamese. Major mistakes were made during the war by everyone concerned. But the manner in which the United States took its leave was more than a mistake; it was an act unworthy of a great power, one that I believe will be remembered long after such unfortunate misconceptions as the search and destroy strategy have been consigned to footnotes.

It was not that the leave-taking itself was a disgrace. The United States fought long and hard in Vietnam, and if in the end circumstances required that it withdraw, it may be considered a tragedy but hardly an act of shame. The same cannot be said, however, for the manipulative and callous manner with which the American administration and the American Congress dealt with South Vietnam during the last years of the war. It was not one of America's finest hours, and there are plenty of lessons in it for both the United States and for other nations, particularly small ones that must rely on the United States for their defense.

As for Henry Kissinger, the architect of the Paris agreement, one can sympathize with his desire for "flexibility," that is, for control. Kissinger was in the middle, attempting to maneuver disparate and obstinate parties (including the North Vietnamese, South Vietnamese, Soviets, Chinese, even, on occasion, his own president) toward the same end. But he had taken on himself an awesome responsibility, negotiating not just for the global interests of the United States but for the existence of South Vietnam. In this context, he and Richard Nixon avoided holding frank discussions on common strategies with the South Vietnamese. They knew that Nguyen Van Thieu could do nothing without American support, yet they chose the unnecessary expedient of keeping developments to themselves until the last moment, then bringing to bear the heavy tactics of promises and threats. They treated a dependent ally of twenty years with finesse and then brutality, instead of with the openness the relationship required.

The fact that Kissinger and Nixon may have believed they had a viable agreement, or at least the best they could get, does not in my view justify their conduct toward South Vietnam. But at the same time, as unique as the Nixon administration's diplomatic style was, it was in effect just another aspect, another face of the American policy that had obtained in Vietnam from the beginning, informed by worthy motives but without an understanding of the human beings who would be affected by its geopolitical goals.

The congresses that in 1973, 1974, and 1975 washed their hands of Vietnam shared fully in this same guilt. Although senators and representatives talked a good deal then about credibility and moral obligation, in fact what they did was to make a geopolitical decision on the basis of what they saw as American self-interest. They did so in callous disregard of the consequences their actions would have on a nation of twenty million people, and they did so although it was no longer a matter of American blood, but only of some hundreds of millions of dollars.

"Is it possible for a great nation to behave this way?" That was the question an old friend of mine asked me in Saigon when news came in August of 1974 that Congress had reduced the volume of aid. He was a store owner whom I had gone to school with in North Vietnam, a totally nonpolitical person. "You are an ambassador," he said. "Perhaps you understand these things better than I do. But can you explain this attitude of the Americans? When they wanted to come, they came. And when they want to leave, they leave. It's as if a neighbor came over and made a shambles of your house, then all of a sudden he decides the whole thing is wrong, so he calls it quits. How can they just do that?" It was a naïve question from an unsophisticated man. But I had no answer for it. Neither, I think, would William Fulbright, or George McGovern, or the other antiwar congressmen.

In the end, though, the culpability is hardly theirs alone. So many thought they knew the truth. The newsmen — as arrogant as any — Kissinger, Thieu, Nixon, myself as well. But none of us knew the truth or, knowing it, took it sufficiently to heart. Not we, and certainly not the implacable and ruthless ideologues who were our enemies. The truth is in the millions of Vietnamese families that have suffered the most horrible tragedies, people who understood what was happening only in the vaguest way. The truth of this war lies buried with its victims, with those who died, and with those who are consigned to live in an oppressed silence, for now and for the coming generations — a silence the world calls peace.

Index

INDEX